Trade Adjustment in Asia: Past Experiences and Lessons Learned

Edited by

Marc Bacchetta and Matthias Helble

Contents

Tables and Figures

Figures

Foreword

Over the last decade, attitudes toward globalization have shifted in a number of developed countries, contributing to rising trade tensions. A growing public perception holds that the integration of goods, services, labor, and capital markets only benefits a happy few while leaving many people behind. This change in attitudes has been an important factor in the transformation of the political landscape with the election in several countries of politicians who question the effects of international cooperation and who have adopted fewer cooperative approaches to trade and migration.

Economists have been actively involved in the public debate, which has shifted the attention of researchers to the labor market effects of trade. New research has contributed to a better understanding of the mechanisms through which firms and workers adjust to trade. Overall, the findings show that although technological advances and trade yield important benefits for economies overall, certain types of workers and/or regions could be negatively affected. They suggest that policies to help workers adjust to changes in the labor market and ensure that the benefits are spread more widely can increase the positive impact of open trade and technological progress. Making trade more inclusive may also help defuse anti-trade sentiment.

Asia, the focus of this book, is a prime example of the positive effects of more open trade. This is reflected in attitudes that are generally more favorable to trade in emerging Asian countries than in developed countries. A 2018 Pew Research Center report shows that adults in emerging economies are more likely to credit trade with boosting wages and creating employment than those in most developed countries. As Asia opened up, the region experienced sustained economic growth that improved the welfare of hundreds of millions of people. Yet, not much is known about how Asian economies have adjusted to trade. Reaping the benefits of trade opening is not automatic. It requires firms and workers to adjust to a new, more competitive environment, including seeking opportunities abroad. Adjustment may have been different and possibly easier in Asian countries, but in the presence of mobility frictions, it is unlikely to have been costless. Moreover, depending on the industry and firm, some workers may have experienced painful declines in pay or even layoffs, while others saw their salaries increase or found new jobs.

The objective of this book is to shed light on the adjustment of labor markets to trade opening in Asian countries. Leading academics around the world have worked on this edited volume to present the latest evidence on the topic. Their contributions illustrate that trade indeed played a transformative role in Asia's development. Trade opening helped reallocate capital and labor to more productive use. Frictions in the movement of capital and labor at times have limited the potential gains. Some groups of workers were less well-prepared to embrace new opportunities. Overall, the book concludes that trade is a powerful source for a more efficient allocation of resources. However, various frictions generate adjustment costs. A better understanding of the adjustment process can lead to policies designed to reduce those costs and ease the process. A re-skilling of workers or the introduction of social safety nets can also help.

Closing the economy to international trade would not achieve the outcomes its advocates promise. It would throw out the substantial gains from trade, while disrupting processes of adjustment that are often fairly well advanced. The question is how to make the adjustment process smoother and relatively frictionless. We hope this book contributes to better understanding of the impact of trade opening on sectors, firms, and labor markets. This will help in designing better policies that ensure that the benefits of trade are enjoyed by all.

Naoyuki Yoshino
Dean
Asian Development Bank Institute

Xiaozhun Yi
Deputy Director-General
World Trade Organization

List of Contributors

Marc Bacchetta is a counsellor in the Economic Research and Statistics Division of the World Trade Organization, Geneva.

Pavel Chakraborty is a lecturer at the Department of Economics, Lancaster University, United Kingdom.

Ian Coxhead is a professor in the Department of Agricultural and Applied Economics, University of Wisconsin-Madison, United States.

Ha Thi Thanh Doan is an economist at the Economic Research Institute for ASEAN and East Asia, Jakarta.

Prachi Gupta is an adjunct professor of political science and international affairs at Temple University, Tokyo.

Matthias Helble is an economist in the Economic Research and Regional Cooperation Department of the Asian Development Bank, Manila, and an adjunct fellow at the Asian Development Bank Institute, Tokyo.

Devashish Mitra is a professor of economics and Gerald B. and Daphna Cramer professor of global affairs at the Maxwell School, Syracuse University, United States.

Dionisius Narjoko is a senior economist at the Economic Research Institute for ASEAN and East Asia, Jakarta.

Marcelo Olarreaga is a professor of economics at the University of Geneva, and a research fellow at the Centre for Economic Policy Research, London.

Roberta Piermartini is a counsellor in the Economic Research and Statistics Division of the World Trade Organization, Geneva.

Guido Porto is professor of economics at Universidad Nacional de *La Plata*, Argentina.

Rashesh Shrestha is an economist at the Economic Research Institute for ASEAN and East Asia, Jakarta.

Shujiro Urata is professor of economics at the Graduate School of Asia-Pacific Studies, Waseda University, Tokyo, senior research advisor to the president of the Economic Research Institute for ASEAN and East Asia, Jakarta, and a visiting fellow at the Asian Development Bank Institute, Tokyo.

Nobuaki Yamashita is a senior lecturer at the School of Economics, Finance and Marketing of the Royal Melbourne Institute of Technology University, Australia.

Isamu Yamauchi is an associate professor at Meiji University, Japan.

Yuan Zi is an assistant professor in the Department of Economics at the University of Oslo, Norway.

Introduction

Marc Bacchetta and Matthias Helble

Context

Asia has successfully integrated into the world economy over the past forty years. After failed attempts to use import substitution strategies to stimulate economic development, most economies in Asia started to adopt export-oriented growth policies in the 1980s. As a consequence, Asia's trade has grown substantially over the past 40 years, reaching well over half the region's gross domestic product in recent years. Similarly, foreign direct investment (FDI) increased steadily in the region, especially after the 1985 Plaza Accord. The surge of FDI flows was linked to the buildup of regional and global value chains (GVCs). More open trade regimes, combined with modern communication and transportation technologies, allowed the setting up of production networks across borders. Subsequently, Asia's trade transformed itself from interindustry trade to intra-industry trade.

Hand in hand with trade opening and economic integration, Asia experienced strong economic growth. The region's gross domestic product (in nominal terms) grew about 15-fold from 1980 to 2016. This exceptional economic progress translated into a substantial improvement of well-being throughout the populations. For example, in 1990, 56% of those living in East Asia lived in extreme poverty, while in South Asia 54% were extremely poor. Within 20 years, those numbers were reduced significantly. By 2010, 12% remained extremely poor in East Asia and 31% in South Asia. Given these impressive achievements and positive experience with globalization, it comes as little surprise that many in Asia strongly embrace globalization. According to the Pew Research Center's Spring 2014 Global Attitudes Survey, a large majority of Asians (about 86%) believe that trade is good, and that it creates jobs and boosts wages.

However, as we know from theory and experience, reaping the benefits from trade opening requires some adjustments. As economies liberalize their trade regimes and trade costs between trading partners decrease, each of the trading partners starts exporting more of those products for which it has a comparative advantage and importing more of the products for which its trading partner has a comparative advantage. Exporting firms tend to grow and hire more workers, while import-competing firms need to adjust or shrink and lay off workers. Some workers need to transition to new positions either within the same company or in other firms. In any case, firms and workers will need to adjust in response to changes in trade costs. This adjustment can be seamless and painless, but it may also be costly and difficult. Overall, the gains from trade are larger than the losses, but some workers bear a disproportionate share of the costs of adjustment and some are left with a lower wage. This also happened in Asia. The success of Asia in integrating into the world economy was not automatic; it required sectors, firms, and workers to cope with more international competition and respond to new opportunities.

While several other developed countries' political developments in the last decade attracted the attention of researchers on adjustment and the labor market effects of trade, there was less interest regarding adjustment to trade in Asia. In developed countries in the mid-2000s, the bright light shed by a number of political campaigns on those left behind by globalization renewed economists' interest in the link between trade and jobs, inciting researchers to reexamine previous findings suggesting that the effect of trade on labor was not significant. Over the past years, researchers have reexamined more closely the adjustment process and the effects of trade opening, using more micro-level data and new methodologies. They found new and more significant effects of trade on labor market outcomes, in particular of trade with the People's Republic of China (Autor, Dorn, and Hanson 2013). The new evidence indicated that labor market adjustments to trade were more difficult and costly than what earlier evidence suggested, and that the adverse impacts of trade are highly concentrated among specific worker groups and locations (World Trade Organization 2017). These studies also suggested that trade had contributed more significantly than earlier studies suggested to the loss of manufacturing jobs in the US. Yet more recent research factoring in GVCs offers a more benign picture of the effects of trade on aggregate employment and wages as well as on manufacturing jobs, but it tends to confirm the findings of previous studies regarding the concentration of adverse effects of trade on certain workers and certain regions (Bacchetta and Stolzenburg 2019). This work focused mainly on the manufacturing sector in developed countries and Latin America. Unfortunately, much less is known about adjustment and the labor market effects of trade in other sectors and regions of the world.

For Asia, relatively little empirical evidence has been emerging on how labor markets and firms in the region have adjusted to trade opening. Topalova and Khandelwal (2011), for example, provided empirical evidence for a procompetitive impact of output tariff liberalization in the case of India. Hasan et al. (2012) found that tariff cuts lead to reductions in unemployment rates in India. Yu (2015) found a positive impact of both input and output tariff reduction on total factor productivity in the People's Republic of China. More recently, McCaig and Pavcnik (2018) showed that the share of manufacturing workers in Viet Nam in the formal sector substantially increased in response to US tariff reductions. This emerging literature suggests that Asia has adjusted well to trade opening.

Our book adds to this relatively new strand of literature by providing additional insights on how Asia has coped with trade opening. As mentioned, substantive research efforts have gone into analyzing the effects of trade opening in developed countries. A particular focus has been on the impact of the People's Republic of China's integration into the world economy on manufacturing jobs in the US. We believe that more research is needed to understand how the economies in developing Asia have handled the adjustment to trade opening.

There are still many open questions regarding the labor market effects of trade in developing countries. Labor markets in developing countries are often dual, with a large share of informal jobs and weaker social safety nets. There is also evidence suggesting that labor mobility costs are higher in developing countries. At the same time, given the speed at which many Asian economies have integrated in world trade and the significant differences between trade developments in Asia compared to the rest of the world, the effects of trade in this region may be different—if not qualitatively then at least quantitatively—from what they are in other regions.

The volume also aims to provide new insights on adjustment to trade by examining both how firms and how labor markets adjust to trade. A better understanding of how firms adjust can help us understand how workers are affected by trade. Firms have different margins of adjustment, and depending on which of those margins they use in reaction to trade shocks, workers will be affected differently. The book shows that there is much to learn from the Asian experience.

Our book comes at a timely moment. In recent years, political developments in the developed countries have drawn increasing attention to the distributional impact of globalization and trade. A number of countries have elected politicians who argue that multilateral and regional trade opening have been harmful to their countries and, in particular, to certain workers in certain regions. Consequently, we have witnessed an increase in trade tensions and in the use of trade restrictive measures. The trend toward less liberal trade policies is not limited to developed countries. In several developing countries, efforts to further open trade have come to a halt or have been even reversed. Our book provides new evidence on how trade opening affects labor markets and firms. We hope it serves as useful guidance to respond to some of the concerns that have been raised and to promote more inclusive trade opening.

Labor Market Adjustment

Trade and Labor: A Review of the Recent Literature

Recent reviews of the literature on the labor market effects of trade show that trade leads to employment and wage gains at the national level, although in the case of employment these are typically small (Bacchetta and Stolzenburg 2019; World Trade Organization 2017). In the first half of the 2010s, a series of empirical studies focusing on import competition from emerging markets and formerly planned Eastern European economies in the 2000s found that trade liberalization episodes had had a detrimental impact on labor market outcomes. These studies suggested that trade was one of the main factors behind the labor market adjustments that have taken place over the last decades. A prominent role in this regard was given to the People's Republic of China's accession to the World Trade Organization in 2001 (Autor, Dorn, and Hanson 2013; Pierce and Schott 2016), the conclusion of the North American Free Trade Agreement in 1994 (Hakobyan and McLaren 2016), and the enlargement of the European Union in 2004 (Braakmann and Vogel 2011). Since the results of these studies were difficult to reconcile with the common view among economists that trade has only minor employment impacts, further research was undertaken, which, among other effects, sheds light on the impact of the expansion of value chains on the relationship between trade and labor markets.

Factoring in GVCs when studying the impact of trade on labor markets reveals that trade has not been a significant contributor to declines in manufacturing jobs in developed economies, and that job gains in services have offset job losses in manufacturing. While import competition can hurt employment in import-competing firms and their suppliers, access to cheaper imported inputs lowers costs in firms that use them, allowing them to expand. Export expansion, which has benefited several manufacturing industries, has been another offsetting factor so that even when considering only manufacturing employment the overall effect of trade is likely to be minor.

There is also empirical evidence showing that GVC integration has supported jobs and earnings as well as other spillovers that operate through labor markets in developing countries (Hollweg 2019). Job and wage gains have been achieved not only within the exporting sector but also indirectly through linkages of exporting firms to domestic input-supplying firms.

Importantly, however, moving from the nationwide and sectoral level to regional and individual outcomes reveals significant heterogeneity both in developed and developing countries. For instance, when local labor markets within countries are not sufficiently diversified, trade can widen regional disparities. Regions specialized in import-competing and upstream industries can fall behind, while areas with industries that export or benefit from cost savings pull away. The result that trade can widen regional disparities in terms of wages and employment seems to be quite general. It has been found both for developed and developing countries such as Brazil, India, and Viet Nam (Dix-Carneiro and Kovak 2017; Topalova 2010; McCaig 2011).

Similarly, while in developed countries trade typically leads to labor market polarization by favoring high-skilled employment over medium-skilled employment, it also seems to raise the demand for skilled workers in developing countries, at least in those for which there is evidence (Bacchetta and Stolzenburg 2019; Bacchetta et al. 2017; Hollweg 2019). Detailed information on the skill structure within French manufacturing firms shows that firms employ relatively more skilled workers in marketing and development when they sell their products outside of France (Maurin, Thoenig, and Thesmar 2002). Other studies show that import competition leads to skill upgrading through its impact on product and process innovation (Bloom, Draka, and Van Reenen 2016; Mion and Zhu 2013). Firm- and worker-level evidence shows that offshoring and import competition have a small positive impact on the demand for nonroutine occupations and thus on job polarization (Becker et al. 2013; Keller and Utar 2016; Hakkala and Huttunen 2016; Utar 2016; Hummels et al. 2014). Two recent studies stand out for accounting explicitly for the rise of GVCs. The first (Reijnders and de Vries 2018) finds that while both automation and offshoring have contributed to polarization in developed economies, the effect of automation is dominant. The results of the second study (Beverelli et al. 2018) suggest that import competition from the People's Republic of China increased the share of low-skilled employment in the US, while participation in GVCs increased the share of high-skilled employment. Trade as a combination of the two has thus contributed to polarization. The results for trade are, however, dwarfed by the estimates for the role of technology.

In developing countries, employment creation and wage gains have been biased toward more skilled workers, which contrasts with the predictions of traditional trade theory. Some early evidence pointed toward skill-biased technical change due to increased competitive pressure brought about by trade liberalization as one of the mechanisms at play (Attanasio, Golderg, and Pavcnik 2004). There is also evidence of a complementary mechanism in which exporters have more incentive to upgrade their technology when trade costs decrease (Bustos 2011a, 2011b).

When they get better access to the markets of rich countries, exporters may also have an incentive to upgrade the quality of their products, which in turn requires more skilled workers (Verhoogen 2008; Brambilla, Lederman, and Porto 2012). Finally, imported technological change may be an important driver of demand for skills in developing countries that rely on imports for most of their capital equipment (Burstein, Cravino, and Vogel 2013). GVCs reinforce this trend by supporting more complex industrial organization and relying on complementary skill-intensive services inputs (Hollweg 2019).

Trade and Labor in Asia

A review of the literature by Devashish Mitra (Chapter 1) confirms that trade has benefited Asian economies through a number of channels and in many different respects—through higher productivity, lower markups through import competition, higher wages, higher employment, lower unemployment, and, above all, lower poverty rates. At the same time, however, studies of the labor market and distributional effects of trade identify a number of challenges. First, trade can increase informality. Second, high adjustment costs can significantly slow down the adjustment process following a trade shock and reduce the benefits from trade opening. Third, rigidities in the labor market may limit the movement of workers and increase the costs of firms to make the necessary adjustments. Fourth, there is evidence that trade raised inequality in some Asian countries but reduced it in others. Finally, evidence suggests that, in some respects, globalization has put pressure on workers, decreasing their bargaining power relative to their employers.

It is important to emphasize that none of these results can be generalized to all countries in the region or beyond the region. The empirical studies in this book focus on a small set of countries, including the People's Republic of China and India, which differ significantly from other countries in the region.

The other studies in this volume examine various dimensions of worker and firm adjustments to trade in Asia. The same caveat regarding generalization of their results applies.

Marcelo Olarreaga, Roberta Piermartini, and Guido Porto (Chapter 2) look systematically and for a large sample of developed and developing countries at the correlation between tariffs faced in the export destination markets and domestic wages. Tariffs are often used as an instrument to protect domestic workers from foreign competition. Arguably, as tariffs protect domestic workers, they also hurt foreign workers. Indeed, using sector-level data across developing and developed countries during 1976–2004, the authors find that an increase of 10 percentage points in tariffs faced in international markets leads on average to a 0.8% reduction in wages at home. They also explore the winners and losers from the observed changes in tariffs of the rest of the world (ROW) and show that, because countries export different products to different countries, there are important differences in terms of changes in market access. This implies that workers in some countries have benefited from better market access, whereas others experienced losses in wages due to a deterioration of their market access abroad. Of the 14 Asian economies in the sample, eight experienced declines in average wages as a result of increases in ROW tariffs, and six experienced wage increases as a result of declines in ROW tariffs. Japan, Malaysia, Pakistan, and Hong Kong, China experienced some of the highest average wage growth due to improvements in market access.

Yuan Zi (Chapter 3) analyzes how the *hukou* system—the People's Republic of China's household registration system—has restricted the geographical mobility of workers, and the spatial adjustments of labor to trade shocks and limited the (re)distribution of the gains from trade. The remarkable expansion of the People's Republic of China's participation in world trade has been accompanied by a high level of internal migration within the country. Hundreds of millions of workers in the People's Republic of China have moved from inland areas to coastal cities, contributing to the country's manufacturing growth and export surges. Zi shows, however, that by prohibiting migrant workers from accessing various social benefits in their actual cities of residence, the *hukou* system limited migration inflows into urban areas experiencing positive trade shocks. At the worker level, a larger proportion of the gains accrued to workers holding local *hukou*. Hence, the uneven regional gains from trade translated into uneven gains across people holding different types of *hukou*.

Prachi Gupta and Matthias Helble (Chapter 4) examine how trade liberalization affected the labor share in India during 1998–1999 to 2007–2008. Overall, they find that a decline in output tariffs led to an increase in the labor share of income, while a fall in input tariffs led to a decrease in the labor share. Interestingly, controlling for factor intensity, they also find that in sectors that are technology and human capital intensive, both declines in input and output tariff rates led to a decline in the labor share. A fall in tariffs only led to an increase in the labor share for labor-intensive and low-technology plants. Finally, the empirical results show that labor adjustment occurred more efficiently in Indian states with flexible labor laws.

Rashesh Shrestha and Ian Coxhead (Chapter 5) analyze the impact of Indonesia's export boom and rapid economic growth on formality in the job market. Indonesia had relatively lower competitiveness in sectors with high formal employment rates. Trade opening triggered some involuntary labor movement from formal to informal modes of employment. Using an econometric model, the authors provide new evidence that the earnings of workers displaced from formal jobs to informal ones are significantly lower than those of workers who remain in the formal market. This finding shows that welfare gains from trade opening and economic growth are not necessarily shared by everyone. Furthermore, they shed some light on the causes of Indonesia's unprecedented increase in inequality during the same growth period.

Firm-level Adjustment

A review by Dionisius Narjoko and Shujiro Urata (Chapter 6) of the recent literature on firm-level adjustments in Asia shows strong evidence of the positive impact of trade opening on productivity as well as a rapid growth in the number of new firms entering the market. More and more studies are finding evidence that exporting increases their process innovation activities and promotes the creation of new products. Finally, several studies show a positive impact of input tariff reduction on quality upgrading.

Nobuaki Yamashita and Isamu Yamauchi (Chapter 7) examine the question whether firms that have been more exposed to import competition from developing countries undertake more innovative activity or less. Using a firm-level panel dataset for Japan for 1994–2005, the authors find that intensified import competition from the People's Republic of China has resulted in more innovative activity of Japanese firms, consistent with similar findings of firms in Europe. Moreover, such competition has also led to both an increase in nonused patents.

Pavel Chakraborty (Chapter 8) analyzes the effect of tariff liberalization in India between 1990 and 2011 on wage inequality, measured as the ratio of managerial to nonmanagerial compensation. India underwent a significant structural transformation through trade liberalization and other reforms (domestic) in the 1990s because of a balance-of-payments crisis. Using this episode to identify the causal effect of a drop in tariffs on wage inequality, he finds that a 10% reduction in input tariffs (and not output) significantly increases the share of managerial compensation by 0.5%–3.5%, raising within-firm wage inequality. His results also suggest that a rise in skill intensity possibly explains the increase in managerial compensation, but only for firms below the median of the size distribution. On the other hand, there is no evidence of a demand shift away from nonmanagers due to the drop in tariffs.

Using firm-level data covering the 2010–2015 period, Ha Thi Thanh Doan (Chapter 9) analyzes the characteristics of multiproduct manufacturing firms in Viet Nam. She finds that multiproduct firms are larger, more capital intensive, more productive, and more likely to export. Looking into the link between tariff reduction and product shedding, her results reveal that exporters have an important role in product adding, which suggests they may contribute to aggregate growth through the channel of product scope expansion. Finally, while she finds that state-owned enterprises are more likely to spread economic activities across products and industries, there is little difference in terms of product churning among FDI, state-owned enterprises, and the domestic private sector.

Main Findings and Policy Conclusions

Mobility frictions prevent necessary adjustments. In the case of the People's Republic of China, for example, the *hukou* system appears to have limited the workers in moving where the demand was. In India, firms in states with rigid labor laws were unwilling to hire more labor and instead replaced labor with capital. Several studies in this volume indicate that mobility frictions can cause important adjustment costs. Identifying these frictions and addressing them can improve overall efficiency but it can also help make trade more inclusive.

Trade opening appears to have the potential to increase informality, but it doesn't necessarily have this effect. In the case of Indonesia, trade opening triggered a movement from formal to informal modes of employment. However, there is also evidence that trade can raise the share of formal employment (Bacchetta et al. 2009). The benefits of trade opening can be more easily shared if a large share of workers are in the formal sector. Being in the formal sector usually means to enjoy benefits that smoothen the adjustment process, such as unemployment insurance. More research is needed to understand how governments can ensure that more trade will not result in more informal employment.

Evidence in this volume also suggests that engaging in exports can stimulate research and development activities, enlarge the product scope, and increase the product quality, which tend to increase the demand for skilled labor. Not having access to skilled labor undermines the competitiveness of firms and entire sectors. Training and education policies play an important role in helping respond to the changes in labor demand induced by trade (Bacchetta et al. 2017).

Trade opening increases competition among firms. At the same time, it allows for improved access to inputs at lower prices. Typically, it therefore results in an increase in productivity of firms.

However, some firms might have to exit the market or are absorbed by other firms. These dynamics suggest that the quick reallocation of capital from less to more productive uses is crucial to achieve high welfare benefits. Well-developed capital markets can help achieve this objective. In Asia, the financing of firms is typically bank dominated, and capital markets are shallow. As Asian economies grow, it is important to deepen their financial markets to ensure an easier redeployment of capital across sectors.

Trade opening is a blessing for some sectors, while others might suffer. It can therefore have a significant impact on income distribution. Despite adjustment costs, trade opening usually yields net overall welfare benefits. While there is an efficiency argument for governments to address mobility frictions and reduce adjustment costs, governments may have different preferences regarding the need to redistribute income between those who lose and those who gain from trade. In developing countries, tax collection can be a challenge for governments that wish to redistribute. For these countries, improving tax collection should therefore become a policy priority. The experience of Asia clearly shows that trade delivers; governments can help ensure that trade delivers for all.

References

Attanasio, O., P.K. Goldberg, and N. Pavcnik. 2004. Trade Reforms and Wage Inequality in Colombia. *Journal of Development Economics*. 74 (2). pp. 331–66.

Autor, D.H., D. Dorn, and G.H. Hanson. 2013. The China Syndrome: Local Labor Market Effects of Import Competition in the United States. *American Economic Review*. 103 (6). pp. 2121–68.

Bacchetta, M., and V. Stolzenburg. 2019. Trade, Value Chains and Labour Markets in Advanced Economies. In World Trade Organization, Institute of Developing Economies – Japan External Trade Organization, Organisation for Economic Co-operation and Development, University of International Business and Economics, and World Bank Group, eds. *Global Value Chain Development Report 2019: Technological Innovation, Supply Chain Trade, and Workers in a Globalized World*. Geneva: World Trade Organization.

Bacchetta, M., C. Gregg, S. Rubínová, and B. Tumurchudur Klok. 2017. *Investing in Skills for Inclusive Trade*. Geneva: International Labour Organization and World Trade Organization.

Bacchetta, M., E. Ernst, and J.P. Bustamante. 2009. *Globalization and Informal Jobs in Developing Countries*. Geneva: International Labour Organization and World Trade Organization.

Becker, S., K. Ekholm, and M.A. Muendler. 2013. Offshoring and the Onshore Composition of Tasks and Skills. *Journal of International Economics*. 90 (1). pp. 91–106.

Beverelli, C., S. Rubinova, V. Stolzenburg, and N. Woessner. 2018. Did Global Value Chains Contribute to Rising Labour Market Polarization? World Trade Organization, unpublished manuscript.

Bloom, N., M. Draka, and J. Van Reenen. 2016. Trade Induced Technical Change? The Impact of Chinese Imports on Innovation, IT and Productivity. *The Review of Economic Studies*. 83 (1). pp. 87–117.

Braakmann, N., and A. Vogel. 2011. How Does Economic Integration Influence Employment and Wages in Border Regions? The Case of the EU Enlargement 2004 and Germany's Eastern Border. *Review of World Economics*. 147 (2). pp. 303–23.

Brambilla, I., D. Lederman, and G. Porto. 2012. Exports, Export Destinations, and Skills. *The American Economic Review*. 102 (7). pp. 3406–38.

Burstein, A., J. Cravino, and J. Vogel. 2013. Importing Skill-Biased Technology. *American Economic Journal: Macroeconomics*. 5 (2). pp. 32–71.

Bustos, P. 2011a. The Impact of Trade Liberalization on Skill Upgrading: Evidence From Argentina. Universitat Pompeu Fabra Economics and Business Working Paper. No. 1189. Barcelona: Universitat Pompeu Fabra.

———. 2011b. Trade Liberalization, Exports, and Technology Upgrading: Evidence on the Impact of MERCOSUR on Argentinian Firms. *American Economic Review*. 101 (1). pp. 304–40.

Dix-Carneiro, R., and B.K. Kovak. 2017. Trade Liberalization and Regional Dynamics. *The American Economic Review*. 107 (10). pp. 2908–46.

Hakkala, K.N., and K. Huttunen. 2016. Worker-Level Consequences of Import Shocks. *VATT* Institute for Economic Research Working Paper. No. 74. Helsinki: VATT Institute for Economic Research.

Hakobyan, S., and J. McLaren. 2016. Looking for Local Labor Market Effects of NAFTA. *Review of Economics and Statistics*. 98 (4). pp. 728–41.

Hasan, R., D. Mitra, P. Ranjan, and R.N. Ahsan. 2012. Trade Liberalization and Unemployment: Theory and Evidence from India. *Journal of Development Economics*. 97 (2). pp. 269–80.

Hollweg, C.H. 2019. Global Value Chains and Employment in Developing Countries. In World Trade Organization, Institute of Developing Economies – Japan External Trade Organization, Organisation for Economic Co-operation and Development, University of International Business and Economics and World Bank Group, eds. *Global Value Chain Development Report 2019: Technological Innovation, Supply Chain Trade, and Workers in a Globalized World*. Geneva: World Trade Organization.

Hummels, D.L., R. Jørgensen, J.R. Munch, and C. Xiang. 2014. The Wage Effects of Offshoring: Evidence from Danish Matched Worker-Firm Data. *American Economic Review*. 104 (6). pp. 1597–629.

Keller, W., and H. Utar. 2016. International Trade and Job Polarization: Evidence at the Worker Level. CESifo Working Paper. No. 5978. Munich: Center for Economic. Studies and Ifo Institute.

Maurin, E., M. Thoenig, and D. Thesmar. 2002. Globalization and the Demand for Skill: An Export Based Channel. CEPR Discussion Paper. No. 3406. Washington, DC: Center for Economic and Policy Research.

McCaig, B. 2011. Exporting Out of Poverty: Provincial Poverty in Vietnam and US Market Access. *Journal of International Economics*. 85 (1). pp. 102–13.

McCaig, B., and N. Pavcnik. 2018. Export Markets and Labor Allocation in a Low-Income Country. *American Economic Review*. 108 (7). pp. 1899–941.

Mion, G., and L. Zhu. 2013. Import Competition from and Offshoring to China: A Curse or Blessing for Firms? *Journal of International Economics*. 89 (1). pp. 202–15.

Pierce, J.R., and P.K. Schott. 2016. The Surprisingly Swift Decline of US Manufacturing Employment. *The American Economic Review.* 106 (7). pp. 1632–62.

Reijnders, L.S.M., and G.J. de Vries. 2018. Technology, Offshoring and the Rise of Non-routine Jobs. *Journal of Development Economics.* 135. pp. 412–32.

Topalova, P. 2010. Factor Immobility and Regional Impacts of Trade Liberalization: Evidence on Poverty from India. *American Economic Journal: Applied Economics.* 2 (4). pp. 1–41.

Topalova, P., and A. Khandelwal. 2011. Trade Liberalization and Firm Productivity: The Case of India. *Review of Economics and Statistics.* 93 (3). pp. 995–1009.

Utar, H. 2016. Workers beneath the Floodgates: Impact of Low-Wage Import Competition and Workers' Adjustment. CESifo Working Paper Series. No. 6224. Munich: Center for Economic. Studies and Ifo Institute.

Verhoogen, E.A. 2008. Trade, Quality Upgrading, and Wage Inequality in the Mexican Manufacturing Sector. *The Quarterly Journal of Economics.* 123 (2). pp. 489–530.

World Trade Organization. 2017. *World Trade Report 2017: Trade, Technology and Jobs.* Geneva.

Yu, M. 2015. Processing Trade, Tariff Reductions and Firm Productivity: Evidence from Chinese Firms. *The Economic Journal.* 125 (585). pp. 943–88.

PART I
Overview: Trade Adjustment in Asia

1

Responses to Trade Opening: Evidence and Lessons from Asia

Devashish Mitra

1.1 Introduction

Over the last 3 decades, several developing countries have liberalized their trade regimes. This may have happened either due partially to conditionalities imposed by international organizations, such as the International Monetary Fund in response to emergency requests for loans, in the context of a country's accession to the World Trade Organization, or as a result of the signature of a preferential trade agreement. In many cases, the reforms may have stemmed from a country's own disappointment with its growth performance during its import substitution phase. While movement toward free trade is expected to expand the size of the overall economic pie, such changes always produce both losers and winners. In fact, it is this creation of winners and losers, along with "individual-specific uncertainty" (Fernandez and Rodrik 1991) about who benefits and who loses from reforms, that has led to the delays in trade reforms, appropriately called "status quo bias."

Guided by theoretical work, a large number of empirical papers focus on identifying the losing and winning sections of society from these reforms and even quantifying the impact of these reforms on the various economic classes, such as the poor relative to the rich and unskilled relative to skilled workers. While there certainly will be winners and losers, who exactly they will be also matters. If the rich benefit and the poor lose, then, despite economic growth, there will be a new situation with higher poverty and inequality. This does not necessarily mean that countries should not open up to trade. It only means that they will have to have social protection schemes in place at the time of trade reforms. Of course, if the incomes of the poor grow along with the overall economic growth brought about by trade opening, then trade reforms will be highly desirable. Even in these situations, social protection and redistributive policies might be necessary to maximize the progress in poverty reduction and minimize any possible increase in inequality.

As will be apparent from the evidence reviewed in this chapter, researchers associate trade liberalization with poverty reduction in Asia. This has probably happened through economic growth. At the same time, they also sometimes and in some countries see a rise in inequality. In the case of the People's Republic of China, there has been a very rapid rise in income inequality but at the same time a particularly impressive reduction in poverty. On the one hand, there is no question about the desirability of poverty reduction. The desirability of lower inequality, on the other hand, is sometimes questionable under certain conditions. For instance, some degree of inequality is optimal to preserve incentives in any economy. However, beyond a point, inequality could lead to social, political, and economic instability that could hurt a country's growth performance. It could also lead to inequality in educational attainment. Especially in the presence of credit market imperfections, inequality reduces a country's aggregate human capital and handicaps local businesses in their expansion (or even in their entry decisions), thereby adversely affecting growth.

In this chapter, I first examine the evidence on the impact of trade opening on productivity, since productivity levels normally determine incomes. A rise in productivity, holding other things equal, improves workers' wages and lifts them out of poverty. In addition, it is always necessary to determine the distribution of any increase in per capita income. The first distribution of importance is that between producers and consumers. While every individual in society is both a producer and a consumer, owners of firms or capitalists actually receive the producer surplus. Thus, looking at the impact of trade on producer and consumer surplus indicates something about the distribution of welfare changes. A reduction in price–cost markups indicates a shift of the surplus from firm owners to consumers, most of whom are ordinary citizens whose primary income source is their raw labor power. Therefore, I also study the impact of trade reforms on markups.

As mentioned, for ordinary citizens, the main source of income is their labor. It is therefore necessary to know whether trade provides a higher or lower reward for their labor and whether it provides greater and better opportunities to use their labor for their livelihoods. Therefore, I next review the evidence on the impact of trade reforms on wages, employment, and unemployment. Productivity and markups are just inputs into these outcomes that matter directly to citizens.

However, it is important to consider not only how many people have jobs but also the quality of their jobs. In developing countries, a large number of people work in the informal sector or informally for formal firms. These workers lack job security, health insurance, a pension plan, and so on. In addition, they receive a wage that is a fraction of the formal worker wage. Therefore, it is important to investigate how trade affects informal employment as a proportion of the overall employment and whether there are any complementary domestic policies and institutions that affect this relationship. Investigating these relationships will allow me to make recommendations on domestic policies such as labor market policies.

In addition, it is necessary to examine the immediate impact of trade reforms or shocks on workers. While workers might move to a better steady state due to trade liberalization, they may incur mobility costs to move to the new steady state. As a result of incurring trade adjustment costs, workers might be hurt in the transition, and they may lose a significant part of the gross welfare gains as a result. I discuss policies aimed at reducing labor mobility costs and minimizing the pain from trade adjustment.

I continue by directly examining the evidence on the impact of trade reforms on poverty, as well as the channels through which this impact takes place. In this regard, I consider rural and urban poverty separately. I also investigate the impact on the people just below the poverty line relative to those far below it. The impact of trade on poverty is important, especially when evaluating social welfare using a Rawlsian welfare function, which measures how well a society is performing by how well the least well-off are performing.

Next, this chapter reviews the impact of trade liberalization on inequality in its various forms. While there are summary measures of inequality, such as the Gini coefficient, every such measure has its weaknesses and no measure is able to capture all aspects of inequality. Therefore, starting with overall inequality, I move to more specific forms of inequality, such as the inequality among workers, which I capture through the ratio of the wages of the skilled to those of the unskilled, often using the ratio of wages of nonproduction workers to those of production workers as a proxy. I also study the interindustry wage differentials and the way in which trade reforms affect them. It is important to analyze this heterogeneity, because different industries receive different amounts of tariff cuts. For example, in most countries, the tariff cuts were deepest in labor-intensive industries, simply because they were the most protected initially.

Another way in which trade affects the distribution of the overall pie is through its impact on the bargaining power of workers relative to their employers. In addition, as mentioned, trade affects the monopoly power of firms, which I measure using the price–marginal cost markups. Apart from affecting the way in which consumers and producers share the surplus, this impact affects the wedge between the value of the marginal product of labor and the wage that labor receives. As a result, this may affect labor's share in the sales or output (and, at the macro level, the national income). It is also important to analyze the impact of trade on these labor shares (along with the bargaining power of workers), since, during the last 2–3 decades, these shares have been falling all over the world, along with countries opening their trade regimes, in the presence of skill-biased technical change. It is important to investigate which of the two (trade or technological change) is the culprit here.

I find that, for Asian countries, on the whole has been able to stimulate productivity and, to a certain extent, discipline firms to reduce their markups (if I focus on the impact of reductions in output tariff cuts). As a result, wages have risen on average. In addition, large reductions in poverty have occurred. However, inequality has increased, for which the blame partially falls on trade. Thus, there is a need for redistributive policies and social protection policies, especially in the form of public works programs.

1.2 Trade Reforms, Productivity, and Markups

The standard gains from trade are those that countries obtain through specialization and exchange. Moving away from free trade to a state of protection leads to production as well as consumption distortion costs. Under protection, for an import-competing good, consumers pay and domestic producers receive a higher price than that under free trade. This distorts both the consumption and the production of the good, with too little of the former and too much of the latter. It is possible to demonstrate these standard costs of protectionism or the standard gains from trade under the very basic conditions of perfect competition. Once countries move to less competitive market structures, allowing firms to have some degree of monopoly power, trade results in another gain. Trade destroys the monopoly power of domestic firms along with the deadweight losses that accompany it. Domestic firms, while still not facing any competition from other domestic firms, now face competition from foreign firms within the same industry. Domestic consumers are no longer at the mercy of domestic firms, and, as a result, firms cannot charge unusually high markups over their costs. In other words, trade has a way of disciplining domestic firms, the extent of which it is possible to estimate by examining the impact of trade on price–marginal cost markups.

In addition to a decline in markups, which benefits consumers for given production costs, import competition can also have an impact on these costs themselves through the induced changes in technology and efficiency. Procompetitive effects of trade lead to an increase in the incentives for import-competing firms to invest in research and development and function more efficiently. The way in which these effects work is that reductions in the production costs of domestic firms relative to those of foreign firms now lead to a gain in the market share of the former at the expense of the latter. This opportunity to grab market share from a foreign competitor or the danger of losing some market share to it due to lagging productivity leads to this procompetitive increase in the incentive for firms to invest in productivity increases. There is also a market size effect in the opposite direction, arising from the fact that the benefits of any reduction in the production costs of a domestic import-competing firm now applies to a smaller domestic market (for any domestic firm) under freer trade, thereby reducing the returns to cost reduction. In addition, the trade and endogenous growth literature highlights several other channels through which trade can affect productivity growth. These effects often move in opposing directions. For example, depending on whether skilled labor becomes more or less expensive through trade due to Stolper–Samuelson-type effects, research and development output may increase or decrease. Trade will also reduce the duplication of research efforts as well as lead to greater knowledge flows, resulting in higher productivity. Grossman and Helpman (1991) describe and rigorously model a number of other channels. Due to these numerous mutually opposing effects, how trade affects productivity and productivity growth becomes an empirical question.

While all the theory on markups points in only one direction, namely that trade reforms, in the form of reductions in import protection for the output of an industry (leading to greater import competition), should unambiguously lower price–cost markups, the various theoretical models on the impact of trade reforms on productivity together predict little. However, it is important to study both empirically for a few reasons. While price depends on cost and markup, cost depends on productivity. In other words, consumer and overall welfare ultimately depends on productivity and markup, and it is thus important to study them, especially to gain some idea of the sizes of the actual changes. Furthermore, inputs may become cheaper due to trade liberalization, and that might have an opposite impact on markups.

In many studies, in the process of estimating productivity and the impact of trade on it, researchers end up measuring markups and the impact of trade on them. It is important to note that, while the latter is often a by-product of the former, markup estimations are sometimes necessary to achieve accurate estimates of productivity and changes in productivity.

Pioneered by Nobel laureate Robert Solow in 1957, the oldest approach to measuring total factor productivity (TFP) growth was called growth accounting. The approach assumed perfect competition and constant returns to scale, with the implication that the share of a factor in the total output equals the elasticity of the output with respect to the factor. This is another way of saying that the reward to the factor equals the value of its marginal product. However, the elasticity of output with respect to this factor, measured as its share in output, would be underestimated in the presence of imperfect competition and increasing returns to scale. This would overestimate the unexplained growth in output or TFP growth. Robert Hall's (1988) pathbreaking work in macroeconomics incorporated imperfect competition and markups as well as nonconstant returns into the analysis of TFP growth. In international trade, Harrison (1994) was the first to incorporate these two features into TFP growth estimation using firm-level data from Côte d'Ivoire. The same regression estimates both markups and productivity growth as well as changes in them in response to trade liberalization. Krishna's and Mitra's (1998) paper was the first to estimate these parameters using the same methodology (though slightly modified to incorporate changes in returns to scale) for an Asian country.

1.2.1 Empirics

I start with the case of India. The oldest study on the impact of trade reforms on markups and productivity in India is the one by Krishna and Mitra (1998). They use firm-level data for a few industries in the period 1986–1993 on output, capital, labor raw materials, energy use, and input shares in output (using the data on input expenditures) to produce estimates of both markups and productivity along with changes in them between the pre- and postreform periods. The idea is that, if they regress the growth rate of output on a weighted sum of the growth rates in the various inputs (the weights being the shares of the various inputs in the value of the output), the coefficient of this variable is the price-to-marginal cost markup and the intercept term is the estimated TFP growth. Additionally, using an interaction dummy variable and the dummy variable itself (where the dummy variable takes the value 1 for the postreform years and 0 otherwise), we can estimate the change in the markup and productivity growth.

Such a study is meaningful only if the trade reform is not endogenous to changes in the relevant economic variables. The Indian trade reforms initiated in 1991 provide such an opportunity, since the reforms, as Krishna and Mitra argue, were unexpected in that the Government of India approached the International Monetary Fund to rescue it from a bad macroeconomic situation. The loans came with the strict conditionality of economic reforms, which included trade liberalization as an important component. There were other reasons as well to believe that the reforms were exogenous.

For three out of the four industries studied—non-electrical machinery, electronics, and transport equipment—Krishna and Mitra find statistically significant reductions in markups. In the pre-reform phase, the markups are in the range of 1–2 percentage points, and they all fall below 1 percentage point after the reforms. This is consistent with the idea that a firm might lose money while adapting to a new and changing environment. In another industry—electrical machinery— the markup is below 1 percentage point initially, and no statistically significant change in the markup is observable.

Moving to productivity growth, in three out of four industries— electrical machinery, non-electrical machinery, and electronics—the point estimates of growth increases are positive, ranging between 3 and 6 percentage points, but these estimates are not as precise as the markups and markup changes. In the case of transport equipment, there is a decline in productivity growth, but the estimate is highly insignificant statistically.

One important point to note is that this method involves choosing inputs and output simultaneously, as a result of which both are correlated with technology shocks. Consequently, the right-hand side input variables are correlated with the error term. Researchers argue that this will lead to biased estimates of productivity growth and markups. Krishna and Mitra assert that the estimates of the change in markup and change in productivity growth will be biased only if the abovementioned correlation changes after the reform. They do not expect this reform to have a systematic impact on this correlation. Krishna and Mitra support their arguments with Monte Carlo simulations.

Since Krishna's and Mitra's study, the methodologies for markup and productivity estimation have improved, and they address the above concerns directly. The recent studies on productivity and markup are separate. Topalova and Khandelwal (2011) use the Levinsohn–Petrin approach to address the simultaneity problem that I described above (as well as the measurement error problem). The approach recognizes that the choice of materials responds to technology shocks and changes in the capital stock. Under such conditions, inverting this function of technology shocks and capital stock gives the technology shocks as a function of material inputs and capital. Further assuming a Markov process for technology, the authors are able to control for simultaneity problems. The authors also have a longer sample period for their firm-level analysis, spanning a 15-year period, 1987–2001. Additionally, they investigate the impact of both tariffs on final goods as well as inputs.

Topalova and Khandelwal find a procompetitive impact of output tariffs in that lower tariffs lead to higher productivity.[1] However, they conclude that the positive impact of an equal input tariff reduction is much greater in size. A 10% reduction in the output tariff increases productivity by 0.3%, while a 10% reduction in the input tariff leads to a 4.8% productivity increase. Between 1989 and 1996, the output and input tariff declines led to about 1.7% and 10.6% increases in productivity, respectively. The authors view this result as indicative of a much stronger impact of trade liberalization through the greater availability of a broader range of inputs of higher quality as well as "exposure to new technologies" rather than through greater competition from final products coming from abroad. Goldberg et al. (2010) confirm this channel, finding that trade liberalization led to a 21% decline in the prices of intermediate inputs and an 8% increase in the variety of intermediate inputs.

De Loecker et al. (2016) rigorously study the impact of trade liberalization on the markups of Indian firms. Using an improved version of the Levinsohn–Petrin approach to deal with the fact that physical quantities of output and inputs are rarely observable (leading to biases in production function estimation), the authors arrive at estimates of the elasticities of output with respect to the various inputs. Under constant returns to scale, the price–marginal cost markup equals the elasticity of output with respect to an input divided by the input's share in the sales of output. They calculate these markups and investigate their relationship to trade liberalization for the period 1989–1997. Reductions in input tariffs increase markups. Average costs are lowered through reductions in input tariffs but partly offset by the fact that only some of these benefits are passed on to consumers as a result of an increase in markups. A 10-percentage-point reduction in input tariffs can lead to an 8% increase in markups; a 10-percentage-point reduction in output tariffs has a procompetitive effect of reducing markups by 1.2%–1.5%. While output tariffs declined on average by 62 percentage points during the 1989–1996 period, input tariffs declined by 24 percentage points. The net impact was an increase in markups during this period of about 13%. Given that costs declined by 31% due to lower input prices as well as a greater variety of inputs (consistent with Goldberg et al. [2010] as well as Topalova and Khandelwal [2011]), this meant that there was an average decline in prices (relative to the overall two-digit sectoral price level) of about 18%. The authors also find that the procompetitive

---

[1]   Note that the new literature, unlike the old literature (Krishna and Mitra 1998; Harrison 1994), focuses on productivity levels rather than productivity growth rates.

effect of output tariff reduction was concentrated in the initially high-markup firms. While a 10-percentage-point reduction in output tariffs led to a 4.4% reduction in markups in firms that were among the top 10% of the initial distribution of markups, the remaining firms, on average, experienced a 1.3% markup reduction.

Nataraj (2011) also examines formal- and informal-sector firms in India separately for the period 1989–2001 and finds that, while mainly output tariff reductions affect informal-firm productivity, input tariff reductions affect only formal-sector firm productivity. A 10-percentage-point reduction in the output tariff increases formal-firm productivity by up to 0.76% but increases informal firm productivity by 4.8%. A 10-percentage-point reduction in the input tariff increases formal-firm productivity by 4.6%, with no statistically significant effect on informal-firm productivity. This makes intuitive sense, since informal sector firms rarely buy imported inputs but might feel the competition from imported final products.

Amiti and Konings (2007) study the impact of the 1990s trade reforms on firm-level productivity in Indonesia. Indonesia's trade reforms are linked to its accession to the World Trade Organization in 1995, and the sample period for this study is 1991–2001. This is, in fact, the first study to investigate the impact of input and output tariffs simultaneously on firm productivity, which it calculates using the Olley–Pakes approach to correct for both simultaneity in input and output choice and sample selection bias. While a 1%–6% increase in productivity is attributable to a 10-percentage-point reduction in the output tariff, they find that firms that import inputs can experience up to a 13% increase in productivity from a 10-percentage-point input tariff reduction. They also find that the Asian financial crisis somewhat muted the latter effect from 1997 onward. This is understandable, since domestic currency devaluations would have led to an increase in the domestic price of inputs. The authors also find the beneficial effects of output tariff reforms to be concentrated in the more competitive industries (as compared with the high-markup ones), while the positive effects of input tariffs on productivity do not vary by the degree of within-industry competition. The results here qualitatively survive correction for endogeneity of trade reforms through an instrumental variable approach in which the initial (1991) tariffs instrument the change in tariffs.

Brandt et al. (2017) study the impact of trade liberalization on firm-level markups and TFP in the People's Republic of China around the time of its accession to the World Trade Organization. As in the case of India, input tariff reductions increase markups, implying an incomplete pass-through of input cost reductions to consumers. On the other hand, output tariff reductions reduce the markups only of the relatively large firms, mainly incumbents, and have no impact on the markups of other firms, especially new entrants. On average, a 10-percentage-point reduction in the output tariff leads to up to a 1% markup reduction, while a 10-percentage-point reduction in the input tariff leads to a 7% markup increase.[2] The authors argue that the endogeneity of the trade liberalization is not a major concern by showing that neither past industry productivity nor past productivity change determine tariff reductions. The procompetitive effects in this study and in that of De Loecker et al. (2016) are not comparable, since the latter observe firm-level prices to which they can apply their estimated markups to compute firm-level marginal costs, which, in turn, they can control for in their estimation of the procompetitive effects of output tariff reductions. To the extent that there are procompetitive effects on productivity and costs that are incompletely passed on to consumers, this study of the People's Republic of China will underestimate the output tariff effects on markups. The procompetitive effect of a 10-percentage-point decline in the output tariff is a 1.7% increase in TFP, while, for the same percentage decline in the input tariff, the TFP gain is 16%–18%. While the bulk of the gain in industry-level productivity comes from increases in within-firm productivity, some of the gains arise through the entry of new productive firms that are flexible enough to incorporate newer, more efficient technology. The exit of relatively low-productivity firms is another channel but is not as strong. The authors also find that the industries that experience deeper input tariff cuts are those that experience a relatively smaller reallocation of output from less to more productive firms.

Yu (2015) also considers the impact of trade liberalization on firm-level TFP in the People's Republic of China for the period 2000–2006. While he also finds a positive impact of both input and output tariff reduction on TFP, in contrast to other studies, he identifies a much bigger impact of output tariff reductions than input tariff reductions. With a 10-percentage-point output tariff reduction, TFP increases by 9%. A 10-percentage-point input tariff reduction increases TFP by only 5%. Many reasons could explain the difference in results. The sample period is slightly different (in Brandt et al. [2017]it is 1998–2007), but the tariff measures are also firm specific in Yu's study, with firm-specific weights based on the multiple product lines that each firm sells in the case of output tariffs and firm-level imports of

---

[2]   Fan et al. (2017) obtain qualitatively similar results on markups. They run regressions separately for firms engaged in processing trade and other firms. As they expect from the theory, these effects empirically do not appear for the former but are apparent in the latter type of firms.

various imported inputs in the case of input tariffs. Another result that Yu obtains is that the impact of these tariff reductions on TFP decreases with an increase in the share of processing imports in total imports. This is not surprising, since these processing imports do not lead to greater import competition nor were they ever subject to tariffs during the author's sample period.

Bas and Causa (2013) examine the impact of input tariff reductions, among many policy changes, on the labor productivity of firms in the People's Republic of China. In this study, they take the productivity heterogeneity among firms quite seriously. Using a sample of firms for 2001–2008, they find that input tariff reductions increase labor productivity and that the effect is stronger for firms at the domestic technological frontier than for other firms. Firms that are on or close to the frontier experience a 0.74% increase in productivity from a 1-percentage-point reduction in the input tariff. Firms whose productivity is half of the domestic technological frontier will experience roughly a 0.5% rise in productivity from the same 1-point-reduction in the input tariff. The procompetitive impact of output tariff reductions seems to be stronger for firms that are relatively distant from the technological frontier.

There is also an industry-level study by Kim (2000) for the Republic of Korea for the period 1966–1988. He finds that a 10-percentage-point reduction in the quota–coverage ratio leads to an increase in TFP growth of about 0.26 percentage points and a reduction in the markup of 1.33 percentage points. A 10-percentage-point reduction in the nominal rate of protection, on the other hand, leads to an increase in the TFP growth rate of only 0.12 percentage points and a reduction in the markup of 0.4 percentage points. Trade liberalization, primarily quota–coverage reduction from 10% to 30%, during the entire sample period raises the annual TFP growth rate permanently by over 2 percentage points.[3]

Thus, we see that trade reforms generally lead to productivity increases and that the reduction in input tariffs has a much bigger productivity-enhancing impact than an output tariff reduction. Pavcnik (2002) for Chile and Fernandes (2007) for Colombia also find a positive impact of trade liberalization on productivity, but, for countries outside Asia, no studies decompose the impacts of output and input tariffs. As regards productivity growth, Harrison (1994) finds support for an increase in firm-level productivity growth as a result of trade reforms in Côte d'Ivoire. At the same time, she concludes that tariff cuts lead to a reduction in markups. Levinsohn (1993) shows a reduction in markups as a result of trade liberalization for Turkey. Overall, through these

---

[3]   The nominal rate of protection actually rose from 36% to 39%.

channels, trade should increase the average income and at the same time improve the distribution of real incomes.

It is important to note that empirical studies on the impact of trade on productivity and/or markups only exist for a handful of Asian countries: India, Indonesia, the People's Republic of China, the Republic of Korea, and Turkey. However, the fact that the results are no different for all the other non-Asian countries should offer a certain degree of confidence that these relationships may be generalizable to other Asian countries.

The next logical point to study is the impact of trade on the two most fundamental labor market outcomes—wages and employment— since both depend on productivity and markups, as will be explained.

1.3 Trade, Wages, and Employment

Trade benefits the abundant factor and hurts the scarce factor. Given that most Asian economies are abundant in labor, in particular low-skilled labor, I expect trade to increase wages, in particular low-skilled wages, in these economies. However, this result (the Stolper–Samuelson theorem) is based on the assumption that factors move freely between sectors, one of the key assumptions of the Heckscher–Ohlin model. This assumption is unlikely to be valid in developing Asia, especially in the short to medium run, thereby reducing the relevance of the Heckscher–Ohlin model to this region. Even with low levels of education, workers need to have sector- or even firm-specific skills, and those take time to acquire. Workers acquire some skills on the job. As a result, workers who become displaced, through import competition, cannot easily find new jobs in the expanding sectors. Those who remain employed in the shrinking sectors may experience wage reductions. Furthermore, if the Stolper–Samuelson effect holds, even weakly, the wage increase can result in many firms reducing their employment in response.

However, the procompetitive productivity effect, for which evidence exists, can result in an increase in firm-level and industry-level employment and wages. In addition, the destruction of monopoly power, brought about by import competition, shrinks the wedge between the price and the marginal cost and thus between the value of the marginal product and the wage, thereby possibly leading to an increase in the wage. However, if there is rent sharing, the decline in the rents can lower the wages that employees receive and/or the employment itself. In addition, the incentive to remain unionized decreases. With de-unionization, workers' bargaining power lessens, representing another channel through which wages can shrink. In addition, in a monopoly situation, the seller produces too little and as a result the employment is low. Trade, by reducing the monopoly power of domestic firms, might be able to increase employment through this channel.

1.3.1 Empirical Evidence from Asia

Amiti and Davis (2012) investigate how the average wage of a firm changes with trade liberalization. They examine the differential effects of output and input tariff cuts on firms that are purely domestic (do not export or import) and those that export and/or import. The theoretical model that guides their estimation is one of fair wages in which workers receive a fraction of the profits. In other words, more profitable firms pay higher wages. As a result, greater openness in trade leads to exporting firms earning higher profits and, therefore, paying higher wages, while those selling only in the domestic market but facing import competition suffer from profit reductions and pay lower wages. Additionally, firms that use imported inputs become more profitable and pay higher wages, with the effect being smaller and statistically not significant for nonimporting firms. A 10-percentage-point output tariff cut leads to a 2.4% reduction in the wage paid by a nonexporting firm but a 2.4% increase in the wage paid by an exporting firm. A 10-percentage-point input tariff reduction results in a 2.3% wage increase in firms that do not import their inputs, while it leads to a 7.5% wage increase in firms that import at least some of their inputs. The reason for firms that do not import any of their inputs possibly ending up paying higher wages due to input tariff cuts might be the competition from other firms in the labor market or a procompetitive effect on upstream industries.

Here again, the results are robust to controlling for endogeneity using an instrumental variable approach, which runs the regression in long differences (5-year differences) and instruments the long-differenced output tariffs using the industry's initial share of production workers in total employment and its interaction with an initial export status indicator and a nontariff barrier dummy (and a few other variables). For the first-differenced input tariff variable, the instrument is the initial input tariff interacted with the initial import status.

Dutt (2003), using industry-level data for India, also finds that real wages rise after liberalization. He further discovers that real wages are positively related to import penetration. While trade protection has no significant effect on the wage level, he finds that wage growth is negatively related to protection: wage growth is higher for relatively less protected industries and during years with lower tariffs.

Relatively little research focuses on the impact of trade on employment at the micro level. Kambhampati, Krishna, and Mitra (1997) find that, controlling for wages and markups, after trade liberalization, the firm-level labor demand increased in India by 4%–9%, depending on the industry. Not controlling for wages and markups produces a statistically insignificant impact of trade reforms on firm-level employment, due to the mutually opposing channels that I have described.

Dutt (2003) finds results for employment and employment growth that are similar to his results for wage and wage growth with respect to import penetration and protection.

In a study on the Republic of Korea, Mitra and Shin (2012) find that a 10-percentage-point reduction in industry-level tariff reduces labor demand at the firm level in the Republic of Korea by about 0.6% and that a 10-percentage-point increase in the ratio of exports to output increases this labor demand by 0.7%.

Hasan et al. (2012) investigate the impact of trade liberalization on industry- and state-level unemployment rates in India. A 10-percentage-point decrease in the state-level employment-weighted average tariff rate leads to a 7.5% decline in the state-level unemployment rate. In addition, a 10-percentage-point reduction in a two-digit industry-level tariff leads to a 0.08-percentage-point reduction in the probability of being unemployed within an industry. An increase in the value of the marginal product of labor brought about by trade liberalization seems to drive all these results.

For all the Asian economies studied so far, it seems that trade does not reduce firm wages or employment. In most cases, trade reforms have led to an increase in wages and employment. In the case of India, it is also apparent that tariff cuts lead to reductions in unemployment rates. Empirical work investigating the impact of trade reforms on wages and employment in non-Asian countries, on the other hand, does not provide such a positive view. For example, Ravenga (1997) finds that, in addition to the reduction in the demand for output of domestic import-competing firms in Mexico, trade reforms led to a destruction of monopoly rents, which firms shared with workers, in turn becoming another wage- and employment-reducing effect. Ravenga finds the overall impact of trade reforms on firm-level wages and employment in import-competing firms to be negative. She is able to break down the overall negative effect into the channel through the destruction of quasi-rents and the remaining ones. Currie and Harrison (1997) find no statistically significant effect of trade reforms on firm-level employment in Morocco. They conclude that, while there are positive effects through markup reductions and productivity increases, there is a negative effect through a switch in demand toward imported substitutes for domestic products.

Clearly, based on my earlier theoretical discussion, there are many channels that flow in different directions. For all the Asian economies, for which rigorous research investigates the wage and employment effects of trade reforms, researchers do not find any adverse impact. For non-Asian countries, however, some adverse effects are apparent, which prompt caution about generalizing the positive effects to the remaining Asian countries. As a result, the use of redistribution and adjustment policies becomes quite important. To add to this, the evidence within Asia that exists on trade adjustment and the impact of trade on informality, which I will discuss next, strengthens the case for such policies. As I will argue, such policies can also create and maintain support for globalization.

1.4 Trade and Informality

Having a job is important for an individual's well-being. However, conditional on having a job, the quality of that job also matters. What determines the quality of a job? One obvious determinant is the wage, but there are other important determinants as well. These include job security, whether the job has a pension plan, whether it provides health insurance, what its working conditions are, and so on.

Some, albeit not all, labor regulations aim to provide some of the elements of job quality. Firms in the formal sector have to follow their country's labor laws and other regulations, such as those related to corporate taxes. However, adherence to these regulations results in additional costs for these firms. Consequently, firms in developing countries often want to remain small and in the informal sector. In addition, firms in the formal sector employ casual or informal short-term workers to gain the flexibility to hire and fire them, which is not possible in the case of permanent workers. Casual or short-term jobs, including those in informal-sector enterprises, lack adequate job security and social insurance. Thus, the fraction of employment that is informal is an important inverse indicator of job quality.

What are the trade-offs here for firms? Remaining small (and in the informal sector) prevents firms from exploiting economies of scale and from using modern technology, which is usually cost-effective only when the scale of production is sufficiently large. In addition, temporary workers have very little incentive to learn on the job and be efficient, since a large proportion of the human capital that they acquire through on-the-job training and experience is firm specific and will not be of much use elsewhere. However, a contraction in demand makes an industry less profitable, and, therefore, it is less cost-effective for any firm in that industry to hire more costly (but more productive) regular (permanent) workers, while an expansion in demand produces the opposite result.

As mentioned earlier, Nataraj (2011), in her study of India's formal and informal manufacturing enterprises, found that a given output tariff reduction increases informal-firm productivity proportionally much more than formal-firm productivity, while the comparison is reversed in the case of an input tariff reduction. This finding is important, as one expects it to result in the expansion of informal relative to formal employment due to the former but a reduction due to the latter. Thus, one expects informality to respond to trade liberalization.

Mitra and Ural (2008), in their study of the Indian manufacturing sector, find that industry productivity, output, value added, and employment increase with tariff reductions, with the impact being relatively greater in states where labor regulations generate relatively flexible labor markets. However, Sundaram, Ahsan, and Mitra (2013) discover the opposite effect of trade openness on informal-sector firms with five or fewer workers. These firms experience a greater increase in output, value added, and employment due to tariff reductions in the relatively rigid labor regulation states compared with others. These results indicate that trade liberalization might reduce informality (the share of employment or output in the informal sector) in states with relatively flexible labor regulations and increase it in other states. This might be driven by the need for formal-sector firms, due to restrictive labor regulations, to outsource some of their work to informal-sector firms.

The results for India are quite consistent with those that Goldberg and Pavcnik (2003) find in their study of how the informal sector in Brazil and Colombia responded to trade liberalization in the 1980s and 1990s. While, in the case of Brazil, Goldberg and Pavcnik do not find any evidence of a relationship between informality and trade liberalization, for Colombia they find evidence of an increase in informality as a result of trade liberalization for only the earlier part of their sample period. This relationship disappears after the implementation of the labor regulation reforms that made the Colombian labor market more flexible, which is the latter part of their sample period.

In another paper, Ahsan and Mitra (2017) find that informality in India was rising in low-productivity sectors relative to high-productivity sectors, which were also the sectors that were expanding in relative output and employment. However, this differential trend disappears with trade liberalization, possibly due to the need for greater flexibility in input choice, which the employment of casual workers can provide, as explained earlier.

McCaig and Pavcnik (2018) study the impact of Viet Nam's exports on informality. They find that, as United States (US) tariffs on exports from Viet Nam to the US fell from 23.4% to 2.4% through the US–Viet Nam Bilateral Trade Agreement, these exports expanded from $1.1 billion in 2001 to $5 billion in 2004, and individuals moved from employment in small, informal enterprises to employment in large, formal firms. Over the first 2 years after the start of the bilateral trade agreement, the proportion of informal workers in the manufacturing sector decreased from 66% to 60%. The authors also find that industries with bigger US tariff cuts experience larger reductions in informality. This movement contributes to aggregate productivity growth of about 1.5%–2.8% annually and economic development.

While it is difficult to find any study that examines the impact of trade on informality in the People's Republic of China, a study by Liang, Appleton, and Song (2016) shows that the proportion of casual employment in urban areas of the People's Republic of China increased from 24% in 2007 to 42% in 2013. The authors put much of the blame for this on the 2008 New Labor Contract Law, which requires all employers to write up contracts for each of their employees and to provide social insurance for workers who have contracts longer than 2 years. However, the implementation and compliance are far from perfect, and formal firms often hire short-term workers without contracts despite the law that prohibits such hiring. In other words, the study shows that a more stringent labor law has resulted in greater evasion and noncompliance with the law, so making the law more stringent has been counterproductive. However, this study does not discuss identification issues. As a result, researchers cannot rule out one of the causes of the increase in employment informality being the opening of the People's Republic of China's economy.

I next look at a cross-economy study by Fiess and Fugazza (2012), whose panel dataset includes, among others, a number of Asian economies such as Bangladesh; Hong Kong, China; India; Indonesia; Japan; Malaysia; Nepal; Pakistan; the Philippines; the People's Republic of China; Singapore; and Sri Lanka. While they find that output informality rises with trade openness, employment informality falls. This is possible if there is a large increase in the relative labor productivity of the informal sector. However, employment informality falling with trade openness is good news from the point of view of job quality. I also believe that it is necessary to separate developed and developing economies or allow an interaction of trade openness or restriction with economy per capita income, as the relationship between trade and informality for developed and developing economies can be quite different. In addition, the interaction of the trade variable with the nature of labor regulations or the flexibility of labor markets will provide valuable insights.

Thus, it seems fairly clear that, in the presence of labor regulations that produce rigid labor markets, import competition increases informality. However, export expansion seems to reduce informality. Labor reforms can contain, or even reverse, the informality-increasing effects of trade liberalization. The fact that researchers find the complementarity between trade and labor market flexibility to hold for all the Latin American countries studied with respect to these issues makes it also plausible for the Asian economies not studied so far.

1.5 Labor Mobility, Trade Shocks, and Adjustment Costs

I next consider the adjustment costs incurred by workers moving from one sector to another in response to trade shocks. Artuc, Lederman, and Porto (2015) carry out pathbreaking work on this issue. In their first step, the authors estimate the average labor mobility costs stemming from labor market frictions using industry-level data (within the manufacturing sector) on employment and wages. They perform this exercise for several countries (31 developing countries and 25 developed countries), using a dynamic model of sectoral employment choices. The labor mobility cost or the cost of moving incurred by a worker in moving to another sector from his or her current sector of employment turns out to be a few multiples of the annual average wage. It is 3.88 times the average wage in South Asia, 3.95 times in Central Asia, and 3.46 times in East Asia and the Pacific. Regarding individual countries, it is 2.71 for the People's Republic of China, 2.87 for India, 3.34 for Iran, 3.46 for Indonesia, 3.77 for the Republic of Korea, 4 for Lithuania, 4.47 for Azerbaijan, and 4.89 for Bangladesh. For most developed countries, the numbers are much lower, for example 1.43 for Finland, 1.70 for Germany, 1.82 for the Netherlands, 2.21 for the US, and so on. The authors also examine the correlations between mobility costs in the various countries and country-specific characteristics. Richer countries have lower mobility costs. The mobility costs are also higher in countries with a larger proportion of their labor force in "vulnerable employment" or low-quality jobs, a higher number of procedures to enforce a contract, and a higher number of days required to export.

Based on these mobility costs, the second stage involves the estimation of the welfare effects on workers in the food and beverage sector, following a 30% decline in the price of food and beverages due to a trade shock. A 9.55% potential welfare increase is reduced to an 8.53% actual welfare increase due to the presence of mobility costs in India. For the People's Republic of China, these numbers are 8.25% and 7.05%, respectively. The difference is greater in Indonesia, with the numbers being 11.28% and 9.02%, respectively. Clearly, the difference is increasing in the mobility costs estimated. If I consider countries with even higher mobility costs, the difference is much bigger between potential and actual welfare gains, respectively 12.87% and 8.16% for Bangladesh and 10.38% and 5.23% for the Philippines. Evidently, mobility costs wipe out a sizable proportion of the welfare gains from trade.

While the initial impact of a food and beverage price decline due to a trade shock is a decline in real wages in the food and beverage sector, the real wage starts to rise after some time and reaches a higher steady state within a few years. The higher the labor mobility cost in a country, the longer it takes to converge to the new steady state. While a country such as the People's Republic of China with a low mobility cost will reach 95% of the new steady-state real wage in about 3 years, it could take 10–11 years in Bangladesh or the Philippines.

Matusz (2003) also provides a calibration of a dynamic multisectoral search model of unemployment. He uses the data from the National Sample Survey Office (NSSO) in India to calculate the duration of unemployment as 4.4 months and the rate of job separation from a firm as 2% per year. He uses these to calibrate his model and finds that the adjustment costs can be up to 60% of the gross benefits from trade liberalization. This is considerably higher than the figures in the previous study, but, in general, the broader point is that mobility or adjustment costs can account for a significant proportion of aggregate welfare changes. After a trade shock, according to the results of Matusz's exercise, it takes the economy over 10 years to reach the new steady state.

The above results are consistent with the cross-country results of Dutt, Mitra, and Ranjan (2009), who study the impact of trade policy on unemployment. The dataset includes a handful of Asian economies in addition to countries from other parts of the world. The authors find a very interesting response of unemployment to trade liberalization. Initially, there is a rise in unemployment in the year of liberalization. However, over a longer period of time, there is a reduction in unemployment relative to the initial level. Trade liberalization leads to immediate dislocations of workers, resulting in a short-term spike in unemployment rates of about 0.6% on average. Over a longer time horizon of 2–3 years, employment recovers and the rise in unemployment reverses, leading to a 2.5% decline in the unemployment rate in the long run. The results are similar at the industry level for India in the study by Hasan et al. (2012).

Thus, informality and labor adjustment costs are real problems in developing Asia. Furthermore, trade reforms can magnify these problems. Therefore, next I discuss policy options to address these problems.

1.6 Policies to Tackle Trade-induced Adjustment and Informality

I have shown that trade adjustment costs, as a result of worker mobility costs, can destroy a significant part of the welfare gains from trade. In addition, these costs can lead to an initial decline in real wages in the sector that is hit with a negative trade shock, followed by a rise to the higher, new steady state. The transition to this new steady state can be slow, the speed being inversely related to the magnitude of labor mobility costs. Hollweg et al. (2014) provide several policy options to tackle the problems associated with adjustment costs. These policies aim to reduce the mobility costs that workers incur, such as subsidizing destination-specific relocation costs, training programs to provide skills specific to destination sectors, unemployment benefits or insurance, job search assistance, subsidized employment through public works programs, announcing trade reforms in advance, or gradual trade liberalization that would allow for advance planning, skill acquisition, searches, and so on. They warn about the dangers of more stringent employment protection laws through more restrictions on the firing of workers, as such policies would slow down the job creation in expanding sectors and the transition to the new, better steady state.

Mitra and Ranjan (2011) discuss social protection policies for workers exposed to external or globalization shocks. They also note the benefits of expanding unemployment benefits and insurance to facilitate job searches to enable efficient matching of workers and jobs but with strict monitoring to ensure that such searches are truly taking place. Like Hollweg et al. (2014), they do not recommend excessive use of employment protection policies in the form of firing restrictions, which often end up being hiring restrictions. The reason for this is that employers are reluctant to hire workers when they know they cannot fire them in the event of a negative shock or in the case of incompetence. Mitra and Ranjan advocate East Asian-style public works programs that serve the twin purpose of providing interim employment for people who have lost their jobs in sectors exposed to adverse external shocks and improving the public infrastructure that is badly needed in many developing countries. They also argue that these various forms of unemployment support will build and sustain support for greater openness of the economy.

As regards informality, there is strong evidence that trade liberalization will increase it in the presence of restrictive labor regulations. This is quite clear from Goldberg and Pavcnik's empirical work on Latin America as well as my own work on India with coauthors. In addition, the People's Republic of China has experienced an increase in informality due to the recent introduction of more rigid labor regulations in the presence of substantial openness. Therefore, reforms of labor regulations are probably the solution.

1.7 Trade, Poverty, and Inequality

Trade can affect poverty and inequality through many channels. According to Bhagwati (2004), trade raises growth, which, in turn, reduces poverty. Researchers often consider trade to be "an engine of growth," especially in the light of the experiences of several Asian economies, including the People's Republic of China and India, which have liberalized their trade regimes during the last few decades. The theoretical literature on trade and growth, however, provides several different channels heading in opposite directions, as the section on trade and productivity explained. However, David Ricardo's work from centuries ago clearly shows that there are "gains from trade" when trade is driven by comparative advantage. For policy purposes, this means that international trade is likely to lead to an increase in real per capita income. In other words, trade expands the size of the pie. This rise in real per capita income is economic growth.

Not only economists but also world leaders have been aware for many decades that growth is a necessary condition for poverty reduction. Especially in the 1950s and 1960s, when many developing countries had abysmally low per capita incomes, it was clear, as a matter of simple arithmetic, that redistribution would not lead to poverty reduction. For example, perfect equality with a very low per capita income can put everyone below the poverty line.

While there is empirical evidence, after controlling for reverse causation through an instrumental variable approach, that trade increases per capita income (Frankel and Romer 1999; Irwin and Tervio 2002), there is also evidence that the poor usually share a country's growth. In fact, the growth in incomes of the poor is no less than the rate of growth of per capita income (Dollar and Kraay 2002). Additionally, there are redistributive effects of trade in that trade redistributes in favor of the abundant factor and away from the scarce factor. In poor countries, the abundant factor is unskilled labor and those below the poverty line are all unskilled workers. Thus, trade, by increasing the incomes of the poor, is expected to raise the poor above the poverty line.

However, the above logic depends very much on intersectoral factor mobility. In the absence of such mobility, workers in declining sectors are trapped there, losing incomes and/or jobs. Trade also makes capital goods cheaper, though these capital goods are often complementary to skilled labor and not unskilled labor, thereby raising wage inequality and poverty under certain conditions (Davis and Mishra 2007). Furthermore, for firms to export successfully, they need to be able to offer goods of higher quality than under autarky. However, higher-quality goods are more intensive in skilled labor; thus, trade can increase the demand for skilled labor and reduce the demand for unskilled labor, thereby raising poverty and inequality. In other words, in such scenarios, simple Heckscher–Ohlin predictions will not hold.

I next look empirically at the impact of trade on poverty and inequality.

1.7.1 India–People's Republic of China Comparisons

I start here by discussing some basic evidence that I present in Mitra (2016), in which I discuss the experiences of two large Asian countries: the People's Republic of China and India. India's trade-to-gross domestic product (GDP) ratio increased from roughly 13% in 1988 to 48% in 2010, while its average tariff rate fell from 80% to 10% during the same period. The $1.25-a-day poverty rate decreased during the period from 53% to 32%. The most rapid decline in poverty, from 41.6% to 32.7%, occurred during 2005–2010, when growth was also the most rapid, in the range of 8%–10% (except for 2008). Based on my cross-country regression, I find in Mitra (2016) that the increase in trade as a fraction of GDP accounts for a fourth of the reduction in poverty in India. The income inequality in India during this period was fairly stable. The Gini coefficient increased only a little from about 32 to 34, the entire blame for this (or even more) falling on trade liberalization, based on Mitra's (2016) cross-country regression analysis.[4] The ratio of the incomes of the top 10% to the bottom 10% rose by only slightly above 10% from 6.9 to 7.7.

In the People's Republic of China, the trade-to-GDP ratio rose from 17% in 1984 to 70% in 2005 but then fell to 62% in 2008 and 49% in 2009 due to the Great Recession. The country's average tariff decreased from 32% to 4% between 1984 and 2010, while its $1.25-a-day poverty rate fell from 69% to 12% during this period. Based on my cross-country regression in Mitra (2016), the increase in trade as a fraction of GDP accounts for one seventh of the reduction in poverty in the People's Republic of China. The residual is possibly attributable to growth that other factors drive, such as infrastructure and skill development, as well as policies to promote labor market flexibility. However, this topic requires rigorous investigation. In addition, the country's Gini coefficient increased from 28 to 42 during 1984–2009, one fifth of which is due to trade liberalization, based on Mitra's (2016) cross-country regression analysis. The ratio of the incomes of the top 10% to the bottom 10% rose from 6 to 18 during the same period.

The comparison makes clear that the People's Republic of China, where inequality increased much more, actually performed much better in poverty reduction than India. While both India and the People's Republic of China have grown rapidly during the last decades, the People's Republic of China's growth performance has been significantly better than India's and has remained steady at that

---

[4]   While the actual increase in inequality, according to the Gini coefficient, was 2 points, the increase predicted by trade liberalization (the tariff reduction that actually took place) was 3.5 points.

rate for a longer period of time. This relatively rapid growth has led to faster poverty reduction. It is possible that the People's Republic of China was spending more of its tax revenues on infrastructure, while India was using them mainly for redistributive purposes and public works programs that were not so productive. Thus, equality was unable to rise substantially in India, but its poor performance with regard to infrastructure probably hurt its growth performance as well as its progress in poverty reduction.

1.7.2 Trade and Poverty: Astructural, Reduced-form Intra-country Studies from Asia

I next look at some intra-country studies on trade, poverty, and inequality. I start with studies based on a direct, astructural, reduced-form approach. Topalova (2007) examines a panel of districts in India by creating measures of rural, urban, and overall poverty rates (the proportion of people below the poverty line) and a measure of district-level protection, which is a weighted average of industry-level tariff rates, the weights being the initial share of the labor force in individual districts (also calculated at the rural, urban, and overall levels). Topalova finds that districts in which rural workers were more exposed to a rise in import competition (in the form of a greater reduction in the weighted average tariff) experienced a relatively slower reduction in rural poverty. Compared with a district that did not experience any change in tariffs, a district that experienced the mean level of tariff reduction witnessed a 2-percentage-point rise in poverty. In the case of urban poverty, Topalova does not find a statistically significant relationship with district-level protection, but the coefficient sign is the same as in the case of rural poverty. In fact, she describes one of her findings as trade liberalization leading to a "significant setback" in rural poverty reduction (equaling about 15% of the poverty reduction that took place in India in the 1990s).

Hasan, Mitra, and Ural (2007), later updated by Cain, Hasan, and Mitra (2012), perform a cross-state panel analysis for India (as opposed to Topalova's cross-district analysis). Apart from considering states, they examine NSSO regions (roughly three times the number of states). Their main finding is that states where workers were more exposed to foreign competition, through a greater employment concentration in industries that were more open to trade, had lower rural, urban, and overall poverty rates. States with greater trade liberalization (a greater reduction in employment-weighted tariffs) also experienced greater poverty reduction. These effects were more pronounced in states with labor laws that allowed more flexible labor markets, greater road density, and greater financial development. The authors find that trade liberalization between 1987 and 2004 led to a 38% reduction in poverty. A 1-percentage-point greater reduction in the employment-weighted average tariff led to a 0.57% additional reduction in the poverty rate.

There could be a number of reasons for the differences in results between Topalova and Hasan and Mitra and their coauthors. First, results can differ because compositional changes can drive poverty reduction (relatively poor districts within a state shrinking and rich districts expanding). This is a plausible story, since researchers find that, while labor is quite immobile between states, there is no such evidence for the lack of mobility of workers between districts within a state. There are other differences, such as differences in the treatment of nontradable sectors in the calculation of the weighted protection, the noninclusion of the 1993 NSSO round in Topalova's study, and the greater variety of protection measures used in the Cain–Hasan–Mitra–Ural studies.

Another study (Mukim and Panagariya 2012) shows that, contrary to the previous claims, socially disadvantaged classes have also experienced declines in poverty rates during the period since the trade reforms, with some evidence existing that trade reforms led to a decline in their poverty.

Kis-Katos and Sparrow (2015) conduct a similar analysis of the impact of the Indonesian trade reforms on poverty for 259 Indonesian districts in the period 1993–2002. One difference between the studies on India and this one on Indonesia is that these authors examine both the employment-weighted output and the input tariffs, with the unit of observation being a district every 3 years from 1993 to 2002. The measures that the authors use are the poverty rate, the poverty gap, and the squared poverty gap. Kis-Katos and Sparrow find that poverty (as defined through any of the three measures) declines with a reduction in the input tariffs, but that output tariff reductions increase poverty. A 1-standard-deviation (or 2-percentage-point) larger reduction in the employment-weighted input tariff leads to a reduction in the poverty rate that is half a standard deviation (6.7 percentage points) greater. Running these regressions for separate education levels (no education, primary education, junior secondary education, and senior secondary education), the two extreme education levels seem to drive the results. Furthermore, the impact of input tariff reductions seems to work through an increase in the share of working adults in the population, and there is some evidence of this happening through an increase in the wage rate, possibly due to an increase in firm productivity, as Amiti and Konings (2007) show for the Indonesian case. In the case of wage increases, the channel is more pronounced for medium-skilled workers, while the worker participation channel works mainly for low-skilled workers.

McCaig (2011) studies the impact of tariff reductions in the US as part of the bilateral trade agreement between the US and Viet Nam on the poverty rates in Viet Nam's provinces. He constructs a province-specific US import tariff using employment levels in various industries within a province as weights. McCaig finds that there is negligible interprovince migration, making this analysis meaningful. A 1-standard-deviation reduction in the weighted average US tariff that a province faces leads to a 33%–40% reduction in poverty within 2 years.

Thus, there seems to be considerable evidence that unilateral trade reforms have reduced poverty at the state level in India (although the district-level evidence available so far is different). In the case of Viet Nam, state-level poverty declined as a result of the US reciprocal tariff cuts. In addition, input tariff reductions have led to poverty reductions in Indonesian provinces, while output tariff reductions have led to slight increases in the incidence of poverty. Research finds that trade liberalization had a poverty-reducing effect in Poland through greater wage increases in labor-intensive industries that also experienced deeper tariff cuts (Goh and Javorcik 2007). Furthermore, in the 1990s, Mexican provinces that were more open to foreign direct investment and imported and exported more relative to the value of their output experienced greater poverty reduction relative to the more closed provinces based on these measures (Hanson 2007). Goldberg and Pavcnik (2007b), on the other hand, find that urban poverty is unrelated to tariffs in the Colombian case but negatively related to the volume of competing imports.

Overall, as long as the right kinds of complementary domestic policies and institutions are in place, trade liberalization has a favorable impact on poverty reduction in Asia, and this also applies to many other parts of the world.

Next, I discuss studies that are more model driven.

1.7.3 Trade and Welfare: Empirical General Equilibrium Studies from Asian Economies

I now move on to studies that use the approach called empirical general equilibrium analysis, which Porto (2006) pioneered. These studies focus on the changes in the cost of consumption as measured using the compensating variation of the various price changes, both in tradable and in nontradable industries, as a consequence of trade liberalization (mainly tariff changes) as well as changes in wages resulting from tariff declines. In the formula for compensating variation, price changes interact with budget shares, which researchers can allow to vary across income classes. Ural Marchand (2012), in an empirical general equilibrium study for India, allows wage responses to vary by skill level and age. For that purpose, she creates a quasi-panel based on skill level, age, and industry over time, since the available data are repeated across sections and not a true panel. She also assumes no interindustry labor mobility, so wages for different skills and ages in an industry respond only to changes in that industry's price. Unlike Porto, she assumes no impact of tariff changes on nontradable prices. However, like most of the literature, Ural Marchand also ignores land and capital income. The benefit of this analysis is that it is possible to compute the welfare changes at each point in the income distribution. The price transmission of tariffs in this analysis can differ between rural and urban areas as well as the remoteness of the location from the nearest port. Overall, Ural Marchand finds a pro-poor effect of trade reforms in India in that the poor benefited proportionally more than others. Her analysis shows that households at all levels of per capita expenditure benefited from the reforms. Both the consumption and the wage effects separately benefit the poor, especially those significantly below the poverty line relative to those just below it. The benefits are greater for households in urban areas than for those in rural areas and for those in relatively less remote areas due to muted transmission of the price effects of tariffs. Over the entire 1988–2000 period studied, the overall estimated welfare gain was 27% for those at the lowest per capita expenditure levels in rural areas and 13% at the highest levels in rural India. For urban areas, these numbers are 40% and 18%, respectively.

Han et al. (2016) evaluate the pass-through of tariff reductions into price reductions and through that the impact on urban poverty in the People's Republic of China. Having calculated the pass-through into tradable prices (allowing for this pass-through to change with the share of the private sector in a city's economy) and the general equilibrium impact of tradable price changes on nontradable prices, it is possible to calculate the percentage welfare change (through a change in the cost of consumption) for each urban household in the People's Republic of China using a compensating variation formula. While the overall percentage increase in welfare is about 7%, poor households experience about a 14% increase in welfare. The percentage gain in welfare keeps decreasing with the overall household expenditure. This is not surprising, since tradables, such as food, clothing, and household appliances, form a bigger share of the household budget in the case of relatively poorer households. Richer households buy relatively more expensive nontradables, such as high-quality education, health care, housing, and entertainment. Both the tariff pass-through and the welfare gain from a given tariff reduction increase with the share of the private sector in the economy.

Seshan (2014) performs a similar empirical general equilibrium analysis for Viet Nam for 1993–1998. The author modifies the approach to incorporate household production in agriculture, in which consumption and supply decisions (including input use decisions) are not separable. This is an important feature of agriculture in Viet Nam. Given that relaxing export restrictions on agricultural products, along with reducing import restrictions on goods such as chemicals and fertilizers, was an important part of the overall trade reforms in Viet Nam, making this change to the model was essential. Seshan finds both overall poverty and inequality reduction arising from trade liberalization. While rural poverty fell by 9 percentage points, urban poverty rose slightly. Moreover, Seshan finds that trade liberalization was responsible for a third of the decline in overall poverty and half of the decline in rural poverty during this period.

Thus, based on the empirical general equilibrium welfare studies, we find that, while the welfare impact of trade reforms in Asia has been positive, it is special in that it has been pro-poor. In fact, Porto (2006) also finds such an impact of Mercosur on Argentina. While Mercosur is a customs union that people expect to lead to both trade creation and diversion, the focus of Porto's study is only trade creation. In that respect, it is not especially different from the studies on Asia. However, certain assumptions of his model differ slightly, especially compared with the Indian study, in that he allows for some intersectoral labor mobility as well as the possibility of tariff cuts to affect nontradable prices. In addition, unlike Ural Marchand, he does not allow the price transmission of tariff cuts to vary by distance from the nearest port or by rural and urban areas, nor the wage responses to vary by age, skill level, and so on. Furthermore, unlike Seshan, he does not allow for household production in agriculture, in which consumption and production decisions occur jointly.

1.7.4 Trade and Inequality: Empirical Evidence from Asia

Overall Income Inequality

While the above studies focus mainly on wage inequality, the question as to whether trade affects overall income inequality is also important. In Mitra (2016), I show, using cross-country regressions for 46 countries over the period 1981–2013, that a 10-percentage-point tariff reduction raises inequality, as measured by the Gini coefficient (on a 0–100 scale), by half a point. Based on these regressions, all the blame (and more) for the slight increase in inequality in India can be placed on trade reforms, while for the People's Republic of China, trade liberalization is responsible for one fifth of the inequality increase. A country-by-country examination of what happened to inequality following trade reforms, however, does not produce any clear patterns (Goldberg and Pavcnik 2007a).

Krishna and Sethupathy (2012) construct the Theil index of inequality for the various states and for rural and urban areas for all the years of the "thick" NSSO rounds in India in 1988–2005. The advantage of this index is that it is additively separable into "within-group" and "between-group" inequality (within and between states and within and between rural and urban areas). The authors find that inequality, 70% of which is within group, immediately after the reforms first decreased during 1988–1994, then increased during 1994–2000, and decreased thereafter. These results are robust to the use of other measures of inequality. In addition, protection does not seem to be significantly related to inequality.

Wage Inequality

Kumar and Mishra (2008) focus on the impact of trade liberalization on the industry wage premium and overall wage inequality in India for 1983–2000. They estimate the value of the three-digit industry fixed effects in Mincerian wage regressions run year by year with individual-level household survey data from the NSSO for each survey round on individual age, employment, and educational and other demographic characteristics. The study controls for state and occupational indicators. The final wage premiums take the form of percentage deviations from the average industry for each year. Pooling all these wage premiums for the various industries over all the years to create a panel, the authors regress the industry wage premium on the nominal rate of protection, the nontariff barrier coverage ratio, and the import penetration ratio. The two preferred specifications are the ones in levels with year and industry fixed effects and those in first differences with year effects. A 1-percentage-point reduction in the industry's import tariff leads to a 0.17% increase in the industry wage premium, which the authors explain using the available evidence on the procompetitive effects of tariff reductions on productivity. To the extent that industries with a larger share of unskilled workers in total employment experienced a greater tariff reduction, the wage inequality must have decreased. The authors confirm this by running the above regression separately for skilled and unskilled workers. The results in Kumar's and Mishra's paper are qualitatively robust to controlling for endogeneity through the use of instrumental variables, namely 1980 nominal rates of protection interacted with foreign exchange reserves as well as the initial share of unskilled workers in employment interacted with foreign exchange reserves. The results are also robust to controlling for gross fixed capital formation.

Amiti and Cameron (2012) study the impact of trade liberalization in Indonesia on wage inequality (measured by the ratio of the wage rate of nonproduction to that of production labor) at the firm level for 1991–2000. Using five-digit output tariff rates and the share of various inputs at the firm level as weights to arrive at input tariffs, the authors find that a 10-percentage-point input tariff reduction lowers wage inequality by 2.6% on average for all firms but by 4.5% for importing firms. For firms with imports as a share of the value of all inputs that are in the top 10%, this effect is 8.5%. This shows that, while imported inputs might be, on average, substitutes for skilled workers, they are probably complements for unskilled workers. The regression of firm-level skill intensity (the ratio of nonproduction to production labor) on the interaction of importing status and input tariff confirms this, showing that importing firms reduce their skill intensity with input tariff liberalization. Output tariffs seem to have no impact on wage inequality.

Chen, Yu, and Yu (2013) investigate the impact of input tariff cuts on wage inequality between skilled and unskilled workers within firms in the People's Republic of China. The authors argue that skilled workers share the profits of the firm primarily so that they are incentivized to perform well rather than due to the presence of firm–worker bargaining. Since input tariff reductions increase profits, skilled workers' wages rise relative to those of unskilled workers, whose wages firms determine in a perfectly competitive labor market. The authors find evidence that input trade liberalization, in the presence of profit sharing between skilled workers and firms, leads to an increase in skilled–unskilled wage inequality. Running equations in first differences, they instrument the first-differenced tariff with the lagged tariff. Interestingly, their result is the opposite of Amiti and Cameron's (2012) finding for Indonesia. The coefficient is smaller when the sample includes processing firms, demonstrating that this channel is not valid for processing firms.

While there is evidence that trade liberalization reduced wage inequality in India and Indonesia, the impact was the reverse in the People's Republic of China. The results from Latin America are similar to those from the People's Republic of China. Feenstra and Hanson (1996, 1997) find that wage inequality rose in response to trade reforms during 1975–1988 in Mexico, primarily from input tariff cuts that resulted in relatively skill-intensive activities in processing these inputs moving to Mexico from the US (where these activities were the least skill intensive in the US but still more skill intensive than the existing production activities that Mexican workers were already undertaking). Attanasio, Goldberg, and Pavcnik (2004) find that trade liberalization increases wage inequality in Colombia. However, Pavcnik et al. (2004) do not find any impact of tariff cuts on wage inequality in Brazil. The difference between these results is attributable to differences in labor market flexibility as well as informal-to-formal sector labor mobility between Colombia and Brazil. Overall, for Asia as well as the rest of the world, researchers find mixed results regarding this question. More recent work by Helpman et al. (2017) and by Krishna, Poole, and Senses (2014) shows that wage inequality can have a nonmonotonic or increasing relationship with respect to trade openness. Openness in trade leads to higher returns to exporting firms from investment in screening to find the best workers. This screening process leads to the recognition of worker characteristics that are usually unobservable (especially to the econometrician). The match quality also improves in exporting firms with greater openness. As a result, exporting firms are able to pay higher wages. As trade costs fall, initially only a few firms export; but with further reductions in trade costs, more and more firms export. This can contribute to a nonmonotonic response of wage inequality to greater trade openness. In fact, it is possible in this case, as Helpman et al. (2017) show, for inequality to increase first and then start to decrease. They show the latter part in their model but not in the data, as trade costs have not yet fallen to that level in Brazil.

I next move on to labor share, which researchers view as being negatively correlated with income inequality.

Labor Share

Recently, there has been an interest in the factor shares or the so-called functional distribution of income. While the share of labor had remained constant for many decades all over the world, the past 2–3 decades have witnessed a decline in this share in many parts of the world, especially in developing countries (International Labour Organization 2011). At the same time, globalization has taken place at a rapid pace all over the world, especially trade reforms. Thus, there is a tendency to blame the declining labor share on trade. The issue of declining labor share needs further investigation for a few reasons. First, the rich derive their income mainly from capital and land, the distribution of which is highly unequal throughout the world. Second, the poor derive their income mainly from their raw labor, and labor incomes are relatively more equally distributed. Third, overall inequality and the share of labor are strongly negatively correlated (Atkinson 2009). Last, while globalization has taken place at a rapid pace, skill-biased technological change has occurred equally rapidly. Therefore, the exact cause of the declining labor share and whether globalization has sped up this decline or whether the decline would have been even greater in the absence of globalization are unknown.

For India, Ahsan and Mitra (2014) use firm-level data to investigate the impact of tariff cuts on the share of the wage bill in firm sales.

This study indicates something quite nuanced. For relatively small firms (those that lie in the bottom third of the distribution), which also turn out to be relatively labor intensive, based on the within-firm variation and controlling for macro effects, the authors find that tariff reductions increase labor share, while for large firms (in the top third of the distribution), which are relatively less labor intensive, labor share decreases with tariff reductions. While the elasticity of the labor share with respect to the industry-level tariff is −0.5 in the former set of firms, it is 0.8 for the latter. The study also finds that there is a decline in the bargaining power of workers in the sharing of profits across the board (as Rodrik [1997] argues and predicts), arising from these tariff cuts, but there is an offsetting force coming from the destruction of the monopoly power of domestic firms, which shrinks the wedge between the value of the marginal product and the wage. The second force is the dominant one in the case of small firms.

Mitra and Shin (2014) find qualitatively similar but quantitatively slightly different results for the Republic of Korea using firm-level survey data both for the labor share and for the bargaining power of workers. Kamal, Lovely, and Mitra (2014), on the other hand, find that in the case of firms in the People's Republic of China between 1998 and 2007, tariff cuts lead to increases in firm-level labor share across the board. This effect is stronger for coastal firms than for interior firms and varies by ownership type (domestic private, foreign, and state owned). Both input and output tariff cuts seem to have qualitatively similar effects. The effective rates of protection have qualitatively similar effects on the share of wages in the firm value added.

Regarding the case of India, while a reduction in the bargaining power of workers (through either direct competition from imported inputs or through indirect competition from goods produced by foreign inputs and labor) is an important force arising from trade liberalization, it is also possible that the decline in rents leads to declining unionization. This can happen due to the reduced incentives to meet the costs of forming new unions and maintaining old ones. Using household survey data for 1993–2004 from India, from which the authors create measures of union presence (the proportion of workers in an industry in unionized activities) and union membership (the proportion of workers in an industry who are union members) in various industries by state, Ahsan, Ghosh, and Mitra (2017) find evidence that, in net-importer industries, a 10-percentage-point reduction in the import tariff led to a 0.8-percentage-point reduction in the proportion of workers working in unionized activities as well as in the proportion of workers who are union members. This investigation also finds evidence from firm-level data that industry quasi-rents per plant declined with tariff cuts (where quasi-rents are total sales minus material and fuel costs minus the wage bill evaluated at the prevailing nonunion wage in the household survey data).

Trade and Labor-demand Elasticities
Rodrik (1997) argues that trade liberalization makes the labor demand more elastic. Through trade liberalization, cheaper and a greater variety of imported substitutes for domestically produced goods are available. This makes the demand for domestically produced goods more elastic. The demand for labor, being derived from the demand for goods and services, also becomes more elastic. In addition, imported inputs can directly substitute domestic labor.

The study of the impact of trade on labor-demand elasticities is important for a few reasons. An increase in the magnitude of labor-demand elasticity results in lower bargaining power for workers relative to employers, greater volatility in employment and wages for the given volatility in productivity, and a greater negative impact of rises in input and fuel costs on workers.

Hasan, Mitra, and Ramaswamy (2007) show that, with tariff cuts, the absolute value of the elasticity of labor demand at the industry level in Indian manufacturing rose from 0.076 to 0.186 in states with labor regulations that ensure a relatively rigid labor market, while in the other states it increased from 0.206 to 0.316. These calculations are based on a change in the average manufacturing tariff from 150% in 1988 to 40% in 1997. In contrast, Slaughter (2001) finds no systematic impact of trade liberalization on labor-demand elasticities for the US, while this impact is statistically insignificant for Turkey (Krishna, Mitra, and Chinoy 2001).

For the Republic of Korea, Mitra and Shin (2012) find weak evidence of trade liberalization increasing labor-demand elasticities. However, there is some evidence that the Republic of Korea's exports have increased their firm-level labor-demand elasticities. A 10-percentage-point increase in the share of exports in firm-level output leads to an increase in absolute labor-demand elasticity of up to 0.04.

1.8 Discussion and Concluding Remarks

As is apparent from the above discussion, trade has been beneficial to Asian economies through a number of channels and in many different respects: through higher productivity, lower markups through import competition, higher wages, higher employment, lower unemployment, and, above all, lower poverty rates.[5] At this juncture, however, two caveats are in order. First, the beneficial impacts might not be generalizable to Asian countries that so far remain unstudied. Second, there are a few adverse consequences of trade even in the Asian countries that are studied rigorously, and public policy needs to address these. First, trade can increase informality, especially in the presence of labor market rigidities. Second, there is an adverse effect stemming from trade adjustment as a result of worker mobility costs. Then, there is rising income inequality. However, the diversion of government funds from social expenditures to infrastructure building during this period of globalization is quite possibly the reason for some countries not being able to contain the rise in inequality. However, at the same time, this could be the reason for rapid growth and, in turn, through its "pull-up" effect (Bhagwati 2004), the reduction in poverty.

My review of the evidence also shows that, in some respects, globalization has put pressure on workers. For example, their bargaining power relative to their employers has decreased, most likely due to the greater options available to employers in terms of obtaining inputs from abroad or even the wider variety of imported final goods and services available to consumers, thereby making the services of domestic workers more replaceable. This reflects in the rise of labor-demand

---

[5]   For a summary of the research discussed here, please see the literature table in the appendix at the end of this chapter.

elasticities in the two Asian countries (India and the Republic of Korea) for which evidence is available and in some other countries outside Asia. As explained earlier, this, apart from reducing the bargaining power of labor, makes workers' incomes more volatile and their jobs more uncertain. In addition, firms have to bear a higher burden of rises in input and fuel costs.

Bhagwati (2004) argues that "appropriate policies" are necessary to reap and harness the gains from trade. For example, he reasons that countries can specialize away from goods for which the world prices are falling steeply but still specialize according to their comparative advantage. He is also in favor of other complementary "appropriate policies," especially with respect to agriculture, financial development, property rights, infrastructure building, and so on. Cain, Hasan, and Mitra (2012) find that Indian states that were financially more developed, had higher road density, were closer to ports, and had labor regulations that enabled more flexible labor markets, were able to achieve a greater reduction in urban poverty as a result of trade reforms. The work of Krishna, Mitra, and Sundaram (2010) also supports this result, finding that "lagging" regions or states (those that are distant from their respective nearest ports) within South Asia have been relatively less successful in reducing poverty through trade reforms.

Thus, the above evidence stresses the need for better infrastructure, especially a denser and better network of roads and greater investment in the building of new ports. Also needed would be a larger number of bank branches and labor regulations that can provide workers with the right kind of protection without sacrificing flexibility for employers to respond nimbly to the demand and supply shocks that they face in a more globalized environment. In addition, social protection and "appropriate" redistributive policies would help make sure that the losers from globalization are appropriately compensated to minimize the chances of a reversal of reforms (which policy makers should not underestimate). Countries could use public works programs, which provide the unemployed and underemployed with productive job opportunities, as much as possible as a means of social protection and, at the same time, infrastructure building, which is essential for maximizing the gains from trade in its many forms. Public works programs can be especially important in Asian developing countries where the informal sector accounts for a substantial share of employment.

References

Ahsan, R. N., A. Ghosh, and D. Mitra. 2017. International Trade and Unionization: Evidence from India. *Canadian Journal of Economics.* 50 (2). pp. 398–425.

Ahsan, R. N., and D. Mitra. 2014. Trade Liberalization and Labor's Slice of the Pie: Evidence from Indian Firms. *Journal of Development Economics.* 108. pp. 1–16.

_____. 2017. Can the Whole Actually Be Greater Than the Sum of Its Parts? Lessons from India's Growing Economy and Its Evolving Structure (with Reshad N. Ahsan). In M. McMillan, D. Rodrik, and C. Sepulveda, eds. *Structural Change, Fundamentals and Growth: A Framework and Country Studies.* Washington, DC: International Food Policy Research Institute. pp. 39–79.

Amiti, M., and L. Cameron. 2012. Trade Liberalization and the Wage Skill Premium: Evidence from Indonesia. *Journal of International Economics.* 87 (2). pp. 277–287.

Amiti, M., and D. R. Davis. 2012. Trade, Firms, and Wages: Theory and Evidence. *Review of Economic Studies.* 79 (1). pp. 1–36.

Amiti, M., and J. Konings. 2007. Trade Liberalization, Intermediate Inputs, and Productivity: Evidence from Indonesia. *American Economic Review.* 97 (5). pp. 1611–38.

Artuc, E., D. Lederman, and G. Porto. 2015. A Mapping of Labor Mobility Costs in the Developing World. *Journal of International Economics* 95 (1). pp. 28–41.

Atkinson, A. B. 2009. Factor Shares: The Principal Problem of Political Economy? *Oxford Review of Economic Policy.* 25 (1). pp. 3–16.

Attanasio, O., P. K. Goldberg, and N. Pavcnik. 2004. Trade Reforms and Income Inequality in Colombia. *Journal of Development Economics.* 74. pp. 331–66.

Bas, M., and O. Causa. 2013. Trade and Product Market Policies in Upstream Sectors and Productivity in Downstream Sectors: Firm-Level Evidence from China. *Journal of Comparative Economics.* 41 (3). pp. 843–62.

Bhagwati, J. 2004. *In Defense of Globalization.* New York: Oxford University Press.

Brandt, L., J. Van Biesebroeck, L. Wang, and Y. Zhang. 2017. WTO Accession and Performance of Chinese Manufacturing Firms. *American Economic Review.* 107 (9). pp. 2784–820.

Cain, J., R. Hasan, and D. Mitra. 2012. Trade Liberalization and Poverty Reduction: New Evidence from Indian States. In J. Bhagwati and A. Panagariya, eds. *India's Reforms: How They Produced Inclusive Growth.* New York: Oxford University Press. pp. 91–185.

Chen, B., M. Yu, and Z. Yu. 2013. Wage Inequality and Input Trade Liberalization: Firm-Level Evidence from China. Mimeo. SSRN: https://ssrn.com/abstract=2329292 or http://dx.doi.org/10.2139/ssrn.2329292.

Currie, J., and A. E. Harrison. 1997. Sharing Costs: The Impact of Trade Reform on Capital and Labor in Morocco. *Journal of Labor Economics*. 15. pp. 44–71.

Davis, D. R., and P. Mishra. 2007. Stolper–Samuelson is Dead: And Other Crimes of Both Theory and Data. In A. Harrison, ed. *Globalization and Poverty*. Chicago, IL: University of Chicago Press. pp. 87–108.

De Loecker, J., P. K. Goldberg, A. K. Khandelwal, and N. Pavcnik. 2016. Prices, Markups, and Trade Reform. *Econometrica*. 84 (2). pp. 445–510.

Dollar, D., and A. Kraay. 2002. Growth Is Good for the Poor. *Journal of Economic Growth*. 7 (3). pp. 195–225.

Dutt, P. 2003. Labor-Market Outcomes and Trade Reforms: The Case of India. In R. Hasan and D. Mitra, eds. *The Impact of Trade on Labor: Issues, Perspectives and Experiences from Developing Asia*. Amsterdam, Netherlands: North Holland. pp. 245–74.

Dutt, P., D. Mitra, and P. Ranjan. 2009. International Trade and Unemployment: Theory and Cross-National Evidence. *Journal of International Economics*. 78 (1). pp. 32–44.

Fan, H., X. Gao, Y. A. Li, and T. A. Luong. 2017. Trade Liberalization and Markups: Micro Evidence from China. *Journal of Comparative Economics*. 46 (1). pp. 103–130.

Feenstra, R. C., and G. H. Hanson. 1996. Foreign Investment, Outsourcing and Relative Wages. In R. C. Feenstra et al., eds. *Political Economy of Trade Policy: Essays in Honor of Jagdish Bhagwati*. Cambridge, MA: MIT Press. pp. 89–127.

———. 1997. Foreign Direct Investment and Relative Wages: Evidence from Mexico's Maquiladoras. *Journal of International Economics*. 42. pp. 371–93.

Fernandes, A. M. 2007. Trade Policy, Trade Volumes and Plant-Level Productivity in Colombian Manufacturing Industries. *Journal of International Economics*. 71 (1). pp. 52–71.

Fernandez, R., and D. Rodrik. 1991. Resistance to Reforms: Status-Quo Bias in the Presence of Individual-Specific Uncertainty. *American Economic Review*. 81 (5). pp. 1146–55.

Fiess, N., and M. Fugazza. 2012. Informality and Openness to Trade: Insights from Cross-Sectional and Panel Analyses. *Margin – The Journal of Applied Economic Research*. 6 (2). pp. 235–75.

Frankel, J., and D. Romer. 1999. Does Trade Cause Growth? *American Economic Review*. 89 (3). pp. 379–99.

Goh, C.-C., and B. S. Javorcik. 2007. Trade Protection and Industry Wage Structure in Poland. In A. E. Harrison, ed. *Globalization and Poverty*. Chicago, IL: University of Chicago Press. pp. 337–72.

Goldberg, P. K., A. K. Khandelwal, N. Pavcnik, and P. Topalova. 2010. Imported Intermediate Inputs and Domestic Product Growth: Evidence from India. *Quarterly Journal of Economics*. 125 (4). pp. 1727–67.

Goldberg, P. K., and N. Pavcnik. 2003. The Response of the Informal Sector to Trade Liberalization. *Journal of Development Economics*. 72 (2). pp. 463–96.

____. 2007a. Distributional Effects of Globalization in Developing Countries. *Journal of Economic Literature*. 45 (1). pp. 39–82.

____. 2007b. The Effects of the Colombian Trade Liberalization on Urban Poverty. In A. E. Harrison, ed. *Globalization and Poverty*. Chicago, IL: University of Chicago Press. pp. 241–89.

Grossman, G. M., and E. Helpman. 1991. *Innovation and Growth in the Global Economy*. Cambridge, MA: MIT Press.

Hall, R. E. 1988. The Relation between Price and Marginal Cost in US Industry. *Journal of Political Economy*. 96 (5). pp. 921–47.

Han, J., R. Liu, B. U. Marchand, and J. Zhang. 2016. Market Competition, Imperfect Pass-Through and Household Welfare in Urban China. *Journal of International Economics*. 100. pp. 220–32.

Hanson, G. H. 2007. Globalization, Labor Income, and Poverty in Mexico. In A.E. Harrison, ed. *Globalization and Poverty*. Chicago, IL: University of Chicago Press. pp. 417–56.

Harrison, A. E. 1994. Productivity, Imperfect Competition and Trade Reform: Theory and Evidence. *Journal of International Economics*. 36 (1–2). pp. 53–73.

Hasan, R., D. Mitra, and K. V. Ramaswamy. 2007. Reforms, Labor Regulations and Labor Demand Elasticities: Empirical Evidence from India. *Review of Economics and Statistics*. 89 (3). pp. 466–81.

Hasan, R., D. Mitra, P. Ranjan, and R. N. Ahsan. 2012. Trade Liberalization and Unemployment: Evidence from India. *Journal of Development Economics*. 97 (2). pp. 269–80.

Hasan, R., D. Mitra, and B. P. Ural. 2007. Trade Liberalization, Labor Market Institutions, and Poverty Reduction: Evidence from Indian States. *India Policy Forum, 2006–07*.

Helpman, E., O. Itskhoki, M. A. Muendler, and S. Redding. 2017. Trade and Inequality: From Theory to Estimation. *Review of Economic Studies*. 84 (1). pp. 357–405.

Hollweg, C. H., D. Lederman, D. Rojas, and E. R. Bulmer. 2014. *Sticky Feet: How Labor Market Frictions Shape the Impact of International Trade on Jobs and Wages*. Washington, DC: World Bank.

International Labour Organization. 2011. *World of Work Report 2011: Making Markets Work for Jobs.* Geneva: International Labour Office.

Irwin, D., and J. M. Tervio. 2002. Does Trade Raise Income? Evidence from the Twentieth Century. *Journal of International Economics.* 58. pp. 1–18.

Kamal, F., M. E. Lovely, and D. Mitra. 2014. Trade Liberalization and Labor Shares in China. Mimeo, Syracuse University.

Kambhampati, U., P. Krishna, and D. Mitra. 1997. The Effect of Trade Policy Reforms on Labor Markets: Evidence from India. *Journal of International Trade & Economic Development.* 6 (2). pp. 287–97.

Kim, E. 2000. Trade Liberalization and Productivity Growth in Korean Manufacturing Industries: Price Protection, Market Power, and Scale Efficiency. *Journal of Development Economics.* 62. pp. 55–83.

Kis-Katos, K., and R. Sparrow. 2015. Poverty, Labor Markets and Trade Liberalization in Indonesia. *Journal of Development Economics.* 117 (C). pp. 94–106.

Krishna, P., and D. Mitra. 1998. Trade Liberalization, Market Discipline and Productivity Growth: New Evidence from India. *Journal of Development Economics.* 56 (2). pp. 447–62.

Krishna, P., D. Mitra, and S. Chinoy. 2001. Trade Liberalization and Labor Demand Elasticities: Evidence from Turkey. *Journal of International Economics.* 55 (2). pp. 391–409.

Krishna, P., J. P. Poole, and M. Senses. 2014. Wage Effects of Trade Reform with Labor Market Frictions and Endogenous Worker Mobility. *Journal of International Economics.* 93 (2). pp. 239–52.

Krishna, P., and G. Sethupathy. 2012. Trade and Income Inequality in India. In Jagdish Bhagwati and Arvind Panagariya, eds. *India's Reforms: How They Produced Inclusive Growth.* New York: Oxford University Press. pp. 247–78.

Krishna, P., D. Mitra, and A. Sundaram. 2010. Do Lagging Regions Benefit from Trade? In Ejaz Ghani, ed. *The Poor Half Billion in South Asia: What Is Holding Back Lagging Regions?* New Delhi and New York: Oxford University Press. pp. 137–77.

Kumar, U., and P. Mishra. 2008. Trade Liberalization and Wage Inequality: Evidence from India. *Review of Development Economics.* 12 (2). pp. 291–311.

Levinsohn, J. 1993. Testing the Imports-as-Market-Discipline Hypothesis. *Journal of International Economics.* 35 (1–2). pp. 1–22.

Liang, Z., S. Appleton, and L. Song. 2016. Informal Employment in China: Trends, Patterns and Determinants of Entry. IZA Discussion Paper. No. 10139.

Matusz, S. J. 2003. Trade Policy Reform and Labor Market Dynamics: Issues and an Agenda for Future Research. In Rana Hasan and Devashish Mitra, eds. *The Impact of Trade on Labor: Issues,*

Perspectives, and Experiences from Developing Asia. Amsterdam: North-Holland Publishers. pp. 99–125.

McCaig, B. 2011. Exporting out of Poverty: Provincial Poverty in Vietnam and US Market Access. *Journal of International Economics.* 85 (1). pp. 102–13.

McCaig, B., and N. Pavcnik. 2018. Export Markets and Labor Allocation in a Low-Income Country. *American Economic Review.* 108 (7). pp. 1899–1941.

Mitra, D. 2016. Trade, Poverty, and Inequality. In J. Bhagwati, P. Krishna, and A. Panagariya, eds. *The World Trade System.* Cambridge, MA: MIT Press. pp. 55–90.

Mitra, D., and P. Ranjan. 2011. Social Protection in Labor Markets Exposed to External Shocks. In M. Bacchetta and M. Jansen, eds. *Making Globalization Socially Sustainable.* Geneva: International Labour Organization and World Trade Organization. pp. 199–231.

Mitra, D., and J. Shin. 2012. Import Protection, Exports and Labor-Demand Elasticities: Evidence from Korea. *International Review of Economics & Finance.* 23 (C). pp. 91–109.

———. 2014. Globalization and Workers: Firm-Level Evidence from Korea. In N. Khor and D. Mitra, eds. *Trade and Employment in Asia.* August 2013. London: Routledge. pp. 204–45.

Mitra, D., and B. P. Ural. 2008. Indian Manufacturing: A Slow Sector in a Rapidly Growing Economy. *Journal of International Trade and Economic Development.* 17 (4). pp. 525–60.

Mukim, M., and A. Panagariya. 2012. Growth, Openness and the Socially Disadvantaged. In J. Bhagwati and A. Panagariya, eds. *India's Reforms: How They Produced Inclusive Growth.* New York: Oxford University Press. pp. 186–246.

Nataraj, S. 2011. The Impact of Trade Liberalization on Productivity: Evidence from India's Formal and Informal Manufacturing Sectors. *Journal of International Economics.* 85 (2). pp. 292–301.

Pavcnik, N. 2002. Trade Liberalization, Exit, and Productivity Improvements: Evidence from Chilean Plants. *Review of Economic Studies.* 69. pp. 245–76.

Pavcnik, N., A. Blom, P.K. Goldberg, and N. Schady. 2004. Trade Liberalization and Industry Wage Structure: Evidence from Brazil. *World Bank Economic Review.* 18 (3). pp. 319–343.

Porto, G.G. 2006. Using Survey Data to Assess the Distributional Effects of Trade Policy. *Journal of International Economics.* 70 (1). pp. 140–60.

Ravenga, A. 1997. Employment and Wage Effects of Trade Liberalization: The Case of Mexican Manufacturing. *Journal of Labor Economics.* 15. pp. 20–43.

Rodrik, D. 1997. *Has Globalization Gone Too Far?* Washington, DC: Peterson Institute for International Economics.

Seshan, G. 2014. The Impact of Trade Liberalization on Household Welfare in a Developing Country with Imperfect Labor Markets. *Journal of Development Studies.* 50 (2). pp. 226–43.

Slaughter, M.J. 2001. International Trade and Labor-Demand Elasticities. *Journal of International Economics* 54(1). pp. 27–56.

Solow, R. 1957. Technical Change and the Aggregate Production Function. *Review of Economics and Statistics.* 39 (3). pp. 312–20.

Sundaram, A., R. Ahsan, and D. Mitra. 2013. Complementarity between Formal and Informal Manufacturing in India. In *Reforms and Economic Transformation in India,* edited by Jagdish Bhagwati and Arvind Panagariya, pp. 49–85. New York: Oxford University Press.

Topalova, P. 2007. Trade Liberalization, Poverty and Inequality: Evidence from Indian Districts. In A. E. Harrison, ed. *Globalization and Poverty,* pp. 291–335. Chicago, IL: University of Chicago Press.

Topalova, P., and A. Khandelwal. 2011. Trade Liberalization and Firm Productivity: The Case of India. *Review of Economics and Statistics.* 93 (3). pp. 995–1009.

Ural Marchand, B. 2012. Tariff Pass-Through and the Distributional Effects of Trade Liberalization. *Journal of Development Economics.* 99 (2). pp. 265–81.

Yu, M. 2015. Processing Trade, Tariff Reductions and Firm Productivity: Evidence from Chinese Firms. *Economic Journal.* 125 (585). pp. 943–88.

Appendix A1

Table A1 Responses to Trade Opening: Summary of Evidence from Asia

Topic	Authors	Economies Covered	Main Finding
Trade reforms, productivity growth, and markups at the firm level	Krishna and Mitra (1998)	India	Statistically significant reductions in markups and increases in productivity growth in firms in majority of industries studied.
Trade and productivity	Topalova and Khandelwal (2011)	India	Procompetitive impact of output tariff reduction: lower tariffs lead to higher productivity. Much greater increase in productivity from an equal input tariff reduction.
Trade, intermediate goods prices, and variety	Goldberg et al (2010)	India	Trade liberalization led to a considerable decline in the prices of intermediate inputs and an increase in their variety.
Trade liberalization and firm-level markups	De Loecker et al. (2016)	India	Output tariff reductions led to a reduction in firm-level price–marginal cost markups, while input tariff reductions led to an increase in these markups.
Trade liberalization and formal- and informal-firm productivity	Nataraj (2011)	India	Output tariff reductions increased informal firm productivity proportionally much more than formal-firm productivity. The reverse was the case with input tariff reductions.
Trade liberalization and productivity	Amiti and Konings (2007)	Indonesia	While a 1%–6% increase in productivity can be attributed to a 10-percentage-point reduction in output tariff, firms importing inputs experience up to a 13% increase in productivity from a 10-percentage-point input tariff reduction.
Trade liberalization, markups, and productivity	Brandt et al. (2017)	People's Republic of China	A 10-percentage-point reduction in output tariff leads to 1% markup reduction, while a 10-percentage-point reduction in the input tariff leads to a 7% markup increase. The procompetitive effect of a 10-percentage-point decline in output tariff is 1.7% increase in total factor productivity (TFP), while for a 10-percentage-point decline in input tariff the TFP gain is 16%–18%.

continued on next page

Table A1 *continued*

Topic	Authors	Economies Covered	Main Finding
Trade liberalization and markups	Fan et al. (2017)	People's Republic of China	Looking separately at firms engaged in processing trade and other firms, effects in Brandt et al. (2017) empirically do not show up for the former but are seen in the latter.
Trade liberalization and firm productivity	Yu (2013)	People's Republic of China	With a 10-percentage-point output tariff reduction, firm TFP increases by 9%. A 10-percentage-point input tariff reduction increases firm TFP by only 5%. These impacts go down with an increase in the share of processing imports in total imports.
Trade liberalization, firm productivity, and technological frontier	Bas and Causa (2013)	People's Republic of China	Firms on or close to the frontier experience a 0.74% increase in productivity from a 1-percentage-point reduction in input tariffs. Firms whose productivity is half of the domestic technological frontier will see roughly a 0.5% rise in productivity from the same tariff reduction. The procompetitive impact of output tariff reductions is stronger for firms relatively distant from the technological frontier.
Trade liberalization, industry productivity, and markups	Kim (2000)	Republic of Korea	A 10-percentage-point reduction in the quota-coverage ratio led to a TFP growth increase of 0.26 percentage points and a markup reduction of 1.33 percentage points. A 10-percentage-point reduction in the nominal rate of protection led to a TFP growth rate increase of only 0.12 percentage points and a markup reduction of 0.4 percentage points. Trade liberalization overall during the entire sample period raised annual TFP growth rate permanently by over 2 percentage points.
Trade liberalization and firm-level wages	Amiti and Davis (2012)	Indonesia	A 10-percentage-point output tariff cut leads to a 2.4% reduction in the average nonexporting firm wage but a 2.4% increase in the average export firm wage. A 10-percentage-point input tariff reduction results in a 2.3% wage increase in nonimporting firms, but a 7.5% wage increase in firms that import at least some of their inputs.
Trade liberalization, firm-level wages, and markups	Kambhampati, Krishna, and Mitra (1997)	India	Controlling for wages and markups, after trade liberalization, firm-level labor demand increased in India by 4%–9%, depending on the industry.

continued on next page

Table A1 *continued*

Topic	Authors	Economies Covered	Main Finding
Trade and industry-level employment and wages	Dutt (2003)	India	Industry-level employment goes up after liberalization and is positively related to import penetration. But there is no significant effect of trade protection on the employment level. However, employment growth is negatively related to protection.
Trade and firm-level employment	Mitra and Shin (2012)	Republic of Korea	A 10-percentage-point reduction in industry-level tariff reduces firm-level labor demand by 0.6%. A 10-percentage-point increase in the ratio of exports to output increases firm-level labor demand by 0.7%.
Trade liberalization and unemployment	Hasan et al. (2012)	India	A 10-percentage-point decrease in the state-level employment-weighted average tariff rate leads to a 7.5% decline in the state-level unemployment rate. Also, a 10-percentage-point reduction in a two-digit industry-level tariff leads to a 0.08-percentage-point reduction in the probability of being unemployed within an industry.
Trade liberalization, labor market flexibility, and informality	Sundaram, Ahsan, and Mitra (2013)	India	Informal sector firms with five or fewer workers experience a greater increase in output, value added, and employment due to tariff reductions in the relatively rigid labor regulation states as compared to others. Trade liberalization might be reducing informality (the share of employment or output in the informal sector) in states with relatively flexible labor regulations and increasing it in other states.
Informality, structural change, and trade liberalization	Ahsan and Mitra (2017)	India	Informality was rising in low-productivity sectors relative to high-productivity sectors which were also the sectors which were expanding in relative output and employment. This differential trend goes away with trade liberalization.
Exports and informality	McCaig and Pavcnik (2018)	Viet Nam	As United States (US) tariffs on exports by Viet Nam to the US were lowered from 23.4% to 2.4% through the US–Viet Nam Bilateral Trade Agreement, individuals moved from employment in small, informal enterprises to large, formal firms. Within the first 2 years, the proportion of informal workers in the manufacturing sector went down from 66% to 60%. Industries with bigger US tariff cuts also experienced larger reductions in informality. This contributed to aggregate productivity growth of about 1.5%–2.8% annually.

continued on next page

Table A1 *continued*

Topic	Authors	Economies Covered	Main Finding
Labor regulations and informality in an open economy	Liang, Appleton, and Song (2016)	People's Republic of China	The proportion of casual employment in urban People's Republic of China increased from 24% in 2007 to 42% in 2013, probably due to the 2008 New Labor Contract Law (in an open economy).
Trade openness and informality	Fiess and Fugazza (2012)	People's Republic of China; India; Indonesia; Japan; Bangladesh; Pakistan; Sri Lanka; Nepal; Malaysia; Hong Kong, China; Singapore; the Philippines; and many non-Asian countries	While output informality rises with trade openness, employment informality falls.
Adjustment costs of trade and worker mobility costs	Artuc, Lederman, and Porto (2015)	People's Republic of China, India, Iran, Indonesia, Republic of Korea, Lithuania, Azerbaijan, Bangladesh, the Philippines, and many non-Asian developed and developing countries	The labor mobility cost is 3.88 times the average wage in South Asia, 3.95 in Central Asia, and 3.46 in East Asia and the Pacific. A sizable proportion of the welfare gains from trade are being wiped out by adjustment costs.
Policies to minimize trade adjustment costs	Hollweg et al. (2014)	Cross-country study, includes above countries	Policies aimed at reducing labor mobility costs include subsidizing destination-specific relocation costs, training programs to provide skills specific to destination sectors, unemployment benefits or insurance, job search assistance, subsidized employment through public works programs, announcing trade reforms in advance or gradual trade liberalization, etc.

continued on next page

Table A1 *continued*

Topic	Authors	Economies Covered	Main Finding
Social protection policies for workers exposed to external	Mitra and Ranjan (2011)	No specific country	The study notes the benefits of expanding unemployment benefits and insurance but with strict monitoring. The study recommends against excessive use of employment protection policies and advocates for East Asian-style public works programs. The authors also argue that various forms of unemployment support will build and sustain support for greater openness of economy.
Trade and per capita incomes	Frankel and Romer (1999)	Cross-country study	Trade increases per capita income.
	Irwin and Tervio (2002)	Cross-country study	Trade increases per capita income.
Growth in incomes of the poor	Dollar and Kraay (2002)	Cross-country study	The growth in incomes of the poor is no less than the rate of growth of per capita income.
Trade, growth, poverty and inequality	Mitra (2016) (first relevant part)	India and the People's Republic of China	The People's Republic of China, where inequality went up much more, actually did much better at poverty reduction than India. While both India and the People's Republic of China have grown quite rapidly during the last decades, the People's Republic of China's growth performance has been quite a bit better, and that has led to a faster reduction in poverty.
Trade and poverty reduction	Topalova (2007)	India	Districts whose rural workers were more exposed to an import competition rise saw a relatively slower reduction in rural poverty. Compared to a district that did not experience any change in this exposure, a district experiencing the mean change saw a 2-percentage-point poverty rise. Urban poverty showed no statistically significant relationship but had the same coefficient sign as rural poverty. Trade liberalization led to a "significant setback" in rural poverty reduction.
Trade and poverty reduction	Hasan, Mitra, and Ural (2007), later updated by Cain, Hasan, and Mitra (2012)	India	States with workers more exposed to foreign competition had lower rural, urban, and overall poverty rates. States with greater reduction in employment-weighted tariffs also experienced greater poverty reduction. These effects were more pronounced in states with labor laws making for more flexible labor markets, greater road density, and greater financial development.

continued on next page

Table A1 *continued*

Topic	Authors	Economies Covered	Main Finding
Trade and poverty reduction of socially disavantaged classes	Mukim and Panagariya (2012)	India	Socially disadvantaged classes also experienced declines in poverty rates during the period since trade reforms, with some evidence that trade reforms led to a decline in their poverty.
Trade and poverty reduction	Kis-Katos and Sparrow (2015)	Indonesia	Poverty declined with a reduction in the input tariffs but increased with output tariff reductions. A 1-standard-deviation larger reduction in the employment-weighted input tariff leads to half a standard deviation greater reduction in the district-level poverty rate. The results seem to be driven by people at the extremes in education levels.
	McCaig (2011)	Viet Nam	A 1-standard-deviation reduction in the employment-weighted average US tariff faced by a province leads to a 33%–40% reduction in poverty within 2 years.
Trade and poverty	Ural Marchand (2012)	India	There was a pro-poor effect of trade reforms in that the poor benefited proportionally more than others. The benefits were greater for households in urban areas than those in rural areas and for those in relatively less remote areas.
	Han et al. (2016)	People's Republic of China	The poor saw a great percentage increase in their real incomes as compared to the rich due to trade liberalization.
Trade, poverty and inequality	Seshan (2014)	Viet Nam	Overall poverty as well as inequality fell due to trade liberalization. While rural poverty fell drastically, urban poverty went up slightly. Trade liberalization has been responsible for a third of the decline in overall poverty and half of the decline in rural poverty during the postreform period.
Trade and inequality	Mitra (2016) (second relevant part)	India and the People's Republic of China (cross-country regressions using data from 42 countries were run)	All of the slight increase in inequality in India over the last decades can be attributed to trade reforms, while in the People's Republic of China trade liberalization is responsible for a fifth of the inequality increase.

continued on next page

Table A1 *continued*

Topic	Authors	Economies Covered	Main Finding
Trade and inequality	Krishna and Sethupathy (2012)	India	Inequality, right after the reforms, first went down during 1988–1994, then went up during 1994-2000, and went down thereafter. Protection does not seem to be significantly related to inequality.
Trade and wage inequality	Kumar and Mishra (2008)	India	A 1-percentage-point reduction in the industry's import tariff leads to a 0.17% increase in the industry wage premium. Bigger tariff reductions and, therefore, bigger wage premium increases in unskilled labor-intensive industries resulted in a reduction in wage inequality.
	Amiti and Cameron (2012)	Indonesia	A 10-percentage-point input tariff reduction lowers wage inequality by 2.6% on average for all firms but by 4.5% for importing firms. For firms whose imports as a share of the value of all input are in the top 10%, this effect is 8.5%.
	Chen, Yu, and Yu (2013)	People's Republic of China	Input trade liberalization, in the presence of profit sharing between skilled workers and firms, leads to an increase in skilled–unskilled wage inequality. This effect is not valid for processing firms.
Trade and labor share	Ahsan and Mitra (2014)	India	For the relatively small and labor-intensive firms, tariff reductions raised labor share, while for the large and relative low labor intensity firms, labor share fell with tariff reductions. While the elasticity of the labor share with respect to the industry-level tariff is -0.5 in the former set of firms, it is 0.8 for the latter.
	Kamal, Lovely, and Mitra (2015)	People's Republic of China	Tariff cuts lead to increases in firm-level labor share across the board. This effect is stronger for coastal firms than for the interior firms and vary by ownership type: domestic private, foreign, and state owned. Both input and output tariff cuts have qualitatively similar effects.
	Mitra and Shin (2014)	Republic of Korea	Results are qualitatively similar but quantitatively different from Ahsan and Mitra (2014).

continued on next page

Table A1 *continued*

Topic	Authors	Economies Covered	Main Finding
Trade and unionization	Ahsan, Ghosh, and Mitra (2017)	India	In net-importer industries, a 10-percentage-point reduction in the import tariff led to a 0.8-percentage-point reduction in the proportion of workers working in unionized activities as well as in the proportion of workers that are union members. Industry quasi-rents per plant were declining with tariff cuts.
Trade and labor-demand elasticities	Krishna, Mitra, and Chinoy (2001)	Turkey	The impact of trade liberalization on firm-level labor-demand elasticities was statistically insignificant.
	Hasan, Mitra, and Ramaswamy (2007)	India	The absolute elasticity of labor demand at the industry level in Indian manufacturing went up, due to trade liberalization, from 0.076 to 0.186 in states with rigid labor regulation and from 0.206 to 0.316 in states with flexible labor regulation.
	Mitra and Shin (2014)	Republic of Korea	There was weak evidence of trade liberalization increasing labor-demand elasticities. However, exports from the Republic of Korea have increased their firm-level labor-demand elasticities. A 10-percentage-point increase in the share of exports in firm-level output led to an increase in absolute labor-demand elasticity by up to 0.04.

PART II
Labor Market Adjustments in Asia

2

Industry Wages and Tariffs of the Rest of the World[1]

Marcelo Olarreaga, Roberta Piermartini, and Guido Porto

2.1 Introduction

There is widespread evidence that countries use trade policy to protect their workers. Sector-level tariffs typically correlate positively with sector wages and employment. This chapter examines the mirror question of how tariffs of other countries of the world affect industry wages at home. To answer this question, we rely on an industry-level analysis of wages in a sample of developing and developed countries spanning from 1976 to 2004. The effect of trade policy is identified through differential exposure of trade policy changes abroad for workers in different industries.

As expected, we find that there is a robust negative correlation between tariffs faced in export markets and sector-level wages. Our estimates suggest that a 10-percentage-point higher tariff in the rest of the world (ROW) implies a 0.8% lower wage at home. Because during the period under study most countries benefited from improvements in market access, sector-level wages tended to increase through this channel. But we uncovered a large degree of heterogeneity across countries. Asian economies such as Japan, Malaysia, Pakistan, and Hong Kong, China are among those in our sample that experienced the highest average wage growth during the period due to improvements in market access. At the other end of the spectrum, Latin American and African countries such as Argentina, Uruguay, Senegal, and Nigeria experienced the largest declines in average wages due to higher ROW tariffs faced by

[1] The authors are grateful to Marc Bacchetta for useful suggestions. Olarreaga and Porto also gratefully acknowledge support from the r4d program on employment funded by the Swiss National Science Foundation and the Swiss Agency for Development and Cooperation.

their exporters. We also find that there is strong heterogeneity within regions. In Asia, countries such as Nepal and Sri Lanka saw their wages decline due to a deterioration of their market access. In Latin America and Africa, some countries experience increases in wages due to declines in the tariffs they face abroad. These results are important for at least three reasons. First, they provide a rationale for trade negotiations based on wages that is probably much easier to grasp than the terms-of-trade rationale offered by the standard trade model (even though they are driven by the same mechanism). Second, it enables us to disentangle the significant heterogeneity across countries in terms of wage growth benefits associated with trade reforms over the period. Workers in some countries have been left behind by the general move toward trade liberalization, and there is a need to address these imbalances if we want those countries and workers back at the negotiating table. Last, but not least, if individuals care about worker welfare not only at home, but also abroad, as the corporate social responsibility literature seems to suggest, then the case for using tariffs to protect workers is seriously undermined by our results.

The literature on trade policy and wages is vast. Earlier studies typically find significant negative effects of removing trade protection on wages, especially for developing countries. For example, in a study on Colombia, Attanasio, Goldberg, and Pavcnik (2004) document a reduction of the skill premium in sectors that face the strongest tariff reduction compared to industries that faced a lower reduction. In her study of the effects of India's liberalization in 1991, Topalova (2010) finds that regions with a higher concentration of industries that lost protection as a result of import tariff reductions experienced a slower decline in poverty. Looking at Brazil's early 1990s trade liberalization, Kovak (2013) estimates a relative fall in wages in regions facing larger liberalization. In general, the literature finds larger employment effects than effects on wages of import tariff reductions in developed countries (Grossman 1986; Trefler 2004; Pierce and Schott 2016, who look at reduction of trade policy uncertainty rather than tariff cuts). McLaren and Hakobyan (2016) find that wages grew significantly less for workers in the United States located in areas more affected by tariff cuts following the implementation of the North American Free Trade Agreement.

We focus on changes in tariffs faced in the export destination markets. To our knowledge, our study is the first to look systematically at how the correlation between tariffs and wages depend on the nature of the tariff change and for a large sample of developed and developing countries. In his study on the United States–Viet Nam free trade agreement, McCaig (2011) finds that provinces in Viet Nam that were more exposed to the United States' tariff cuts experience greater declines in poverty rates. Similarly, Porto (2010) predicts that the elimination of trade and barriers on exports of agro-manufactures to industrialized countries would cause poverty to decline in Argentina. These studies, however, do not look at wages.

2.2 Data

Our main source of data is the Trade, Production and Protection database put together by Nicita and Olarreaga (2007). The cross-country data include information on export values and export quantities, production, value added, employment, wages, and number of establishments for 28 manufacturing industries corresponding to the three-digit level of the International Standard Industrial Classification (ISIC), Revision 2. The database is available at the World Bank trade website (www. worldbank.org/trade). We combine the Nicita and Olarreaga data with supplementary data on country characteristics from the World Development Indicators. These characteristics include per capita gross domestic product (GDP), GDP, population, and bilateral exchange rates.

The basic premise of our analysis is the correlation between the average tariff across export destinations and the level of wages. Using the Nicita and Olarreaga (2007) data, we calculate the average industry wage for each source country as the ratio of total industry wage bill to total employment. Using w_{ic} as the average wage in industry i in country c, we construct a measure of exposure to foreign tariffs by computing the average tariff across export markets. We define the average tariff of an industry's exports as:

$$\tau_{ict} = \sum_d s_{icdt} * \tau_{idt} \tag{1}$$

where τ_{idt} is the tariff faced by industry i in destination country d at time t and s_{icdt} the share of destination d in exports of industry i of source country c. Average tariffs abroad vary by industry, source country, and year through differences in tariffs themselves and the export-share weights.

Figure 2.1 showcases our basic hypothesis for four Asian countries in our sample: the Republic of Korea, India, Indonesia, and Singapore. In these cases, there is clear negative correlation between the log of the average wage paid in industry i in country c and the average tariff across export destinations. Higher tariffs in the rest of the world de-protect Asian workers and make them worse-off in terms of wages. Figure 2.2 displays this negative correlation for four developed countries: the United States, Denmark, Finland, and Norway.

Figure 2.1 Correlations between Wages and Tariffs in Asia

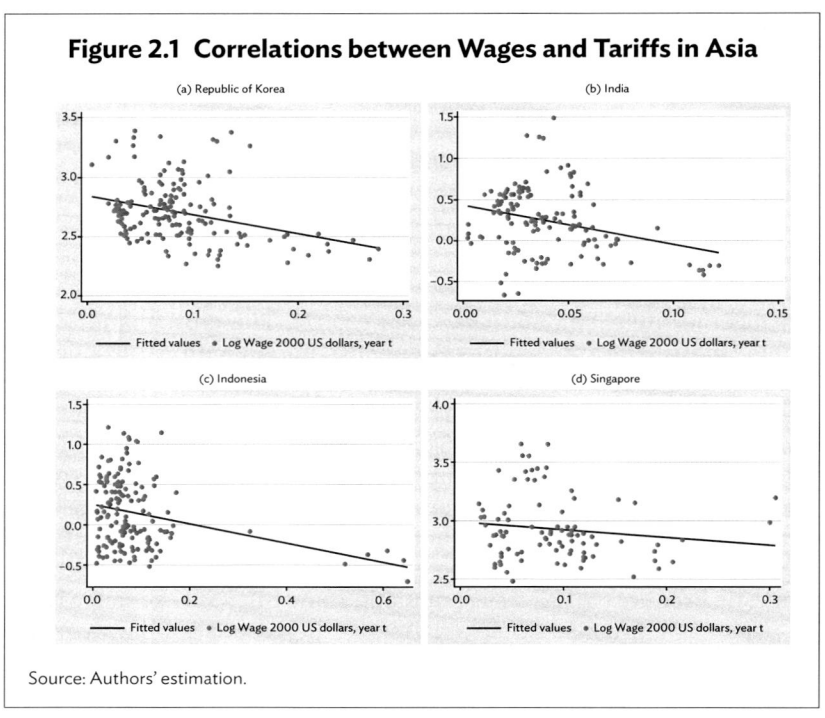

Source: Authors' estimation.

Figure 2.2 Correlations between Wages and Tariffs in Developed Countries

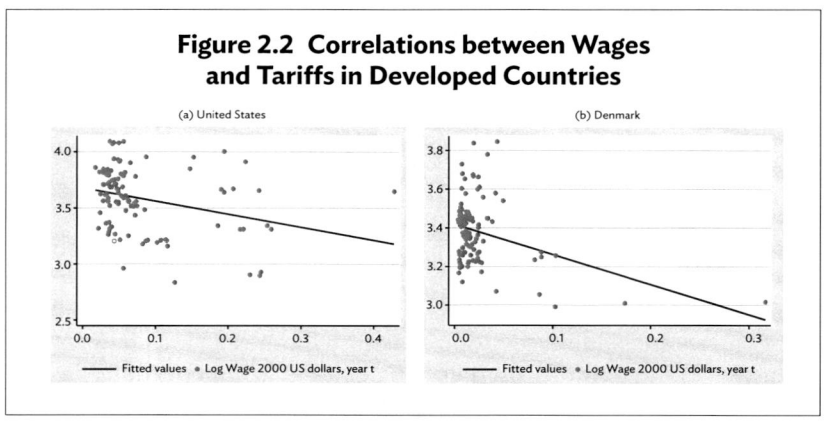

continued on next page

Figure 2.2 *continued*

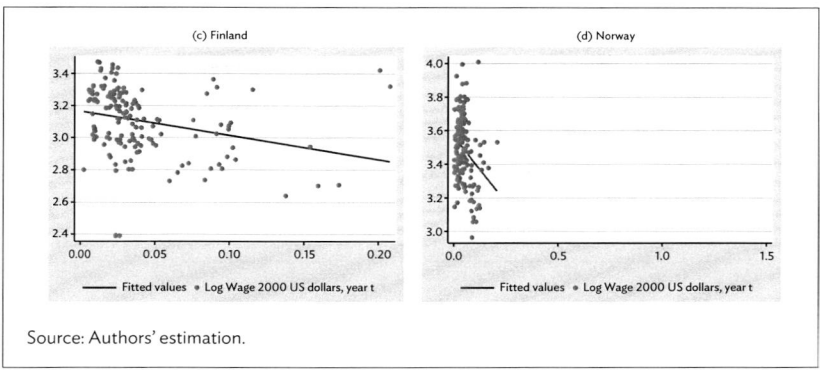

Source: Authors' estimation.

Figure 2.3 shows examples for Latin America (Colombia, Chile, Peru, and Uruguay) and Figure 2.4 for Africa (Ethiopia, Cameroon, Malawi, and Nigeria). In these countries, the data reveal that industries that faced higher tariffs in the rest of the world paid lower wages, on average.

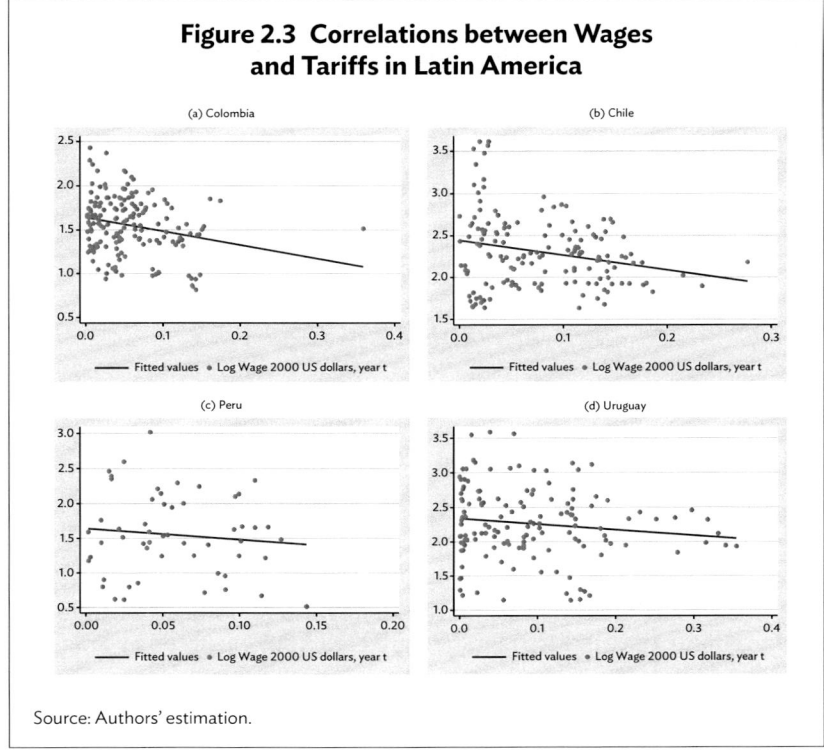

Figure 2.3 Correlations between Wages and Tariffs in Latin America

Source: Authors' estimation.

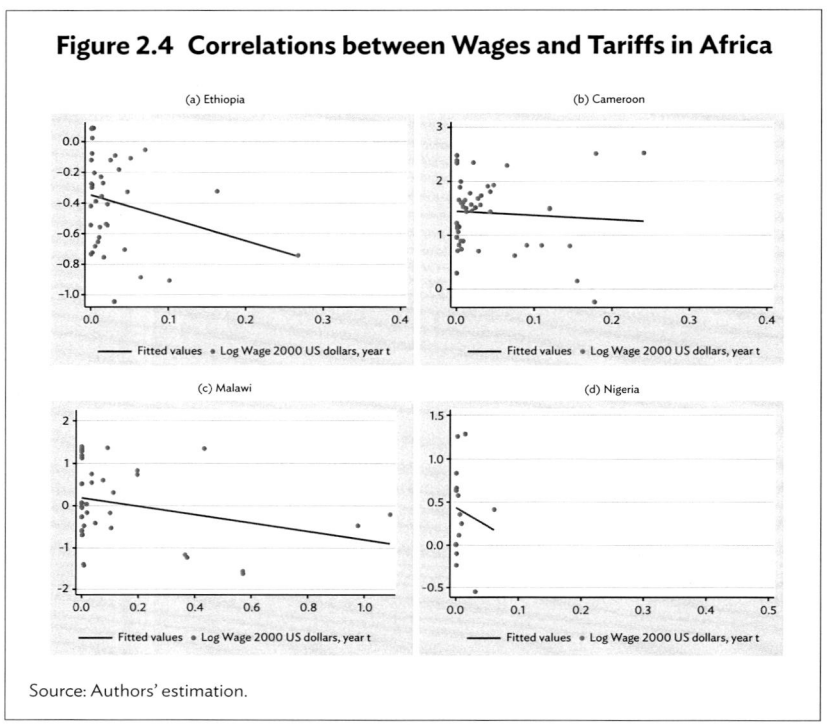

Figure 2.4 Correlations between Wages and Tariffs in Africa

Source: Authors' estimation.

2.3 Econometric Model and Results

To study these questions formally, we set up the following regression specification for wages:

$$log\ w_{ict} = \beta\tau_{ict} + x_{ict}^i\gamma + \varphi_t + \varphi_{ict} + u_{ict}, \qquad (2)$$

where log w_{ict} is the log of the average wage paid in industry i in country of origin c at time t, τ_{ict} is the export-share weighted average foreign tariff across destination markets as defined in equation (1), x_{ict} is a vector of controls that varies across several specifications, φ_t are year fixed-effects, φ_{ic} are country of origin-industry fixed effects, and u_{ict} is the error term. Given the set of fixed effects used in equation (2), the coefficient of interest β, which captures the impact of tariffs abroad on sector wages is identified using the average variation across time and within country and industries. Standard errors are clustered by industry-country (source). Because we are looking at the impact of changes in trade protection abroad on home wages, we do not expect endogeneity to be an important problem and estimate equation (2) using ordinary least squares.

Table 2.1 presents our results. Conditioning only on the fixed effects φ_t and φ_{ic}, the coefficient is negative and statistically significant (column 1). An industry facing an average tariff across destinations which is 10 percentage points higher pays on average almost 1% lower wages. Since this model includes year effects, any aggregate shock is accounted for, while the origin-industry effects control for time-invariant characteristics of an industry in a given country (such as certain technological characteristics or policies that remain constant).

This negative correlation between wages and foreign tariffs is robust to the inclusion of various important controls. Following Brambilla and Porto (2016), we add the log of the per capita GDP of the origin

Table 2.1 Average Wages and Average Tariffs in ROW: OLS-FE Estimation

	(1)	(2)	(3)	(4)	(5)	(6)
Average ROW Tariff	−0.0984** [0.0496]	−0.0976** [0.0483]	−0.0972* [0.0497]	−0.0835* [0.0495]	−0.0806** [0.0400]	−0.0808** [0.0400]
Log Origin p/c GDP		0.459*** [0.101]		0.338*** [0.103]	0.410*** [0.0884]	0.412*** [0.0883]
Log Industry Exports			−0.000104 [7.19e-05]	−1.4e-04** [6.96e-05]	−0.000121* [6.78e-05]	−0.000122* [6.80e-05]
Log Industry Output				0.145*** [0.0333]	0.0300 [0.0229]	0.0300 [0.0229]
Productivity					0.189*** [0.0250]	0.190*** [0.0250]
Average p/c GDP						0.00852 [0.0119]
Observations	7,083	7,083	7,083	6,795	6,166	6,166
R-squared	0.016	0.024	0.016	0.072	0.154	0.154
Origin-Industry Groups	1,539	1,539	1,539	1,539	1,539	1,539

FE = fixed effects, GDP = gross domestic product, OLS = ordinary least squares, p/c = per capita, ROW = rest of the world.

Significance at 1%, 5%, and 10% levels indicated by ***, **, and *.

Note: Proportional changes in average wages caused by the observed change in ROW tariffs, 2000–1995.

Source: Authors' estimation.

country in column 2. Higher income implies a higher domestic demand and thus higher wages. The level of per capita GDP also accounts for differential country effects across time, such as periods of booms or crises. In column 3, we exclude per capita GDP but include the log of industry exports. In column 4, we further control for per capita GDP in the country of origin, the log of industry exports and the log of industry output (column 4). The results are robust: in column 4, for instance, $\hat{\beta}$ = –0.0835, which is smaller but similar to the $\hat{\beta}$ estimated when conditioning only on the fixed effects (column 1). Finally, we control for the average productivity of an industry (output per worker) in column 5 and for the average GDP of the export destination (as in Brambilla and Porto 2016) in column 6. These controls do not affect the results either, with an estimate $\hat{\beta}$ = –0.0808 so that a 10-percentage-point higher tariff in the rest of the world implies 0.8% lower industry wages.

If the impact of foreign tariffs on domestic wages is on average relatively small, the impact of foreign trade reforms on home wages will depend on the change in tariffs in foreign countries faced by each country's exporters. As discussed in the next section, there are some important differences.

2.4 Wages and Rest of the World Tariff Changes

In this section, we explore the winners and losers from the observed changes in ROW tariffs. To this end, we compute for each country in our sample the observed change in the average tariff faced in the rest of the world from 1995 to 2000. Then, we use the estimated coefficient in column 5 of Table 2.1 and make predictions for the change in average log wages.

The average impacts on wages in Asia are shown in Table 2.2. There are 14 Asian economies in our sample, with eight losers (those with increases in ROW tariffs and declines in average wages) and six winners (those with ROW tariff declines and wage increases). The largest loss is estimated for Nepal, at 0.61% decline in wages. In Sri Lanka, Bangladesh, and Thailand, the losses are –0.19%, –0.17%, and –0.10%, respectively. In Jordan, Singapore, the Philippines, and India, the losses become smaller and are negligible. The largest increase in wages is observed in Hong Kong, China, at 1.23%. In Malaysia with an increase of 0.52%, Pakistan with 0.36%, Japan with 0.29%, and Indonesia with 0.18%, the impacts are sizable, but the gains in the Republic of Korea are small.

These differences in the impact of foreign tariffs on home wages in Asia are simply explained by differences in changes in ROW tariffs faced by each of these countries. The largest reductions in ROW tariffs are experienced by exporters in Hong Kong, China with declines in average

Table 2.2 Average Wages and Average Tariffs in ROW: Asian Economies

	ROW Tariff Changes	Change in Log Wages
Nepal	0.0759	−0.0061
Sri Lanka	0.0240	−0.0019
Bangladesh	0.0214	−0.0017
Thailand	0.0125	−0.0010
Jordan	0.0063	−0.0005
Singapore	0.0012	−0.0001
Philippines	0.0007	−0.0001
India	0.0006	−0.0000
Republic of Korea	−0.0026	0.0002
Indonesia	−0.0226	0.0018
Japan	−0.0358	0.0029
Pakistan	−0.0451	0.0036
Malaysia	−0.0639	0.0052
Hong Kong, China	−0.1519	0.0123

ROW = rest of the world.

Notes: Dependent variable is average wage. Controls in all columns: origin-industry effects, year effects. Standard errors clustered at origin-industry level.

Sources: Data from A. Nicita and M. Olarreaga. 2007. Trade, Production and Protection Database, 1976–2004. *World Bank Economic Review* 21 (1). pp. 165–171; and World Bank. World Development Indicators. http://datatopics.worldbank.org/world-development-indicators/ (accessed June 2017).

tariffs of 15 percentage points, followed by Malaysia (6 percentage points) and Pakistan (5 percentage points). Sri Lanka, Bangladesh, and Thailand have the largest increases in ROW tariffs with increases in average tariffs of 2, 2, and 1 percentage point(s), respectively. Note that these changes in foreign trade protection only include tariffs. If nontariff measures were to be included, it is likely that we would observe larger changes in foreign trade protection.

The estimated impacts on wages for the remaining 16 losing countries are reported in Table 2.3. ROW tariffs increase in these countries, and this creates losses in real wages ranging from −0.43% in Argentina to very negligible losses in Ireland. This again is simply explained by the degree of ROW tariff increases experienced in each of these countries varying from an increase of 5 percentage points in Argentina to 0.05 percentage points in Ireland. In the remaining 52 countries in our sample (Table 2.4), real wages increase following reduction in foreign

Table 2.3 Average Wages and Average Tariffs in ROW: Losers from Higher Tariffs

	ROW Tariff Changes	Change in Log Wages
Argentina	0.0532	–0.0043
Uruguay	0.0508	–0.0041
Senegal	0.0496	–0.0040
Nigeria	0.0482	–0.0039
Oman	0.0363	–0.0029
Iran	0.0354	–0.0029
Ethiopia	0.0351	–0.0028
Chile	0.0144	–0.0012
Malawi	0.0100	–0.0008
Egypt	0.0092	–0.0007
Côte d'Ivoire	0.0071	–0.0006
Guatemala	0.0068	–0.0005
Brazil	0.0022	–0.0002
Kyrgyz Republic	0.0017	–0.0001
Venezuela	0.0013	–0.0001
Ireland	0.0005	–0.0000

ROW = rest of the world.
Note: Proportional changes in average wages caused by the observed change in ROW tariffs, 2000-1995.
Source: Author's calculation using the data in A. Nicita and M. Olarreaga. 2007. Trade, Production and Protection Database, 1976–2004. *World Bank Economic Review* 21 (1). pp. 165–171.

Table 2.4 Average Wages and Average Tariffs in ROW: Winners from Lower Tariffs

	ROW Tariff Changes	Change in Log Wages
El Salvador	–0.0004	0.0000
United Kingdom	–0.0035	0.0003
Latvia	–0.0037	0.0003
Peru	–0.0040	0.0003
Ecuador	–0.0047	0.0004
Gabon	–0.0050	0.0004
Greece	–0.0052	0.0004
Finland	–0.0054	0.0004

continued on next page

Table 2.4 *continued*

	ROW Tariff Changes	Change in Log Wages
Colombia	−0.0055	0.0004
United States	−0.0057	0.0005
Kenya	−0.0062	0.0005
Netherlands	−0.0063	0.0005
Sweden	−0.0067	0.0005
Bolivia	−0.0068	0.0005
Honduras	−0.0072	0.0006
Portugal	−0.0072	0.0006
United Republic of Tanzania	−0.0077	0.0006
Cameroon	−0.0079	0.0006
Canada	−0.0082	0.0007
Denmark	−0.0092	0.0007
Italy	−0.0106	0.0009
Mexico	−0.0135	0.0011
Slovenia	−0.0149	0.0012
Spain	−0.0154	0.0012
Australia	−0.0176	0.0014
Germany	−0.0191	0.0015
Austria	−0.0194	0.0016
France	−0.0200	0.0016
Slovakia	−0.0209	0.0017
South Africa	−0.0224	0.0018
Lithuania	−0.0227	0.0018
Botswana	−0.0239	0.0019
New Zealand	−0.0240	0.0019
Costa Rica	−0.0277	0.0022
Ukraine	−0.0293	0.0024
Algeria	−0.0306	0.0025
Russian Federation	−0.0313	0.0025
Bulgaria	−0.0352	0.0028
Azerbaijan	−0.0368	0.0030
Armenia	−0.0373	0.0030
Hungary	−0.0423	0.0034
Trinidad and Tobago	−0.0425	0.0034

continued on next page

Table 2.4 *continued*

	ROW Tariff Changes	Change in Log Wages
Czech Republic	−0.0442	0.0036
Panama	−0.0454	0.0037
Poland	−0.0555	0.0045
Mauritius	−0.0585	0.0047
Israel	−0.0593	0.0048
Norway	−0.0662	0.0054
Morocco	−0.0722	0.0058
Moldova	−0.0724	0.0058
Tunisia	−0.1084	0.0088
Turkey	−0.1110	0.0090

ROW = rest of the world.

Notes: Dependent variable is average wage. Controls in all columns: origin-industry effects, year effects. Standard errors clustered at origin-industry level.

Sources: Data from A. Nicita and M. Olarreaga. 2007. Trade, Production and Protection Database, 1976–2004. *World Bank Economic Review* 21 (1). pp. 165–171; and World Bank. World Development Indicators. http://datatopics.worldbank.org/world-development-indicators/ (accessed June 2017).

tariffs. The gains range from very small increases in real wages due to very low cuts in ROW tariffs in El Salvador to more sizable real wage increases of 0.9% in Turkey.

2.5 Conclusions

We show that industries that face higher tariffs in their export markets pay lower wages. We show that this result is robust and holds for both developed and developing countries. However, because countries export different products to different countries, there are important differences in terms of changes in market access, which implies that workers in some countries have benefited from better market access, whereas others experienced losses in wages due to a deterioration of their market access abroad. Even though there are important intraregional differences, workers in parts of Asia seem to be among those that have benefited the most from wage increases associated with trade reforms during the period under study, whereas workers in Latin America and Africa are among those that have actually experienced wage losses due to trade reforms during the same period.

Differences in sector specialization and trading partners explain our results, but differences in the impact that changes in market access have on wages at home are also likely explained by labor market frictions, different types of worker endowments, product market power, and taxation and redistribution that we leave for further research. There is definitely a need for within-country studies to further disentangle differences across countries in terms of benefits accruing to workers from trade reforms abroad.

Our findings further suggest that there is a positive international spillover from unilateral liberalization that countries do not internalize when setting their trade policies to protect workers' wages. As a result, the level of protection that countries individually set to protect workers employed in the industry with low wages is inefficiently high. Existing evidence supports this prediction. In their study of tariffs faced in international markets by Indian workers, Mendoza, Nayyar, and Piermartini (2018) show that trade barriers tend to be increasingly higher for workers earning lower wages. More research is needed to assess the general equilibrium effects of a global reduction of tariffs for the goods produced by low-wage workers. However, the analysis of existing tariff profiles and our results appear to suggest the need to further international cooperation.

References

Attanasio, O., P. K. Goldberg, and N. Pavcnik. 2004. Trade Reforms and Wage Inequality in Colombia. *Journal of Development Economics.* 74 (2). pp. 331–66.

Brambilla, I., and G. Porto. 2016. High-Income Export Destinations, Quality and Wages. *Journal of International Economics.* 98 (C). pp. 21–35.

Grossman, G. M. 1986. Imports as a Cause of Injury: The Case of the US Steel Industry. *Journal of International Economics.* 20 (3). pp.201–23.

Kovak, B. 2013. Regional Effects of Trade Reform: What Is the Correct Measure Of Liberalization? *American Economic Review.* 103 (5). pp. 1960–76.

McCaig, B. 2011. Exporting Out of Poverty: Provincial Poverty in Vietnam and US Market Access. *Journal of International Economics.* 85 (1). pp. 101–13.

McLaren, J., and S. Hakobyan. 2016. Looking for Local Labor Market Effects of the NAFTA. *The Review of Economics and Statistics.* 98 (4). pp. 728–41.

Mendoza, A., G. Nayyar, and R. Piermartini. 2018. Are the "Poor" Getting Globalised? In World Trade Organization and World Bank Trade and Poverty Reduction: New Evidence of Impacts on Developing Countries. Mimeo, WTO.

Nicita, A., and M. Olarreaga. 2007. Trade, Production and Protection Database, 1976–2004. *World Bank Economic Review.* 21 (1). pp. 165–71.

Pierce, J., and P. Schott. 2016. The Surprisingly Swift Decline of US Manufacturing Employment. *American Economic Review.* 106 (7). pp. 1632–62.

Porto, G. 2010. International Market Access and Poverty in Argentina. *Review of International Economics.* 18 (2). pp. 396–407.

Topalova, P. 2010. Factor Immobility and Regional Impacts of Trade Liberalization: Evidence on Poverty from India. *American Economic Journal: Applied Economics.* 2 (4). pp. 1–41.

Trefler, D. 2004. The Long and Short of the Canada–US Free Trade Agreement. *American Economic Review.* 94 (4). pp. 870–89.

World Bank. World Development Indicators. http://datatopics.worldbank.org/world-development-indicators/ (accessed June 2017).

3

Trade Liberalization and the *Hukou* System of the People's Republic of China: How Migration Frictions Can Amplify the Unequal Gains from Trade

Yuan Zi

3.1 Introduction

The emergence of the People's Republic of China as a great economic power has stimulated an epochal shift in patterns of world trade, in contradiction to the conventional wisdom regarding the impact of trade on labor markets in developed countries (Autor, Dorn, and Hanson 2016). The global effects of the People's Republic of China's trade and economic growth has been widely documented (Autor, Dorn, and Hanson 2013; Bugamelli, Fabiani, and Sette 2015; Balsvik, Jensen, and Salvanes 2015; Giovanni, Levchenko, and Zhang 2014; Hsieh and Ossa 2011), reshaping our understanding of the consequences of trade for wages, unemployment, and other labor market outcomes.

On the other hand, equally significant transformations can be identified within the People's Republic of China itself, including the remarkable degree of internal migration occurring within the country. Hundreds of millions of the workers have moved from inland areas to coastal cities, contributing to manufacturing growth and export surges. However, the extent to which they have benefited from the country's trade liberalization remains less clear: migrant workers are usually treated as second-class citizens and are prevented from accessing various social benefits provided at the local level due to the country's unique household registration system (*hukou*). Does the *hukou* system contribute to the unequal distribution of gains from trade? Does this labor market distortion prevent the People's Republic of China from fully reaping the gains from trade reforms? These are relevant policy questions that require empirical underpinning.

From a theoretical point of view, trade liberalization is often considered an important driver of economic development, as it can raise a country's income through increasing specialization in sectors with a comparative advantage, providing access to cheap foreign inputs, and facilitating the adoption of new technologies. However, prominent trade theories typically focus on long-run equilibria, assuming that the reallocation of resources across economic activities is frictionless. However, in reality, factor adjustments tend to be slow, costly, and heterogeneous across firms, sectors, and space. As long as some production factors are spatially immobile and trade is not frictionless, the extent to which a country can gain from trade is ultimately contingent on labor mobility. This point has long been recognized but has become increasingly emphasized by trade and labor economists, as we find more and more evidence regarding the adverse impact of trade shocks on labor market outcomes.

Nevertheless, demonstrating this empirically is not easy. First, it is very difficult to find a clear measure of migration friction, as most factors or policy shocks affect both goods and people at the same time. Second, according to most studies, internal migration reacts negligibly to trade shocks. Some indirect evidence exists that labor immobility can explain a large proportion of the negative impact of trade,[1] but owing to the aforementioned difficulties, a direct test remains missing. I exploit the People's Republic of China's liberalization episode following its accession to the World Trade Organization (WTO) to test how its internal migration reacts to trade shocks. Using a *hukou* friction measure constructed in Zi (2018), I shed light on the interaction between trade and migration frictions.

Drawing on a rich dataset that I assembled on the People's Republic of China's regional economy, I find that prefectures that experience more positive trade shocks have seen a relative increase in employment, and the effect is strongest in provinces with a lower amount of *hukou* friction. A prefecture at the 75th percentile of effective tariff exposure experiences an employment increase 3.4 percentage points greater (or smaller decrease) than a prefecture at the 25th percentile. In a prefecture

---

[1]   See, for instance, Autor, Dorn, and Hanson (2013); Topalova (2010); Dix-Carneiro and Kovak (2017) for the cases of the United States (US), India, and Brazil, respectively.

with the lowest amount of *hukou* friction, the effect is three times larger than the average effect. On average, over 30% of the regional variation in employment changes can be attributed to trade liberalization. Moreover, the total population and the working-age population of prefectures react to trade shocks and their interaction with the *hukou* measure in a quantitatively similar way to employment, suggesting that the observed regional employment changes are primarily driven by interregional labor adjustments. Direct focus on migration flows yields similar results. Most importantly, I only find that trade shocks result in increases in the population holding local *hukou* in prefectures where *hukou* frictions are low. This result suggests that in spite of labor mobility between prefectures, migrant workers can only obtain a local *hukou* in prefectures with less stringent *hukou* systems. This supports the validity of my *hukou* measure and confirms the existence of *hukou* frictions.

Although the focus of this chapter is on the People's Republic of China, the message and policy implications are not limited to this country. According to World Population Policies 2013 (United Nations 2013), 60% of governments in the world desired a major change in their spatial labor distribution and 80% of these countries had policies in place to influence internal migration. In general, gaining a greater understanding of when and where trade is costly and how various domestic frictions shape the impact of trade on workers, individuals, and/or households of different groups is central to the research agenda of trade economists. Implementing effective policies to eliminate or mitigate these frictions and effectively targeting the most adversely affected individuals should represent a salient issue to policy makers and applied economists.

The content of this chapter is based on the analysis of Zi (2018). I begin by discussing the People's Republic of China's trade reforms since the late 1970s and their acceleration following the country's accession to the WTO. I then provide a detailed description of the country's various *hukou* reforms. In the following section, I identify the trade shocks and migration frictions embedded in the *hukou* system at the local level, present evidence regarding the ways in which trade shocks have stimulated a substantial degree of spatial labor reallocation in the People's Republic of China, as well as how regional *hukou* frictions influence this effect. I subsequently offer a simple conceptual framework that guides our inquiry on measuring and interpreting the welfare impacts of the observed labor reallocation. Finally, I present welfare calculations from Zi (2018), demonstrating how the *hukou* system has prevented optimal spatial adjustments of labor to trade shocks in the country, and how this in turn amplifies the negative distributional consequences of trade.

3.2 The Trade and *Hukou* Reforms of the People's Republic of China

3.2.1 Trade Liberalization in the People's Republic of China: Before and after the WTO

Prior to its economic reform in the early 1980s, the average tariff level in the People's Republic of China was 56%.[2] This tariff schedule was implemented in 1950, with almost no change since, partly due to the relative unimportance of trade policy under the centrally planned economy. Under the planned economy, import and export quantities represented government decisions rather than reflections of market supply and demand (Ianchovichina and Martin 2001). During this period, the People's Republic of China's trade was run by 10 to 16 foreign-trade corporations that were de facto monopolies in their specified product ranges (Lardy 1991).

In 1982, the People's Republic of China commenced its first tariff modification, and gradually reduced its average tariff by 13% in the following 5 years. From 1992 onward, in order to pave the way for the country's accession to the WTO, the government engaged in a series of voluntary tariff cuts on over 5,000 products, driving the simple average tariff down from 43% in 1992 to 24% in 1996 (Li 2013).

However, these episodes of tariff reductions were accompanied by pervasive and complex import and export controls. Import quotas, licenses, designated trading practices, and other nontariff barriers were widely used (Blancher and Rumbaugh 2004). There was also a substantial level of tariff redundancy resulting from various preferential arrangements. To name a few, imports for processing purposes, for military uses, by special economic zones (SEZs), and in certain areas near the People's Republic of China's border were subject to waivers or reductions in import duties. According to Ianchovichina and Martin (2001), only 40% of imports were subject to official tariffs. In addition, the renminbi depreciated by more than 60% in the 1980s, and a further 44% in 1994 to help firms export (Li 2013). As a result, changes in tariff duties do not fully reflect the changes in actual protection faced by firms or the accessibility of imported inputs during these periods.

In 1996, the government implemented substantial reforms that removed most restrictive nontariff barriers to fulfill the preconditions of WTO accession. Trade licenses, special import arrangements,

---

[2]   This is the 1982 unweighted average tariff documented by Blancher and Rumbaugh (2004).

and discriminatory policies against foreign goods were reduced or eliminated to render tariffs the primary instruments of protection. The share of all imports subject to licensing requirements fell from a peak of 46% in the late 1980s to less than 4% of all commodities by the time the People's Republic of China acceded to the WTO. The state abolished import substitution lists and authorized tens of thousands of companies to engage in foreign trade transactions, undermining the monopoly powers of state trading companies for all but a handful of commodities. The transformation was similarly far-reaching on the export side (Lardy 2005). The duty-free policy on imports for personal use by SEZs was gradually abolished in the 1990s, and preferential duty in some border provinces were abolished in 2001. Moreover, the People's Republic of China also abolished, modified, or added over 1,000 national regulations and policies. At the regional level, more than 3,000 administrative regulations and about 188,000 policy measures implemented by provincial and municipal governments were ceased.

From 2001, phased tariff reductions were implemented following the People's Republic of China's WTO accession, with the goal of reducing both the average tariff levels and the dispersion of tariffs across industries. In 2000, the People's Republic of China's simple average applied tariff was 17%, with a standard deviation across the Harmonized System six-digit level (HS6) products of 12%. By the end of 2005, the average tariff level was reduced to 6%, and the standard deviation had almost halved. The average tariff level stabilized after 2005.[3]

3.2.2 The *Hukou* System

A *hukou* is a household registration record that identifies a person as a resident of a particular area in the People's Republic of China. It officially identifies a person as a resident of an area in the country and determines where he or she is officially allowed to live. The *hukou* system was introduced in the early 1950s to harmonize the old household registration systems across regions. However, under the centrally planned economy, economic resources were mostly devoted to urban areas, as the government hoped to extract the country's agricultural economic surplus to fuel urban industrialization. This uneven allocation of resources led to a massive influx of migrants into the main cities, which in turn resulted in substantial unemployment in urban areas while threatening agricultural production in rural areas (Kinnan, Wang, and

---

[3]   All numbers are calculated using the simple average of most-favored nation applied tariffs at the Harmonized System six-digit level (HS6) from the United Nations Conference on Trade and Development Trade Analysis Information System database.

Wang 2015). As a result, the *hukou* system was soon repurposed to restrict both interregional and rural-to-urban migration. In 1958, the Standing Committee of the National People's Congress adopted the Household Registration Regulations. According to the regulations, citizens could only apply to move after the registration authority had granted them the local *hukou*. From then on, the People's Republic of China entered an era with strict internal migration controls, with the *hukou* being at the center of the migration control system.

By the end of the 1950s, free migration became extremely rare. Migrant workers would require six passes to work in provinces other than their own. Moreover, rural-to-urban migrants would have to adhere to the above restrictions and also first acquire an urban *hukou*, the annual quota of which was 0.15% to 0.2% of the nonagricultural population of each city (Cheng 2007). Under the central planning system, coupons for consumption goods, employment, housing, education, health care, and other social benefits were entirely allocated based on the local *hukou*, and urban dwellers without a local *hukou* would be fined, arrested, and deported. Thus, it was impossible for people to work and live outside their authorized domain (Cheng and Selden 1994).

In the early 1980s, the People's Republic of China latched onto a labor-intensive, export-oriented development strategy that created increasingly large labor demand in cities. Accordingly, migration policy began to relax over time. In 1984, the State Council allowed rural populations to reside in villages with self-sustained staples. In the following year, the Ministry of Public Security allowed people to migrate freely conditional on applying for a temporary residential permit upon arrival. In 1993, the People's Republic of China officially ended the food rationing system, and internal migration was no longer limited by *hukou*-based consumption coupons. Gradually, the distinction between the rural and urban *hukou* also became less important (Bosker et al. 2012). The rural-to-urban migration quotas were officially abolished in 1997; for many cities and towns, the rural/urban distinction of the *hukou* type was also eliminated (Chan 2009).

Nevertheless, the *hukou* system continues to serve as the primary instrument for regulating interregional migration. Certain cities have limited capacity for large quantities of labor due to historical or environmental issues, so they continue to seek to keep migration under tight control. Some regions that are close to national borders or that contain large proportions of ethnic minority groups are also sensitive to migration inflows, largely due to stability concerns. In addition, without fiscal transfers from the central government, prefectures generally have very little incentive to provide public services to migrant workers. Consequently, discrimination against migrant workers on the basis of the *hukou* status remains widespread. Individuals who do not have a local *hukou* in the place where they live are not able to access certain jobs, schooling, subsidized housing, health care, and other benefits enjoyed by those who do. As a result, the ease of obtaining a local *hukou* still influences one's migration decisions to a considerable extent.

Importantly, as part of a contemporaneous reform devolving fiscal and administrative powers to lower-level governments, local governments have largely acquired the authority to determine the number of *hukou* to issue in their jurisdictions. Since 1992, some provinces have introduced temporary resident permits for anyone with a legitimate job or business in one of their major cities, and some grant a *hukou* to high-skilled professionals or businesspeople who make large investments in their region (Kinnan, Wang, and Wang 2015). The most significant change is the introduction of two types of residential registration, the so-called temporary residential permit and the blue-stamp *hukou*. Unlike the regular *hukou*, these are not administered by the central government; instead, their design and implementation are determined by local governments. While the temporary resident permit can be issued to anyone who has a legitimate job or business in the city, citizens who want a blue-stamp *hukou* are usually required to pay a one-time entry fee called the urban infrastructural construction fee, which varies between a few thousand yuan in small cities and CNY50,000 in more "attractive" cities. However, the stringency of these policies and general *hukou*-issuing rules differ significantly across regions. For instance, it is notoriously difficult to obtain a *hukou* in Beijing or Shanghai, while Dongguan, a coastal city in Guangdong province, offers relatively generous granting rules to attract low-skilled migrants for its booming manufacturing sectors. It is this heterogeneity in *hukou*-granting practices that provides variation in the *hukou* friction measure.

The aforementioned practices resulted in formal *hukou* reform, launched by the central government in 1997. The major aspects of the reform included officially abolishing the rural-to-urban migration quotas and approving the selective migration policies in cities. Following an experimental period, a national implementation of the reform began in 2001. However, this reform, which is largely an affirmation of local policies that were already in place, has been largely put on hold since mid-2002 due to stability concerns (Wang 2004). According to Chan and Buckingham (2008), it only had a small impact in facilitating internal migration. In spite of the general increase in the number of migrants in the country during the last quarter century, the annual number of *hukou* migrants recorded by the Ministry of Public Security remained stable between 1992 to 2008 (Chan 2013). In 2011, "a *hukou* reform" was mentioned again in the country's Five-Year Plan, but the exact plan only began to take shape in 2014.

3.2.3 Exogeneity of Trade Liberalization

The validity of the empirical analysis relies on the variation in tariff changes across industries. To draw any causal implications of input trade liberalization, tariff changes must be unrelated to counterfactual industry employment growth. As discussed in Kovak (2013), such a correlation may arise if trade policy makers impose smaller tariff cuts to protect weaker industries, or if larger industries lobby for smaller tariff cuts (Grossman and Helpman 1994).

There are several reasons to believe that these concerns are less important for the People's Republic of China. Viewing WTO membership as a means of locking the country on a path of deepening economic reform and openness, the government has demonstrated a greater desire to open rather than protect its domestic industries (Woo 2001). Additional supporting evidence comes from examining the relationship between tariff cuts and preliberalization employment. If policy makers had permitted "stronger" industries to bear larger tariff

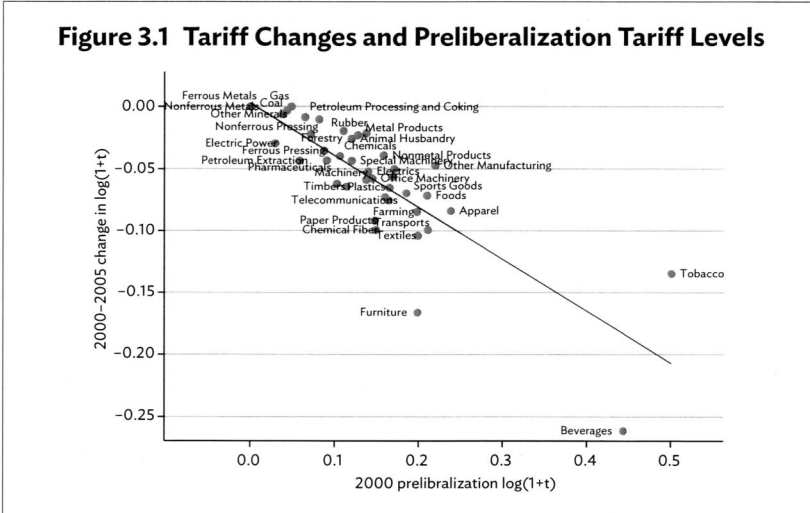

Figure 3.1 Tariff Changes and Preliberalization Tariff Levels

Notes: This figure plots log tariff changes over 2000–2005 against the log 2000 tariff levels. The sectoral tariff is calculated based on the simple average of most-favored nation applied tariff rates at the Harmonized System HS6 product level from the Trade Analysis Information System database. Correlation: –0.84; regression coefficient: –0.43; standard error: 0.044; t: –9.60.

Source: Author's calculation.

cuts, industries with higher employment *growth* between 1990 and 2000 would have experienced greater tariff reductions; if large industries lobbied more or were more likely to be protected due to employment concerns, industries with larger employment (in *levels*) in 2000 would have experienced lower tariff cuts. However, I find only marginal and statistically insignificant correlation between tariff changes and pre-WTO industry employment in both *changes* and *levels*, the simple correlations being 0.13 and 0.16, respectively.

Following the approach of Goldberg and Pavcnik (2005), Figure 3.1 demonstrates that industries with high tariffs in 2000 experienced the largest tariff cuts, with the correlation between the 2000 tariff levels and the change in tariffs being −0.84. The fact that the pre-WTO tariff levels largely determined the tariff changes following the People's Republic of China's WTO accession implies that the primary goal of policy makers was to reduce tariff rates and to smoothen cross-industry variations. This rules out the industry protection and political economy concerns.

Most importantly, even after rounds of voluntary tariff reductions, the country's tariff structure in 2000 remained similar to that of 1992,[4]

Table 3.1 Imports and Tariffs

	Import Values		Varieties		Unit Values	
	All Products	Intermediates	All Products	Intermediates	All Products	Intermediates
	(1)	(2)	(3)	(4)	(5)	(6)
Output tariff	−0.22***	−0.16***	−1.06***	−1.01***	0.02	0.05**
	(0.05)	(0.06)	(0.12)	(0.13)	(0.02)	(0.02)
Year fixed effect	Yes	Yes	Yes	Yes	Yes	Yes
HS6 fixed effect	Yes	Yes	Yes	Yes	Yes	Yes
Observations	35,457	26,380	35,457	26,380	33,695	25,193
R-squared	0.08	0.09	0.27	0.29	0.10	0.09
Number of hs2002	5,222	3,904	5,222	3,904	5,124	3,830

HS = Harmonized System.

Notes: Coefficient on tariffs from HS6 product level regression of log import value, HS8 variety numbers, unit value on lagged output tariffs, HS6 product fixed effects, and year fixed effects. An observation is HS6-year. The data cover nonprocessing trade in 2000–2006. Robust standard errors in parentheses. *** $p < 0.01$, ** $p < 0.05$, * $p < 0.1$.

Source: Author's calculation.

---

4   1992 is the earliest year that tariff data for the People's Republic of China at the HS6 level are available.

with a correlation of 0.93. On the other hand, the *bound* duties after joining the WTO were largely imposed externally, benchmarking the tariff levels of other WTO members. Unlike in many other developing countries, there is almost no gap between the People's Republic of China's *bound* and *applied* duties, and the binding coverage is 100%. This implies that the preliberalization tariffs in the People's Republic of China were based on a protection structure that was set a decade earlier, while postliberalization tariffs were externally set. Therefore, it is highly unlikely that tariff reductions between 2000 and 2005 are correlated with counterfactual industry employment changes.

3.2.4 Tariff Reductions, Trade Surge, and Employment Changes

Before analyzing the relationship between input tariff reduction and labor reallocation, I first examine whether the tariff reduction induced by the People's Republic of China's WTO accession was systematically related to its trade expansion. To summarize the findings, I find that (i) lower tariffs led to an overall increase in trade values, (ii) lower tariffs led to an increase in imports in the number of varieties within HS6 categories, and (iii) lower tariffs resulted in lower unit values of existing product lines, with particularly pronounced effects on intermediate products.

These results are summarized in Table 3.1. I begin by examining the responsiveness of import values to tariffs by regressing the log import value of an HS6 product on HS6 log tariff levels, HS6 fixed effects, and year fixed effects. I restrict my analysis to the period 2000–2006, in which I have access to customs data to calculate HS6 product variety numbers. Extending the analysis to the period 2000–2010 yields similar results. For all regressions, I exclude processing trade flows as they are not affected by tariff reductions. Column (1) of Table 3.1 reports the coefficient estimates of tariffs for all sectors, and column (2) for intermediate sectors based on the Broad Economic Categories classification. In both cases, we can note that declines in tariffs are associated with higher import values.

Recent theory also emphasizes the benefits gained by increasing the imported varieties. As we can see from columns (3) and (4), this channel also plays a role in our context. I define varieties as the number of distinct HS8 products within a given HS6 product category. I then regress the number of varieties on the tariff, HS6 fixed effects, and year fixed effects. For all sectors and only intermediate sectors, a decline in tariffs is associated with an increased number of varieties. Lastly, I examine the impact of tariff reduction on the unit price of imports. The estimation results are presented in columns (5) and (6). Tariff declines are associated with decreases in import unit values, but this relationship

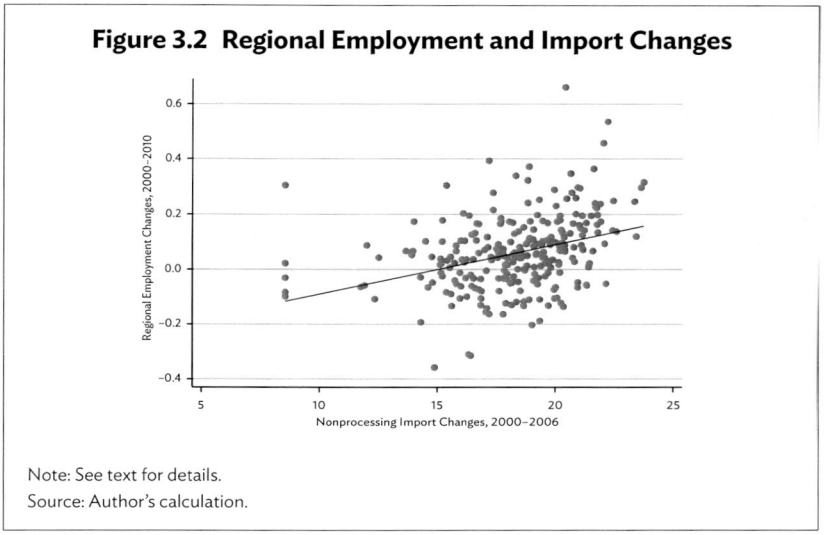

Figure 3.2 Regional Employment and Import Changes

Note: See text for details.
Source: Author's calculation.

is only statistically significant for intermediate sectors. That is, the benefits from trade that occur through increasing imports at a lower price are particularly true of intermediate goods, consistent with the beneficial effects of input tariff reduction on regional employment, which I probe formally in later sections.

Next, I examine the relationship between increased imports and employment changes across cities in the People's Republic of China. In Figure 3.2, I plot the difference in log employment between 2000 and 2010 against the change in log nonprocessing imports between 2000 and 2006 at the prefecture city level. As we can see from Figure 3.2, cities with larger import increases are also associated with larger increases in regional employment. Combining the examination of the relationships between tariff reductions and trade surges, we can be confident that the impact of input tariff reductions on spatial labor reallocation is indeed channeled through changes in trade flows.

3.3 Measurements and Specifications

3.3.1 Local Labor Markets

Throughout the empirical analysis, local labor markets are defined as prefectures. A prefecture is an administrative division of the People's Republic of China that ranks below a province and above a county. Given that most regional policies, including the overall planning of public transportation, are conducted at the prefecture level (Xue and Zhang 2001), I expect counties within the same prefecture to have strong commuting ties and to be economically integrated. In order to account for prefecture boundary changes, I use information concerning the administrative division changes published by the Ministry of Civil Affairs of the People's Republic of China to create time-consistent county groups based on prefecture boundaries in the year 2000. This results in 337 geographic units, which I describe as prefectures or regions, including four direct-controlled municipalities and 333 prefecture-level divisions that cover the entire country. Relative to commuting zones in the United States, the prefectures in the People's Republic of China are about twice as large on average and 1.5 times the size when the 10 largest (but sparsely populated) prefectures in autonomous regions are excluded.

The empirical analysis in this chapter studies 10-year changes in prefecture employment, total and working-age populations, the most recent 5-year migrant inflows from other provinces, and the population holding local *hukou* in each prefecture. I collect these variables at the county level from the Tabulation on Population Census of the People's Republic of China by county for 2000 and 2010, and then aggregate them to prefectures based on the time-consistent county groups. Notably, the employment measure includes informal workers, the lion's share of whom are migrants.[5] Between 2000 and 2010, the People's Republic of China underwent a significant change in its spatial distribution of employment, with some prefectures seeing over a 50% increase in local employment, while others experienced more than a 30% decrease.

3.3.2 Regional Trade Shock Exposures

To construct the exposure of local labor markets to *input tariff reductions*, I combine data on regional industry employment with data on tariffs and industry cost shares. Data on regional employment by industry in 2000 were collected from the Tabulation on the 2000 Population Census published by each province. The original data are by county

---

[5]   According to Park, Wu, and Du (2012), informal employment in the People's Republic of China is defined either based on (i) whether or not the employer fails to provide all of the three most important types of social insurance that employers are expected to provide in the People's Republic of China (i.e., pensions, health insurance, and unemployment insurance), or (ii) whether workers have a labor contract. Migrant workers contribute to 49.0% of the informal employment in the People's Republic of China under the first definition and 65.7% under the second. The employment data from population census include all informal workers, as long as they engaged in at least 1 hour of paid work the week before the survey date, or were on leave.

and by 92 two-digit 1994 Chinese Standard Industrial Classification (CSIC1994), which I aggregate to prefecture level.[6] I use the simple average of most-favored nation applied tariffs at the HS6 product level from the United Nations Conference on Trade and Development Trade Analysis Information System database to calculate tariff changes. The cost share of each industry is constructed as its share of value in the output industry using the 2002 Chinese national input–output (IO) table.[7] To utilize these various datasets, I also construct a common industry classification, which consists of 71 industries, including five agricultural and 28 nontraded industries.[8]

As is standard in the literature, I measure input tariff cuts (ΔIT) as the input-cost weighted average of tariff reductions:

$$\Delta IT_s = \sum_{k \in K} \alpha_s(k) d\ln(1 + t_k), \tag{1}$$

where $\alpha_s(k)$ represents the cost share of industry s due to purchases from industry k, t_k is the tariff rate of industry k, and d represents the long-difference (Autor, Dorn, and Hanson framework) between 2000 and 2005. Following Kovak (2013) and Dix-Carneiro and Kovak (2017), I calculate the regional input tariff cuts (ΔRIT) as follows:

$$\Delta \text{RIT}_i = \sum_{s \in K} \delta_{is} \Delta \text{IT}_s, \tag{2}$$

where $\delta_{is} = \dfrac{L_{is} \frac{1}{\phi_s}}{\sum_{s \in K} L_{is} \left(\frac{1}{\phi_s}\right)}$, L_{is} is the initial amount of labor allocated to industry s in region i, and ϕ_s is 1 – the wage bill share of the industry value added. In a specific-factor model with a constant returns production function, $\frac{1}{\phi_s}$ represents the labor demand elasticity (Kovak 2013). The weight δ_{is} captures the intuition behind the construction of ΔRIT: a prefecture will experience a larger increase in employment if its workers are specialized in industries with large input

---

[6]   The 2010 employment by industry has many missing values, so I perform all analyses at the regional rather than the region-industry level.

[7]   Given that trade liberalization began in 2001, I use the IO table of the closest year. I do so under the assumption that industries' cost structures adjust slowly to trade reforms. I do not use the 1997 IO table for two reasons: first, the 1997 IO table uses an industry classification that is less consistent with employment data; second, it might understate the importance of tradable inputs due to the Asian financial crisis.

[8]   The common industry classification is created to achieve the maximum disaggregation between different classifications; the 2002 IO table consists of 122 industries and is coded similarly to the 1994/2002 Chinese Standard Industrial Classification (CSIC1994/CSIC2002).

tariff declines, and more so if these industries are elastic in labor demand. Nevertheless, my empirical results are robust to using a weight that is based on employment only.

Disparities in industry weights across regions generate substantial variations in their exposure to input trade liberalization. The three hubs of the People's Republic of China's trade and economic growth—the Bohai Economic Rim, the Yangtze River Delta, and the Pearl River Delta—are among the top beneficiaries of input trade liberalization. Western prefectures that are specialized in animal husbandry or basic food processing and manufacturing benefited greatly from tariff cuts in farming industries, and hence also experienced large reductions in regional input tariffs.

Similarly to calculating the regional *input tariff cuts*, I compute regional *output tariff reductions* as a δ_{is}-weighted average of industry-specific tariff reductions over 2000–2005. In order to calculate external tariff reductions, I first use customs data for the People's Republic of China for 2000 to compute prefecture exports and calculate the export share by destination country for each industry and prefecture. I then take the export-share weighted average of the tariff changes across destination countries to obtain prefecture industry-specific tariff reductions. In the final step, I compute the weighted average tariff changes across industries using δ_{is} for each prefecture.

3.3.3 The *Hukou* Measure

The primary dataset that I use to construct the *hukou* measure is the 0.095% random sampled data of the Population Census in 2000. The complete dataset covers the entire population of the for the People's Republic of China, and the sample was randomly drawn at the household level, with a unique identifier linking individuals in the same household. The dataset contains rich individual-level information including one's *hukou* registration status and migration history in the last 5 years, from which I can infer the stringency of a prefecture's *hukou* system based on the likelihood of an individual obtaining a local *hukou* after settling in that prefecture. In reality, the likelihood of an individual acquiring or being granted a local *hukou* also depends on various individual characteristics. In order to draw out these effects, I calculate the *hukou* measure as follows. I focus on individuals who moved between 1995 and 2000 to a prefecture that is not their birthplace.[9] I regress a dummy equal to 1

---

[9]   In the early 1990s, most internal migration was state planned, guaranteeing local *hukou* to migrants. I therefore focus on the most recent 5 years. The raw dataset contains 1,180,111 observations; given that most people never migrate, the number of observations in my regressions is 62,289.

if the individual had already obtained a local *hukou* before November
2000 (when the census was conducted) on age, age squared, gender,
ethnicity (Han versus other), marriage status (ever married), difference
in log gross domestic product (GDP) per capita between the migrate-out
and migrate-in provinces,[10] migrate-from-rural-areas dummy, migrate-
within-province dummy, categorical variables for education and for
the years of residence in the current city, and prefecture fixed effects.
I then take a simple average of the estimated prefecture fixed effects by
province and normalize it from 0 to 1 to obtain the final measure.

The *hukou* measure is an *inverse* indicator of migration frictions
associated with the *hukou* system: it equals 0 if a province has the most
stringent *hukou*-granting practice. Consistent with common knowledge,
my *hukou* measure suggest that Beijing, Shanghai, and Guangdong are
among the most difficult provinces to obtain a local *hukou*. In addition,
there is no correlation between the GDP per capita of a province and
its *hukou* policy. For instance, Qinghai and Xinjiang have very stringent
hukou policies, which are more likely driven by limited farming land and
political stability concerns. *Hukou* stringency is not determined by the
initial population density of a region either, with some densely populated
provinces such as Henan having a rather liberal *hukou* system, while
other densely populated regions such as Beijing have a stringent system.

3.3.4 Empirical Specification

Given the regional input tariff cuts and the *hukou* measure at hand,
I estimate the following equations in the next subsection:

$$\Delta Y_i = \beta_1 \Delta \text{RIT}_i + D_p + \mathbf{X}'_1 \gamma + \epsilon_i \qquad (3)$$

and

$$\Delta Y_i = \beta_2 \Delta \text{RIT}_i + \beta_3 \Delta \text{RIT}_i * Hukou_p + D_p + \mathbf{X}'_2 \gamma + \epsilon_i, \qquad (4)$$

where the second specification explores the heterogeneous regional
effect of input tariff reductions depending on the *hukou* frictions. Here,
ΔY_i is the decadal change of the log value of a regional outcome variable
such as employment or total population; β_1 captures the regional effect
of input trade liberalization on the variable of interest during the
2000–2010 period, while β_2 and β_3 represent the heterogeneous impact

---

[10]   I obtain GDP per capita data from the 2000 provincial statistical yearbooks. Note that
it is important to control for GDP differences, as a migrant from a more developed
area might not be willing to switch and acquire a local *hukou*.

of input tariff reductions depending on *hukou* frictions; D_p are province fixed effects; and **X** represents a set of additional controls. In the main specification, **X** includes regional output tariff reductions, external tariff reductions, and the preliberalization level of the outcome variable to control for increased import competition, improved market access,[11] and possible mean convergence. *Hukou_p* is the *hukou* friction measure; in equation (4), I also control for its interaction with external and output tariff reductions.

3.3.5 Empirical Results

The impacts of input tariff cuts on the People's Republic of China's regional labor adjustments are summarized in Table 3.2. In columns (1) and (2), I first present the results of regressing employment changes on regional input tariff cuts. The standard errors are clustered at the provincial level, accounting for the possible covariance between the error terms across prefectures within the same province. Regressions are weighted by the log of the employment in the initial period. As we can see from column (1), the coefficient of ΔRIT is significant at the 1% level and has the expected positive sign. The estimate of 4.92 implies that a prefecture facing a 1-percentage-point regional input tariff cut experiences an almost 5-percentage-point employment increase. The difference between regional input tariff cuts in regions at the 25th and 75th percentiles is 0.7 percentage points. Evaluated using the estimate in column (1), a region at the 75th percentile experiences a 3.4-percentage-point larger employment increase than a region at the 25th percentile. Consistent with the existing literature, I find that regional output tariff reductions have a negative impact on employment, although at a smaller magnitude compared to the impact of input tariff cuts. The effect of external tariff reductions has the expected positive sign but is statistically insignificant.

In column (2), I add the interaction term between input trade liberalization and the *hukou* measure, probing whether input liberalization-induced employment adjustments are more pronounced in provinces with relatively free *hukou* systems. Given that I normalized my *hukou* measure to the unit interval, coefficients of ΔRIT directly reflect the impact of input tariff cuts in prefectures with the highest *hukou* frictions. The coefficient for the interaction term is positive

---

[11]   External tariff reductions capture the positive impact of tariff reductions by the People's Republic of China's trading partners following its WTO accession. However, this is less of a concern as most countries had already granted the People's Republic of China most-favored nation status prior to 2001.

and statistically significant. Input tariff reductions have no impact on regional employment in the provinces with the most stringent *hukou* systems. In contrast, in regions with the most relaxed *hukou* systems, a 1-percentage-point increase in input tariff cuts leads to a 16-percentage-point relative increase in employment, which is much larger than the 5-percentage-point average found in column (1). I also find a weak relationship between the effect of output tariff reductions and *hukou* stringency, although the result is only significant when fixed effects are included. This is consistent with the fact that the *hukou* system is primarily designed to control for migration inflows. On the other hand, the interaction terms between external tariff change and *hukou* frictions have the opposite sign. Calculated based on the specification in column (2), the partial R-squared of regional input tariff cuts, regional output tariff cuts and their interactions with the *hukou* measure is 0.35. This suggests that when considering both input and output channels, over 30% of the regional variation in employment changes could be accounted for by trade liberalization.

Table 3.2 Effect of Input Tariff Cuts

	Employment		Working-Age Population	
	(1)	(2)	(3)	(4)
Regional input tariff cuts (ΔRIT)	4.92***	−0.06	4.33***	−1.00
	(1.44)	(1.53)	(1.46)	(1.50)
Regional input tariff cuts x *Hukou*		15.70***		16.43***
		(4.45)		(4.31)
Regional output tariff change	−2.73***	−3.81**	−2.20***	−2.83***
	(0.67)	(0.92)	(0.59)	(0.83)
Regional output tariff change x *Hukou*		4.52**		3.53*
Regional input tariff cuts (ΔRIT)		(2.04)		(1.88)
External tariff change	0.10	0.73	0.16	1.10*
	(0.19)	(0.54)	(0.22)	(0.54)
Controls	Yes	Yes	Yes	Yes
Province fixed effects (31)	Yes	Yes	Yes	Yes
Observations	337	337	337	337
R-squared	0.62	0.65	0.58	0.63

continued on next page

Table 3.2 *continued*

	Migrant Inflows		Hukou Population	
	(5)	(6)	(7)	(8)
Regional input tariff cuts (ΔRIT)	13.16**	−5.55**	1.25	−2.51
	(5.56)	(2.05)	(0.77)	(2.59)
Regional input tariff cuts x *Hukou*		61.99***		10.23**
		(15.41)		(4.65)
Regional output tariff change	−3.73	−2.92	−2.84***	−2.06
	(2.49)	(2.61)	(0.70)	(1.35)
Regional output tariff change x *Hukou*		3.14		−1.26
Regional input tariff cuts (ΔRIT)		(5.39)		(2.66)
External tariff change	0.72	−0.06	0.17	0.68*
	(1.23)	(3.76)	(0.12)	(0.36)
Controls	Yes	Yes	Yes	Yes
Province fixed effects (31)	Yes	Yes	Yes	Yes
Observations	337	337	337	337
R-squared	0.41	0.44	0.70	0.72

Notes: The dependent variable is the difference in log employment, log working-age population (15 to 64 years old), log population that migrated from other provinces between 2005–2010 and 1995–1990, and the 10-year change in log prefecture population holding local *hukou* permit for columns (1) and (2), (3) and (4), (5) and (6), and (7) and (8), respectively. The sample contains 333 prefectures and four direct-controlled municipalities. All regressions include the full vector of control variables; models with interaction terms further include the interaction between the *hukou* measure and other tariff changes as in column (6) of Table 3.1. Prefecture birth and death rates are also controlled in columns (7) and (8). Robust standard errors in parentheses are adjusted for 31 province clusters. Models are weighted by the log of beginning-period prefecture population. *** p<0.01, ** p<0.05, * p<0.1.

Source: Author's calculation.

In combining the results from columns (1) and (2), we know that prefectures facing larger input tariff cuts experience a relative increase in employment, and the effect is stronger in provinces with a lower amount of *hukou* friction. This observed change in regional employment can be caused by both intra- and interregional adjustments. A positively affected region may experience a decline in unemployment and an increase in labor force participation, both of which may result in an increase in local employment. To ensure that it is the spatial reallocation of labor that drives the employment adjustment, I next look at how working-age (15 to 64 years) populations respond to input tariff reductions. If the observed employment changes are mainly due to intraregional adjustments, trade shocks should have no impact on the local population, whereas if the change is primarily due to interregional adjustments, the local population should react to trade shocks in a quantitatively similar way to that of employment.

Columns (3) and (4) report the results of regressing the regional change of log working-age populations on regional input tariff cuts, with and without interactions. I include the full set of controls and cluster standard errors at the provincial level. The results strongly support interregional labor reallocation: column (3) shows that prefecture-level working-age populations react positively and significantly to input tariff cuts, and the coefficients are quantitatively similar to those of employment. On average, a 1-percentage-point increase in regional input tariff cuts leads to a 4.33-percentage-point increase in the working-age population of a prefecture. In a prefecture with the least *hukou* frictions, a 1-percentage-point increase in regional input tariff cuts leads to a 16.43-percentage-point increase in the working-age population, which reinforces the notion that the observed regional employment adjustment is due to interregional labor reallocation.

Compared to indirectly inferring spatial adjustments in labor from regional population changes, it would be preferable to examine migration directly. However, the ideal measure, i.e., the decadal change in net migration inflows, is not available. Therefore, I instead consider the most similar variable available in the census: the number of migrants from other provinces in the past 5 years. It is important to note that compared to the ideal measure, this variable is likely to provide an insignificant estimate. First, interregional migration occurs much more frequently within provinces than across them. Second, since this variable counts migrant inflows in 5-year periods, I compare the number of migrants between 1995 and 2000 with those between 2005 and 2010. As tariff reductions began in 2001, if their impact levels off quickly, I will not be able to find a significant result.

With the above concerns in mind, I regress the change in the log 5-year inflow of population from other provinces on regional input tariff reductions, with and without interactions. The results are presented in columns (5) and (6) of Table 3.2, respectively. Column (5) reports that a 1-percentage-point increase in regional input tariff reduction leads to a 13.16-percentage-point increase in migrant inflows from other provinces. Column (6) confirms that input tariff cuts result in larger migrant inflows when the *hukou* system is less stringent. Both estimates are significant at the 5% level. Since migration is a flow rather than a stock variable, the magnitude of the estimates is much larger. These results provide additional support to the finding that regional input tariff cuts increase local employment through attracting labor from other locations, and this effect crucially depends on frictions caused by the *hukou* system.

Interestingly, I find that neither the regional output tariff reductions nor the external tariff changes have a significant effect on migrant inflows, nor does their impact heterogeneously depend on *hukou* frictions. These results further suggest that among various trade shocks associated with the accession to the WTO, input tariff liberalization seems to have played the dominant role in shaping labor reallocation in the country.

Finally, columns (7) and (8) of Table 3.2 show how the number of individuals holding local *hukou* (*hukou* population) in a prefecture responds to input tariff reductions. In these regressions, I further control for prefecture birth and death rates to address two additional concerns. One is that input tariff cuts may generate different life expectancies across regions, affecting *hukou* population changes. The second concern is that it may generate different family planning behavior across regions (i.e., in positively affected areas, families may be willing to have more children). The latter is going to impact the *hukou* population via birth rate changes, as the children of local *hukou* holders are automatically granted a local *hukou*.

If a local *hukou* can be obtained without cost, the *hukou* population should be highly correlated with total population in a given region, and hence react positively to input tariff reductions. The empirical results, however, point to the contrary: column (7) indicates that on average, reductions in regional tariffs do not cause significant changes in the *hukou* population. However, in prefectures with less stringent *hukou* systems, the *hukou* population does increase in positively affected regions. Column (8) indicates that in a prefecture with the freest *hukou* system, a 1-percentage-point increase in regional input tariff cuts leads to a 10.23-percentage-point increase in the *hukou* population. The magnitude, however, is only two-thirds of the input liberalization-induced increase in the working-age population (column (4), Table 3.2). This implies that *hukou* frictions are substantial even in regions with the least stringent system. This represents evidence that even though many migrant workers moved to cities that were positively affected by trade shocks, few were able to obtain a local *hukou*.

3.4 Welfare Quantifications

The empirical results presented in the previous section can be viewed through the lens of a multisector spatial equilibrium model, which allows for IO linkages and migration frictions. Falling trade costs allow firms to access cheaper intermediate inputs and hence produce less expensive final goods. As a result, demand for local production increases.

Regions whose labor is concentrated in industries facing larger input tariff reductions are more positively affected, thus pushing up wages and attracting workers from other places. Immigration increases the price of nontradables and depresses wages until the economy reaches a new equilibrium. When migration frictions are high, employment changes are small due to limited migration, and real wages instead react strongly to trade shocks. In contrast, when migration friction is low, employment reacts more strongly to trade shocks and real wages react less.

In standard economic geography models with no migration frictions, workers will move to arbitrage away the utility difference of living in different cities. When we allow for amenity or productivity difference across locations and heterogeneous workers, real wages can differ across cities. In this case, a city with a high wage in equilibrium either reflects its relative technology superiority, or the fact that it is less livable than the other cities, and so people demand higher wages to compensate for the relatively poor local amenities. In equilibrium, we may observe that some cities offer more employment than others, but from the workers' perspective, they are indifferent about where to live given the equilibrium wage and amenity in each location. Therefore, when the economy is hit by a trade shock, the expected utility change will be the same among all workers.

However, with the presence of the *hukou* system, a larger fraction of the gains accrues to workers with a local *hukou*. This is intuitive: as migrant inflows are limited in positively affected regions when *hukou* friction is high, real wages increase. Workers with a local *hukou* face no constraints on living in the particular region, and hence benefit more significantly from the local wage increase. In other words, the presence of a *hukou* affects the welfare distribution across otherwise identical worker groups.

In Table 3.3, I present the quantification of the welfare change of workers holding a *hukou* of different provinces in the People's Republic of China, and the simulated regional adjustment in other margins following trade liberalization. The five provinces with the largest increases in employment are Beijing, Shanghai, Guangdong, Tianjin, and Fujian, with Beijing experiencing an increase in employment of 0.55% and Shanghai of 0.40%. The five provinces with the lowest employment increase are Hubei, Hunan, Sichuan, Anhui, and Jiangxi, consistent with our observations in the real data. These simulations are based on static models, hence the magnitudes of adjustments are smaller than our observations from real data.[12]

---

[12]   The simulated numbers may change slightly depending on model assumptions; see Zi (2018) for details.

Table 3.3 Regional Adjustments to Trade Liberalization

Province or Autonomous Region	(1) Employment	(2) Real Wage	(3) GDP	(4) Price	(5) Exports	(6) Imports	(7) Welfare
Guangdong	0.19	0.95	1.12	−1.77	5.27	7.05	0.93
Beijing	0.55	1.80	2.27	−2.06	9.62	3.34	1.69
Shanghai	0.40	1.61	1.93	−1.85	6.30	4.02	1.50
Tianjin	0.17	1.43	1.57	−1.96	7.62	4.65	1.38
Fujian	0.08	0.97	1.04	−1.69	6.67	7.14	0.96
Zhejiang	0.06	0.89	0.93	−1.60	5.18	5.69	0.87
Jiangsu	0.05	1.14	1.17	−1.79	9.40	6.85	1.12
Xinjiang Uygur	0.03	0.67	0.67	−1.53	6.42	5.25	0.64
Liaoning	0.02	0.96	0.97	−1.76	8.12	6.50	0.95
Hainan	0.01	0.74	0.76	−1.66	2.76	6.44	0.75
Jilin	0.00	0.73	0.73	−1.74	6.71	5.08	0.73
Yunnan	−0.01	0.49	0.48	−1.49	7.48	5.15	0.49
Shandong	−0.01	0.70	0.68	−1.71	5.92	8.72	0.69
Inner Mongolia	−0.02	0.52	0.50	−1.54	4.76	6.75	0.52
Ningxia Hui	−0.02	0.40	0.38	−1.51	9.17	3.99	0.41
Qinghai	−0.02	0.40	0.38	−1.51	6.72	5.12	0.40
Shanxi	−0.02	0.37	0.35	−1.48	7.23	4.27	0.37
Shaanxi	−0.02	0.46	0.43	−1.60	5.15	5.58	0.46
Heilongjiang	−0.03	0.59	0.56	−1.66	4.06	6.97	0.59
Chongqing	−0.03	0.48	0.45	−1.54	2.67	4.32	0.48
Gansu	−0.03	0.31	0.28	−1.52	5.72	3.82	0.31
Hebei	−0.05	0.41	0.36	−1.62	5.20	7.88	0.42
Henan	−0.05	0.38	0.33	−1.56	5.15	5.23	0.40
Hubei	−0.05	0.48	0.43	−1.59	5.14	5.13	0.50
Guangxi Zhuang	−0.05	0.55	0.50	−1.50	6.59	4.81	0.57
Guizhou	−0.05	0.40	0.35	−1.53	4.76	4.50	0.42
Hunan	−0.07	0.46	0.39	−1.53	7.48	5.12	0.49
Sichuan	−0.08	0.47	0.39	−1.58	4.27	4.81	0.49

continued on next page

Table 3.3 *continued*

Province or Autonomous Region	(1) Employment	(2) Real Wage	(3) GDP	(4) Price	(5) Exports	(6) Imports	(7) Welfare
Anhui	−0.11	0.52	0.41	−1.53	4.34	5.18	0.55
Jiangxi	−0.12	0.39	0.28	−1.47	3.85	5.36	0.44
Weighted average							0.63
Standard deviation							0.27

GDP = gross domestic product.

Notes: Counterfactual percentage changes in regional employment, real wage, real GDP (total value added divided by local consumption price index), consumption price index, exports, and imports when the tariff structure of the People's Republic of China changed from its 2000 to 2005 level, holding *hukou* frictions constant. The nominal wage of the constructed rest of the world is the numeraire.

Source: Author's calculation.

Column (2) shows that real wages increase in all provinces and that they are positively correlated with changes in employment. When comparing changes in real wages and employment, two patterns stand out. First, regional employment reacts less to trade shocks than do wages (regressing employment changes on wage changes yields coefficient of 0.47), indicating substantial internal migration frictions in the People's Republic of China. Second, a region with a larger real wage increase is not necessarily a region with a greater increase in employment. To see this dynamic, compare Fujian with Guangdong. The latter has a smaller rise in real wage in equilibrium, but its labor inflows rise twice as much. This suggests that migration frictions differ significantly across regions in the People's Republic of China.

Column (3) presents changes in provincial real GDP, adjusted for the local price index. Every region gains from tariff reductions, but the level differs significantly across regions. The most positively affected provinces are those that were the most developed before the introduction of tariff reductions, implying that trade liberalization has exacerbated regional inequality in the People's Republic of China. Column (4) presents changes in the local consumption price index. Beijing, Tianjin, and Shanghai experienced the largest price decrease, suggesting that they are the top beneficiaries of cheaper foreign goods. Columns (5) and (6) present the total changes in exports and imports, and show that both increased in all provinces, with some provinces experiencing a larger increase in total exports than imports. There are two main economic forces behind these changes in trade flows. The first is related to industry composition. When sectors with limited regional importance experience substantial tariff cuts, limited import competition is introduced but a broad range of sectors may benefit. This boosts local exports more than imports. The other subtler force works through trade diversion. Cheaper intermediates directly lower production costs in all regions in the People's Republic of China. For a Chinese province, it therefore becomes optimal to source more intermediates locally and from other provinces in the country. This also suppresses growth in imports from the rest of the world.

As suggested by the last column of Table 3.3, all regions (in terms of people's *hukou* status) gain from tariff reductions, but the distribution of the gains is uneven. Individuals with a Beijing and Shanghai *hukou* experience welfare improvements of 1.69% and 1.50%, respectively, while individuals holding a *hukou* from Shanxi and Gansu provinces only gain 0.37% and 0.31%, approximately 80% less. The *hukou* population-weighted average welfare increase is 0.63%, with the standard deviation being 0.27%.

Note that when labor is perfectly mobile, workers may choose to move to different places due to idiosyncratic amenity draws, but the welfare changes should be equal across individuals due to migration. When labor is perfectly immobile, the labor reallocation term equals 0,

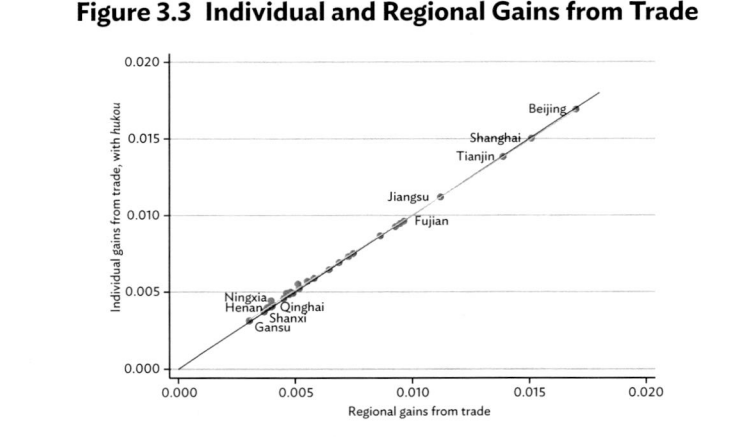

Figure 3.3 Individual and Regional Gains from Trade

Notes: This figure plots individual welfare changes in terms of *hukou* provinces (individual gains from trade) against the changes in provincial real income per capita, i.e., regional gains from trade). The lighter line is the linear fit and the darker is the 45-degree line. Correlation: 1.00; regression coefficient: 0.97; t: 178.04; R-squared: 0.999.

Source: Author's calculation.

and hence individual gains from trade equal the real income increase of the individual's *hukou* province. To explore the extent to which internal migration has alleviated the uneven welfare gains, Figure 3.3 plots individual welfare changes in terms of their *hukou* (individual gains from trade) against the changes in provincial real income per capita (regional gains from trade). The relationship is strikingly linear with the data points lying around the 45-degree reference line. This suggests that the redistribution of wealth via migration is limited: although we can see large changes in real income, most of the gains in booming areas accrue to local *hukou* holders due to the high costs of migration.

3.5 Counterfactual *Hukou* Abolishment

The empirical exercise in section 3.3 suggests that the People's Republic of China's internal labor reallocation over 2000–2010 can be explained in large part by its integration into the global economy. Moreover, the labor market distortion caused by the *hukou* system has a significant impact in shaping the effects of trade on migration. A question that naturally follows is, what would happen if the People's Republic of China abolished the *hukou* system? In particular, what is its direct impact on wages, employment, trade, and GDP growth in different regions? What are its distributional consequences? Would the country have reaped more gains from trade reforms if the *hukou* system had been abolished before its accession to the WTO? These are intriguing questions not only of academic interest but also relevant for today's policy debate. For example, reforming this system appears high on the agenda of the government today, but the exact road map is much less clear. Exploring the counterfactual result of *hukou* abolishment could provide valuable guidance regarding the ongoing *hukou* reforms.

3.5.1 Effects of *Hukou* Abolishment

Table 3.4 presents the regional adjustments that would have taken place following the abolishment of the *hukou* system. I report the five provinces that would experience the most significant expansions or contractions. Beijing, Shanghai, and Guangdong are the top migrant-receiving provinces, with an employment increase of more than 10%. Jiangxi, Sichuan, Anhui, Hunan, and Guangxi Zhuang Autonomous Region have the largest migrant outflows. The large migrant outflows in Guangxi and Jiangxi are (among other factors) due to their geographic proximity to Guangdong, while for Anhui these outflows are due to its proximity to Shanghai. In the case of Hunan and Sichuan, locals may face fewer migration frictions for other reasons, such as their strong historical ties with Guangdong. This is also reflected in the fact that their regional employment reacts strongly to tariff reductions (Table 3.3). In expanding provinces, increased labor supply lowers real wages and boosts local GDP; given the increased economic size, more intermediates can now be sourced locally with a cost advantage, hence the local consumption price decreases.

There are two forces that govern changes in trade flows. A province experiencing expansion requires more intermediate inputs, which implies an increase in both exports and imports; at the same time, increased economic size also means the region gains a cost advantage in producing a wider range of intermediates, suggesting an increase in exports and a decrease in imports. These two forces work in the opposite direction in contracting provinces. Therefore, exports should always rise while the changes in imports are ambiguous in provinces with worker inflows, and the opposite is true in provinces with worker outflows. The calibration exercise shows that imports in all top expanding provinces decrease, suggesting that the latter force prevails. On the other hand, imports increase in some contracting provinces but decrease in others.

In the last column of Table 3.4, I present the individual welfare changes. Although increased regional employment hurts local *hukou* holders by bidding up structure rents and lowering wages, relaxations in the system makes it easier for individuals to move to provinces where they have higher amenity draws, which always improves welfare. Therefore, while individuals holding a *hukou* from provinces with worker outflows benefit from *hukou* reforms unambiguously, those with a *hukou* from migrant-receiving provinces may not necessarily lose. As shown in the last column of Table 3.4, the top expanding provinces' *hukou* holders do

Table 3.4 Regional Effects of *Hukou* Abolishment

Province or Autonomous Region	(1) Employment	(2) Real Wage	(3) GDP	(4) Price	(5) Exports	(6) Imports	(7) Welfare
Beijing	18.99	−5.68	11.75	−1.43	17.47	−2.57	−5.93
Shanghai	18.33	−5.45	11.47	−1.31	13.80	−2.89	−5.52
Guangdong	13.20	−0.37	8.90	−1.23	10.46	−2.55	−3.62
Tianjin	5.26	−1.48	3.62	−0.46	3.54	−1.17	−1.24
Xinjiang Uygur	4.69	−0.73	3.91	−0.57	4.61	−1.25	−0.46
Hainan	4.36	−0.77	3.44	−0.33	3.22	−0.97	−0.27

continued on next page

Table 3.4 *continued*

Province or Autonomous Region	(1) Employment	(2) Real Wage	(3) GDP	(4) Price	(5) Exports	(6) Imports	(7) Welfare
Zhejiang	3.42	-0.91	2.46	-0.39	1.97	-1.03	0.27
Fujian	2.85	-0.64	2.18	-0.48	1.16	-0.96	0.23
Qinghai	2.09	-0.34	1.77	-0.44	3.00	-1.27	0.21
Yunnan	1.26	0.25	1.47	-0.21	1.10	-0.82	0.46
Inner Mongolia	0.60	0.39	0.94	-0.07	0.26	-0.62	0.98
Liaoning	0.53	0.01	0.54	-0.19	0.52	-0.47	0.31
Shanxi	0.48	0.40	0.83	-0.24	1.04	-1.08	0.66
Jiangsu	0.08	0.04	0.12	-0.20	-0.15	-0.56	0.94
Ningxia Hui	0.02	0.39	0.36	-0.14	-0.03	-0.70	0.88
Shandong	-0.46	0.39	-0.09	-0.11	-1.35	-0.47	0.78
Jilin	-0.59	0.71	0.07	-0.07	-0.49	-0.54	1.32
Hebei	-0.81	0.78	-0.09	-0.03	-2.51	-0.82	1.39
Shaanxi	-1.10	0.67	-0.48	0.02	-0.99	-0.24	1.32
Heilongjiang	-1.26	0.79	-0.48	-0.05	-0.87	-0.38	1.69
Gansu	-1.39	0.84	-0.60	-0.03	-1.36	-0.48	1.49
Chongqing	-1.83	1.37	-0.59	0.06	-2.91	-0.90	2.26
Henan	-2.44	1.03	-1.48	0.08	-3.31	-0.25	2.04
Guizhou	-2.67	1.41	-1.36	0.08	-3.21	-0.51	2.73
Hubei	-3.12	0.99	-2.20	0.26	-4.20	0.05	2.44
Guangxi Zhuang	-3.46	1.66	-1.91	0.10	-4.80	-0.88	3.34
Hunan	-4.73	1.82	-3.10	0.60	-8.54	0.32	3.76
Anhui	-5.06	2.38	-2.90	0.46	-6.17	-0.21	4.40
Sichuan	-5.37	2.02	-3.60	0.82	-8.10	0.72	4.21
Jiangxi	-6.17	2.08	-4.30	0.63	-8.65	0.05	4.66
Weighted average							1.51
Standard deviation							2.22

GDP = gross domestic product.

Notes: Counterfactual percentage changes in regional employment, real wage, real GDP (total value added divided by local consumption price index), consumption price index, exports, imports, and *hukou* population's welfare when *hukou* frictions are reduced to 0 in all provinces, holding tariffs constant. The nominal wage of the constructed rest of the world is the numeraire.

Source: Author's calculation.

experience significant welfare losses. However, of the 17 provinces that experience employment increases, their *hukou* holders' welfare only decreases in six. The average gains across provinces is 1.56%, which is twice as high as the gains from trade reforms.

3.5.2 Effects of Tariff Reductions Given the Elimination of *Hukou* Frictions

I next explore whether the impact of trade liberalization would be different if the *hukou* system had been abolished before the People's Republic of China's accession to the WTO. Starting from the postabolishment equilibrium, I repeat the first quantitative exercise by shocking the system with tariff changes. Table 3.5 presents the regional effects for the five provinces with the biggest and smallest increases in employment. Comparing these results with those in Table 3.3, we observe that regional employment reacts more strongly to trade shocks with the elimination of *hukou* frictions, while real wages react less. For instance, the change in Beijing employment increases by more than 50%, while the change in its real wage declines by 6%. The absolute changes, however, remain small. One plausible explanation regards data aggregation: calibrating the initial labor distribution at the province level overestimates the initial migration frictions, therefore abolishing the *hukou* system seems to have only a marginal effect in shaping the impact of trade as the model suggests very high migration frictions in levels even after abolishing the *hukou*.

Table 3.5 Regional Adjustments to Tariff Reductions, without *Hukou* Frictions

Province or Autonomous Region	(1) Employment	(2) Real Wage	(3) GDP	(4) Price	(5) Exports	(6) Imports	(7) Welfare
Beijing	0.84	1.68	2.44	−2.07	9.97	3.36	1.57
Shanghai	0.58	1.51	2.01	−1.85	6.39	4.00	1.40
Tianjin	0.27	1.39	1.62	−1.96	7.65	4.70	1.33
Guangdong	0.25	0.92	1.15	−1.76	5.12	7.01	0.89
Fujian	0.12	0.95	1.07	−1.68	6.50	7.15	0.94
Zhejiang	0.09	0.87	0.94	−1.59	5.09	5.71	0.86
Jiangsu	0.07	1.13	1.19	−1.79	9.36	6.90	1.11
Liaoning	0.03	0.96	0.98	−1.75	8.11	6.54	0.94

continued on next page

Table 3.5 *continued*

Province or Autonomous Region	(1) Employment	(2) Real Wage	(3) GDP	(4) Price	(5) Exports	(6) Imports	(7) Welfare
Xinjiang Uygur	0.03	0.66	0.67	−1.52	6.39	5.32	0.64
Hainan	0.02	0.73	0.77	−1.65	2.76	6.48	0.75
Jilin	−0.01	0.73	0.72	−1.73	6.55	5.11	0.73
Shandong	−0.02	0.70	0.67	−1.70	5.82	8.79	0.70
Yunnan	−0.02	0.49	0.48	−1.48	7.40	5.20	0.50
Ningxia Hui	−0.03	0.41	0.37	−1.50	9.09	4.04	0.41
Inner Mongolia	−0.03	0.53	0.49	−1.53	4.60	6.83	0.53
Shaanxi	−0.04	0.46	0.42	−1.59	4.99	5.62	0.47
Shanxi	−0.04	0.37	0.33	−1.48	6.99	4.37	0.38
Qinghai	−0.04	0.41	0.36	−1.50	6.69	5.20	0.41
Heilongjiang	−0.04	0.59	0.54	−1.65	3.94	7.04	0.60
Gansu	−0.05	0.31	0.26	−1.52	5.55	3.86	0.32
Chongqing	−0.05	0.49	0.44	−1.53	2.59	4.37	0.50
Guangxi Zhuang	−0.08	0.56	0.49	−1.49	6.44	4.90	0.59
Henan	−0.08	0.40	0.31	−1.55	5.04	5.30	0.42
Hubei	−0.08	0.49	0.41	−1.58	5.05	5.17	0.52
Hebei	−0.08	0.42	0.33	−1.61	4.98	7.98	0.44
Guizhou	−0.09	0.42	0.32	−1.52	4.63	4.56	0.44
Hunan	−0.11	0.48	0.37	−1.52	7.27	5.16	0.52
Sichuan	−0.12	0.49	0.36	−1.57	4.16	4.87	0.53
Anhui	−0.17	0.54	0.36	−1.52	4.14	5.23	0.60
Jiangxi	−0.19	0.42	0.23	−1.45	3.68	5.41	0.49
Weighted average							0.64
Standard deviation							0.25

GDP = gross domestic product.
Notes: This table presents the counterfactual percentage changes in regional employment, real wage, real GDP (total value added divided by local consumption price index), consumption price index, exports, and imports when the tariff structure of the People's Republic of China changed from its 2000 to 2005 level after eliminating *hukou* frictions, holding tariffs constant. The nominal wage of the constructed rest of the world is the numeraire.
Source: Author's calculation.

The final column of Table 3.5 presents the changes in welfare of *hukou* holders of a given province. Comparing these results to those in Table 3.3, we can see that the top five beneficiaries remain *hukou* holders from Beijing, Shanghai, Tianjin, Jiangsu, and Fujian. However, they gain less due to the larger increase in migrant inflows. On the other hand, provinces with net migration outflows also experience an increase in regional employment response to trade shocks, and this is associated with larger welfare improvements.

The last two rows of column (7) of Table 3.5 report the weighted average and the standard deviation of welfare increases. Average gains from trade increase by about 2%, from 0.71% in the case with *hukou* frictions to 0.72%. Compared with Monte, Redding, and Rossi-Hansberg (2015), who demonstrate that by permitting commuting across counties in the United States, gains improve from a 20% reduction in domestic trade costs by 0.8%, the additional gains from trade due to *hukou* friction elimination are considerable. In addition, calibrating the model at the prefecture city level would likely produce larger estimates. Therefore, we can interpret the 2% gains from trade due to *hukou* abolishment as a lower bound estimate.

The standard deviation of welfare gains across worker types falls from 0.24% to 0.22%. Freer migration leads to greater employment

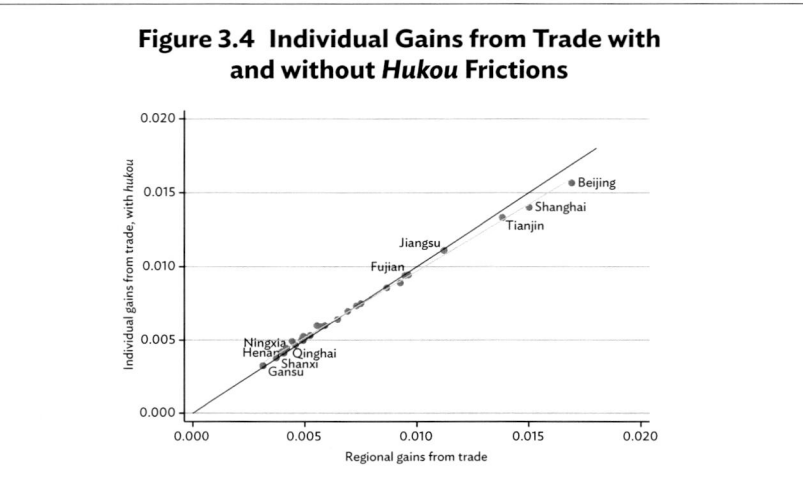

Figure 3.4 Individual Gains from Trade with and without *Hukou* Frictions

Notes: This figure plots individuals' welfare changes from tariff reductions in terms of *hukou* provinces (individual gains from trade) with *hukou* abolishment against the changes without. The lighter line is the linear fit and the darker line is the 45-degree line. Correlation: 0.999 Regression coefficient: 0.9; t: 101.55; R-squared: 0.997.

Source: Author's calculation.

increases in more positively affected regions, and the opposite in less positively affected regions. This narrows the spatial wage gap, meaning that individuals who stay in contracting regions are less negatively affected. In addition, freer migration makes individuals migrate to booming areas to improve their welfare. Both effects lead to more evenly distributed gains. Figure 3.4 plots individual gains from tariff reductions without *hukou* frictions to those with; the plot is flatter than the 45-degree line, suggesting that the elimination of *hukou* frictions alleviates the distributional effects of trade.

3.5.3 The Role of Internal Geography: General Assessment

I now investigate the importance of accounting for internal geography in computing gains from trade. I compare the results of my model (benchmark) to a multiregion model with no internal migration, as well as to a two-country model treating the People's Republic of China as a unit of analysis. I calibrate each of these models to the year 2000 and compute the welfare response and its decomposition to the tariff reductions from the country's WTO accession. Table 3.6 presents the simulated welfare effects implied by different models. The first row presents the benchmark results, the second row the welfare results for the no-migration model, and the third row the results for the model treating the People's Republic of China as a whole.

Table 3.6 suggests that the welfare effects are smaller for the model without migration compared to the benchmark model. The average gain decreases from 0.63% to 0.61%. It is also distributed more unevenly, with the standard error rising from 0.27% to 0.31%. Allowing interregional migration diminishes both effects.

When treating the People's Republic of China as a unit of analysis, the welfare increases substantially to 0.80%, almost 30% more than the

Table 3.6 Gains from Tariff Reductions: Role of Internal Geography

Model	Average (%)	Standard Deviation (%)
Benchmark	0.63	0.27
No migration	0.61	0.31
People's Republic of China as a whole	0.80	0.00

Notes: Average of counterfactual percentage changes in welfare in terms of individual *hukou* provinces and its standard deviation. In models with many regions in the country, both the average and standard deviation of welfare changes are *hukou* population weighted.

Source: Author's calculation.

benchmark model. The results reflect the importance of accounting for domestic geography. The intuition for this result is related to that of the no-migration model. By treating the People's Republic of China as a unit of analysis, I implicitly assume that both goods and factors are perfectly mobile within the country, and thus I get much larger gains from trade. In short, the results from this subsection illustrate the importance of accounting for economic geography within a country to evaluate the effect of trade policies, especially where the country has significant spatial heterogeneities.

3.6 Conclusion

Trade liberalization can lead to significant spatial labor adjustment within a country, and internal migration frictions are important in shaping the impact of trade. In the context of the People's Republic of China, input-liberalization has stimulated significant labor reallocation across prefectures, as well as the presence of migration frictions caused by the *hukou* system. Quantitatively, tariff reductions improve the People's Republic of China's aggregate welfare by 0.71%, but magnify regional disparities. Abolishing the *hukou* system leads to a sizable improvement in aggregate welfare, but it also has a strong distributional impact. In addition, it increases the gains from trade and alleviates its negative distributional consequences. These results shed light on the benefits of eliminating migration frictions and the importance of taking these frictions into account when evaluating both aggregate and distributional consequences of trade reforms.

While the focus of this chapter has been on the People's Republic of China, the existing literature suggests that migration frictions are pervasive in many other countries. According to the World Population Policies 2013 (United Nations 2013), 60% of governments around the world desired a major change in their spatial labor distribution, and 80% of these had policies to influence internal migration. Therefore, this chapter's exercises may inform migration policy and stimulate further studies in other national contexts.

References

Autor, D. H., D. Dorn, and G. H. Hanson. 2013. The China Syndrome: Local Labor Market Effects of Import Competition in the United States. *The American Economic Review*. 103 (6). pp. 2121–68.

———. 2016. The China Shock: Learning from Labor-Market Adjustment to Large Changes in Trade. *Annual Review of Economics*. 8 (1). pp. 205–40.

Balsvik, R., S. Jensen, and K. G. Salvanes. 2015. Made in China, Sold in Norway: Local Labor Market Effects of an Import Shock. *Journal of Public Economics*. 127. pp. 137–44.

Blancher, N.R., and R. Rumbaugh. 2004. China: International Trade and WTO Accession. IMF Working Paper. No. WP/04/36. Washington, DC: International Monetary Fund.

Bosker, M., S. Brakman, H. Garretsen, and M. Schramm. 2012. Relaxing Hukou: Increased Labor Mobility and China's Economic Geography. *Journal of Urban Economics*. 72 (2). pp. 252–66.

Bugamelli, M., S. Fabiani, and E. Sette. 2015. The Age of the Dragon: The Effect of Imports from China on Firm-Level Prices. *Journal of Money, Credit and Banking*. 47 (6). pp. 1091–118.

Chan, K. W. 2009. The Chinese Hukou System at 50. *Eurasian Geography and Economics*. 50 (2). pp. 197–221.

———. 2013. China: Internal Migration. In I. Ness, ed. *The Encyclopedia of Global Human Migration*. Malden, MA: Blackwell Publishing. doi:10.1002/9781444351071.wbeghm124

Chan, K. W., and W. Buckingham. 2008. Is China Abolishing the Hukou System? *The China Quarterly*. 195. pp. 582–606.

Cheng, M. 2007. How Do We Lose the Freedom of Movement: Formation of China's Household Registration System in the 1950s and Its Evolution. *Modern China Studies*. 4. pp. 6.

Cheng, T., and M. Selden. 1994. The Origins and Social Consequences of China's Hukou System. *The China Quarterly*. 139. pp. 644–68.

Dix-Carneiro, R., and B. K. Kovak. 2017. Trade Liberalization and Regional Dynamics. *American Economic Review*. 107 (10). pp. 2908–46.

Giovanni, J. D., A. A. Levchenko, and J. Zhang. 2014. The Global Welfare Impact of China: Trade Integration and Technological Change. *American Economic Journal: Macroeconomics*. 6 (3). pp. 153–83.

Goldberg, P. K., and N. Pavcnik. 2005. Trade, Wages, and the Political Economy of Trade Protection: Evidence from the Colombian Trade Reforms. *Journal of International Economics*. 66 (1). pp. 75–105.

Grossman, G. M., and E. Helpman. 1994. Protection for Sale. *The American Economic Review*. 84 (4). pp. 833–50.

Hsieh, C.-T., and R. Ossa. 2011. A Global View of Productivity Growth in China. NBER Working Paper. No. 16778. Cambridge, MA: National Bureau of Economic Research. doi:10.3386/w16778

Ianchovichina, E., and W. Martin. 2001. Trade Liberalization in China's Accession to WTO. *Journal of Economic Integration*. 16 (4). pp. 421–45. http://www.jstor.org/stable/23000767

Kinnan, C., S.-Y. Wang, and Y. Wang. 2015. Relaxing Migration Constraints for Rural Households. NBER Working Paper. No. 21314. Cambridge, MA: National Bureau of Economic Research. doi:10.3386/w21314

Kovak, B. K. 2013. Regional Effects of Trade Reform: What Is the Correct Measure of Liberalization? *The American Economic Review*. 103 (5). pp. 1960–76.

Lardy, N.R. 1991. *Foreign Trade and Economic Reform in China, 1978–1990*. Cambridge, UK, and New York, NY: Cambridge University Press.

_____. 2005. Trade Liberalization and Its Role in Chinese Economic Growth. In W. Tseng and D. Cowen, eds. *India's and China's Recent Experience with Reform and Growth*. Procyclicality of Financial Systems in Asia. London: Palgrave Macmillan. pp. 158–69.

Li, X. 2013. China as a Trading Superpower. Mimeo, London School of Economics and Political Science, 1–7.

Monte, F., S. J. Redding, and E. Rossi-Hansberg. 2015. Commuting, Migration and Local Employment Elasticities. NBER Working Paper. No. 21706. Cambridge, MA: National Bureau of Economic Research. doi:10.3386/w21706

Park, A., Y. Wu, and Y. Du. 2012. *Informal Employment in Urban China*. Technical Report. Washington, DC: World Bank. http://documents.worldbank.org/curated/en/383331468220789675/pdf/777370WP0Infor00Box377299B00PUBLIC0.pdf

Topalova, P. 2010. Factor Immobility and Regional Impacts of Trade Liberalization: Evidence on Poverty from India. *American Economic Journal: Applied Economics*. 2 (4). pp. 1–41.

United Nations. 2013. *World Population Policies 2013*. Technical Report. New York, NY: United Nations. http://www.un.org/en/development/desa/population/publications/pdf/policy/WPP2013/wpp2013.pdf

Wang, F. 2004. Reformed Migration Control and New Targeted People: China's Hukou System in the 2000s. *The China Quarterly*. 177. pp. 115–32.

Woo, W. T. 2001. Recent Claims of China's Economic Exceptionalism: Reflections Inspired by WTO Accession. *China Economic Review*. 12. pp. 107–36.

Xue, L., and H. Zhang. 2001. Shaping Up Sustainable Urban Transport Authorities in China: Status Quo Assessment and Reforming Solutions. Working Paper, World Resources Institute.

Zi, Y. 2018. Trade Liberalization and the Great Labor Reallocation. Mimeo, University of Oslo.

4

The Impact
of Tariff Liberalization
on the Labor Share in India's
Manufacturing Industry

Prachi Gupta and Matthias Helble

4.1 Introduction

India opened its domestic market to international trade in the early 1990s. The decision had profound implications on the development trajectory of the country. Trade opening allowed the country's firms to source inputs more cheaply and increase their competitiveness. At the same time, it meant that firms in India were exposed to increased competition from abroad, while consumers enjoyed lower prices for final goods. While the trade opening helped boost economic growth, it required an adjustment of capital and labor within and across sectors.

In this chapter, we aim to uncover how the labor share in the manufacturing sector changed after the trade opening. We use highly disaggregated plant-level data covering the period 1998–2008 to study the overall effect, as well as the effect across different manufacturing sectors. We find that a decline in output tariffs increased the labor share in manufacturing, whereas a fall in input tariffs led to a decrease in the labor share. This general result becomes more nuanced once we take into account the factor intensity of sectors. In technology-intensive and human capital resource-intensive sectors, both a decline in input and output tariff rates led to a decline in labor share. Separating the sample into the Indian states with flexible and inflexible labor laws, our results suggests that Indian plants subject to inflexible labor laws adjusted to trade opening by systematically replacing labor with capital. Our study significantly adds to the existing literature by studying the effect of both output and input tariff liberalization. Furthermore, ours is the first study to control for different levels of technology across sectors.

4.2 Background

Until the early 1990s, the Government of India pursued a policy of import substitution. The underlying idea was that a protectionist trade regime would insulate the domestic industry from the rigors of market competition. As imports would be very expensive, domestic production and industrialization would be promoted, and Indian firms would sooner or later become competitive, including internationally. The public sector was given a central role in running the economy. However, in contrast to the economic objective of rapid industrialization with equitable growth, this policy regime created an economy of complacent rentiers rather than competitive entrepreneurs, and it stifled the growth of the industry sector. In addition, government expenditures spiraled and made the Indian economy vulnerable to external shocks.

When external economic shocks did hit the country's economy in 1991, the Indian government approached the International Monetary Fund and the World Bank for support. The two international organizations made their assistance conditional on the implementation of profound structural reforms. This created a milieu for the political will to undertake large-scale economic reforms, which had already been discussed in economic circles in India in the 1980s. Starting in 1991, the government started a comprehensive liberalization strategy that gradually dismantled the protective shield for domestic producers. One important pillar of the new strategy was the opening up of India's highly protected trade regime. The government first

Table 4.1 Economic Growth and Openness in India, 1960–2010 (%)

Time Period	GDP per Capita Growth	Trade % of GDP	Manufacturing Output Growth
1960/61 to 1969/70	1.7	9.6	4.7
1970/71 to 1979/80	1.0	11.3	5.1
1980/81 to 1989/90	2.9	14.0	5.9
1990/91 to 1999/2000	3.6	21.2	7.0
2000/01 to 2009/10	5.0	39.3	8.5

GDP = gross domestic product.
Sources: World Bank Development Indicators (2019) and authors' calculations using data from National Income Accounts, India.

started by opening its market for raw materials, intermediate goods, and capital goods. The market for consumer goods remained highly protected throughout the 1990s.

Table 4.1 compares the economic growth rate of India and the share of trade in gross domestic product (GDP) from 1960 to 2010. While the 3 decades from 1960 to 1990 were marked by low growth and low trade-to-GDP ratios, the latter 2 decades saw a sharp increase in both. Similar to overall growth, the growth rate in manufacturing was boosted after the trade opening.

Figure 4.1 illustrates how the average and weighted tariff rates for industrial products were drastically reduced, respectively, from 81.9% and 49.5% in 1990 to 57.4% and 27.8% in 1992. The process of tariff rationalization continued over the next 2 decades. By 1999, the average and weighted tariff rates stood at 33.0% and 28.6%, respectively, and the peak tariff was reduced to 35.1%. The effective rate of protection was reduced from 125.9% in 1986–1990 to 80.2% in 1990–1995 and further to 40.4% in 1996–2000 (Das 2003).

While in the 1990s, during the first decade of reforms, tariff rates declined substantially, some experts argued that the level was still sufficiently high to substantially discourage imports (Goldar 2012). Furthermore, imports of most products were still subject to a range of nontariff measures. Das (2003) estimated the nominal and effective rates of protection and found that they remained high until 2000, reaching almost 100% for intermediate and final goods.

Figure 4.1 Average Tariff (Weighted Average) for Industrial Products, 1990–2008 (%)

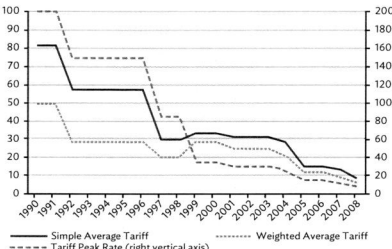

Source: Authors' calculation based on R. Banga and A. Das, eds. 2012. *Twenty Years of India's Liberalization: Experiences and Lessons*. Geneva: United Nations Conference on Trade and Development. Http://unctad.org/en/PublicationsLibrary/osg2012d1_en.pdf. p. 8.

It was only in 2000, after India lost a World Trade Organization dispute against the United States on quantitative restrictions, when the Indian government decided to remove a large number of nontariff restrictions (Banga and Das 2012). In the 2000s, the long-protected consumer sector was opened to trade, which led to a sharp rise in India's imports of final goods, leading in turn to a significant increase in competition for domestic producers. At the same time, the fall in the price of intermediate inputs allowed Indian manufacturers to boost their productivity. Figure 4.2 shows the fall in tariffs for the 10 most important industries in India. The decline was most dramatic in the apparel sector, which employed roughly a quarter of the workers in the manufacturing sector.

The trade opening also contributed to a change of the import and export basket of India. Table 4.2 lists the share of each industry (following the National Industrial Classification of India, or NIC) in total manufactured imports and exports. In textiles, wearing apparel, and leather (NIC17–19) the export shares fell from close to 40% in 1990 to 13.7% in 2010. All three industries are labor intensive, and they collectively employed about one quarter of total workers in 2010. At the same time, we notice a sharp rise in the export of coke and refined petroleum products, a very capital-intensive industry. In terms of imports, India saw a sharp increase in furniture imports. Depending on the technological sophistication, the furniture industry can be labor intensive.

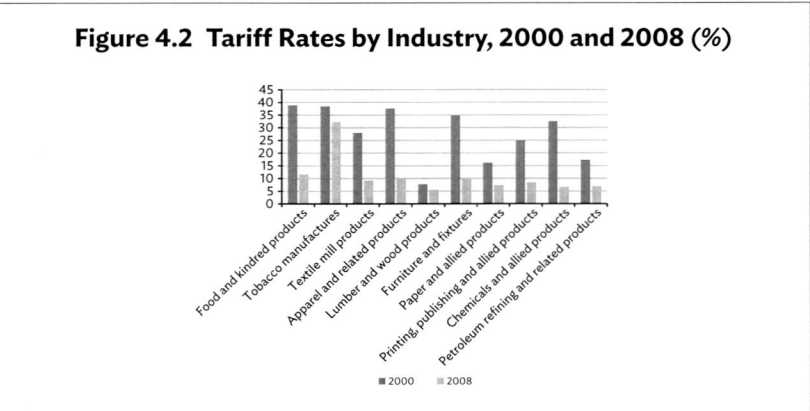

Figure 4.2 Tariff Rates by Industry, 2000 and 2008 (%)

Source: Author's calculation based on R. Banga and A. Das, eds. 2012. *Twenty Years of India's Liberalization: Experiences and Lessons.* Geneva: United Nations Conference on Trade and Development. http://unctad.org/en/PublicationsLibrary/osg2012d1_en.pdf. p. 10.

Table 4.2 Share in India's Manufacturing Export and Import by NIC-2 Digit Classification (%)

NIC Industry	Imports			Exports		
	1990	2000	2010	1990	2000	2010
NIC 15: Food Products and Beverages	2.8	6.1	4.1	10.1	9.3	6.0
NIC 16: Tobacco	0.0	0.0	0.0	0.3	0.1	0.1
NIC 17: Textiles	1.7	2.1	1.3	15.7	16.0	7.3
NIC 18: Wearing Apparel	0.0	0.1	0.1	16	13.7	4.7
NIC 19: Leather	0.6	0.6	0.4	7.8	3.8	1.7
NIC 20: Wood	0.1	0.1	0.2	0.1	0.1	C.1
NIC 21: Paper	3.0	2.1	1.2	0.1	0.4	C.4
NIC 22: Publishing	0.5	1.9	0.3	0.3	1.0	C.2
NIC 23: Coke, Refined Petroleum Products	19.0	8.1	4.7	3.5	3.6	1E.9
NIC 24: Chemicals	23.8	20.7	17.3	9.1	11.6	12.5
NIC 25: Rubber	0.9	1.3	1.3	1.4	1.6	˙.7
NIC 26: Non-metallic Mineral Products	0.8	0.7	0.8	0.6	1.5	˙.0
NIC 27: Basic Metals	12.6	21.4	25.3	3.0	4.5	9.8
NIC 28: Fabricated Metal Products	1.2	1.5	1.6	2.7	3.2	2.2
NIC 29: Machinery and Equipment	13.5	9.8	10.3	3.2	2.5	3.7
NIC 30: Office, Accounting and Computing Machinery	1.7	5.1	2.1	0.8	0.6	0.3
NIC 31: Electrical Machinery	3.1	3.2	3.3	1.2	1.5	2.2
NIC 32: Radio, Television and Communication Equipment	3.5	4.7	7.6	0.6	0.6	2.0
NIC 33: Medical, Precision and Optical Instruments	4.1	3.5	2.6	0.4	0.7	0.8
NIC 34: Motor Vehicles	2.2	1.9	2.3	1.9	1.7	4.3
NIC 35: Transport Equipment	4.6	2.7	3.7	1.1	1.0	3.6
NIC 36: Furniture	0.3	2.3	9.6	20.0	21.0	15.7

NIC = National Industrial Classification (2004).

Source: Authors' calculation based on data from World Integrated Trade Solution.

Table 4.3 Average Labor Share of Income, 1999–2008

	Mean	Standard Deviation
1999	0.126	0.130
2000	0.132	0.135
2001	0.124	0.131
2002	0.124	0.130
2003	0.124	0.129
2004	0.119	0.123
2005	0.108	0.113
2006	0.106	0.111
2007	0.100	0.106
2008	0.100	0.104

Source: Authors' estimates.

In our study, we define the labor share as the total wage bill (product of wages and number of employees) divided by total sales. Table 4.3 shows a tendency of a falling labor shares during the period of trade liberalization. This is a rather unexpected outcome with respect to theory given the comparative advantage of India in labor-intensive sectors.

The labor share can fall in two cases, holding all other variables constant. First, when the total sales increase faster than the wage bill. Second, in the case of a contraction—that is, the total sales fall more slowly than the wage bill. To better understand the three variables involved in the labor share, Table 4.4 gives an overview of how employment, the wage rate (inflation adjusted), and sales revenue (inflation adjusted) evolved.

In our data of large manufacturing plants, we find that the average employment size fell by 1.1% annually during the period of our analysis. Overall, the census sector witnessed a growth in employment of 4.9% per year during the period. Given that firing workers in census plants is not very easy due to stringent labor laws in India, the numbers in columns (1) and (2) imply that the new entrant plants had a smaller labor force. This is not surprising since there is substantial evidence in the literature with respect to "jobless" growth and capital intensification in the case of Indian manufacturing (Kannan and Raveendran 2009; Thomas 2013). We also see that wages grew by 4.1%, while plant revenue grew at a much higher rate of 7.0%. Studies that have analyzed wages and productivity in the case of Indian manufacturing have found that capital intensification

Table 4.4 Average Employment and Wages/Sales Ratio

Year	Average Number of Workers per Plant	Total Number of Workers Employed	Wage Rate (₹ per day)	Sales Revenue (₹ million)
	(1)	(2)	(3)	(4)
1999[a]	391.3	3,179,513	NA	4.28
2000[a]	357.9	3,100,965	131.7	4.43
2001	241.1	3,722,010	130.1	3.05
2002	233.7	3,601,330	137.7	3.06
2003	237.1	3,691,729	143.2	3.48
2004	202.3	3,882,585	145.3	3.20
2005	258.1	4,026,021	154.4	4.59
2006	233.2	4,348,107	157.7	4.37
2007	220.6	4,688,096	165.0	4.52
2008	214.0	5,124,493	176.5	4.51
Growth[b]	–1.1%	4.9%	4.1%	7.0%

NA = not available.

Note: Wage rate and sales revenue numbers have been deflated using the wholesale price index with base year 2004/05.

[a] The definition of the census sector was changed in 2001 to include plants with more than 100 workers, which earlier was capped at 200 workers. Hence, the figures for 1999 and 2000 are not comparable with the later years.

[b] We have excluded 1999 and 2000 for the purpose of growth estimation.

Source: Authors' estimates.

in the Indian manufacturing sector has increased, though a large share of the resultant labor productivity growth has been retained by employers with little growth in the wages of workers (Kannan and Raveendran 2009). Overall, the numbers suggest that the main driver of the fall in labor share was the smaller increase in the wage bill compared to sales. The question that follows is what the impact of tariff liberalization has been on labor share. In the analysis that follows, we try to answer this.

4.3 Literature Review

The case of India's experience with trade opening has attracted scholarly attention for many years. Development economists have attempted to evaluate the impact of trade opening on various socioeconomic outcomes in India.

With respect to the impact on poverty, the evidence remains mixed. Using four rounds of household survey data (1983–1984, 1987–1988, 1993–1994, and 1999–2000), Topalova (2007) finds that districts that were more exposed to tariff reductions experienced a lower reduction in rural poverty. Contrary to her study, Cain, Hasan, and Mitra (2012), also using household survey data, undertook a state-level analysis with no evidence for worsened poverty due to the reductions in trade protection. Instead, they find that states whose workers were on average more exposed to foreign competition had lower rural, urban, and overall poverty rates.

Another dimension covered was the impact on inequality. Using Indian household expenditure survey data from 1988 to 2005, Krishna and Sethupathy (2011) find that income inequality fell between 1988 and 1994, rose between 1994 and 2000, and fell again after 2000. They find that the changes to the state-level measures for trade protection had no significant impact on changes in inequality across households within states. This is in line with the findings of Topalova (2007) that there is no discernible effect of trade reforms on rural and urban inequality in India.

More closely related to our study are the empirical papers that evaluate the impact on firms. One strand of literature looks at the link between trade and firm productivity. Sivadasan (2009) analyzes the impact of tariff reduction and foreign direct investment reforms on cross-sectional data of manufacturing plants during 1986–1987 to 1994–1995. The study finds a positive impact of foreign direct investment and tariff reforms on plant-level productivity toward the end of the observation period. Topalova and Khandelwal (2011) use firm-level data for 1989–2001 and analyze the impact of the reduction in output and input tariffs on firm-level productivity growth. The study finds the reduction in both tariffs to have had a significant impact on firm-level productivity growth, and gains are found to be larger with respect to the fall in input tariffs. Gupta (2016) uses plant-level data of Indian manufacturing for 1997–1998 to 2007–2008 and analyzes the channels through which trade can drive productivity growth. Her study finds that technology spillovers, in addition to input and output variety growth, significantly contributed to higher plant-level productivity in the case of India. In contrast to the above, the studies by Balakrishnan, Pushpangadan, and Babu (2000) and Bollard, Klenow, and Sharma (2013) find no significant role for trade reforms in generating productivity gains in Indian manufacturing.

Our study builds on previous attempts to gauge the impact of trade opening on employment and labor shares. Hasan et al. (2012) find urban unemployment to have declined after trade opening in states with more flexible labor markets and larger employment shares in net export industries. Workers in industries experiencing greater reductions in trade protection were less likely to become unemployed, especially in net export industries. Using aggregate industry-level data, Hasan et al. (2012) find evidence that trade liberalization had a positive impact on labor demand elasticity. They also show that trade reforms led to a reduction in labor share due to a decline in the bargaining power of workers. However, using micro-level data, Ahsan and Mitra (2014) uncover variation in terms of the impact of trade liberalization on labor shares. For small and labor-intensive firms, the trade reforms seemingly led to an increase in labor share, while the impact was found to be the opposite for the larger and less labor-intensive firms. Mishra and Kumar (2005) use household survey data and find that a negative relationship forms over time between changes in trade policy and changes in industry wage premiums. Since tariff reductions were proportionately larger in sectors that employ a larger share of unskilled workers, their findings imply that unskilled workers experienced an increase in their relative incomes due to the trade reforms.

Traditional trade theory (the Heckscher–Ohlin model) predicts that gains from trade favor abundant factors. In the case of a developing country with abundant low-skilled labor like India, this would imply that unskilled labor would benefit the most from globalization. However, new theories such as Marjit, Beladi, and Chakrabarti (2004) suggest that, even in a labor-abundant country, trade liberalization can reduce the wages of unskilled labor, thereby widening the gap between the rich and the poor. Moreover, such adjustments may be costly, with the burden falling disproportionately on the poor (Banerjee and Newman 2004).

4.4 Data and Variables

4.4.1 Plant-level Data

The Indian government has relatively recently released plant-level data for manufacturing firms. The data are collected through the Indian Annual Survey of Industries (ASI). The ASI is the principal source of industrial statistics in India and extends to almost the entire country.[1]

---

[1]   Many studies in the Indian context have earlier used industry-level and plant-level cross-sections from the ASI (Hasan, Mitra, and Ramaswamy 2007; Hsieh and Klenow 2009; Sivadasan 2009; Harrison, Martin, and Nataraj 2012; Bollard, Klenow, and Sharma 2013), but the earlier data of the ASI did not disclose plant identifiers. This study uses the recently released data with plant identifiers launched by the ASI which enable us to create a panel of manufacturing plants in India.

It covers all factories that are registered under sections 2(m) (i) and 2(m) (ii) of the Factories Act of 1948. This implies that all factories employing 10 or more workers using power and those employing 20 or more workers without using power are surveyed under the ASI. The primary unit of enumeration is a plant or factory in the case of the manufacturing industry. The plant-level panel data of the ASI included in our sample cover the period between 1998–1999 and 2007–2008.

The ASI data are collected annually by the Field Operations Division of the National Sample Survey Office in consultation with the Chief Inspector of Factories in the states. Under the ASI framework, factories are classified into two sectors: Census and Sample. In the "Census" sector, the data from all the factories employing 100 (or 200 up to the accounting year 2002–2003) workers are collected on a complete enumeration basis. The remaining factories fall under the "Sample" sector, for which data are collected by drawing a representative sample using sampling techniques. Since continuous data are only available for this set, our study covers only those plants that fall under the "Census" sector of the ASI and can be successfully analyzed in a panel form. The data are an unbalanced panel and contain detailed information on production-related factors such as output, fixed assets, inventories, working capital, inputs, employment, labor costs, raw materials, electricity, power and fuel consumption, location, ownership, year of incorporation, and so on.

As per the National Industrial Classification (NIC), factories are classified into industry categories up to the four-digit level of disaggregation in the ASI.[2] In this study, we only focus on those plants that operate in the manufacturing sector (i.e., belong to the NIC15 to NIC36 two-digit industry groups). Table 4.5 provides the summary statistics of the key variables included in the regressions.

Table 4.5 Summary Statistics

	Mean	Standard Deviation
Age (years)	22.02	22.06
No. of workers	313.93	851.17
Capital stock (₹ million)	544.14	4,172.80
Output (₹ million)	1,146.53	9,619.45

Source: Authors' estimates.

---

[2]   NIC classification of Indian industries closely corresponds to the International Standard Industrial Classification of All Economic Activities classification.

4.4.2 Tariff Data

In order to gauge the impact of trade opening on the labor share, we use the applied tariff as a proxy. Nontariff measures are often similarly important, but we only take into account tariffs due to data constraints. We also do not consider any preferential tariffs, as by the early 2000s, India had not yet signed preferential trade agreements with significant trading partners.

Trade liberalization affects firms mainly in two ways. First, as tariffs are lowered, the firms typically face more foreign competition for their final goods. Second, lower tariffs allow them to source their inputs at a lower price. As these two channels might affect labor shares differently, we introduce them as separate variables.

Output tariffs. To measure the trade openness of a given industry, we use the most disaggregate output tariff data possible. In our study, this corresponds to the four-digit level data as per the International Standard Industrial Classification of All Economic Activities, or ISIC Rev 3. Since the ASI categorizes factories in this panel data per the NIC 1998 classification, we construct a concordance table between the four-digit ISIC Rev 3 and four-digit NIC 1998 classifications in order to match the tariff data with the ASI panel. The primary data series of tariffs was obtained from the Trade Analysis Information System (TRAINS) database of the United Nations Conference on Trade and Development. However, tariff data were not available in TRAINS for some of the years, for which instances we used data obtained from the Integrated Data Base of the World Trade Organization.

Input tariffs. In addition to output tariffs, which measure competition faced by domestic producers from the import of final goods, trade liberalization also facilitates access to cheaper and advanced intermediate inputs. To capture the impact of improved access to advanced intermediate input, we construct a measure of input tariffs following Topalova and Khandelwal (2011). It is defined as follows:

$$In\_tariff_{it} = \Sigma_j \alpha_{ij} \, Out\_tariff_{jt}. \qquad (1)$$

For example, if we assume that the shoe manufacturing industry i uses two intermediates j (leather and rubber with tariffs of 10% and 20%, respectively) and value shares of 0.8 and 0.2, respectively, then, using the above formula, the input tariff faced by the shoe industry stands at 12%. The input share, α_{ij}, is the share of input j in the total input cost of industry i. We estimate the input shares in this study by using the Input–Output Transactions Table 2003–04 for India obtained from

Table 4.6 Average Tariff for Manufacturing Industry Groups Analyzed in the Study, 1997–2008

Year	Average Output Tariff	Average Input Tariff
1997	32.58	14.97
1998	33.86	15.83
1999	35.02	16.47
2000	34.90	16.60
2001	33.84	16.14
2002	30.94	14.81
2003	30.76	14.71
2004	30.87	14.73
2005	20.50	8.83
2006	17.96	8.51
2007	18.52	7.75
2008	14.90	5.78

Source: Authors' estimates using the Trade Analysis Information System database and Integrated Data Base accessed through the World Integrated Trade Solution software of the World Bank.

the Central Statistics Office. Table 4.6 displays the average output and input tariffs for the manufacturing sector in India during the period 1997–2008.

4.4.3 Controls

Worker-days lost. We suspect that the conditions of labor market regulations may affect labor share adjustment due to trade liberalization. Different states in India have different levels of labor market flexibility because industrial relations fall under the concurrent subject in the Indian Constitution. This allows state governments to make their own amendments to the Industrial Disputes Act, which is the key regulation that governs industrial relations in India. As a result, labor markets have evolved differently across the various states in India (Besley and Burgess 2004). To measure state-level labor market frictions (condition), we estimate an index named worker-days lost in strikes and lockouts per industrial worker, which is the ratio of the total number of days lost in strikes and lockouts to the total number of industrial workers in the state. Data on worker-days lost have been obtained from the Indian

Labour Bureau, while data on the state-wise number of industrial workers employed have been obtained from the aggregate ASI data.

Export intensity. Exporting patterns of industries can impact employment and wages of the sector and hence labor share. To control the same, we include a measure of export intensity of the industry at the two-digit level. We define export intensity as the ratio of exports to domestic output, that is $Export\_intensity_{it} = X_{it}/Q_{it}$, where Q is the domestic output and X is gross exports. The impact can be either negative or positive depending on the industry characteristics and hence remains an empirical issue.

Factor intensity dummies. Labor share adjustment may vary across industries depending on the factor intensity of their production. To analyze this, we use the Hinloopen and Marrewijk (2008) classification to group industries on the basis of their factor intensities. Hinloopen and Marrewijk's classification corresponds to three-digit Standard International Trade Classification (SITC) level, with 240 items classified into five categories (number of items in each category in parentheses): primary (83), natural resource intensive (21), unskilled labor intensive (26), human capital resource intensive (43), technology intensive (62), and unclassified (5). To match this classification with our panel data, we construct a concordance table between SITC three-digit and NIC three-digit levels to segregate plants based on the factor intensities of their production.

Technology intensity dummies. In addition to factor intensity-based classification, we also use the technology intensity classification of industries based on the Organisation for Economic Co-operation and Development (OECD) ISIC Rev 3. This classification primarily corresponds to the two-digit level and classifies manufacturing industries into four subgroups: high technology, medium-high technology, medium-low technology, and low technology.[3]

4.5 Estimation Strategy

We start with a constant elasticity of substitution or CES production function of the following form:

$$Y_i = [\alpha(A_iK_i)^\theta + (1-\alpha)(B_iL_i)^\theta]^{1/\theta}. \qquad (3)$$

---

[3]   Since "Manufacturing n.e.c industry" at the two-digit level has been allocated to more than one category, we leave it as "unclassified" for our analysis.

Assuming that labor is paid its marginal product, and following Bentolila and Saint-Paul (2003), we get:

$$LS_i = 1 - \alpha(A_i k_i)^\theta. \tag{4}$$

By log-linearizing equation (4) and putting in additional variables that can drive the labor share of income, we derive the following empirical estimation model:

$$lnLS_{ijt} = \beta_0 + \beta_1 lnA_{ijt} + \beta_2 lnk_{ijt} + \beta_3 X_{ijt} + \beta_4 T_{jt} + P_i + Y_t + \epsilon_{ijt}, \tag{5}$$

where LS_{ijt} is the labor share (total wages divided by the net total sales revenue) of plant i in industry j at time t; A_{ijt} is the plant productivity; k_{ijt} is the plant capital output ratio; X_{ijt} are other plant-specific controls, such as age, man-days lost in strikes and lockouts, state where the plant is located, etc.; T_{jt} are industry-level trade openness related variables; and P_i and Y_t are plant and year dummies, respectively. Labor share (LS) in this study is defined as the share of wages in the net sales revenue of the plant. Plant age has been calculated based on the year of establishment as reported by the plant managers. Plant capital has been estimated using the perpetual inventory method following Balakrishnan, Pushpangadan, and Babu (2000). Plant productivity has been estimated following the technique of Levinsohn and Petrin (2004).

4.6 Results

The regression results of estimating equation (5) are displayed in Tables 4.7–4.11. The baseline results are shown in Table 4.4. In column (1) we start with a simple model with both input and output tariff variables. The coefficient of output tariff is found to be negative and highly significant, suggesting that a decline in output tariffs led to a rise in labor share of income. This result suggests that increased foreign competition triggered firms to hire additional workers. This result hints toward a Heckscher–Ohlin finding that India expanded the use of its relatively abundant endowment, namely labor.

However, with respect to input tariffs, the coefficient is positive and significant at 1%, suggesting that a fall in input tariffs led to a fall in labor share. This suggests that firms substituted labor with other capital inputs, such as machinery and equipment, when the policy with respect to imports of inputs was relaxed.

In the subsequent models in columns 2–4, we introduce several plant-level and industry-level controls. Note that the results with respect to input and output tariffs in all the models remain consistent.

In column (2), we introduce plant-level (*lnk_int*, *lnp*) and state-level variables (*lnmlpw*). The coefficients of *lnk_int* and *lnp* are both negative, as expected, and highly significant, at the 1% level. This result indicates that a rise in capital input and a rise in productivity both lead to a decline in the labor share of income. The coefficient of *lnmlpw* is positive and highly significant. In the case of India, this variable is closely associated with union strength; hence, a positive coefficient of *lnmlpw* is indicative of a positive impact of union strength and further a higher labor share of income. From the estimation results of column (2), we can say that a 10% decline in output tariffs led to a 0.24% rise in the labor share of income. On the other hand, a 10% decline in input tariffs led to a 0.12% decline in the labor share of income for large manufacturing plants in India. The coefficient of *export_intensity* is negative and significant, at the 5% level. This reflects the inherent capital-intensive export bias in the case of Indian manufacturing (Veeramani, Aerath, and Gupta 2018).

While our estimates show that there was a decline in the average number of workers employed per plant as displayed in Table 4.7, this does not necessarily imply that tariff reforms had a negative impact on plant-level employment. To check for this, we run our regression by replacing the dependent variable with number of workers in equation (5). All the

Table 4.7 Trade Liberalization and Labor Share

Variables	Model			
	(1) ln_LS_w1	(2) ln_LS_w1	(3) ln_LS_w1	(4) ln_LS_w1
out_tariff	−0.0179***	−0.0244***	−0.0321***	−0.0203**
	(0.00617)	(0.00803)	(0.00868)	(0.00808)
in_tariff	0.0261***	0.0125*	0.0149**	0.0144**
	(0.00624)	(0.00675)	(0.00695)	(0.00675)
lnk_int		−0.0267***	−0.0292***	−0.0250***
		(0.00700)	(0.00785)	(0.00705)
lnp		−0.132***	−0.134***	−0.131***
		(0.00737)	(0.00839)	(0.00740)
export_intensity			−0.0710**	
			(0.0301)	
lnmlpw		0.0128**	0.00960*	0.0142***
		(0.00500)	(0.00517)	(0.00498)

continued on next page

Table 4.7 *continued*

Variables	Model			
	(1) ln_LS_w1	(2) ln_LS_w1	(3) ln_LS_w1	(4) ln_LS_w1
lnage				0.0825***
				(0.0134)
Constant	−2.627***	−1.549***	−1.498***	−1.818***
	(0.0176)	(0.0706)	(0.0782)	(0.0832)
Year fixed effect	Yes	Yes	Yes	Yes
Observations	67,275	67,275	57,573	67,275
R-squared	0.007	0.066	0.069	0.068
Number of plants	13,353	13,353	11,859	13,353

Notes: Dependent variable is plant labor share. *out_tariff* is 1-year lagged output tariff; *in_tariff* is 1-year lagged input tariff; *lnk_int* is plant capital intensity; *lnp* is plant productivity; *lnage* is plant age; *lnmlpw* is man-days lost in strikes and lockouts; and *export_intensity* is export intensity of the industry group to which the plant belongs. All values are in natural logarithms. Clustered standard errors are in parenthesis. All regressions include firm and year fixed effects and constant.
*** p<0.01, ** p<0.05, * p<0.1.
Source: Authors' calculations.

results in Table 4.8 indicate that a decline in both types of tariffs led to a rise in employment. The coefficient of both input and output tariffs is negative and highly significant across all models. The coefficients of the other variables are as expected. A rise in capital intensification (*lnk_int*) of the plant is associated with decline in employment. The rise in productivity (*lnp*) has a negative and highly significant coefficient, indicating that as total factor productivity grows less labor is employed. Older plants tend to have higher levels of employment as reflected by the positive and highly significant coefficient for the plant age variable (*lnage*). The coefficients of man-days lost due to strikes and lockouts (*lnmlpw*) and export intensity are statistically insignificant (*export_intensity*).

In Table 4.9, we analyze how tariff liberalization had an impact on various industries based on their factor intensity of production. For this, we classify industries at the three-digit level into five subgroups. In our regression model, however, we use four dummies: natural resource intensive (*FI_nat*), labor intensive (*FI_lab*), technology intensive (*FI_tech*), and human capital resource intensive (*FI_hri*). Using the four dummies and interactions with tariff rates, we find that the different subgroups adjust the labor share of income in very different ways.

Table 4.8 Impact of Tariff Reforms on Employment
(Plant Fixed Effects Model)

	Model		
Variables	(1) employment	(2) employment	(3) employment
out_tariff	−0.0445***	−0.0225***	−0.0436***
	(0.00671)	(0.00616)	(0.00943)
in_tariff	−0.0165**	−0.0330***	−0.0185**
	(0.00688)	(0.00632)	(0.00873)
lnk_int		−0.347***	−0.362***
		(0.00390)	(0.0141)
lnp		−0.303***	−0.320***
		(0.00395)	(0.0152)
lnage		0.368***	
		(0.00813)	
lnmlpw		0.00603	−0.00269
		(0.00463)	(0.00544)
export_intensity			0.0305
			(0.0329)
Constant	5.117***	6.802***	8.051***
	(0.0192)	(0.0478)	(0.134)
Year fixed effect	Yes	Yes	Yes
Observations	71,257	71,257	59,782
R-squared	0.030	0.179	0.146
Number of plants	13,945	13,945	12,287

Notes: Dependent variable is plant labor employment. *out_tariff* is 1-year lagged output tariff; *in_tariff* is 1-year lagged input tariff; *lnk_int* is plant capital intensity; *lnp* is plant productivity; *lnage* is plant age; *nmlpw* is man-days lost in strikes and lockouts; and *export_intensity* is export intensity of the industry group to which the plant belongs. All values are in natural logarithms. Robust standard errors are in parentheses.
*** $p<0.01$, ** $p<0.05$, * $p<0.1$
Source: Authors' calculations.

Across all specifications, the coefficient of the *FI_lab* dummy has a positive and significant sign, as expected. Although positive in most cases, the coefficient of the *FI_tech* and *FI_hri* dummies are insignificant. In column (2) of Table 4.9, as we interact *out_tariff* and *in_tariff* with the *FI_lab* dummy, the coefficients of both interaction terms are negative and significant. This indicates that a decline in both kinds of tariffs led to an increase in the labor share of income in the labor-intensive sector. Columns (3) and (4) display the interaction of *out_tariff* and *in_tariff* with the *FI_tech* and *FI_hri* dummies, respectively. Unlike the labor-intensive sector, the interactions are positive and significant, indicating that a decline in both input and output tariff rates led to a decline in the labor share in the technology-intensive and human capital resource-intensive sectors.

Table 4.9 Trade Liberalization, Labor Share, and Factor Intensity of Production (Plant Fixed Effects Model)

	Model			
Variables	(1) In_LS	(2) In_LS	(3) In_LS	(4) In_LS
out_tariff	−0.0318***	−0.0123	−0.0279***	−0.0350***
	(0.00832)	(0.00859)	(0.00841)	(0.00882)
in_tariff	0.0143**	0.0284***	0.0136**	0.0162**
	(0.00674)	(0.00692)	(0.00681)	(0.00675)
lnp	−0.109***	−0.109***	−0.109***	−0.110***
	(0.00307)	(0.00308)	(0.00308)	(0.00308)
lnage	0.0900***	0.0830***	0.0850***	0.0846***
	(0.0134)	(0.0134)	(0.0134)	(0.0134)
lnmlpw	0.0141***	0.0116**	0.0139***	0.0137***
	(0.00496)	(0.00496)	(0.00497)	(0.00498)
FI_nat	−0.317***	0.147	0.155	0.135
	(0.110)	(0.0977)	(0.0967)	(0.0962)
FI_lab	0.0382	0.649***	0.0607	0.0363
	(0.0971)	(0.112)	(0.0978)	(0.0973)
FI_tech	0.0182	0.0251	−0.0712	0.0148
	(0.0912)	(0.0930)	(0.0982)	(0.0915)
FI_hri	0.0708	0.0701	0.0838	−0.0714
	(0.0932)	(0.0950)	(0.0940)	(0.103)
out_tariff * FI_nat	0.0967***			
	(0.0166)			
in_tariff * FI_nat	0.0773***			
	(0.0123)			

continued on next page

Table 4.9 *continued*

	Model			
Variables	**(1)** **ln_LS**	**(2)** **ln_LS**	**(3)** **ln_LS**	**(4)** **ln_LS**
out_tariff * Fl_lab		−0.136***		
		(0.0154)		
in_tariff * Fl_lab		−0.0772***		
		(0.00877)		
out_tariff * Fl_tech			0.0173	
			(0.0131)	
in_tariff * Fl_tech			0.0210**	
			(0.00824)	
out_tariff * Fl_hci				0.0265**
				(0.0129)
in_tariff * Fl_hci				0.0209**
				(0.00925)
Year fixed effect	Yes	Yes	Yes	Yes
Observations	67,275	67,275	67,275	67,275
R-squared	0.070	0.074	0.068	0.063
Number of plants	13,353	13,353	13,353	13,353

Notes: Dependent variable is plant labor share in all regressions. *out_tariff* is 1-year lagged output tariff; *in_tariff* is 1-year lagged input tariff; *lnp* is plant productivity; *lnage* is plant age; *lnmlpw* is man-days lost in strikes and lockouts; *Fl_nat* is the natural resource-intensive industry dummy; *Fl_lab* is the labor-intensive industry dummy; *Fl_tech* is the technology-intensive industry dummy; and *Fl_hci* is the human capital resource-intensive dummy. All values are in natural logarithms. Clustered standard errors are in parenthesis All regressions include firm and year fixed effects and constant.
*** p<0.01, ** p<0.05, * p<0.1.
Source: Authors' calculations.

In Table 4.10, we use another classification of industries to separate the plants based on their technology intensity. This corresponds to the OECD two-digit technology intensity classification, which comprises five subgroups: low-technology industries, medium-low-technology industries, medium-high-technology industries, high-technology industries, and unclassified. The literature suggests that the labor share should be affected negatively in the medium-technology-intensive industries, where labor has an easy and high substitutability with capital. In column (1), we interact the *tech_low* dummy with the corresponding output and input tariffs. The interaction term with the output tariff is negative and significant, suggesting that, as output tariffs fall, the labor share rises in low-technology industries. The interaction term with the input tariffs is positive but insignificant. In column (2), we interact the *tech_midlow* dummy with output and input tariffs. Similar to low-technology industries, the interaction term with output tariffs is negative and significant. Also, the interaction with input tariffs is negative and significant, indicating that a decline in input tariffs leads to a rise in the labor share in medium-low-technology industries. In column (3), we interact the *tech_midhigh* dummy with output and input tariffs. Both coefficients are positive and significant, indicating that the labor share falls as technology intensity rises. As we move to column (4), which corresponds to the industries with the most advanced technology, both the interactions remain positive with higher levels of significance. Overall, these results suggest that as industries become more technology intensive, tariff liberalization leads to a decline in the labor share of income.

Table 4.10   Trade Liberalization, Labor Share, and Technology Intensity of Production (Plant Fixed Effects Model)

	Model			
Variables	(1) ln_LS	(2) ln_LS	(3) ln_LS	(4) ln_LS
out_tariff	−0.0193**	0.0157	−0.0433***	−0.0373***
	(0.00802)	(0.0106)	(0.00885)	(0.00819)
in_tariff	0.0192***	0.0585***	0.0203***	0.00615
	(0.00672)	(0.00854)	(0.00681)	(0.00675)
lnp	−0.117***	−0.116***	−0.117***	−0.117***
	(0.00320)	(0.00319)	(0.00320)	(0.00319)
lnage	0.0863***	0.0882***	0.0888***	0.0811***
	(0.0134)	(0.0133)	(0.0134)	(0.0134)
lnmlpw	0.0140***	0.0124**	0.0137***	0.0135***
	(0.00497)	(0.00495)	(0.00497)	(0.00495)
tech_ low	0.112	−0.137**	−0.0891	−0.0943
	(0.159)	(0.0660)	(0.0657)	(0.0659)
tech_ midlow	0.0298	0.510***	0.0462	0.0304
	(0.0769)	(0.0872)	(0.0761)	(0.0767)
tech_ midhigh	0.108*	0.0796	−0.147**	0.111*
	(0.0582)	(0.0580)	(0.0680)	(0.0581)

continued on next page

Table 4.10 *continued*

	Model			
	(1)	(2)	(3)	(4)
Variables	**ln_LS**	**ln_LS**	**ln_LS**	**ln_LS**
tech_high	−0.261***	−0.291***	−0.251***	−0.766***
	(0.0555)	(0.0557)	(0.0551)	(0.0724)
out_tariff * tech_low	−0.0793*			
	(0.0444)			
in_tariff * tech_low	0.0173			
	(0.0249)			
out_tariff * tech_midlow		−0.110***		
		(0.0129)		
in_tariff * tech_midlow		−0.0615***		
		(0.00790)		
out_tariff * tech_ midhigh			0.0742***	
			(0.0119)	
in_tariff * tech_midhigh			0.0138*	
			(0.00805)	
out_tariff * tech_high				0.121***
				(0.0152)
in_tariff * tech_high				0.0538***
				(0.00922)
Year fixed effect	Yes	Yes	Yes	Yes
Observations	67,275	67,275	67,275	67,275
R-squared	0.072	0.078	0.074	0.077
Number of plants	13,353	13,353	13,353	13,353

Notes: Dependent variable is plant labor share in all regressions. *out_tariff* is 1-year lagged output tariff; *in_tariff* is 1-year lagged input tariff; *lnp* is plant productivity; *lnage* is plant age; *lnmlpw* is man-days lost in strikes and lockouts; *tech_low* is the low-technology-intensive industry dummy; *tech_midlow* is the medium-low-technology-intensive industry dummy; *tech_midhigh* is the medium-high-technology-intensive industry dummy; and *tech_high* is the high-technology-intensive industry dummy. All values are in natural logarithms. XXX standard errors are in parenthesis. All regressions include firm and year fixed effects and constant.

*** $p<0.01$, ** $p<0.05$, * $p<0.1$.

Source: Authors' calculations.

In the case of India, labor laws fall under the concurrent list and are hence controlled both by the center and the state. As a result, Indian states vary significantly from each other in terms of the conditions of their labor laws, which makes some states more flexible (employer friendly) than others. To analyze whether state-level differences in labor market flexibility affect the labor share of income, we ran separate regressions for plants located in states with flexible labor laws (column (1) of Table 4.11) and plants located in states with inflexible labor laws (column (2) of Table 4.11). In the case of states with flexible labor laws, the sign and significance of *out_tariff* remains similar to the baseline results; *in_tariff* is, however, insignificant. In the case of states with inflexible labor laws, the coefficients are positive and significant, indicating that a decline in both types of tariff rates led to a decline in the labor share of income. This reflects plant-level decisions in favor of less labor-augmenting methods of production.

Table 4.11 Trade Liberalization, Labor Share, and Labor Market Flexibility

Variables	Model	
	(1) ln_LS	(2) ln_LS
out_tariff	−0.0666***	0.0215**
	(0.0142)	(0.0107)
in_tariff	−0.0130	0.0377***
	(0.0106)	(0.00914)
lnk_int	−0.0197	−0.0327***
	(0.0126)	(0.00904)
lnp	−0.124***	−0.128***
	(0.0134)	(0.00935)
lnmlpw	0.0210**	−0.00304
	(0.00939)	(0.00684)
Constant	−1.397***	−1.743***
	(0.127)	(0.0911)
Year fixed effect	Yes	Yes
Observations	23,155	36,238
R-squared	0.063	0.068
Number of plants	4,579	7,149

Notes: Dependent variable is plant labor share in all regressions. *out_tariff* is 1-year lagged output tariff; *in_tariff* is 1-year lagged input tariff; *lnk_int* is plant capital intensity; *lnp* is plant productivity; and *lnmlpw* is man-days lost in strikes and lockouts. All values are in natural logarithms. Clustered standard errors are in parenthesis. All regressions include firm and year fixed effects and constant.
*** p<0.01, ** p<0.05, * p<0.1.
Source: Authors' calculations.

4.7 Conclusion

This chapter analyzed the impact of input and output tariff liberalization on the labor share in the Indian manufacturing sector. We use data on large Indian manufacturing plants for the period 1998–1999 to 2007–2008. Overall, we find a decline in the labor share during the period of our analysis. As to whether this implies that tariff liberalization made the workers worse-off, our econometric analysis suggests that a reduction in output and input tariffs had a differential impact on the labor share. A fall in output tariffs led to a rise in the labor share. Given that labor is abundant in India, this trend falls in line with the predictions of the Heckscher–Ohlin model. In contrast, a fall in input tariffs led to a decline in the labor share, which suggests that as accessibility to cheaper inputs increased, Indian manufacturers substituted labor with capital.

We then extend our analysis to incorporate sector-level differences across plants in factor intensity and technology intensity of production. Segregating industries based on factor intensity and technology intensity classifications yields a different picture. On the one hand, we find that the overall decline in both input and output tariffs led to a decline in the labor share in technology-intensive and human capital resource-intensive sectors. On the other hand, it led to a rise in the labor share for labor-intensive and low-technology plants. However, given India's manufacturing sector has a bias in favor of capital-intensive manufacturing, the overall labor share on average has declined. A plausible explanation of this capital-intensive manufacturing bias is that India's rigid labor laws discourage firms from hiring and firing easily and hence employing labor more freely. To investigate if labor law differences across states account for losses to workers, we run separate regressions for plants based on their location. Our results suggest that workers employed in states with flexible labor laws gained from tariff reductions while workers employed in states with rigid labor laws witnessed losses in labor share. These findings are crucial given that India has a large unskilled and semi-educated population, with its comparative advantage in labor-intensive sectors. Labor law rigidity has likely done more harm than good to Indian workers. Further, gains from trade liberalization were attenuated due to the capital-intensive production bias in Indian manufacturing.

Our research has certain limitations that should be kept in mind when interpreting and possibly generalizing the findings. First, our sample only includes relatively large plants. These firms tend to be more capital intensive and more productive. In a Melitz-type trade model, these firms are more likely to benefit from trade liberalization compared to smaller firms. Due to increased foreign competition induced by trade opening, smaller, less productive firms might be forced to shrink or even exit the market. Our results only reflect the adjustment that occurred in large firms. Furthermore, our data at the plant level do not reveal how plants are linked. Trade opening might have led to a reorganization of activities across plants, but within the same firm. Firms might use profits earned by one activity to subsidize other loss-making activities. Such firm behavior might bias our estimation results, although, in the long run, firms can only survive if they are able make profits.

The research results presented in this chapter answered several important questions, but many remain. For example, our measurement of the labor share is rather crude. It would be interesting to distinguish the wage bill for skilled and unskilled labor. We have evidence for other countries that trade opening benefited high-skilled labor more. Knowing which group of workers benefited most from the trade opening in India would be important for policy makers. In case high-skilled workers benefited most, more investment in education may be warranted. Furthermore, the plants in our sample are different not only in terms of size but also in the number of products they produce. It would be worthwhile testing whether the labor adjustment was different in firms with multiple products compared to those selling few products. In case of multiple products, labor could be reallocated more easily. Many other pertinent questions can be answered using this rich dataset. We hope that this chapter will prod other economists to undertake additional research on the trade opening of India.

References

Ahsan, R.N., and D. Mitra. 2014. Trade Liberalization and Labor's Slice of the Pie: Evidence from Indian Firms. *Journal of Development Economics.* 108 *(C).* pp. 1–16.

Balakrishnan, P., K. Pushpangadan, and M.S. Babu. 2000. Trade Liberalization and Productivity Growth in Manufacturing: Evidence from Firm-Level Panel Data. *Economic and Political Weekly.* 35 (41). pp. 3679–82.

Banerjee, A., and A. Newman. 2004. Notes for Credit, Growth, and Trade Policy. Massachusetts Institute of Technology.

Banga, R., and A. Das. eds. 2012. *Twenty Years of India's Liberalization: Experiences and Lessons.* Geneva: United Nations Conference on Trade and Development. http://unctad.org/en/PublicationsLibrary/osg2012d1_en.pdf

Bentolila, S., and G. Saint-Paul. 2003. Explaining Movements in the Labor Share. *Contributions in Macroeconomics.* 3 (1). pp. 1–33.

Besley, T., and R. Burgess. 2004. Can Labor Regulation Hinder Economic Performance? Evidence from India. *The Quarterly Journal of Economics.* 119 (1). pp. 91–134.

Bollard, A., P.J. Klenow, and G. Sharma. 2013. India's Mysterious Manufacturing Miracle. *Review of Economic Dynamics.* 16 (1). pp. 59–85.

Cain, J., R. Hasan, and D. Mitra. 2012. Trade Liberalization and Poverty Reduction: New Evidence from Indian States. In J. Bhagwati and A. Panagariya, eds. *India's Reforms: How They Produced Inclusive Growth.* New York: Oxford University Press. pp. 91–185.

Das, D.K. 2003. Manufacturing Productivity under Varying Trade Regimes: India in the 1980s and 1990s. Working Paper No. 107. New Delhi: Indian Council for Research on International Economic Relations.

Goldar, B. 2012. Productivity in Indian Manufacturing in the Post-Reform Period: A Review of Studies. In V. Kathuria, Rajesh Raj S.N., and K. Sen, eds. *Productivity in Indian Manufacturing: Measurement, Methods and Analysis.* New Delhi: Routledge.

Gupta, P. 2016. Trade, Productivity and Markups: Analysis of Indian Manufacturing Plants (PhD thesis). Mumbai: Indira Gandhi Institute of Development Research.

Harrison, A.E., L.A. Martin, and S. Nataraj. 2012. Learning versus Stealing: How Important Are Market-Share Reallocations to India's Productivity Growth? *The World Bank Economic Review.* 27 (2). pp. 202–28.

Hasan, R., D. Mitra, and K.V. Ramaswamy. 2007. Trade Reforms, Labor Regulations, and Labor-Demand Elasticities: Empirical Evidence from India. *The Review of Economics and Statistics.* 89 (3). pp. 466–81.

Hasan, R., D. Mitra, P. Ranjan, and A. Reshad. 2012. Trade Liberalization and Unemployment: Theory and Evidence from India. *Journal of Development Economics.* 97 (2). pp. 269-80.

Hinloopen, J., and C. van Marrewijk. 2008. Empirical Relevance of the Hillman Condition for Revealed Comparative Advantage: 10 Stylized Facts. *Applied Economics.* 40 (18). pp. 2313–28.

Hsieh, C.T., and P.J. Klenow. 2009. Misallocation and Manufacturing TFP in China and India. *The Quarterly Journal of Economics.* 124 (4). pp. 1403–48.

Kannan, K.P., and G. Raveendran. 2009. Growth sans Employment: A Quarter Century of Jobless Growth in India›s Organised Manufacturing. *Economic and Political Weekly.* 44 (10). pp. 80-91.

Krishna, P., and G. Sethupathy. 2011. Trade and Inequality in India. NBER Working Paper No. 17257. Cambridge, MA: National Bureau of Economic Research.

Levinsohn, J., and A. Petrin. 2003. Estimating Production Functions Using Inputs to Control for Unobservables. *The Review of Economic Studies.* 70 (2). pp. 317–41.

Marjit, S., H. Beladi, and A. Chakrabarti. 2004. Trade and Wage Inequality in Developing Countries. *Economic Inquiry.* 42 (2). pp. 295–303.

Mishra, P., and U. Kumar. 2005. Trade Liberalization and Wage Inequality: Evidence from India. IMF Working Paper WP/05/20. Washington, DC: International Monetary Fund.

Sivadasan, J. 2009. Barriers to Competition and Productivity: Evidence from India. *The BE Journal of Economic Analysis & Policy.* 9 (1). pp. 1935–62.

Thomas, J.J. 2013. Explaining the "Jobless" Growth in Indian Manufacturing. *Journal of the Asia Pacific Economy.* 18 (4). pp. 673–92.

Topalova, P. 2007. Trade Liberalization, Poverty and Inequality: Evidence from Indian Districts. In A. Harrison, ed. *Globalization and Poverty.* Chicago, IL: University of Chicago Press for National Bureau of Economic Research. pp. 291–336.

Topalova, P., and A. Khandelwal. 2011. Trade Liberalization and Firm Productivity: The Case of India. *Review of Economics and Statistics.* 93 (3). pp. 995–1009.

Veeramani, C., L. Aerath, and P. Gupta. 2018. Intensive and Extensive Margins of Exports: What Can India Learn from China? *The World Economy.* 41 (5). pp. 1196–222.

World Bank. 2019. World Development Indicators. https://datacatalog .worldbank.org/dataset/world-development-indicators

5

Export Boom, Employment Bust? The Paradox of Indonesia's Displaced Workers, 2000–2014

Rashesh Shrestha and Ian Coxhead

5.1 Introduction

Charles Dickens' phrase "it was the best of times; it was the worst of times" is for many Indonesian workers an apt summary of their experience during the early 2000s. While the national economy and especially its resource-exporting sectors enjoyed trade-driven growth of unprecedented magnitude and duration, millions of blue-collar workers and labor market entrants found themselves paradoxically sidelined from well-paid jobs in manufacturing, and instead forced to seek livelihoods in low-paid, low-skill service sector jobs. This happened at a time when many Asian countries, led by the People's Republic of China, were enjoying (continued) expansion of manufacturing trade by participating in global production networks, which in turn created better employment opportunities for their less-skilled agricultural workforces. For many Indonesians, on the other hand, the boom was a period of stagnating real wages and diminished earnings prospects, even as national income and spending surged ahead and overall expectations for the future became increasingly bright. For workers, the consequence of job displacement due to structural change would have been particularly severe during this time.

The phenomenon of job displacement accompanied by earnings losses is familiar from studies of developed country labor markets. A substantial literature has explored the causes, duration, and implications of job displacement in developed countries (e.g., Jacobson, LaLonde, and Sullivan 1993; Kletzer 1998; Couch and Placzek 2010; Korkeamäki and

Kyyrä 2014). In some developed countries, trade-related "downskilling" (Modestino, Shoag, and Balance 2016) and declining real earnings, especially for blue-collar workers, has become increasingly widespread, and has been linked to competition from lower-cost manufacturers, including in the People's Republic of China (Autor et al. 2014; Autor, Dorn, and Hanson 2016).[1] Widespread job displacement has also been a concern in Latin American countries undergoing major trade policy adjustments, typically under highly adverse macroeconomic conditions (Goldberg and Pavcnik 2005, 2007; McMillan and Rodrik 2011). In most developing countries, however, job displacement has not been at the forefront of issues studied by economists, likely because in these countries structural change usually involves a transition to better jobs.

In contrast to the foregoing, Indonesian data reveal job displacement in a setting that differs in one very visible way: It occurs not during a negative trade shock or a period of crisis-induced macroeconomic adjustment, but against a background of rapid economic expansion. Studies of comparable "job displacement" in the United States (US) and Europe dwell almost without exception on the aftereffects of *negative* shocks, whether caused by recessions or by trade competition from emerging economies such as the People's Republic of China. Indonesia's manufacturing industries have also been impacted by external competition (Coxhead 2007). But in addition, Indonesia—along with Brazil and numerous other developing economies—has experienced strong and sustained growth in global demand for its energy and natural resource products. It is this resource export growth that has been the dominant driver of structural change since about 2000.

There is in addition another subtler set of differences in the Indonesian case. These arise from the fact that Indonesia, unlike even the large Latin American economies, was (at least at the beginning of this period) a low-income economy. While the *rate* of Indonesia's economic growth during the recent export boom was high, the boom induced changes in the *structure* of economic activity—and thus of employment— that were biased against high-wage jobs for blue-collar workers and were sufficiently large to deny many poor Indonesians a share in the proceeds of the boom. The paradox is solved by noting that during this structural change, industries (largely in manufacturing) offering "good" semi-skilled jobs, and especially industries in which *formal* employment is widespread, contracted sharply relative to industries (largely services) in which skills are seldom rewarded and in which regulation of wages and employment conditions is almost totally lacking. Increased labor

---

[1]   This has directly contributed to current political backlash against globalization and trade in the United States and Europe.

market rigidity due to new regulations were likely contributing factors. As a result, new labor market entrants and workers displaced from the former types of jobs could still find employment. However, they could do so only in sectors and occupations paying less, and offering few prospects for promotion and no contractual security.

Each of these features of the Indonesian experience is salient to the analysis we conduct, as will become clear. In this chapter, we explore how workers who started out in formal employment fared several years later, and how their transition out of the sector affected earnings. We use the 2000, 2007, and 2014 rounds of the Indonesian Family Life Survey (IFLS) data, research that tracks individual workers over time. We find that transition out of formal employment, which is strongly associated with manufacturing jobs, leads to substantial loss of earnings. The results demarcate an episode of job displacement and earnings losses during "the best of times" not previously examined in a rigorous fashion. Building on our previous work examining the consequences of Indonesia's palm oil export boom for the structure of the labor market, inequality, and educational incentives (Coxhead and Shrestha 2016), we show that high growth does not automatically translate into positive labor market changes for workers. One implication is that high growth not matched by increased formalization or the creation of more formal jobs could be a reason for the exacerbation of inequality in Indonesia.

5.2 Trade Shocks and Job Displacement

Given the seemingly strong symbiosis between the growth of labor-intensive manufacturing and increases in income, it is not surprising that development economists have expressed concern over two phenomena that appear to indicate an ongoing structural change in this relationship. One of these is "premature deindustrialization," wherein (for reasons including policy changes and loss of global competitiveness) the gross domestic product (GDP) share of manufacturing peaks at a lower value and at a lower level of income per capita than was the case in earlier development experiences (Rodrik 2015). The underlying notion is that economic growth led by labor-intensive manufacturing is preferable for countries with a large pool of less-skilled labor. Loss of momentum in labor-intensive manufacturing is unlikely to cause overall employment to drop; rather, it is part of a structural shift in which job opportunities in "good" (mainly formal) employment are replaced by the growth of less productive, poorly paid, and insecure jobs, mainly in informal services.

Concerns over job displacement have long been widespread in developed economies, and a large literature has explored its causes, duration, and implications (e.g., Jacobson, LaLonde, and Sullivan 1993; Kletzer 1998). In early contributions to this literature, job displacement was typically observed during macroeconomic downturns resulting from the internal dynamics of the business cycle (Jacobsen, LaLonde, and Sullivan 1993; Couch and Placzek 2010). Because business cycle recessions are typically brief, the main policy concern was less with temporary earnings drops and spells of unemployment, but rather with persistent loss of individual earning power over longer periods (Jacobson, LaLonde, and Sullivan 1993). Persistent losses from job displacement were explained by loss of job-specific human capital and loss of returns to job tenure (Carrington and Fallick 2014).

More recently, attention has shifted from business cycle displacement to deeper structural causes associated with changes in the relative competitiveness of domestic and foreign industries. Studies of the effects of People's Republic of China-related trade shocks on US workers (Autor et al. 2014; Autor, Dorn, and Hanson 2016) have found that US workers who are more exposed to a trade shock from the People's Republic of China have worse outcomes in terms of cumulative earnings growth and employment. There is a substantial amount of switching between jobs, industries, and sectors, but a surprisingly low rate of geographical relocation. Because of this, trade-related job displacement can have prolonged negative effects on welfare, especially among less-skilled workers. Splitting their labor market sample by terciles of pre-exposure earnings to capture the heterogeneity of impact on workers with different earnings capabilities, Autor et al. (2014) find that workers in the lowest tercile face a larger effect from exposure to a negative shock than workers at the top end. Furthermore, this effect is driven by a lower ability of low-earnings workers to adjust at the extensive margin, that is, to exit from sectors with greater exposure and find jobs in less exposed sectors. Thus, the capacity to recover from a negative labor market shock is positively correlated with initial earnings. This result is less surprising when we consider that variation in initial earnings is itself a measure of individual education and ability.

The majority of the literature focuses on developed economy cases in which labor markets are typically more complete, with lower search-and-matching costs than in developing countries. Earnings losses associated with job displacement are likely to be much more severe in the context of a developing country, where the coexistence of formal and informal labor market institutions greatly increases the significance of job displacement. Displacement from formal employment could result in large losses in individual welfare due to low earnings in informal employment. The existing literature has focused on understanding the characteristics of formal and informal workers, and in particular on whether informality is voluntary or forced (see discussion in Gindling

2014). However, we know much less about how transition between formality and informality affects individuals.

Likewise, the welfare implications of job displacement are arguably more important in the case that unemployment insurance is lacking. In addition, analysis of labor market adjustments is more complicated because it typically takes place in an economy undergoing a secular process of structural change in addition to short-run macroeconomic shocks. Distinguishing these and their effects on labor demand and returns to specific worker characteristics is an important task.

5.3 Indonesia's Recent Trade and Employment Trends

Indonesia is a relatively poor country—GDP per capita was just 31% of the world average in 2017—but since 2001 its economy has grown at 5%–6% per year, about double the world average. At this rate, aggregate labor demand growth should be correspondingly rapid, and with labor force growth much slower at about 2% per year, real wages should rise. However, growth has been accompanied by significant changes in the structure of production and employment. Notably, manufacturing, a prominent driver of growth in the 1990s, has been sluggish, while output and employment in a wide range of services industries has expanded (Aswicahyono, Hill, and Narjoko 2011).

Although Indonesia's exports are now dominated by primary commodities, manufacturing trade was a major source of job creation in the decade prior to the Asian financial crisis. During the 1980s and early 1990s, the manufacturing industry (especially labor-intensive, export-oriented sectors such as textiles, garments, and footwear) expanded much faster than GDP. Between 1980 and 1991, the share of production of these sectors in total manufacturing value added increased from 19% to 30% (Sjöholm 1999). In 1996, just before the Asian financial crisis, textiles and garments accounted for over 10% of Indonesian exports (Figure 5.1). Subsequently, however, their share steadily declined as that of primary commodities rose, as shown in Figure 5.2. While the total value of their exports grew, their share in Indonesia's total exports and also in world exports both fell sharply. The commodity boom caused substantial real exchange rate appreciation, rendering Indonesian exports less competitive.[2] Product market competition from low-cost

---

[2]   A more positive interpretation of the Indonesian experience in the 2000s follows the Balassa–Samuelson hypothesis, in which productivity growth in tradable sectors drives up real wages across the entire economy, combined with income-elastic preference for nontradable services (Dornbusch 1988). However, there is no evidence either of differential productivity growth or of rising real wages.

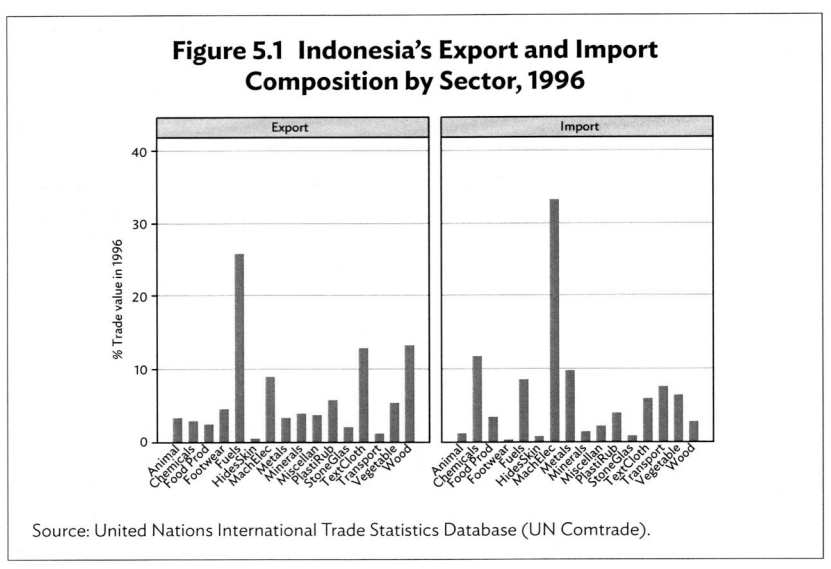

Figure 5.1 Indonesia's Export and Import Composition by Sector, 1996

Source: United Nations International Trade Statistics Database (UN Comtrade).

Figure 5.2 Trends in Indonesia's Exports of Key Products, 1990–2016

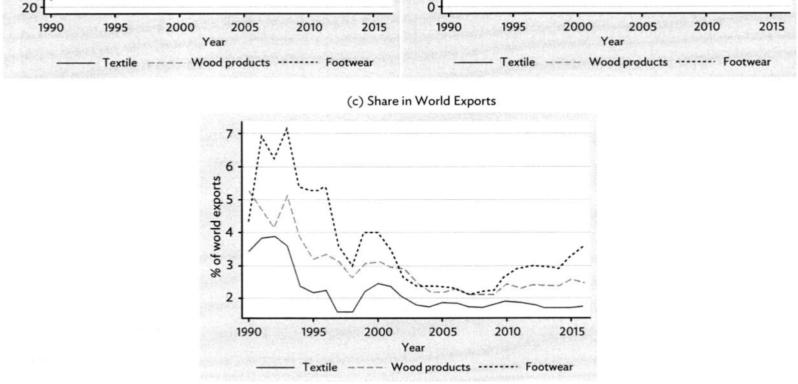

(a) Total Value

(b) Share in Total Domestic Exports

(c) Share in World Exports

Source: United Nations International Trade Statistics Database (UN Comtrade).

manufacturers in the People's Republic of China further depressed what had been an important source of employment growth in the 1990s. Both of these channels led to specialization in nontradable sectors.[3]

From an employment perspective, labor-intensive manufacturing is crucial to the development of nearly all emerging countries. Labor-intensive sectors tend to have a higher employment elasticity of output and, as such, their expansion leads to greater job creation. The mid-1990s, as it happens, was the high-water mark of Indonesia's manufacturing job expansion. According to data in Aswicahyono, Hill, and Narjoko (2011), employment growth in manufacturing, which had averaged 6% per year in 1990–1996, fell to an average rate of just 0.9% per year in 2000–2008, less than half the overall employment growth rate. The fastest rates of job growth in 2000–2008 were in construction (5.7% per year), transport (3.9%), and other services (3.6%), as well as mining (3.7%). Census data obtained from IPUMS International (Minnesota Population Center 2017) show that the share of males and females aged 20–49 years working in manufacturing peaked in the 1990s, but in 2000, following the 1997–1999 Asian financial crisis, it was once again below its 1990 level. It recovered slightly between 2000 and 2010 but did not regain the 1995 peak (Figure 5.3).

The precrisis manufacturing expansion was beneficial in terms not only of the numbers of jobs created but also of their characteristics. For given labor quality and production technology, growth of workers' earnings depends heavily on complementarities between labor and other factors of production, such as land and capital. For countries with low-skilled labor, investment in the manufacturing sector, by increasing the stock of capital, provides a direct path to higher labor productivity and thus labor earnings.

In addition to higher unit earnings, labor-intensive manufacturing provided an opportunity for many workers to be formally employed. In Indonesia, as in other developing countries, formal employment means a great deal but is quite rare among blue-collar workers. One recent survey estimated that labor productivity in a median informal firm in

---

[3]   In the case of Indonesia, trade shocks may also interact with labor market regulations. Indonesian labor market reforms introduced in 2003 are thought to have discouraged expansion of formal jobs (Garnaut 2015; World Bank 2010). These reforms included greater freedom to unionize and bargain collectively for wages, higher minimum wages, stricter hiring and firing rules, and increased severance pay and long service pay requirements upon job separation (Manning and Roesad 2007). Stringent labor laws have been proposed as an explanation for low rates of formal sector job creation in general (World Bank 2010). The labor regulations in Indonesia increased the costs associated with both hiring and firing, making it harder for displaced workers to find other formal jobs. If workers are unable to access formal jobs upon displacement, labor market regulations such as these are likely to create segmentation in the labor market and protect the lucky few who can maintain formal employment status.

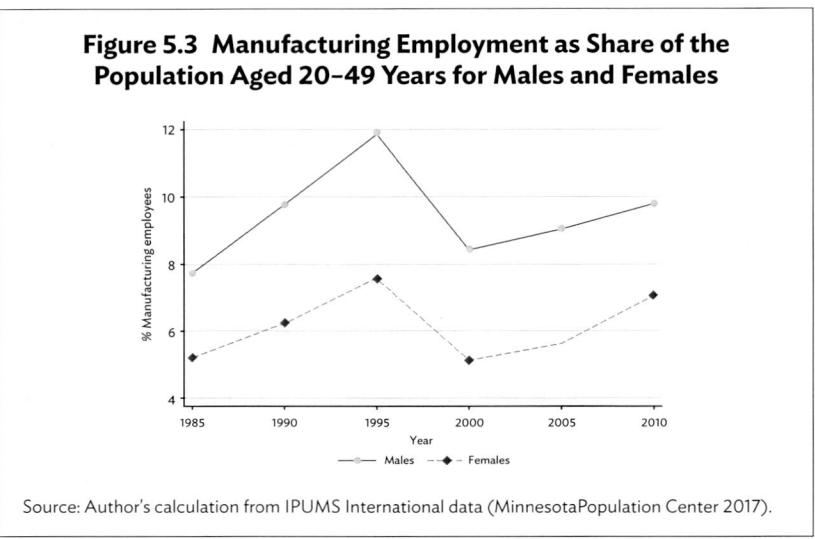

Figure 5.3 Manufacturing Employment as Share of the Population Aged 20–49 Years for Males and Females

Source: Author's calculation from IPUMS International data (MinnesotaPopulation Center 2017).

Indonesia is just 4.5% that in an average formal firm; labor productivity in the two sectors converges only in the top few percentiles (Rothenberg et al. 2016). Nearly all informal firms are tiny (under five workers); the 1990s manufacturing boom was dominated by growth in relatively large firms. As such, it is no surprise that the share of Indonesia's labor force recorded as engaged in formal employment reached a peak of about 45% immediately prior to the Asian financial crisis and has declined since (World Bank 2010).

Other surveys allow us to study further the characteristics of the jobs created by Indonesia's manufacturing growth prior to the Asian financial crisis. According to our analysis of the Survei Angkatan Kerja Nasional (SAKERNAS), the Indonesian labor force survey, at the peak of the manufacturing boom in 1997 over 5% of the Indonesian workforce was engaged in the "textile, ready to wear clothes and leather" industry and the "wooden commodities industry including furniture."[4] Among younger workers (aged 15–29 years), the proportion was higher at 9%, thus providing opportunities for Indonesia's younger population to engage in stable work outside agriculture. Geographically, these jobs were highly concentrated, with over 50% of employment in these two sectors located on Java. In terms of education, workers in these sectors

---

[4]   The corresponding industry codes are 32 and 33 in SAKERNAS 1997.

were slightly more educated than the overall population, but not by much. These sectors had slightly higher concentrations of workers with junior high school-level schooling. They also had slightly better gender ratios than overall nonagricultural work, so they were also crucial for improved participation of women in formal work. By 2007, however, less than 4% of workers were involved in these sectors.[5] The concentration of younger workers had also declined to 5.3%.

Studies on job transitions in Indonesia have by and large focused on the secular movement of labor out of agriculture and into "modern" sectors, such as manufacturing or urban services. Suryahadi, Hadiwidjaja, and Sumarto (2012) and Suryadarma, Suryahadi, and Sumarto (2013) both find that service sector growth made a substantial contribution to poverty reduction in Indonesia in the 2000s. A few studies have examined labor market responses to macroeconomic shocks, such as the Asian financial crisis (e.g., Manning 2000), but these studies are more descriptive than quantitative. Our own previous work (Coxhead and Shrestha 2016) provides causal connections from trade shocks to structural change in the labor market, notably the shift from formal to less formal employment.

The fact that formal jobs in labor-intensive sectors provide opportunities for low-skilled individuals to raise their earnings and move out of poverty motivates our exploration of the consequences of slower growth in high-productivity sectors and occupations, especially in a developing country with a relatively large endowment of low-skilled workers. The possible effects of slow growth include the relegation of some less-skilled workers into low-productivity sectors due to lack of opportunities, and/or reduced earnings and job security for workers who get displaced by the shrinking of these sectors. The situation for individual workers is much more difficult when slow job creation is coupled with structural change that increases the rate of job separation or reduces growth in formal jobs.

At the aggregate level, we can study patterns of job displacement by tracking employment patterns for the same age cohorts across time. For example, workers aged 20–24 years in 1985 would be aged 25–29 in 1990, 30–34 in 1995, and so on. By comparing the sectoral distribution of employment of the same initial cohort, we can see how structural change over time affects employment patterns. Stark evidence of structural change can especially be found in data for younger workers, as first-time job seekers are most likely to enter the sector that has been

---

[5]   The industry classification codes used in SAKERNAS 2007 differ from SAKERNAS 1997 as it uses three-digit classification codes rather than two-digit codes. The relevant sectors have codes between 171 and 210 in 2007.

expanding. Thus, a growing manufacturing sector would attract more young workers. We can observe this in repeated cross-sectional data by focusing on successive cohorts of labor market entrants.

Figure 5.4 plots the share of manufacturing employment among cohorts aged 20–24 years in the initial year (either 1985, 1990, 1995, 2000, or 2005) between 1985 and 2010. First, the share of new job market entrants finding employment in manufacturing fell sharply after 1995. Furthermore, each line in the figure tracks a cohort of individuals initially aged 20–24 in the beginning year. These data show a rise in the share of manufacturing employment in the 1990s followed by a sharp decline in the early part of the 2000s within the same age cohort. For the male cohort aged 20–24 in 1985, at least 12% worked in manufacturing until 1995, after which the share fell to less than 10%. More than 13% of the 1995 urban cohort started out in manufacturing, but by 2010 only 10% remained in this sector. By 2005, only 8% of men aged 20–24 had manufacturing jobs, although this number had increased slightly by 2010.

What can be inferred from these patterns? Overall, these figures demonstrate that, since the late 1990s, not only were new entrants in the labor market less likely than their predecessors to land manufacturing jobs, but workers already holding manufacturing jobs were also transitioning out of the sector. This trend in manufacturing jobs comes despite growth in sector output, albeit at a rate much lower than in the 1990s (Aswicahyono, Hill, and Narjoko 2011). Part of the reason could also be that this cohort stayed in school to a greater extent than previous cohorts, but lack of opportunity in manufacturing is likely to be a major factor.

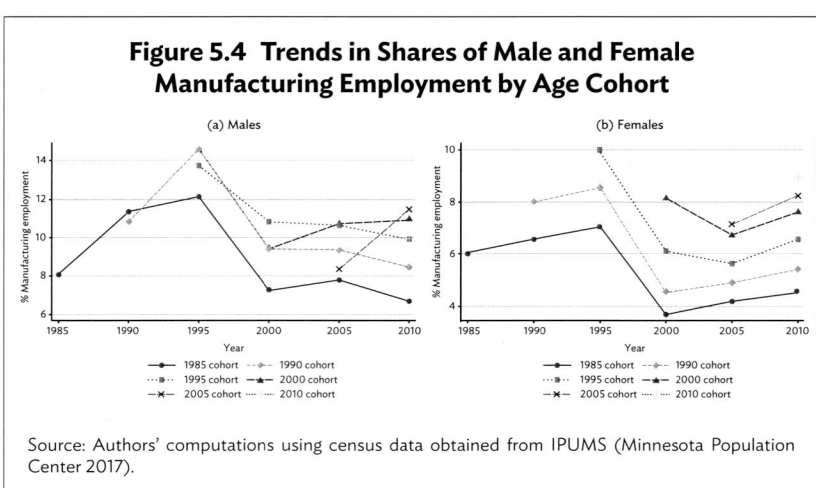

Figure 5.4 Trends in Shares of Male and Female Manufacturing Employment by Age Cohort

Source: Authors' computations using census data obtained from IPUMS (Minnesota Population Center 2017).

5.4 Data and Estimation

To understand the impact of such displacement on worker earnings, we require panel data tracking individual workers over time. The IFLS provides such an opportunity to explore the Indonesian case. The IFLS is a panel study that began in 1993, with follow-up rounds in 1997, 2000, 2007, and 2014 (for a detailed description of the surveys, see Strauss et al. 2004, 2009). We perform two different analyses, making use of two features of the IFLS data. The panel nature of the IFLS enables us to track the evolution of labor market status of individual workers over time. In addition, in a module concerning each worker's displacement experience over the past 5 years, added in 2007, respondents were asked to report any termination from a salaried job in the previous 5 years. Although the Indonesian structural change is one of declining manufacturing competitiveness in textile, footwear, and wood products, unavailability of detailed data (industry codes in the IFLS are only available at the one-digit level) means that we use information on all formal workers.

The pattern over time in the IFLS employment data matches closely that observed in national surveys. Panels (a) and (b) of Table 5.1 show the distribution of workers by occupation and sector, respectively. In terms of occupation, the proportions of production and semi-skilled

Table 5.1 Employment Characteristics
in Indonesian Family Life Survey Data, 1993–2014 (%)

(a) Distribution of Workers Aged 20–65 by Occupation

	1993	1997	2000	2007	2014
Professional	4.59	5.28	4.81	5.09	5.37
Admin	1.92	0.24	0.37	0.32	0.41
Clerical	3.62	5.21	4.38	4.24	5.74
Sales	18.69	22.19	16.28	19.02	19.73
Service	6.76	5.09	14.71	15.26	15.72
Agriculture	38.90	33.37	32.83	30.07	25.73
Production	8.13	9.75	8.28	7.70	7.58
Semi-skilled	3.21	4.44	3.00	3.07	3.23
Laborer	12.32	12.54	13.52	13.29	15.01
Others	1.85	1.90	1.83	1.94	2.08
N	9,064	10,540	14,899	18,174	21,819

continued on next page

Table 5.1 *continued*

(b) Distribution of Workers Aged 20–65 by Sector

	1997	2000	2007	2014
Agriculture	33.56	33.06	30.25	25.76
Mining	0.62	0.55	0.64	1.30
Manufacturing	15.64	13.88	13.34	13.07
Utilities	0.51	0.34	0.32	0.51
Construction	5.58	4.50	4.78	5.00
Wholesale/retail trade	22.52	22.20	24.69	25.52
Transport	4.54	4.19	3.51	2.45
Financial services	0.85	0.78	0.89	4.70
Social services	16.18	20.50	21.57	21.68
N	10,540	14,896	18,174	21,819

Source: Authors' calculation from various Indonesian Family Life Survey rounds. The 1993 survey did not contain sector categories.

workers, who are mostly associated with the manufacturing sector, remain unchanged or decline slightly between 1993 and 2014, after a slight increase in 1997. Likewise, sectoral distribution moves toward greater concentration in the services sector, and declines in agriculture and manufacturing.

The core empirical task is to compare the earnings growth of workers who remained formally employed to that of those who moved out of formal employment, conditional on the observable characteristics of workers and their initial jobs. Consider a labor market in which there are two types of jobs, denoted by 0 and 1. In the first period, all workers hold jobs of type 0. In the second period, some of these workers are found to have moved to jobs of type 1. Each worker possesses a set of general characteristics X with returns α, and also an endowment of job type-specific human capital denoted by vector $A = (a_0, a_1)$.

The first-period earnings of a worker i are determined by:

$$Y_{i0} = \beta + X_i'\alpha + \theta_0 a_0 + e_{i0}. \qquad (1)$$

Due to structural change, both the returns to general characteristics, α, and returns to specific human capital, a_0, can change. In the second period, worker i's earnings in job j are given by:

$$Y_{ij} = \bar{\beta} + X_i'\bar{\alpha} + \bar{\theta}_j a_j + e_{ij}. \qquad (2)$$

Therefore, if individual i stays in job 0, the difference in earnings over time is:

$$dY_i = (\bar{\beta} - \beta) + X_i'(\bar{\alpha} - \alpha) + (\bar{\theta}_0 - \theta_0)a_0 + v_{i0}, \qquad (3)$$

and if worker i switches to job, it is:

$$dY_i = (\bar{\beta} - \beta) + X_i'(\bar{\alpha} - \alpha) + \bar{\theta}_1 a_1 - \theta_0 a_0 + v_{i1} \qquad (4)$$

The differential earnings growth between switchers and stayers is thus given by:

$$D_i = (\bar{\theta}_1 a_1 - \theta_0 a_0) - (\bar{\theta}_0 - \theta_0)a_0. \qquad (5)$$

The second term in equation (5) measures the change in returns to workers who remain in job 0. The first term captures the effects on workers who are displaced to job 1. For this group, not only do returns to human capital change, but the value of their human capital may differ in the new occupation. On the other hand, the second term is hypothetical for those displaced from job 0. We can estimate this term from data on stayers if the unobserved characteristics are similar for switchers and stayers, that is, $E(a_0|S_i = 1) = E(a_0|S_i = 0)$, where $S_i = 1$ if the individual switches employment and 0 otherwise.

In general, there are reasons to believe that switchers will be different from stayers. If the transition is voluntary, Roy's (1951) self-selection model implies that individuals select into occupations in which the returns to their skills are highest. Thus, the earnings potential of switchers may be different than that of stayers. For example, those with high a_0 may be more likely to stay in job 0 if growth in returns to skills is positive. These unobserved skills might drive both switching out of formal employment and earnings conditional on switching. This means that the observed earnings of switchers provides a biased estimate of the potential earnings of nonswitchers.

On the other hand, if job changes are involuntary, workers with a low a_0 might be the first to be laid off from jobs of type 0, which means that the expected a_0 among switchers and stayers is different. At this time—and in contrast to the much richer datasets available for displacement studies on wealthy countries—we lack the data needed to provide an adequate resolution to this selection issue.[6] What we do know, however, is that among workers who self-report displacement from a formal job (defined here as earning a salary), the rate of formal employment in a subsequent survey round is much lower than for workers who do not switch, and median hourly earnings, while still much higher than for workers who were never formally employed, are 20%–30% lower than for workers who did not switch. Adding to this the likely loss of job security, fringe benefits, and better-regulated working conditions, it seems plausible that among blue-collar workers with formal employment, only an exceptional few would *voluntarily* choose to move to informal employment. We analyze these data in greater detail later in section 5.5.

In translating these concepts into statistical analysis, we focus on workers aged 20–53 years old who are employed formally in the baseline year (2000 or 2007, analyzed separately) and analyze their labor market outcomes in the next survey wave. The reason for focusing on those aged 20–53 in the baseline year is to minimize the possibilities of job transition through retirement after age 60. We still have to worry about the issues related to the endogenous labor force participation of women.

We classify workers as formal if they are private employees (thus excluding government workers) who work in firms comprising at least five workers. Larger firm size is associated with greater productivity and compliance with labor market regulation, including job stability and benefits. However, a heavy concentration of small firms with low productivity is a feature of developing countries, including Indonesia (Hsieh and Olken 2014). In such a setting, displacement can easily result in a large loss in earnings. In the IFLS, the highest rates of formal employment among low-skilled occupations are found in the manufacturing sector (Table 5.2).

We focus on formal workers as these are the individuals who are most obviously vulnerable to displacement. In the data, formal workers earn at a higher rate and are more likely to receive benefits such as medical insurance (Table 5.3). This is true even if we focus only on employees (thus excluding the self-employed) or on specific sectors such as manufacturing. Therefore, movement out of formal jobs is more

---

[6]   Systematic selection of displaced workers is an important issue in the job displacement literature. One way of tackling this issue is to include worker-specific time trends to account for unobserved worker characteristics that evolve linearly over time (Jacobson, LaLonde, and Sullivan 2005; Couch and Placzek 2010). The US literature finds that point estimates on earnings losses are slightly smaller, but not statistically different when using matching estimators that compare workers with a similar ex ante probability of being displaced (Couch and Placzek 2010).

Table 5.2   Share of Formal Jobs by Occupation and Sector (%)

(a) Share of Formal Jobs by Occupation

	2000	2007	2014
Professional	26	29	36
Admin	25	24	51
Clerical	41	44	52
Sales	11	12	13
Service	17	19	24
Agriculture	10	09	13
Production	39	39	48
Semi-skilled	45	53	58
Laborer	31	35	39
Others	30	27	37
N	14,899	18,174	21,819

(b) Share of Formal Jobs by Sector

	2000	2007	2014
Agriculture	10	10	12
Mining	48	34	48
Manufacturing	43	46	56
Utilities	24	41	54
Construction	37	43	46
Wholesale/retail trade	11	12	17
Transport	17	20	32
Financial services	61	63	49
Social services	24	26	27
N	14,896	18,174	21,819

Note: A worker is classified as formal if they are private employees in firms with five or more workers.

Source: Authors' calculation from various Indonesian Family Life Survey (IFLS) rounds. Sample includes workers aged 20–65 years in each survey. The IFLS did not collect firm size information to measure formality in 1993 and 1997.

likely to be involuntary. Furthermore, workers in informal employment in the initial period are very likely to remain so in the subsequent period as well. Between 2000 and 2007, only 10% of informal workers transitioned into formal employment.

Table 5.3 Characteristics of Formal Jobs—Earnings and Benefits

	2000		2007	
	Informal	Formal	Informal	Formal
Med. log hourly earnings	7.13	7.38	7.96	8.34
Job benefits[a]				
Housing benefits	4%	6%	4%	6%
Car	2	4	1	3
Transport allowance	9	22	7	17
Health expense	12	30	10	22
Insurance policy	04	22	8	24
Clinic	05	22	6	15
Credit	26	38	21	28
Number of observations	9,695		11,732	

[a] Benefits questions were only asked of employees (N=4,910 in 2000 and 6,646 in 2007).
Notes: Informal excludes government employees. Number of observations pertains to earnings data.
Source: Authors' calculation from the Indonesian Family Life Survey 2000 and 2007.

The IFLS employment module asked individuals to report, among other things, sector, occupation, hours worked per week, number of weeks worked per year, the number of workers in their place of employment, and yearly earnings. For our purposes, the main outcome of interest is growth of hourly earnings. We calculate this by dividing yearly salaries for wage workers (or yearly profits for self-employed workers) by the total number of hours worked in a year. We use annual rather than monthly earnings, because the latter could fluctuate on a seasonal basis.

A major empirical challenge in the study of displacement is constructing counterfactual earnings for displaced workers. Some studies, especially those with richer datasets, have used the workers' predisplacement wage trajectory and information on nondisplaced workers (Carrington and Fallick 2014). However, due to selection, choosing an appropriate comparison group is still a challenge. Couch and Placzek (2010) use a panel estimator with individual fixed effects and propensity score matching, but this is a data-intensive approach not feasible in our study.

We use two different regression approaches. In the first, we regress log earnings per hour on lagged log earnings, formality status, and other control variables that measure workers' human capital in terms of education, gender, and tenure. The inclusion of lagged earnings, while not uncontroversial econometrically, allows us to control for all human capital rewarded in the market. In the second approach, we regress change in log earnings over time on formality status, adding other controls. Both approaches provide similar results but with slightly different point estimates.

In the earnings regression, we control for workers' variables measured in 2000, including age (dummies for bins of age), educational status (dummies for less than elementary, junior, senior, and tertiary), and occupation in the baseline year. Standard errors are robust to heteroskedasticity.

To address endogeneity due to the unobserved ability of workers correlated with formality status in the subsequent year, we check the robustness of our estimates across multiple specifications.

5.5 Results

5.5.1 Descriptive Statistics for the 2000–2007 Sample

In the 2000 survey, there are 2,750 formal workers who meet the demographic criteria and report positive earnings (1,773 men and 977 women). This constitutes 25.7% of all workers in the age group. The rate of formality varies greatly by sector and education level. Mining (54%), manufacturing (49%), and financial services (62%) have the highest rates of formal employment. Likewise, more educated workers are more likely to hold formal jobs: their formal employment rate is 35%, against just 19% among those with no more than primary education.[7]

Table 5.4 shows the distribution of formal workers by occupation, sector, and education level for workers who meet our sampling criteria. Most formal workers are performing low-skilled and semi-skilled tasks—about 45% of formal workers fall within the last three occupational categories, broadly described as "production and related workers, transport operators, and laborers." Taking advantage of the two-digit classification of occupations in the IFLS, we find that the largest shares of male formal workers are in construction (11.3% as "stone-layers, carpenters, and other building workers"), transportation (6.3% as "sea and land transportation workers"), and plantation

---

[7]   The informal employment rate among the highest educated workers in our dataset is biased upward by inclusion of some government employees classed as being in informal employment. Excluding government employees from the sample increases the formality rate among tertiary educated workers from 30% to 46%.

Table 5.4 Distribution of Formal Workers
by Occupation, Sector, and Education Level in 2000

Occupation	%	Sector	%	Education	%
Professional	5.93	Agriculture	15.74	≤ Primary	36.74
Clerical	0.51	Mining	1.35	Junior high school	16.08
Admin	9.17	Manufacturing	30.86	Senior high school	33.90
Sales	9.03	Utilities	0.36	≥ College	13.28
Service	11.98	Construction	8.49		
Agriculture	15.51	Wholesale/ retail trade	12.35		
Production	16.89	Transport	3.68		
Semi-skilled	6.99	Financial services	2.48		
Laborer	21.15	Social services	24.70		

Note: Total number of observations is 2,749.
Source: Authors' calculation from the Indonesian Family Life Survey 2000.

agriculture (6.2% as "agriculture and animal husbandry workers"). For females, the most common formal occupation is plantation work (17.4%), followed by sales (9.7%), tailoring (7.4%), and teaching (6.9%). A relatively large share of formal work created in the agriculture sector is explained by the development of large plantation estates for oil palm production. It also seems that sources of formal jobs are quite distinct for males and females, indicating some segregation in the labor market by gender.

The other occupational category includes service workers (e.g., maids, barbers, and housekeepers). This is also confirmed by looking at the sectoral distribution of these workers; the majority are employed in manufacturing and social services. Within manufacturing, food and beverage processing workers are the most prevalent, comprising over 16% of formal workers in the manufacturing sector. In terms of education, there seem to be two modes: those with primary or less education and those with senior high school-level education. This indicates heterogeneity in skill requirements within the formal sector, with some formal work requiring little education. These low-skilled formal jobs may contribute greatly to poverty reduction, but they are also likely to be more vulnerable to a slowdown in economic growth.

The IFLS 2007 contains detailed labor market information for 2,140 of these individuals, of whom 1,892 report being employed.

We lose some observations because entire households could not be tracked and others because they had moved out of the household. As a result, we have earnings information for 2,130 individuals, reducing the sample by 23%.[8]

The main explanatory variable of interest is formal status in 2007. We create a dummy variable taking the value 1 if displaced and 0 otherwise. Unlike existing work on job displacement, which uses administrative data, we do not know directly whether an individual changed employers between 2000 and 2007.[9] The results should be interpreted accordingly. We estimate earnings loss associated with moving out of formal employment.

Transition out of formality is large. Just over 42% of workers are still classified as formal in 2007, while more than 50% are classified as employees. The transitions are slightly different for males and females. Men transition into self-employment and casual nonagricultural employment to a greater extent than other job types, whereas women transition into unemployment and unpaid family work.

Table 5.5 reports the share of formal workers in 2000 who were still formal in 2007, by sector and education. Those in manufacturing in 2000 had a slightly greater chance of staying formally employed than in other sectors besides financial services (which is relatively small). Formal workers in wholesale or retail trade and social services in 2000 are also more likely to be found in either informal or formal work in 2007. In contrast, agricultural workers were more likely to transition from formal to informal employment. In terms of educational achievement, all those who transitioned out of formal employment had primary or lower levels of education; formal employment rates were higher for all higher education levels.

The heterogeneity within formal jobs is again apparent in the variation in transition rates across different demographics.

---

[8]   Attrition could lead to some issues. The distribution of workers in the baseline year, divided by those in and out of the sample in the subsequent year, shows some divergence. This is reported in Appendix Table A5.1. Those not in the 2007 sample are more likely to come from the agriculture sector. Younger workers are also more likely to be missing, possibly due to migration. A similar pattern of attrition is evident between 2007 and 2014, shown in Appendix Table A5.2. Similarly, those with junior- or college-level education tend to be missing from the sample. This may lead to possible bias in the estimates, but the direction of this bias is a priori uncertain.

[9]   Each IFLS round contains a module on employment history for the previous 8 years based on recall data. Due to the lack of information necessary to construct our formality measure, we do not use this information.

**Table 5.5 Likelihood of Staying Formally Employed
by Education Level and Sector in 2000**

Sector in 2000	N	% Formal	Education	N	% Formal
Agriculture	340	31	≤ Primary	841	38
Mining	30	33	Junior high school	333	38
Manufacturing	683	47	Senior high school	721	49
Utilities	9	44	≥ College	244	47
Construction	188	40			
Wholesale/retail	269	46			
Transport	71	42			
Financial services	40	60			
Social services	507	41			

Note: Total number of observations is 2,137.
Source: Authors' calculation from Indonesian Family Life Survey 2000 and 2007.

5.5.2 Descriptive Statistics for the 2007–2014 Sample

We now examine trends for those formally employed at the later baseline, 2007. There are 3,569 such individuals in the sample, comprising 27.5% of total workers fulfilling the demographic criteria. Similar to 2000, formality rates are higher in manufacturing (54%), among those with senior high school-level schooling (36%), and for those aged 20–29 years (36%). The earnings differential between formal and informal workers is slightly higher in 2007 than in 2000, ranging from a 0.26 log difference in hourly earnings among those aged 20–29 to 0.46 among those aged 40–53.

Table 5.6 presents the distribution of formal workers meeting our sampling criteria by occupation, sector, and education level. Compared with 2000 (Table 5.3), we note that the construction and wholesale or retail trade sectors comprise a greater share of formal jobs in 2007. Analyzing the distribution of formal workers at two-digit occupation levels, we find that while construction still accounts for the largest share of formal workers in 2007 (12.7%), the second largest formal occupation is now sales (7%). For females, plantation work (12%), teaching (9.6%), and sales (9.4%) are the top three formal occupations. The increase in education composition is also noticeable. Formal workers comprise a greater proportion of senior high school- and college-educated workers.

Once again, we lose a significant portion of this sample between survey waves. Out of the 3,569 workers in 2007, 2,512 are still employed

Table 5.6 Distribution of Formal Workers
by Occupation, Sector, and Education Level in 2007

Occupation	%	Sector	%	Education	%
Professional	7.23	Agriculture	13.17	≤ Primary	27.29
Clerical	0.34	Mining	1.01	Junior high school	15.77
Admin	8.85	Manufacturing	29.48	Senior high school	38.64
Sales	11.24	Utilities	0.48	≥ College	18.30
Service	13.51	Construction	9.53		
Agriculture	12.75	Wholesale/retail	14.54		
Production	14.35	Transport	3.25		
Semi-skilled	7.82	Financial services	2.63		
Laborer	21.49	Social services	25.92		

Note: Total number of observations is 3,569.
Source: Authors' calculation from Indonesian Family Life Survey 2007.

in 2014, and we do not have information on 734. Among those with job status information, 57% are reported as working in the formal sector, a much larger proportion than in the 2000–2007 sample.[10] This could partly be due to higher levels of reported formal employment overall in 2014: among males aged 20–53 years, 34.9% are formally employed, a much higher share than in 2000 or 2007.

The importance of education in maintaining formal employment status becomes clear by comparing the last two columns of Table 5.7. Less-educated workers are less likely to continue in formal employment than high educated workers. The difference between the formality rate of the lowest and highest educated workers is over 15 percentage points. In 2000–2007, this difference was just under 9 percentage points.

Our analysis suggests that attrition could lead to some potential issues. In Appendix Tables A5.1 and A5.2, we report the shares of worker status (unemployed, employed, missing) in the subsequent year by sector and education levels of the workers for the baseline years 2000 and 2007, respectively. We find that workers in skill-intensive sectors, those with higher education, are missing to a greater extent. For example, in both samples, over 30% of higher-educated workers are missing from the sample. These workers are likely to have maintained formal jobs had they been in the sample. This may lead to

---

[10]   In comparison, about 16% of workers transitioned from nonformal to formal work.

**Table 5.7 Likelihood of Staying Formally Employed
by Education Level and Sector in 2007**

Sector in 2007	N	% Formal	Education	N	% Formal
Agriculture	343	45	≤ Primary	733	48
Mining	26	46	Junior high school	407	55
Manufacturing	740	63	Senior high school	955	64
Utilities	12	75	≥ College	416	63
Construction	261	49			
Wholesale/retail	350	59			
Transport	84	49			
Fin. services	58	53			
Social services	637	64			

Note: Total number of observations is 2,511.
Source: Authors' calculation from the Indonesian Family Life Survey 2007 and 2014.

possible bias in the estimates, but the direction of this bias is a priori uncertain.

5.5.3 Earnings Function Estimates

We estimate the earnings equations separately for 2000–2007 and for 2007–2014. The observations concern workers aged 20–53 years who were formally employed in the base year (either 2000 or 2007) and have non-zero earnings in the survey year (either 2007 or 2014). The variable of interest is the indicator for formal employment in the later year. This takes the value 1 if an individual is still in formal employment and 0 otherwise.

We use two different dependent variables. In one specification, we use the log of earnings in the current year (2007 or 2014) as the dependent variable. In this set of models, we also control for lagged earnings (2000 for the 2007 model, 2007 for the 2014 model). In the other specification, we use the change in log earnings over time as the dependent variable.

The results are shown in Tables 5.8 and 5.9. In each table, we report first a basic model without controls other than for the log of baseline earnings, then add age, sex, education controls and region fixed effects, and finally occupation controls. Choice of occupation is arguably endogenous, so among the three models, the second is to be preferred on a priori grounds. The last three columns of the tables show results in first-difference form.

The results are quite consistent across models. The dummy for formal employment in the survey year is very precisely estimated in each case, and its coefficient values diminish only slightly with the addition of controls. As we use a semilog specification with a dummy variable, the elasticity of earnings in the survey year with respect to formal employment status is calculated as e^{b-1}, where b is the coefficient estimate. For values in the range of our estimates, the elasticities are slightly larger than the coefficient estimates. In Table 5.8, model (2), formal status is associated on average with per hour earnings 25% higher than those of informal status ($e^{0.224-1} = 0.25$). In the differenced version (model 5), the elasticity is 0.22. In Table 5.9, model (2), the same elasticity is 0.4, or a 40% premium.

Comparing these results with those from previous studies, we can draw a few tentative conclusions. First, the estimated magnitudes of earnings loss are comparable with those from studies of involuntary displacement. Studies of developed economies, with access to annual

Table 5.8 Impact of Displacement on Earnings in 2007

	Hourly Earnings (logs)			Difference		
	(1)	(2)	(3)	(4)	(5)	(6)
Formal	0.260***	0.224***	0.210***	0.198***	0.172***	0.164***
	(0.0546)	(0.0536)	(0.0535)	(0.0596)	(0.0603)	(0.0605)
Lagged log earnings per hour	0.467***	0.300***	0.288***			
	(0.0366)	(0.0352)	(0.0347)			
Constant	4.695***	5.675***	5.870***	0.790***	0.958***	0.928***
	(0.273)	(0.258)	(0.288)	(0.0454)	(0.109)	(0.167)
Demographic variables	No	Yes	Yes	No	Yes	Yes
Education	No	Yes	Yes	No	Yes	Yes
Occupation	No	No	Yes	No	No	Yes
Region	No	Yes	Yes	No	Yes	Yes
Observations	1,761	1,760	1,758	1,761	1,760	1,758

Notes: Robust standard errors in parenthesis. Sample includes workers in 2007 with positive earnings who were aged 20–53 years and formally employed in 2000. Age dummies include 30–39 and 40–53 with 20–29 as base group. Region dummies include indicators for Java, Kalimantan, Sulawesi, and Papua, with Sumatra as base group. Demographic variables include male dummy, age dummies, and education. Occupation variables includes indicators for nine categories of occupation. * p<.1, ** p<.05, *** p<.01.

Source: Indonesian Family Life Survey 2000 and 2007.

Table 5.9 Impact of Displacement on Earnings in 2014

	Hourly Earnings (logs)			Difference		
	(1)	(2)	(3)	(4)	(5)	(6)
Formal	0.343***	0.313***	0.301***	0.257***	0.258***	0.343***
	(0.0646)	(0.0642)	(0.0643)	(0.0679)	(0.0697)	(0.0646)
Lagged log earnings per hour	0.429***	0.309***	0.291***			0.429***
	(0.0379)	(0.0376)	(0.0381)			(0.0379)
Constant	5.278***	5.848***	6.419***	0.616***	0.705***	5.278***
	(0.305)	(0.319)	(0.361)	(0.0607)	(0.123)	(0.305)
Demographic variables	No	Yes	Yes	No	Yes	Yes
Education	No	Yes	Yes	No	Yes	Yes
Occupation	No	No	Yes	No	No	Yes
Province dummies	No	Yes	Yes	No	Yes	Yes
Observations	2,336	2,336	2,336	2,336	2,336	2,336

Notes: Robust standard errors in parenthesis. Sample includes workers in 2007 with positive earnings who were aged 20–53 years and formally employed in 2000. Age dummies include 30–39 and 40–53 with 20–29 as base group. Region dummies include indicators for Java, Kalimantan, Sulawesi, and Papua, with Sumatra as base group. Demographic variables include male dummy, age dummies, and education. Occupation variables includes indicators for nine categories of occupation. * $p<.1$, ** $p<.05$, *** $p<.01$.

Source: Indonesian Family Life Survey 2007 and 2014.

data, typically show a sharp earnings drop following displacement, followed by a partial recovery over several subsequent years. Our survey waves are 7 years apart, and we do not know with any precision when in that interval each worker changed jobs or employment status. Therefore, our results are best understood as an average of short- and long-term impacts.

Second, displaced workers in developed economies typically have access to at least partial income insurance through unemployment benefits or other social safety net instruments. Because of this, estimates of wage declines are likely to be greater than the change in actual income. These mechanisms do not apply in Indonesia, or at least not through official channels, although households may engage in less formal sharing behaviors. Thus, our estimates are likely to be closer to actual income changes than seen in developed economy studies.

Third, although we do not as yet have the means to decompose our results, our estimates of earnings differences in the survey year must reflect a combination of factors. Among these are losses due to frictional or cyclical unemployment; losses due to reduced returns to sector-specific human capital, and losses due to movement across the extensive margin of formal labor market institutions. Because our data are from an economy undergoing rapid expansion, the first type of earnings loss is likely to be small relative to findings from developed economies. Moreover, since most of the workers in our sample are blue-collar wage earners with little formal education, we can speculate with some confidence that the second type of loss is also small relative to other studies. If so, we may hypothesize that the third institutional effect is a more important driver of observed earnings differences. If this is confirmed, it sharply refocuses attention on labor market policies, since the more stringent of these may cause employers to limit their offers of formal labor contracts (as has been argued for Mexico; see Hanson 2010). This is a topic for deeper investigation in the future.

5.6 Self-reported Displacement and Earnings

The foregoing analysis yields estimates of an average earnings effect of movement from the formal to informal sector, but we are unable to establish a rigorous chain of causality. In this section, we explore an alternative approach. IFLS 2007 and 2014 asked some detailed questions about an individual's job history over the preceding 5 years The surveys asked whether the individual held any salaried positions over the previous 5 years and, if yes, whether he or she had been fired or had quit. The survey also inquired about the year of the latest job termination and the primary reason for termination.

Based on the responses to these questions, we can get one step closer to identifying exogenous job displacement and its impact on earnings. We create a categorical variable "displacement status" to indicate the status of the workers: (1) never held a salaried position; (2) held a salaried position that terminated due to firing;[11] (3) held a salaried job that terminated due to other reasons; and (4) held a salaried position and never terminated. This variable is closer to the true notion of displacement that has been used in the current literature as it captures separation from an employer. The goal is to relate this variable to differences in earnings.

---

[11]   The list of possible reasons included in the surveys are as follows: fired by the company because the business was closed down/relocated/restructured; fired for another reason; wage/salary was too low; nonconducive working environment; refused to be relocated; prolonged sickness; marriage; childbirth; other family reason. We consolidate workers experiencing displacement into "fired" (first two reasons) and "other reasons."

To keep these results comparable with the earlier work, we focus on workers aged between 27 and 60 years in the survey year. This keeps the sample's age consistent with the earlier analysis. Second, our estimation sample is limited to workers who are (1) currently formal and never displaced (assuming they were also formal before),[12] or (2) displaced from a formal job, for which we use the same definition of formality as before.[13]

One issue is that earnings information from previous jobs is asked only of those who report being displaced, which means we cannot compare earnings growth due to lack of information on the past earnings for workers who are never displaced. We address this issue by merging information from the previous survey for workers who appear in both years. The second caveat is that workers are displaced at different times within the previous 5 years. Due to the small sample, we pool all workers who are displaced into the aforementioned categories without distinguishing the timing of displacement.

Before exploring the earning patterns, we look at worker characteristics and labor market status by displacement status for all workers. These are shown in Tables 5.10 and 5.11. The first three columns in each table report demographic characteristics, the next column employment status, and the final column median earnings. Our 2007 sample comprises 2,593 individuals,[14] of whom almost 10% reported displacement due to firing or business closure. Our 2014 sample comprises 4,275 workers, of whom 220 (5%) reported being displaced involuntarily and 1,040 reported voluntary job changes.

Tables 5.10 and 5.11 show that gender and education are highly correlated with displacement status. The sample of workers reporting involuntary displacement predominantly comprises men. Those with tertiary education tend to have stable salaried jobs or voluntarily switch employment. Only 14% of workers involuntarily displaced have tertiary-level education compared to over 21% for the other two categories. Furthermore, those experiencing displacement present less than 60%

---

[12]   This may not be exactly accurate as the size of these workers' firms may have expanded over time.

[13]   The workers who reported being displaced were asked about the size of their firm and whether they worked in the government or private sector.

[14]   To arrive at the respective sample for each year, we start with the individuals who appeared in the displacement module. We exclude workers who did not fall into our age range or those who never held salaried jobs. If the worker reported being displaced, we check to ensure that they were nongovernment workers employed at a firm with at least five workers. If they reported never being displaced, we check their current formality status and remove those currently with informal status.

Table 5.10 Characteristics of Workers by Displacement Category in 2007

	Age	Male	Tertiary Education	Formal	Median Earnings
Displaced last 5 years – fired	36.53	0.81	0.13	0.52	3,571.43
Displaced – other reason	34.54	0.74	0.25	0.50	3,900.00
Not displaced	36.45	0.67	0.20	1.00	4,813.16
N		2,593			

Notes: Sample includes workers aged 27–60 years. For earnings, only those with non-missing earnings information and nongovernment workers are included.
Source: Authors' calculations from the Indonesian Family Life Survey 2007.

Table 5.11 Characteristics of Workers in 2014 by Displacement Category

	Age	Male	Tertiary Education	Formal	Median Earnings
Displaced last 5 years - fired	37.45	0.80	0.14	0.59	7,694.13
Displaced - other reason	35.25	0.73	0.22	0.58	9,209.04
Not displaced	37.50	0.63	0.21	1.00	9,558.82
N		9,987		9,263	8,470

Notes: Sample includes males aged 25–60 years. For earnings, only those with non-missing earnings information are included.
Source: Authors' calculations from the Indonesian Family Life Survey 2014.

formal employment in both years. The current formal employment rate is similar for workers who were displaced, regardless of the stated reason. Conditional on employment, median earnings are much higher than the median earnings of workers who have never experienced displacement.

Comparing these statistics across years, we find a greater share of formal workers reporting involuntary displacement in 2007. Furthermore, the median earnings of those changing jobs voluntarily are very similar to those never displaced in 2014. However, it is not clear whether this suggests an improvement in the health of the Indonesian labor market as the sample is highly self-selected and not representative of the Indonesian economy in these years.

In Figure 5.5 we look at the cumulative distribution of log hourly earnings by displacement status in 2007. While continued employment dominates displacement at the lower end in terms of expected earnings,

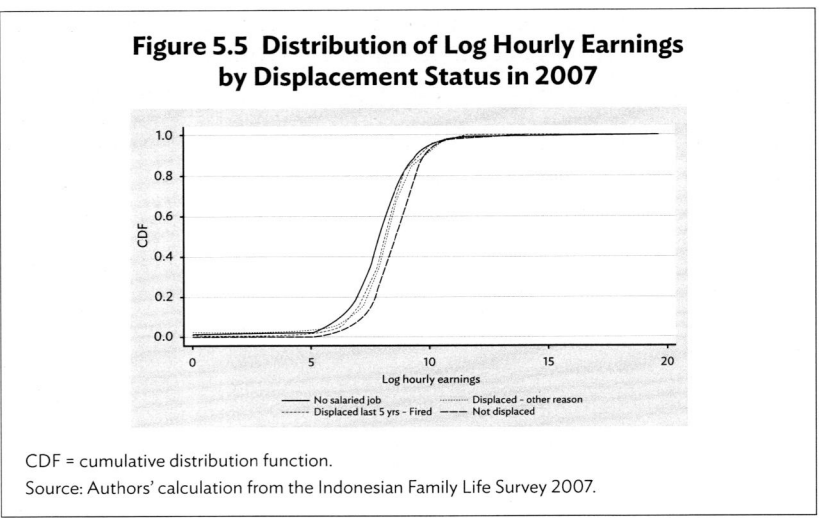

Figure 5.5 Distribution of Log Hourly Earnings by Displacement Status in 2007

CDF = cumulative distribution function.
Source: Authors' calculation from the Indonesian Family Life Survey 2007.

there is a considerable overlap in the distribution at the upper tail of the graph. This is illustrative of the two broad types of individuals who make up the displaced sample, namely a very small number who left their original employment for a better opportunity (or who were exogenously displaced but "landed on their feet"), and those forced or sorted into lower earnings work. Similar patterns are also evident in 2014, as shown in Figure 5.6.

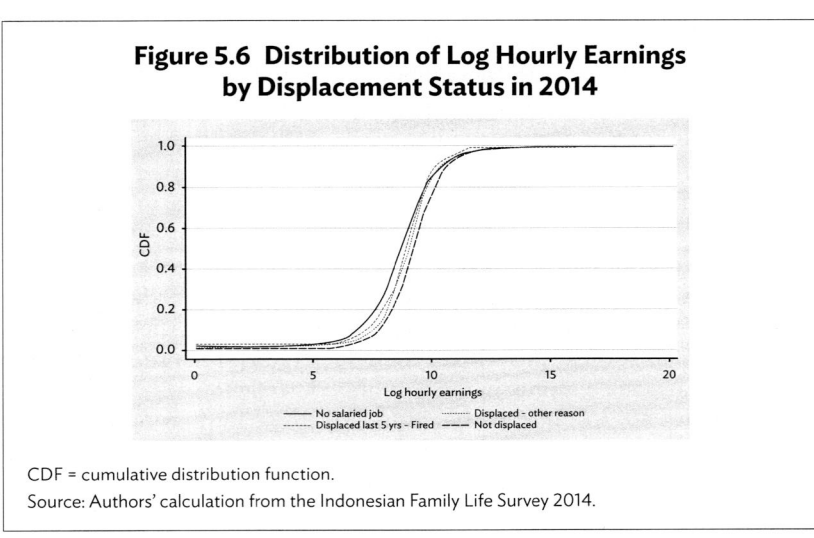

Figure 5.6 Distribution of Log Hourly Earnings by Displacement Status in 2014

CDF = cumulative distribution function.
Source: Authors' calculation from the Indonesian Family Life Survey 2014.

We now analyze the impact of displacement status on earnings in a regression setting. The dependent variable is the log of hourly earnings, and the main explanatory variable is displacement status. As in the previous section, we control for human capital variables, including gender, age categories, and education, and lagged earnings information from the preceding survey (2000 or 2007). Merging with previous surveys inevitably leads to loss of some observations as they do not appear in these surveys.

Tables 5.12 and 5.13 report the results from the 2007 and 2014 samples, respectively. In 2007, we find that those with stable formal jobs had greater earnings compared to those involuntarily displaced. In this case, the results are robust to the inclusion of additional controls and alternative dependent variables. In 2014, the results are similar when we use the estimation with lagged earnings as one of the controls, but the statistical significance of the results disappears in the difference model. This could again indicate some improvement in labor market conditions and post-Asian financial crisis recovery. However, we still need to interpret the results with caution due to the small sample size.

Table 5.12 Regression Results from Self-Reported Displacement, 2007

	(1)	(2)	(3)	(4)
Displaced – other reason	0.225	0.150	0.261	0.223
	(0.155)	(0.157)	(0.160)	(0.163)
Not displaced	0.473***	0.454***	0.425***	0.394***
	(0.130)	(0.131)	(0.135)	(0.133)
Log earnings 2000	0.494***	0.333***		
	(0.0375)	(0.0426)		
_cons	4.344***	5.175***	0.649***	0.762***
	(0.310)	(0.340)	(0.132)	(0.173)
Human capital variables	No	Yes	No	Yes
Region dummies	No	Yes	No	Yes
Observations	1,519	1,519	1,519	1,519

Notes: Robust standard errors in parenthesis. Sample includes workers in 2007 who were salaried 5 years before and aged 27–60 years. Age dummies include 40–49 and 50–60 with 27–39 as base group. Region dummies include indicators for Java, Kalimantan, Sulawesi, and Papua, with Sumatra as base group. Human capital variables include male dummy, age dummies, and education in 2007. * $p<.1$, ** $p<.05$, *** $p<.01$.

Source: Indonesian Family Life Survey 2000 and 2007.

Table 5.13 Earnings Growth and Displacement, 2014

	(1)	(2)	(3)	(4)
Displaced – other reason	0.320**	0.329**	0.292	0.265
	(0.154)	(0.149)	(0.213)	(0.214)
Not displaced	0.372**	0.414***	0.241	0.246
	(0.147)	(0.143)	(0.201)	(0.203)
Log earnings 2007	0.195***	0.139***		
	(0.0215)	(0.0190)		
_cons	7.185***	7.142***	0.747***	1.074***
	(0.226)	(0.208)	(0.198)	(0.246)
Human capital variables	No	Yes	No	Yes
Region dummies	No	Yes	No	Yes
Observations	2,545	2,545	2,545	2,545

Notes: Robust standard errors in parenthesis. Sample includes workers in 2014 who were salaried 5 years before and aged 27–60 years. Age dummies include 40–49 and 50–60 with 27–39 as base group. Region dummies include indicators for Java, Kalimantan, Sulawesi, and Papua, with Sumatra as base group. Human capital variables include male dummy, age dummies, and education in 2014. * $p<.1$, ** $p<.05$, *** $p<.01$.
Source: Indonesian Family Life Survey 2007 and 2014.

5.7 Conclusions

Indonesia is a developing economy which by virtue of its specialization in natural resources, minerals, and labor-intensive manufactures is especially vulnerable to shocks from the global market. In the 2000s, Indonesia experienced rapid growth and equally rapid structural change, largely as a consequence of global market trends. Both the overall growth of the economy and price-induced changes in the structure of production led to large changes in the vitality and composition of labor demand. Textbook models of economic growth and trade predict that greater openness and more growth should increase labor demand and productivity in low-income, labor-abundant economies. Yet in Indonesia, an export boom and rapid GDP growth in the decade after 2000 was accompanied by real wages that were flat on average, as well as declining earnings for a large number of workers. This is likely because the source of growth was not low-skilled manufacturing, as was the case before the Asian financial crisis, but exports of natural resources.

We have explored these seemingly paradoxical trends using individual employment data from the IFLS. We hypothesized that observed trends in wages and earnings may be connected to involuntary changes in sector or occupation. We found that the earnings of workers with informal jobs who had held formal jobs in a previous survey round were significantly lower relative to those of workers who remained in the formal market, and that this effect appears to be much larger than any effect due to changing returns to sector-specific skills. This distinction adds an important developing country dimension to the job displacement literature.

Our findings in this research add one piece to the puzzle of the causes for a startling increase in inequality in Indonesia during the same decade. In 2003–2013, Indonesia's Gini coefficient for individual income inequality rose one third, from 0.32 to 0.43 (Yusuf, Sumner, and Rum 2014). This rise has many possible causes, both related to income changes and fiscal and other policies, but a formal decomposition of changes in the Gini index has yet to be conducted. However, the magnitude of the shift away from formal employment and the earnings drop experienced by workers so displaced are undoubtedly a strong contributing factor.

The phenomenon of job displacement and what appears as "jobless growth" during an economic boom may be a uniquely Indonesian paradox, but the conditions in which they become possible are broadly shared in the developing world. While displacement to informal employment is almost certainly part of the explanation, the constraint of working with a dataset that is designed for other purposes means that the task of establishing a rigorous *causal* connection remains incomplete. At an individual level, more work is needed to identify characteristics that may predict job displacement. At the labor market level, the apparent displacement of workers from formal sector jobs has several possible causes. These include secular changes in economic structure, trade-induced changes in industry-level activity and employment, and domestic policy innovations. Identifying these and distinguishing between them is an important task for future work.

References

Aswicahyono, H., H. Hill, and D. Narjoko. 2011. Indonesian Industrialization: A Latecomer Adjusting to Crises. WIDER Working Paper. No. 2011/53. Helsinki: United Nations University World Institute for Development Economics Research.

Autor, D. H., D. Dorn, G. H. Hanson, and J. Song. 2014. Trade Adjustment: Worker-Level Evidence. *Quarterly Journal of Economics.* 129 (4). pp. 1799–860.

Autor, D. H., D. Dorn, and G. H. Hanson. 2016. The China Shock: Learning from Labor Market Adjustment to Large Changes in Trade. *Annual Review of Economics.* 8 (1). pp. 205–40.

Carrington, W. J., and B. C. Fallick. 2014. Why Do Earnings Fall with Job Displacement? Federal Reserve Bank of Cleveland Working Paper 14-05.

Couch, K. A., and D. W. Placzek. 2010. Earnings Losses of Displaced Workers Revisited. *American Economic Review.* 100 (1). pp. 572–89.

Coxhead, I. 2007. A New Resource Curse? Impacts of China's Boom on Comparative Advantage and Resource Dependence in Southeast Asia. *World Development* 35 (7). pp. 1099–119.

Coxhead, I., and R. M. Shrestha. 2016. Could a Resource Export Boom Reduce Workers Earnings? The Labor Market Channel in Indonesia. *Bulletin of Indonesian Economic Studies.* 52 (2). pp. 185–208.

Dornbusch, R. 1988. Real Exchange Rates and Macroeconomics: A Selective Survey. NBER Working Paper. No. 2775. Cambridge, MA: National Bureau of Economic Research.

Garnaut, R. 2015. Indonesia's Resources Boom in International Perspective: Policy Dilemmas and Options for Continued Strong Growth. *Bulletin of Indonesian Economic Studies.* 51 (2). pp. 189–212.

Gindling, T. 2014. Self-Employment in the Developing World. *World Development.* 56 (C). pp. 313–31.

Goldberg, P. K., and N. Pavcnik. 2005. Trade, Wages, and the Political Economy of Trade Protection: Evidence from the Colombian Trade Reforms. *Journal of International Economics.* 66 (1). pp. 75–105.

——. 2007. Distributional Effects of Globalization in Developing Countries. *Journal of Economic Literature.* 45 (1). pp. 39–82.

Hanson, G. 2010. Why Isn't Mexico Rich? NBER Working Paper. No. 16470. Cambridge, MA: National Bureau of Economic Research.

Hsieh, C.-T., and B. Olken. 2014. The Missing "Missing Middle." *Journal of Economic Perspectives.* 28 (3). pp. 89–98.

Jacobson, L. S., R. J. LaLonde, and D. G. Sullivan. 1993. Earnings Losses of Displaced Workers. *American Economic Review.* 83 (4). pp. 685–709.

———. 2005. Estimating the Returns to Community College Schooling for Displaced Workers. *Journal of Econometrics*. 125 (1). pp. 271–304.

Kletzer, L. G. 1998. Job Displacement. *Journal of Economic Perspectives*. 12 (1). pp. 115–36.

Korkeamäki, O., and T. Kyyrä. 2014. A Distributional Analysis of Earnings Losses of Displaced Workers in an Economic Depression and Recovery. *Oxford Bulletin of Economics and Statistics*. 76 (4). pp. 565–88.

Manning, C. 2000. Labour Market Adjustment to Indonesia's Economic Crisis: Context, Trends and Implications. *Bulletin of Indonesian Economic Studies* 36 (1). pp. 105–36.

Manning, C., and K. Roesad. 2007. The Manpower Law of 2003 and Its Implementing Regulations: Genesis, Key Articles and Potential Impact. *Bulletin of Indonesian Economic Studies*. 43 (1). pp. 59–86.

McMillan, M., and D. Rodrik. 2011. Globalization, Structural Change, and Productivity Growth. NBER Working Paper. No. 17143. Cambridge, MA: National Bureau of Economic Research.

Minnesota Population Center. 2017. *Integrated Public Use Microdata Series, International: Version 6.5* [dataset]. Minneapolis: University of Minnesota.

Modestino, A. S., D. Shoag, and J. Balance. 2016. Downskilling: Changes in Employer Skill Requirements over the Business Cycle. John F. Kennedy School of Government, Harvard University: Faculty Research Working Paper Series RWP16-014.

Rodrik, D. 2015. Premature Deindustrialization. *Journal of Economic Growth*. 21 (1). pp. 1–33.

Rothenberg, A. D., A. Gaduh, N. E. Burger, C. Chazali, I. Tjandraningsih, R. Radikun, C. Sutera, and S. Weilant. 2016. Rethinking Indonesia's Informal Sector. *World Development*. 80 (C). pp. 96–113.

Roy, A. D. 1951. Some Thoughts on the Distribution of Earnings. *Oxford Economic Papers*. 3 (2). pp. 135–46.

Sjöholm, F. 1999. Productivity Growth in Indonesia: The Role of Regional Characteristics and Direct Foreign Investment. *Economic Development and Cultural Change*. 47 (3). pp. 559–84.

Strauss, J., K. Beegle, B. Sikoki, A. Dwiyanto, Y. Herawati, and F. Witoelar. 2004. The Third Wave of the Indonesia Family Life Survey (IFLS3): Overview and Field Report. WR-144/1-NIA/NICHD.

Strauss, J., F. Witoelar, B. Sikoki, and A. Wattie. 2009. The Fourth Wave of the Indonesian Family Life Survey (IFLS4): Overview and Field Report. WR-675/1-NIA/NICHD.

Suryahadi, A., G. Hadiwidjaja, and S. Sumarto. 2012. Economic Growth and Poverty Reduction in Indonesia before and after the Asian Financial Crisis. *Bulletin of Indonesian Economic Studies*. 48 (2). pp. 209–227.

Suryadarma, D., A. Suryahadi, and S. Sumarto. 2013. Sectoral Growth and Job Creation: Evidence from Indonesia. *Journal of International Development*. 25 (4). pp. 549–61.

World Bank. 2010. Indonesia Jobs Report: Towards Better Jobs and Security for All. World Bank Working Paper 56348. Washington, DC.

Yusuf, A. A., A. Sumner, and I. A. Rum. 2014. Twenty Years of Expenditure Inequality in Indonesia, 1993–2013. *Bulletin of Indonesian Economic Studies*. 50 (2). pp. 243–54.

Appendix A5

Table A5.1 Distribution of Workers in 2000 across Sector and Schooling by Their Presence in the 2007 Sample (%)

Sector in 2000	Unemployed	Employed	Missing	Education	Unemployed	Employed	Missing
Agriculture	9.95	68.75	21.30	Primary or less	10.10	73.17	16.73
Mining	2.70	78.38	18.92	Junior high school	10.63	64.71	24.66
Manufacturing	12.63	68.00	19.36	Senior high school	8.37	68.99	22.64
Utilities	0.00	90.00	10.00	College	5.75	61.10	33.15
Construction	4.29	76.39	19.31				
Wholesale/ retail trade	11.80	67.55	20.65				
Transport	0.99	69.31	29.70				
Financial services	2.94	55.88	41.18				
Social services	6.49	68.29	25.22				

Note: Rows sum to 100%.
Source: Authors' calculation from IFLS 2000 and 2007.

Table A5.2 Distribution of Workers in 2007 across Sector and Schooling by Their Status in the 2014 Sample (%)

Sector in 2007	Unemployed	Employed	Missing	Education	Unemployed	Employed	Missing
Agriculture	12.13	72.98	14.89	Primary or less	10.68	75.36	13.96
Mining	0.00	72.22	27.78	Junior high school	9.59	72.29	18.12
Manufacturing	11.22	70.44	18.35	Senior high school	9.21	69.25	21.54
Utilities	0.00	70.59	29.41	College	5.82	63.71	30.47
Construction	3.82	76.76	19.41				
Wholesale/ retail trade	10.60	67.44	21.97				
Transport	6.03	72.41	21.55				
Financial services	8.51	61.70	29.79				
Social services	7.03	68.86	24.11				

Source: Authors' calculation from IFLS 2007 and 2014.

PART III
Firm-level Adjustments in Asia

6

Firm Adjustment to Trade Policy Changes in East Asia

Dionisius Narjoko and Shujiro Urata

6.1 Background

Trade and investment liberalization has been one of the key features of economic policy in many developing countries since the 1990s. A new understanding of the benefits of international trade triggered unilateral tariff reductions from countries throughout the world. As a result, the global economy in the early 21st century has seen significantly reduced barriers, creating much larger trade volumes between countries. This has promoted globalization, as the increasingly borderless countries have nurtured the growth of production networks between countries. It has also made exports an engine of growth and a strategy to foster industrialization.

Economic literature on international trade closely follows globalization, and research has consistently produced more evidence on the benefits of globalization. Undertaking economic analysis of globalization has been facilitated by access to more sophisticated or detailed data (i.e., microdata at firm or plant level). In this context, the recent theoretical literature on heterogeneous firms and trade has emphasized a couple of new mechanisms through which changes in trade policy (trade liberalization) increase aggregate productivity and welfare. While this development has revolutionized our view of how an economy responds to trade and trade policy changes, our understanding is still only partial.

This chapter reviews some recent studies on the subject of firms in a globalized economy to enable us to understand more about how firms respond to globalization or changes in trade and investment liberalization. It focuses on presenting or explaining the underlying mechanisms through which the effects are realized. The studies summarized in this chapter generally confirm the positive impact of trade liberalization on productivity or the spectrum of measures reflecting productivity, such as product quality, firm size, or skill intensity. The positive impact goes through various channels, including competition and industry dynamics, exporting and innovation decisions, and production or investment decisions.

This chapter is organized by broad topics commonly adopted by studies in the literature: productivity, competition, product dynamics, technology and innovation, and product fragmentation. Table 6.1 provides a summary of key empirical findings organized by these topics. The chapter concludes with a section on policy implications.

6.2 Productivity

Voluminous amounts of research have addressed the impact of globalization on productivity. While the benefits of globalization on productivity gains across sectors are relatively clear and well-documented, little is known about the impact at the plant or firm level. There is more variation on the impact when using more disaggregated or micro-level data.

Recent theoretical developments in international trade allow us to understand more about what happens regarding productivity change within an industry when trade and investment liberalization occurs. Departing from the standard trade models, the new wave of trade models recognizes the impact of firm heterogeneity, particularly in terms of productivity, within an industry (Pavcnik 2002). These models point to the importance of firm dynamics (i.e., entry, exit, and growth of the survivors) in shaping both aggregate- and plant-level productivity change. In an environment with heterogeneous firms, trade and investment liberalization induces the entry of more capable firms, forces less-productive firms to exit, and triggers a reallocation of market share toward more productive firms. The disappearance of less-productive firms is reflected by an increase in the level of industry productivity (or "between" firms' productivity growth).

Trade and investment liberalization encourages firms to adopt new technology to ensure their survival, either in domestic or foreign markets. Firms, however, perceive such encouragement differently, as some firms choose to adopt the new technology but others do not. In other words, there is variation between firms, even within the same industry, in responding to liberalization.

A new wave of theoretical developments underlines the importance of firm, or plant, heterogeneity in shaping firms' productivity within an industry, pioneered by Melitz (2003). This developed from growing evidence that the variation of exporting firms cannot be derived from

Table 6.1 Summary of Key Findings

Productivity	Exporting	Competition
Competition, measured typically by dynamics of firms (i.e., firm entry, exit, and growth), increases productivity and improves resource reallocation (e.g., Liu 1993; Liu and Tybout 1996; Olley and Pakes 1996; Aw, Chen, and Roberts 2001; and Narjoko 2012). Aw, Chen, and Roberts (2001) found that in a newly industrialized economy in Asia, new manufacturing firms have lower average productivity than incumbents, although productivity varies significantly across the firms. They also found that the more productive entrants survive, and their productivity converges to the level of incumbents. Narjoko (2012) found a positive relationship between firm entry and industry productivity growth in Vietnamese manufacturing. Rapid trade and investment liberalization occurring in Viet Nam since the early 1990s has substantially reduced the cost of establishing private enterprises and of exporting, and it has triggered rapid growth in a number of firms entering the country's manufacturing and services sectors. There was a reallocation of resources across firms within Viet Nam's manufacturing toward the more productive firms, which has resulted in higher industry-level productivity growth.	There is robust evidence on the self-selection hypothesis to exporting in the literature. One implication of the hypothesis is the significant difference between exporters and nonexporters. Bernard, Jensen, and Lawrence (1995) and Bernard and Jensen (1999) documented that exporters in manufacturing in the United States (US) are larger, more productive, and more capital intensive; pay higher wages; and employ more skilled workers than nonexporters. Sjoholm and Takii (2003) also observed that exporting plants in Indonesian manufacturing are larger and more productive; the labor productivity of these plants was about twice as high as nonexporting plants. Another implication is that firms prepare for exporting. Bernard and Jensen (1999) found that exporters in US manufacturing are more efficient, are larger, and grow faster several years before they become exporters. For the manufacturing industry in the Republic of Korea, Aw, Chung, and Roberts (2000) found that the average productivity of continuing exporters and new entrants as exporters is significantly higher than exiting exporters and nonexporters.	Trade liberalization has a positive impact on competition. One argument is due to the mechanism of imports as a competitive discipline, whereby greater trade inhibits domestic firms to conduct anticompetitive practices. Erdem and Tybout (2003) showed that trade liberalization negatively affects the price-cost margins of firms, which was also found by Harrison (1994) and Krishna and Mitra (1998) for the case of manufacturing in Côte d'Ivoire and India, respectively. Further impacts are positive performance and stronger innovation outcome, as was found by Pavcnik (2002) for Chile and Amiti and Konings (2007) for Indonesia. Trade also positively affects innovation, since trade liberalization stimulates competition, which forces firms to become more efficient and productive through innovation. Fernandes and Paunov (2009) showed that trade liberalization stimulates product quality upgrading in Chilean manufacturing, while Bloom, Draca, and Van Reenen (2010) found a similar relationship between trade liberalization and innovation in the People's Republic of China using patent, information technology (IT), research and development (R&D), and total factor productivity (TFP) as the indicators. Aldaba (2012) found for manufacturing in the Philippines that trade liberalization increases competition in the domestic market, and this forces firms to increase their R&D.

continued on next page

Table 6.1 *continued*

Productivity	Exporting	Competition
Choi and Hahn (2013) examined the relationship between trade liberalization and productivity at firm and product level. They found that the increase in intermediate input variety via trade reduces the cost of R&D, and hence induces new product introduction and TFP improvement. At the product level within firms, they found that the increase in imported intermediate input increases the extent of product switching within firms, defined as simultaneous product adding and dropping. The finding suggests the existence of a "creative destruction" process within firms, which implies a better reallocation of resources.	The alternative hypothesis, i.e., learning by exporting, is growing in terms of evidence collected by cases around the world. For economies in East Asia, for example, a Japanese case study (Ito 2011) showed that first-time exporters increased their R&D expenditure immediately after they exported, although the increase varies by export market destinations. A study in the Republic of Korea (Hahn and Park 2011) showed that exporting promotes the creation of new products, while an Australian study (Palangkaraya 2011) showed that exporters in the services sector increase their process innovation activities.	

Product Dynamics	Technological Change and Innovation	International Production Networks
The heterogeneous firm theory has become more advanced by adopting models with multiproduct firms. It produces predictions on the optimal solution concerning dynamics of product portfolio within a firm. Theories have been developed to predict the impact of trade liberalization on product scope of a firm (e.g., Feenstra and Ma 2008; Eckel and Neary 2010; and Bernard, Redding, and Schott 2011).	International trade or foreign direct investment (FDI) plays a role in promoting R&D to generate innovation. Engagement in exporting stimulates R&D activities of exporters and increases exporters' productivity, within the learning-by-exporting hypothesis. Ito (2011) found that the decision to export by new Japanese exporters increases their R&D spending. Hahn and Park (2011) found evidence to support the role of innovation in the learning-by-exporting hypothesis—that is, a statistically significant positive impact of exporting on product creation. Product creation here is defined to involve strong innovation activities.	International production networks (IPNs) began to be developed as multinational enterprises (MNEs) adopted a fragmentation strategy, under which they break up an entire production system into various processes or production blocs, which are then relocated to different countries where a particular process can be undertaken most efficiently. IPNs have been formed by connecting or linking the production blocs located in different countries.

continued on next page

Table 6.1 *continued*

Product Dynamics	Technological Change and Innovation	International Production Networks
All these predict that trade liberalization reduces product scope, which was evident in Baldwin and Gu (2009); Bernard, Redding, and Schott (2011); and Mayer, Melitz, and Ottaviano (2014). These studies suggest that dropping products is the most immediate (and easy) response to fiercer competition resulting from trade liberalization. The evidence is, however, not yet robust. Qiu and Zhou (2013) found increased product scope as an impact of trade liberalization in manufacturing in the People's Republic of China. Hahn, Ito, and Narjoko (2016) in a comparative study of three countries (Japan, the Republic of Korea, and Indonesia) found that firm product scope increases, rather than decreases, with export participation. Trade liberalization improves product quality. Hayakawa, Matsuura, and Takii (2015), using a case study of Indonesian manufacturing, found that reduction in input tariffs generally boosts quality upgrading, whereas the decrease in output tariffs does not have a significant impact. This is consistent with the view that imported inputs are high in quality.	As for FDI, firm-specific advantages of MNES—in the form of knowledge-based assets, managerial know-how, quality of the workforce, and marketing and branding—are expected to promote R&D activity in the host countries and hence, generate innovation. Kohpaiboon and Jongwanich (2013) found that foreign investment encourages firms to commit investment in R&D. They found that the investment tends to be imported—embodied in imported capital goods—rather than invested in R&D in host countries. Regardless, a positive impact is still observed, including evidence that the presence of MNEs stimulates locally owned firms to conduct R&D activities. Kuncoro (2011), meanwhile, found that foreign ownership of firms in Indonesian manufacturing determines the R&D decisions of the firms but not the scale of the R&D investment.	Critical to IPNs is liberalization of trade and FDI, and evidence of this is strong in cases of Southeast Asian countries. Kohpaiboon and Jongwanich (2013) found that firms participating in IPNs are more active in R&D activities than those not participating. Aldaba (2017) showed that the expansion of the global value chain index in electronic industries in the Philippines is closely related to the opening of intermediate-input sectors of the industries, as well as privatization and fiscal incentives provided for MNEs invested in economic zones, a key element of FDI liberalization. IPNs change the production structure in the medium and longer term, especially because they increase the demand for skilled workers in participating developing countries, due to greater use of more technology-intensive imported input and of more advanced technology embodied in imported capital goods such as machineries. Kohpaiboon and Jongwanich (2013) showed that engagement in IPNs increases the demand for skilled workers, albeit only in firms that are already skill intensive. Thangavelu (2013) found that firms in Viet Nam participating in IPNs restructure their production methods by installing machines with more advanced technology, suggesting a higher demand for skilled workers for these firms.

Source: Authors' compilation.

a random sample, since not all firms within an industry export. Eaton, Kortum, and Kramarz (2004), for example, highlight this for French manufacturing, while Helpman, Melitz, and Yeaple (2004) did so for the data on manufacturing in the United States (US).

Melitz built a theoretical model that takes into account the importance of productivity differences across firms in an imperfect competition setting. As explained and summarized by Helpman (2006), Melitz's model predicts that firm dynamics created by trade liberalization reduce the productivity threshold for any firm to export, implying that any firm now has a higher probability of exporting compared with the situation before the liberalization. At the same time, however, trade liberalization increases the productivity threshold for the survival selection of any operating firm. This means that only more productive firms survive after the trade liberalization. Industry output is hence reallocated to these survivors. What we should ideally observe then is a situation where the overall industry productivity improves.

The Melitz model has been extended by including technology adoption and innovation to reflect technology upgrading by firms. Some of these models are Bustos (2011), Yeaple (2005), and Ekholm and Midelfart (2005). The Bustos model overall predicts that only a fraction of firms—that is, firms with an intermediate level of productivity—respond to trade liberalization by upgrading their technology (Helpman 2006). This comes as a result of both the coexistence of firms within the industry with different levels of productivity and the existence of different types of technology adopted by firms in the industry. Less-productive firms, meanwhile, continue to use traditional technology.

It is important to mention the existence of a closely related strand of literature that examines the relationship between firm dynamics and economic performance. Certain theoretical works, in particular Jovanovic (1982) and Hopenhayn (1992), model the interrelationship between entry–exit and firm heterogeneity in terms of productivity. These models detail how competitive struggle, reflected by firm dynamics (i.e., entry, exit, and growth), affect productivity growth. Empirical studies on this issue include Olley and Pakes (1996), Liu (1993), Liu and Tybout (1996), and Aw, Chen, and Roberts (2001). Aw and her coauthors, for example, found that new manufacturing firms in a newly industrialized economy in Asia have lower average productivity than incumbents, although productivity varies significantly across the firms. They also found that the more productive entrants survive, and their productivity converges to the level of incumbents (Aw, Chen, and Roberts 2001).

More recent studies from research projects run by the Economic Research Institute for ASEAN and East Asia (ERIA) provide more evidence on the positive impact of globalization on productivity and, more importantly, provide more knowledge on the underlying mechanisms creating the impact.

Taking the heterogeneous firm theory as the basis, Narjoko (2012) examined whether trade and investment liberalization in Viet Nam improved industry productivity by improving resource allocation across firms within industries. This study is motivated by the observation that Viet Nam underwent rapid trade and investment liberalization during the 1990s and experienced a massive firm entry in the 2000s. The study asked whether trade and investment liberalization contribute to the entry of firms, whether more firm entry is associated with greater industry productivity growth, and whether the productivity level before trade reforms matters for the extent of the productivity growth.

The study establishes a positive relationship between firm entry and industry productivity growth in Viet Nam's manufacturing. The rapid trade and investment liberalization occurring in Viet Nam since the early 1990s, which has substantially reduced the cost of establishing private enterprises and of exporting, seems to have triggered rapid growth in the number of firms entering the country's manufacturing and services sectors. This finding suggests a reallocation of resources across firms within Viet Nam's manufacturing toward the more productive firms, which has resulted in higher industry-level productivity growth.

Narjoko further examined the within-sector impact of firm entry. Plotting the change in the distribution of productivity growth over time, there is evidence that many firms have become more productive. The productivity improvements, however, vary across firms. The study shows that the entry of firms lowered the productivity of firms located at the bottom of the distribution but increased the productivity of firms located at the center of the distribution. It suggests that the increase in productivity, as a result of the high entry rate, only applies to the firms that have already acquired some intermediate level of productivity before trade reform.

Hahn and Choi (2013) examined the effect of trade liberalization on plant total factor productivity (TFP) growth and within-plant across-product reallocation behavior in manufacturing in the Republic of Korea during 1991–1998. They took the variety-based endogenous growth models, which suggest that the increase in intermediate input variety via trade reduces the cost of research and development (R&D), and hence induces new product introduction and TFP improvement. They examined whether the increase in imported intermediate input variety increased plant TFP growth and the extent to which products are switched (simultaneously added or dropped).

Hahn and Choi showed some evidence that tariff liberalization in the Republic of Korea contributed to the growth of input variety during the period studied. They found that plants belonging to industries with higher variety growth in imported intermediate inputs experienced higher productivity growth.

Hahn and Choi further elaborated the variety–productivity relationships by testing the relationship between the imported intermediate variety and product switching. Product switching, defined as simultaneously adding and dropping products, can be understood as part of a continuous process of "creative destruction" within plants. Active product-switching behavior can enhance the resource allocation process within firms and thereby improve their production efficiency. The empirical results support the hypothesis, suggesting that the increase in imported intermediate variety has a positive impact on stimulating product switching by domestic plants.

6.3 Exporting

One of the most immediate implications of the Melitz (2003) approach, commonly known as heterogeneous firm theory, is that it is easier for firms to engage in the international market after trade liberalization. Existing exporters can expand their export sales, and some firms start to export for the first time.

Consistent with this prediction is the self-selection hypothesis, which existed before Melitz's heterogeneous firm theory. This is based on the presumption that participating in export markets brings additional costs, which usually involve high fixed costs. These include transport costs and expenses related to establishing distributional channels and production costs in adapting products for foreign tastes (Bernard and Jensen 1999). Trade liberalization in export-destination countries reduces the total costs of firms exporting to these countries, in addition to providing more access markets. This is reflected in Melitz's framework by a reduced threshold for firms to export.

Both Melitz's framework and self-selection theory imply that exporters and nonexporters are different. Studies support this, and exporters are considered better performers. For developed countries, Bernard, Jensen, and Lawrence (1995) and Bernard and Jensen (1999) documented that exporters in US manufacturing are larger, more productive, and more capital-intensive; pay higher wages; and employ more skilled workers than nonexporters. Aw and Hwang (1995) and Berry (1992) observed a similar finding for developing countries. Sjoholm and Takii (2003) also observed that exporting plants are larger and more productive; the labor productivity of these plants was about twice as high as nonexporting plants, and this difference seemed to increase during the 1990s.

The essence of self-selection means that firms prepare for exporting. Supporting evidence for this hypothesis exists (e.g., Bernard and Jensen 1999; Clerides, Lach, and Tybout 1998; Aw, Chung, and Roberts 2000; Hallward-Driemeier, Iarossi, and Sokoloff 2002). Bernard and Jensen found that exporters in US manufacturing are more efficient and larger, and they grow faster several years before they become exporters. For the manufacturing industry in the Republic of Korea, Aw, Chung, and Roberts (2000) found that the average productivity of continuing exporters and new entrants as exporters is significantly higher than exiting exporters and nonexporters.

Melitz's heterogeneous firm theory more recently introduced a self-selection mechanism and analyzed the effects of liberalized trade (e.g., Melitz 2003; Bernard et al. 2007). In these models, trade liberalization raises aggregate productivity by inducing resource reallocation across firms—that is, the contraction and exit of low-productivity firms as well as the expansion and entry into export markets of high-productivity firms—even if there is no change in firm-level productivity.

The self-selection hypothesis focuses on action *before* exporting. The difference in performance between exporters and nonexporters can also be explained by actions *after* exporting. Participating in export markets creates a learning effect for firms, as exporters gain access to technical expertise, including product design and method, from their foreign buyers (Aw, Chung, and Roberts 2000). The learning process accumulates knowledge acquired by firms and increases the productivity of exporters over time, widening the performance gap between exporters and nonexporters. This is often termed the learning-by-exporting hypothesis.

The more recent ERIA project provides evidence supporting the learning-by-exporting hypothesis in terms of a firm's innovation responses after engaging in exporting. A Japanese case study (Ito 2011) showed that first-time exporters increased their R&D expenditure immediately after they exported, although the increase varies by export market destinations. A study of the Republic of Korea (Hahn and Park 2011) showed that exporting promotes the creation of new products, while an Australian study (Palangkaraya 2011) showed that exporters in the services sector increase their process innovation activities. All these studies show that the innovation response improves performance of the exporters.

6.4 Competition

Globalization increases competition in the domestic market and triggers dynamism in the survival and creation of new firms. Innovation links competition and firm dynamics.

Competition and innovation have a mixed relationship. The most recent theoretical framework suggests an inverted U-shaped relationship between competition and innovation (Aghion et al. 2002). The framework correlates firms' market power with their level of innovation. In this framework, firms facing intense competition will innovate more, as innovation serves as a method to escape from the fierce competition. In contrast, on the other end of the spectrum, firms facing weak competition do not have the incentive to innovate because firms with market power do not need to win in competing with other firms in the market. Evolution in the competitive struggle that moves between these two extremes creates the inverted U-shaped relationship. Innovation goes up when the market is very competitive, but greater innovation generates market power for some firms; this reduces the incentive to innovate, resulting in less innovation.

This theoretical framework has been reinforced by empirical evidence from Aghion et al. (2002) and Aghion and Burgess (2003). However, several studies find that the inverted U-curve relation is not generally applied in several countries. Creusen et al. (2006) did not find an inverted U-curve relation, although the relation between competition and innovation was found to be positive. Hopman and Rojas-Romagosa (2010) found a negative relationship between competition and innovation, as well as insufficient evidence on the inverted U-curve relation.

Meanwhile, an extensive amount of studies have found strong evidence regarding the positive effect of trade on competition. The most prevalent argument on this relationship is that trade fosters competition and constrains domestic firms in conducting anticompetitive activities (Cadot, Grether, and de Melo 2000). This is known as the "imports as competitive discipline" hypothesis, which has found robust empirical evidence. For instance, Erdem and Tybout (2003) have shown that trade liberalization negatively affects the price-cost margins of firms. This was reinforced by Harrison (1994), who found the same evidence in the Côte d'Ivoire, and Krishna and Mitra (1998) in India. Trade liberalization is also found to increase productivity, as exhibited by several empirical studies, such as Pavcnik (2002) for Chile and Amiti and Konings (2007) for Indonesia. Trade also positively affects innovation since trade liberalization stimulates competition, which forces firms to become more efficient and productive through innovation. Earlier work by Aghion and Burgess (2003) showed the positive effect of reduced trade barriers on the economic performance of firms close to the technological frontier. Fernandes and Paunov (2009) presented evidence that trade liberalization stimulates product quality upgrading using Chilean manufacturing data, while Bloom, Draca, and Van Reenen (2010) found a similar relationship between trade liberalization and innovation in the People's Republic of China using patents, information technology (IT), R&D, and TFP as the indicators.

Recently, more evidence was gathered for the Association of Southeast Asian Nations (ASEAN) and East Asian economies from ERIA's microdata research projects on the impact of globalization. Aldaba (2012), among others, examined the impact of competition on innovation for manufacturing firms in the Philippines, using firm-level panel data over 1996–2006. She examined the impact of trade barrier removal on innovation activities and questioned whether an increase in competition increased the innovation activities.

Aldaba found that trade reforms (i.e., reductions in tariff and/or nontariff barriers), conducted several times in the Philippines from the 1990s to the 2000s, have had a strong impact on the country's manufacturing sector by increasing competition in domestic markets. The tariffs are found to be positively related to the price-cost margin. This is the finding from the first step of Aldaba's econometric estimation. The second step of the estimation revealed that profitability is negatively related to R&D expenditure. In other words, higher competition stimulates R&D. Thus, overall, trade liberalization positively affects R&D through the product market competition channel. All these findings are generally the same even after she controls for firm entry and exit, which are proxies for the industry selection impact arising from competition. Further, from the results of her estimation in the "mixed" sector (i.e., a broad sector group that consists of mostly exporting and importing industries), she found that the net-entry variable is negatively related to profitability. Together with a negative relationship between profitability and R&D expenditure, this indicates that as more firms exit (presumably the inefficient ones), the surviving firms tend to engage in R&D to outcompete the new firms entering the market.

Another example is the study by Nguyen et al. (2011), which examined the determinants of innovation by Viet Nam's small and medium-sized enterprises (SMEs) in the context of increased competition resulting from rapid trade expansion in the 2000s. The authors used data for 2007 and 2009 from the Viet Nam SME Survey. The years of the data are chosen to capture the period when Viet Nam experienced rapid trade liberalization. Unlike the approach taken by other studies, Nguyen and his coauthors used information on pricing strategies to capture the extent of competition among firms. The use of this information was driven by the availability of information in the data.

Nguyen and his coauthors found moderately important effects of competition, both domestic and international. Specifically, matching the price of competitors has a positive impact on product innovation using the 2007 data and on product improvement using the 2009 data. As for the impact of international competition, they found that pressure from foreign firms—in terms of the price set by them—improves all kinds of innovation activities (i.e., product innovation, product modification, and process innovation) by Viet Nam's SMEs. The finding differs slightly when the study uses the 2009 data. The authors not only addressed the globalization impact through the competition channel but also tested whether linkages with foreign firms help SMEs to increase their innovation activities. They found rather convincing evidence for this, using both years of the data and examining other innovation activities.

6.5 Product Dynamics

The literature on heterogeneous firms has gone on to consider the models of multiproduct firms, motivated by an observation that trade is now dominated by firms producing (and trading) more than one product. Research for these models is also developing because of the greater availability of product-level data by firm or plant. Theory based on the multiproduct model suggests that trade liberalization changes firms' product portfolios and increases productivity.

Bernard, Redding, and Schott (2011) developed a model that interacts firm-level productivity with firm-product-specific expertise, which allows a firm to endogenously choose the range of products it exports. The general equilibrium setting of the model results in a prediction for adjustment at both industry and firm level. The adjustment at industry level is the general result of the heterogeneous firm model, which predicts that inefficient firms will exit the exporting market. Adjustment at firm level—across a product range—enables firms with greater ability (or productivity) to produce more products, extending the scope of products that the firm can produce.

Trade liberalization pushes the firm to focus on its "core competence" resulting from the change in focus of the firm on producing only higher-expertise products because of the much higher export opportunities of these products. This is reflected in the dropping of the lower-, or lowest-, expertise products from the range of products for export. Unlike the prediction of the other models, these products are still produced but sold only in domestic markets. Thus, the scope of the products of the firm increases as the firm becomes more productive over time. The decision of the firm to drop its lowest-expertise products raises the productivity of the surviving products and increases the overall firm-level productivity. The model hence predicts a monotonic relationship between productivity and product scope, as illustrated in Figure 6.1.

Figure 6.1 Theoretical Prediction of the Relationship between Productivity and Product Scope

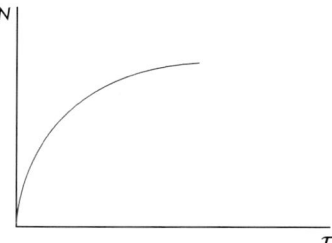

Note: N is the number of products (product scope) and τ is the level of productivity.
Source: A. W. Bernard, S. J. Redding, and P. K. Schott. 2011. Multiproduct Firms and Trade Liberalizat on. *The Quarterly Journal of Economics*. 126 (3). pp. 1271–318.

Eckel and Neary (2010) built a model that recognizes (i) the "cannibalization effect," which is defined as the impact coming from the internalization of demands within the firm across products the firm produces; and (ii) "flexible manufacturing" (reflecting flexible technology in machineries), which allows firms to produce a range of products containing the firm's core competence. Eckel and Neary's model predicts that globalization makes a firm "leaner and meaner" in its product scope, which means that its range of products is pruned to focus on its core competence.

Feenstra and Ma (2008) built a model with a similar prediction to the one built by Eckel and Neary, that is, a firm produces (at the end) only within the range of its core competence. The Feenstra and Ma model can say more about what happens in the process. That is, the lowered costs, caused by trade liberalization or a more open trade regime, expand the range of products produced by the firm. The cannibalization effect becomes unbearable for the firm when the market size grows, however, since globalization forces the firm to start dropping products. This results in a leaner product scope, as predicted by Eckel and Neary (2010).

All the theoretical mechanisms above point to a reduced product scope (i.e., product rationalization) because of trade liberalization. This is evident in the studies conducted by Baldwin and Gu (2009), Bernard, Redding, and Schott (2011), and Mayer, Melitz, and Ottaviano (2014), suggesting that dropping products is the most immediate (and easy) response to fiercer competition resulting from trade liberalization. However, robust evidence of this is not yet available. Qiu and Zhou (2013), for example, found increased product scope as an impact of trade liberalization in the People's Republic of China's manufacturing. Another study with similar results is Hahn, Ito, and Narjoko (2016).

Hahn and his coauthors examined the impact of exporting on product portfolio upgrading, using plant-and-product level data from Indonesia, Japan, and the Republic of Korea. The upgrading is defined technically by the increase in the attributes of a product of a firm (or a plant). The analysis was conducted in two steps: (i) the relationship between exporting and product scope is examined, and (ii) after measuring the attributes for products, the relationship between product dynamics (product adding or dropping) and product attributes is examined. The second step addresses whether changes in the product extensive margin (product adding or dropping) reflect the resource reallocation from products with lower product attributes to those with higher product attributes.

The results provided evidence that changes in the product composition are associated with the exporting activity. Evidence also shows that plants' total product scope increases, rather than decreases, with export participation, though the results are not statistically significant. These results are broadly in line with several recent empirical studies that find that trade liberalization causes firms to add products and expand product scope (Iacovone and Javorcik 2010; Berthou and Fontagne 2013; and Qiu and Yu 2014). With respect to product portfolio upgrading, Hahn, Ito, and Narjoko (2016) found that added products have higher or better product attributes than dropped products.

More specific on the impact on quality of the product, more recent studies point to an improvement in product quality as a result of trade liberalization, which should be able to be traced back to improved productivity.

Hayakawa, Matsuura, and Takii (2015) examined the effect of tariff reductions on firms' quality upgrading in Indonesia's apparel industry. The empirical results suggest that the reduction in input tariffs generally boosts quality upgrading, whereas the decrease in output tariffs does not have a significant impact. The results also suggest that the positive impact of input tariff reduction on quality upgrading is greater, particularly for firms importing intermediate inputs. This is consistent with the view that imported inputs are high in quality. These results show that imported products, especially imported intermediate inputs, are an important factor for productivity growth. The reduction in imported input prices due to tariff reduction encourages firms to increase imports of foreign materials, resulting in an upgrade of output quality.

The positive impact extends to nonimporters, suggesting the presence of positive technology spillovers. Local suppliers learned from the increased foreign inputs and improved the quality of the inputs they use. The improvement thus may boost quality upgrading by the nonimporters.

6.6 Technological Change and Innovation

Innovation has been widely recognized as a key factor in generating industrial development and promoting sustainable economic growth. As in many innovation-based endogenous growth models, firms' innovation activity drives productivity growth as does the introduction of new products or varieties (e.g., Romer 1990; Grossman and Helpman 1991). In an open economy setting, international trade or foreign direct investment (FDI) also play a role in promoting R&D to generate innovation.

Regarding the role of international trade, recent literature points to the engagement in exports, which would help stimulate the R&D activities of exporters and increase exporters' productivity, as a mechanism within the framework of the learning-by-exporting hypothesis. As for the role of FDI, firm-specific advantages of multinational enterprises (MNEs)—in the form of knowledge-based assets, managerial know-how, quality of the workforce, and marketing and branding—are expected to promote R&D activity in the host countries and hence generate innovation. Therefore, competition has been strong among developing countries to attract R&D-intensive FDI through fiscal incentives and high-quality infrastructure at subsidized prices (Athukorala and Kohpaiboon 2010).

6.6.1 Exporting and Innovation

More evidence on the impact of exporting (as a response to trade liberalization elsewhere) is identified for East Asian countries, such as those highlighted in studies from the microdata project of ERIA. Ito (2011) addressed the role of innovation in the context of the learning-by-exporting hypothesis. She asks whether learning by exporting has an effect on innovation and, subsequently, whether and how the impact of exporting on innovation affects productivity. Ito attempts to find answers to these questions by examining the behavior and performance of first-time exporters in Japanese manufacturing. The study, therefore, not only seeks evidence for the positive impact of learning by exporting on innovation, but also moves deeper to find insights on the source of the learning by exporting.

Ito found that first-time exporters are able to increase their sales and employment growth more than firms serving domestic markets. More importantly, the decision to begin to export promotes innovation, as first-time exporters record an increase in R&D intensity and volume. Going deeper into the mechanism of learning by exporting, the study examined whether there are differences in the performance of innovation and other variables, which arise from engaging in exporting to different destinations. The evidence showed that starting to export to North America or Europe has larger positive effects on productivity than starting to export to Asia. This difference is also observed for other performance variables (i.e., sales and employment growth), innovation variables, and some characteristics of the firms. This finding is ascribed to differences in absorptive capacity, in that first-time exporters to North America or Europe have greater absorptive capacity than those exporting for the first time to Asia.

Hahn and Park (2011) used a rich combination of plant- and product-level manufacturing data from the Republic of Korea in their investigation. Unlike the previous studies, however, they adopt a different approach in defining product innovation. They use plant-and-product matched data to distinguish two types of product innovations: those that are new to the plant (termed "product addition") and those that are new to the country's economy (termed "product creation"). The former tends to capture imitation by domestic competitors or the process of domestic knowledge diffusion, while the latter reflects product cycle phenomenon or international knowledge spillover. Product creation could mean product addition, although this does not necessarily work the other way around.

Hahn and Park found evidence to support the learning-by-exporting hypothesis for the role of innovation in the export–productivity relationship. Using propensity score matching, they found a statistically significant positive impact of exporting on product creation. They cannot, however, infer the existence of this relationship when innovation is defined by product addition; the impact of exporting on product addition is not statistically significant, although it shows the same (positive) sign. The study was not able to find evidence to support the selection hypothesis. More specifically, it could not find any significant effect of innovation (for both product creation and addition) on exporting. The investigation was extended by using the vector autoregressive (VAR) method. This route is taken to examine the dynamic interdependence between export and innovation, as well as productivity. The key results are consistent with the key finding that exporting significantly affects product creation. The finding from the VAR indicates that this impact is quite persistent; it takes more than

5 years for the impact on product creation to die out. The VAR results also show that productivity significantly and positively affects both exporting and product creation.

Palangkaraya (2011) investigated the direction of the causality between exporting and innovation using firm-level data from Australian SMEs. His investigation also looks at the direction of causality for the group of new exporters and new innovators, to ensure the robustness of the results. The sample of the study comprises not only manufacturing firms, but also enterprises in the services and other nonmanufacturing sectors. This offers distinct added value to the research, considering the lessons from the usual samples from the manufacturing sector may not be valid for the other sectors.

Palangkaraya found evidence that the relationship between exporting and innovation runs in both directions: both reflecting the self-selection and learning-by-exporting hypothesis. However, this only appears for process innovation in the services sector, not for product innovation and not in the manufacturing or other nonmanufacturing sectors. The investigation also finds that the positive two-way relationship varies across industries. Palangkaraya attributes all these results to the uniqueness of the innovation characteristics of SMEs and the importance of services in the Australian economy. Process innovation matters more than product innovation, because SMEs are usually financially constrained and product innovation is arguably substantially more expensive than process innovation.

6.6.2 Foreign Direct Investment and Innovation

FDI plays a role in promoting R&D through the knowledge and technology brought by MNEs to host countries. FDI liberalization, therefore, is expected to be positively related to the extent of innovations. The following section presents the findings of a few studies emanating from the ERIA research project on the topic.

Kohpaiboon and Jongwanich (2013) examined the roles of MNEs and exporting in determining the decision to carry out R&D, as well as the intensity of R&D activities, in firms in the Thai manufacturing sector, using the most recent (2006) industrial census data. Unlike the other studies, which measure different types of R&D in their total value terms, this study disaggregated R&D activities into three categories: (i) R&D leading to improved production technology, (ii) R&D leading to product development, and (iii) R&D leading to process innovation. The study examines not only the direct effect of MNEs on R&D activities, but also the indirect effect of MNEs on the presence and intensity of R&D in locally owned plants (termed "R&D spillovers").

Kohpaiboon and Jongwanich found that globalization, through exporting and FDI, can play a role in encouraging firms to commit to R&D investment. The role played by FDI, however, seems to be different from the role of exporting. The study found that the R&D propensity of MNE affiliates is lower than that of locally owned firms. This suggests that MNE affiliates in Thailand prefer to import technology from their parent companies rather than investing in R&D in the host country (Thailand). Nonetheless, this does not mean that no effect arises from MNE presence on firm R&D propensity and intensity. In fact, the study found that the presence of MNEs stimulates locally owned firms to conduct R&D activities.

Kuncoro (2011) examined the globalization determinants of the decision to invest in R&D and the intensity of R&D expenditure, of medium-sized and large manufacturing firms in Indonesia. The study considers export participation, foreign investment, and trade protection as the variables that represent globalization. In addition, it looked at the impact of the spatial concentration of MNEs on a firm's R&D investment decisions and expenditure. The author uses data from the mid-1990s to the mid-2000s in his empirical investigation.

The study found that being an exporter significantly affects a firm's decision to invest in R&D, as well as the extent of a firm's R&D expenditure. Foreign ownership was found to be an important determinant only for the R&D investment decision, but not for the amount of R&D expenditure the firm commits. In terms of testing the potential R&D spillover effect arising from the concentration of MNEs in a location, the study found that R&D activities tend to be higher in big urban areas, not in a specialized or agglomerated location. In the interpretation of the findings related to foreign ownership and the presence of MNEs, Kuncoro asserts that a critical mass of MNEs may be needed in a location or agglomeration area for these MNEs to have a meaningful impact in terms of innovation or R&D performance.

6.7 International Production Networks

International production networks (IPNs) began to be developed as MNEs adopted a fragmentation strategy, under which they break up an entire production system into various processes or production blocs, which are then relocated to different countries where a particular process can be undertaken most efficiently. IPNs have been formed by connecting or linking the production blocs located in different countries.

The extent or degree of fragmentation depends mostly on the cost of establishing and managing production blocs and the cost of the service link that connects production blocs. The cost of establishing and managing production blocs depends largely on the labor cost, the quality of infrastructure (including the supply of electricity, transportation, and communication services), openness to foreign firms, and others, while the cost of the service link depends on the cost of international transportation and communication services, which are affected by the international trade policies of the countries involved.

The expansion of IPNs has been aided by the liberalization of trade and FDI policies implemented by Southeast Asian economies, as the governments of these countries recognized the beneficial impacts of hosting MNEs with extensive IPNs.[1] IPNs bring not only export sales and import procurement networks, which enable host countries to import high-quality intermediate and capital goods, but also technology, which contributes to an improvement in productivity. Since rapid and extensive development of IPNs is partly due to MNEs' response to the liberalization of trade and FDI policies, we examine the impacts of IPNs on firm behavior and the development of industries in East Asia.

The importance of FDI and an open trade regime is confirmed by Kohpaiboon and Jongwanich (2013), who found that firms participating in IPNs are more active in R&D activities than those not participating. The dynamism of industries engaged in IPNs required firms populating the industries to keep the industries competitive in international markets.

Aldaba (2017) provided more evidence on the role of trade and investment liberalization for participation of firms in IPNs. The Philippine electronic industry has transformed to become deeply integrated within networks of industries in East Asia. Analyzed using the global value chain (GVC) participation index and length, Aldaba showed that the Philippines increased participation in the backward linkage of GVC over time.[2] The share of foreign inputs in Philippine electronic exports (looking backward along the value chain) increased from 8.5% in 1995 to 32.5% in 2000 and 34.4% in 2008. The trend is the same for the forward GVC participation of the sector. The share of domestically

---

[1]   IPNs involving Southeast Asian countries were triggered by the currency appreciation of industrialized East Asian economies in the 1980s. The appreciation of the yen in the latter half of the 1980s prompted a massive outflow of Japanese FDI by Japanese MNEs, which adopted the fragmentation strategy and relocated production processes from Japan to Southeast Asian economies.

[2]   The GVC participation index is defined as the share of foreign inputs (backward participation) and domestically produced inputs used in third countries' exports (forward participation), expressed as a percentage of gross exports (De Backer and Miroudot 2013).

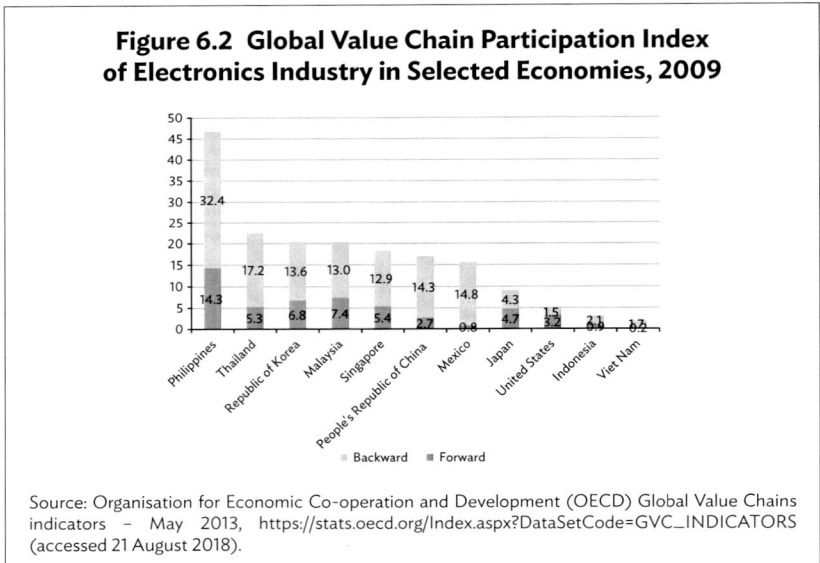

Figure 6.2 Global Value Chain Participation Index of Electronics Industry in Selected Economies, 2009

Source: Organisation for Economic Co-operation and Development (OECD) Global Value Chains indicators – May 2013, https://stats.oecd.org/Index.aspx?DataSetCode=GVC_INDICATORS (accessed 21 August 2018).

produced inputs used in third-country exports (looking forward along the value chain) increased from 2.2% in 1995 to 8.4% in 2000 and 16.2% in 2008. Reflecting this, the GVC participation of the industry in the Philippines is among the highest in the region, as indicated in the cross-country comparison of the GVC index in Figure 6.2.

Aldaba (2017) further explained that the development of the Philippine electronics industry to the level seen in the 2000s can be attributed to reforms to liberalize the investment and trade regime that took place since the 1990s. Development of the industry is argued to have been the result of both privatization of economic zone management and fiscal incentives applied exclusively for investment in economic zones, both of which have been elements of FDI liberalization since the 1990s. The Philippine Economic Zone Authority granted significant incentives for investment in the electronics industry, such as tax- and duty-free importation of capital goods and intermediate inputs, and defining the electronics industry as a preferred area of investment from 1988 to 1994 and from 2006 to 2007.

The electronics industry has benefited from trade liberalization through tariff cuts or the removal of import restrictions for the import of material inputs and finished goods. Liberalization of the import regime for material inputs contributes directly to competitiveness by reducing the price of final products produced domestically, while the liberalization of finished goods affects indirectly by improving efficiency as a result of greater competition from imports.

IPNs change the production structure in the medium and longer term. The basic proposition is that the networks increase the demand for skilled workers in participating developing countries. Feenstra and Hanson (1996, 1997) predict this to come from greater usage of imported intermediate inputs, which are typically skill-intensive inputs performed by MNEs in IPNs. They argue that while IPNs shift production blocs that are unskilled or less technology-intensive from developed countries, they are still considered skill- or technology-intensive production blocs from developing countries' perspective.

In the context of Feenstra and Hanson's "outsourcing" or "production sharing" theory, skill-biased technological change is another explanation. Skill-biased technological change argues that the new technology embodied in imported capital goods—through a more open trade regime or an increase in FDI as a result of investment liberalization—increases the demand for skilled workers (in host countries). In other words, the technical changes induced by trade and FDI liberalization have some effect (i.e., the "bias") to increase the demand for skilled workers.

Kohpaiboon and Jongwanich (2013) provided some support for the predicted higher demand for skilled workers for firms participating in IPNs. They found that engagement in IPNs increases the demand for skilled workers, but this only applies to firms that are already skill-intensive. Thangavelu (2013) found that firms in Viet Nam participating in IPNs restructure their production methods by installing machines with more advanced technology, suggesting higher demand for skilled workers for these firms.

6.8 Policy Implications

This chapter presents several key topics on the responses of firms to globalization, in responding to a more open trade or investment regime between countries. All these have policy implications, and the discussion below presents some of these.

First, most previous studies suggest that a country should continue with ongoing trade liberalization and maintain a relatively open trade regime. Strong domestic market competition drives firms to engage in innovation-enhancing activities, through the ability of the competition to create a contestable market situation. A liberalized trade regime could be even more beneficial in the framework of a deepened integration of a country in Southeast Asia or East Asia. Some studies underline this in the context of linking firms to established IPNs in these regions.

They found a positive relationship between participation in production networks and increased R&D activities by firms.

To complement trade liberalization, a reduction in trade costs (commonly done via trade facilitation reform) should be a high priority on the policy agenda for countries that have yet to join IPNs. Improving trade-related infrastructure is likely to be an important ingredient of policy. In many developing countries, transport costs remains a key bottleneck. Poor transport infrastructure raises transport costs and isolates markets. Such isolated markets may also feature minimal competition, and this will worsen within-country poverty and distribution issues.

Second, it is necessary to ensure that the forces of competition are at work in domestic markets. Some of the dynamic gains from trade are realized through reallocation across firms and industries, and even across products within firms. It is therefore necessary to focus on the elimination or reduction of existing regulations, such as entry regulations, strong employment protection, and business regulations based on firm size, which inhibit the reallocation of resources by market forces. In cases where proper institutions or markets are lacking, such as bankruptcy laws and procedures, building and improving these institutions or markets should be a top priority.

Third, policies to promote exports encourage firm innovation. Thus, policies to assist firms to export more, as well as to cause more firms to engage in exports, seem warranted. Several findings on the positive relationship between exporting and innovation activities and/or performance support this. Among others, and perhaps most importantly, is evidence of the positive effect of learning-by-exporting on exporters' innovation—for instance, exporting encourages the creation of new products as well as the expansion of export markets over time.

Fourth, policies for stronger foreign participation in industrialization should be encouraged. The justification for this comes mostly from evidence of the impact of R&D spillovers on domestically owned firms. For example the presence of MNEs encourages locally owned firms to gain technological knowledge and capability from various possible channels, such as demonstration and the competition effect. From a macro and practical perspective, encouraging a higher presence of foreign ownership or MNE units requires a policy to sustain excellent infrastructure quality, both physical and institutional. The logic is clear; MNEs would consider investing in host countries if they are able to operate efficiently, and one of the key factors is supportive infrastructure. It is also important to achieve and/or maintain a stable macroeconomic environment to attract MNEs.

It is useful to comment here that a unique characteristic of countries in East Asia and Southeast Asia is that they are very flexible and welcoming to the evolving production networks between countries orchestrated by MNEs. Very open trade and investment regimes, with the help of sizable fiscal incentives sometimes, plus the typically flexible labor market, seem to have strongly facilitated formation of IPNs within East Asia and Southeast Asia. This marks a significantly different model of industrialization to that adopted by other regions in the world, such as the one typically adopted by countries in Latin America.

Fifth, findings from the research suggest that globalization seems to benefit not only large firms but also SMEs. While this is encouraging, if one considers affirmative action policies for SMEs in the context of increased globalization in a country's economy, the more important question perhaps is how to devise policies that could harness the benefits of globalization. Conceptually, the policies should be to equip SMEs to learn more about process innovation, rather than product innovation, from using globalization forces. This approach is sensible given the natural disadvantages of SMEs, vis-à-vis their larger counterparts, in terms of financial resources and economies of scale. Further, given the usual assistance-type policy for SMEs, export promotion policies for SMEs in general would be most effective if they were integrated with policies to promote SMEs' innovation activities, which in this case should focus more on process innovation activities.

References

Aghion, P., N. Bloom, R. Blundell, R. Griffith, and P. Howitt. 2002. Competition and Innovation: An Inverted U Relationship. NBER Working Paper Series No. 9269. Cambridge, MA: National Bureau of Economic Research.

Aghion, P., and R. Burgess. 2003. Liberalization and Industrial Performance: Evidence from India and the UK. In E. Zedillo, ed. *The Future of Globalization: Explorations in Light of Recent Turbulence.* London: Routledge. pp. 557–92.

Aldaba, R. M. 2012. Trade Reforms, Competition, and Innovation in the Philippines. ERIA Discussion Paper Series No. 5. Jakarta: Economic Research Institute for ASEAN and East Asia.

———. 2017. The Philippines in the Electronics Global Value Chain: Upgrading Opportunities and Challenges. In L. Y. Ing and F. Kimura, eds. *Production Networks in Southeast Asia (Routledge-ERIA Studies in Development Economics).* London: Routledge. pp. 161–84.

Amiti, M., and J. Konings. 2007. Trade Liberalization, Intermediate Inputs, and Productivity: Evidence from Indonesia. *American Economic Review.* 77 (5). pp. 1611–38.

Athukorala, P., and A. Kohpaiboon. 2010. Globalization of R&D by US-based Multinational Enterprises. *Research Policy.* 39 (10). pp. 1335–47.

Aw, B. Y., X. Chen, and M. J. Roberts. 2001. *Journal of Development Economics.* 66 (1). pp. 51–86.

Aw, B. Y., S. C. Chung, and M. J. Roberts. 2000. *The World Bank Economic Review.* 14 (1). pp. 65–90.

Aw, B. Y., and A. R. Hwang. 1995. Productivity and Export Market: A Firm-Level Analysis. *Journal of Development Economics.* 47 (2). pp. 313–32.

Baldwin, J., and W. Gu. 2009. The Impact of Trade on Plant Scale, Production-Run Length, and Diversification. In T. Dunne, J.B. Jensen, and M. Roberts, eds. *Producer Dynamics: New Evidence from Micro Data.* Chicago: University of Chicago Press. pp. 557–92.

Bernard, A. B., and J. B. Jensen. 1999. Exceptional Exporter Performance: Cause, Effect, or Both? *Journal of International Economics.* 47 (1). pp. 1–25.

Bernard, A. B., J. B. Jensen, and R. Z. Lawrence. 1995. Exporters, Jobs, and Wages in U.S. Manufacturing: 1976–1987. *Brookings Papers on Economic Activity, Microeconomics.* pp. 67–119.

Bernard, A. W., J. B. Jensen, S. J. Redding, and P. K. Schott. 2007. Firms in International Trade. *Journal of Economic Perspective.* 21 (3). pp. 105–30.

Bernard, A. W., S. J. Redding, and P. K. Schott. 2011. Multiproduct Firms and Trade Liberalization. *The Quarterly Journal of Economics.* 126 (3). pp. 1271–318.

Berry, R. A. 1992. Firm (or Plant) Size in the Analysis of Trade and Development. In G. K. Helleiner, ed. *Trade Policy, Industrialization, and Development: New Perspectives.* Oxford: Clarendon Press. pp. 46–88.

Berthou, A., and L. Fontagne. 2013. How Do Multiproduct Exporters React to a Change in Trade Costs? *Scandinavian Journal of Economics.* 115 (2). pp. 326–53.

Bloom, N., M. Draca, and J. Van Reenen. 2010. Trade Induced Technical Change? The Impact of Chinese Imports on Innovation, IT and Productivity. NBER Working Paper Series. No. 16717. Cambridge, MA: National Bureau of Economic Research.

Bustos, P. 2011. Trade Liberalization, Exports, and Technology Upgrading: Evidence on the Impact of MERCOSUR on Argentinean Firms. *American Economic Review.* 101 (1). pp. 304–40.

Cadot, O., J-M. Grether, and J. de Melo. 2000. Trade and Competition Policy: Where Do We Stand? *Journal of World Trade.* 34 (3). pp. 1–20.

Choi, Y.-S., and C. H. Hahn. 2013. Effects of Imported Intermediate Varieties on Plant Total Factor Productivity and Product Switching: Evidence from Korean Manufacturing. *Asian Economic Journal.* 27 (2). pp. 125–43.

Clerides, S., S. Lach, and J. R. Tybout. 1998. Is "Learning-by-Exporting" Important?: Micro-Dynamic Evidence from Colombia, Mexico and Morocco. *Quarterly Journal of Economics.* 113 (3). pp. 903–47.

Creusen, H., B. Vroomen, H. van der Wiel, and F. Kuypers. 2006. Dutch Retail Trade on the Rise? Relation Between Competition, Innovation and Productivity. CPB Document. No. 137. The Hague: CPB Netherlands Bureau for Economic Policy Analysis.

De Backer, K., and S. Miroudot. 2013. Mapping Global Value Chains. OECD Trade Policy Paper. No. 159. Paris: OECD Publishing.

Eaton, J., S. Kortum, and F. Kramarz. 2004. Dissecting Trade: Firms, Industries, and Export Destinations. *American Economic Review.* 94 (2). pp. 150–54.

Eckel, C., and J. P. Neary. 2010. Multiproduct Firms and Flexible Manufacturing. *Review of Economic Studies.* 77 (1). pp. 188–217.

Ekholm, K., and K. Midelfart. 2005. Relative Wages and Trade-induced Change in Technology. *European Economic Review.* 49. pp. 1637–63.

Erdem, E., and J. Tybout. 2003. Trade Induced Technical Change? The Impact of Chinese Imports on Innovation, IT and Productivity. NBER Working Paper Series. No. 16717. Cambridge, MA: National Bureau of Economic Research.

Feenstra, R., and H. Ma. 2008. Optimal Choice of Product Scope for Multiproduct Firms under Monopolistic Competition. In H. Helpman, D. Marin, and T. Verdier, eds. *The Organization of Firms in a Global Economy.* Cambridge, MA: Harvard University Press. pp. 173–99.

Feenstra, C. and G. Hanson. 1996. Globalization, Outsourcing, and Wage Inequality. NBER Working Paper Series. No. 5424, Cambridge, MA: National Bureau of Economic Research.

———. 1997. Foreign Direct Investment and Relative Wages: Evidence from Mexico's Maquiladoras. *Journal of International Economics.* 42 (3-4). pp. 371–93.

Fernandes, A., and C. Paunov. 2009. Does Tougher Import Competition Foster Product Quality Upgrading? Policy Research Working Paper. No. 4894. Washington, DC: World Bank.

Grossman, G., and E. Helpman. 1991. Trade, Knowledge Spillovers, and Growth. *European Economic Review.* 35 (2–3). pp. 517–26.

Hahn, C. H., and Y-S. Choi. 2013. Trade Liberalization and the Wage Skill Premium in Korean Manufacturing Plants: Do Plants' R&D and Investment Matter? In C. H. Hahn and D. A. Narjoko, eds. *Impact of Globalization on Labor Market.* ERIA Research Project Report 2012, No. 4. Jakarta: Economic Research Institute for ASEAN and East Asia. pp. 15–37.

Hahn, C. H., K. Ito, and D. Narjoko. 2016. Exporting and Upgrading of Product Portfolio: Evidence from Korea, Japan, and Indonesia. *Asian Economic Journal.* 30 (4). pp. 349–73.

Hahn, C. H., and C.-G. Park. 2011. Direction of Causality in Innovation-Exporting Linkage: Evidence on Korean 79 Manufacturing. In C.H. Hahn and D. Narjoko, eds. *Globalization and Innovation in East Asia.* ERIA Research Project Report 2010, No. 4. Jakarta: Economic Research Institute for ASEAN and East Asia. pp. 79–115.

Hallward-Driemeier, M., G. Iarossi, and K.L. Sokoloff. 2002. Exports and Manufacturing Productivity in East Asia: A Comparative Analysis with Firm-level Data. NBER Working Paper Series. No. 8894. Cambridge, MA: National Bureau of Economic Research.

Harrison, A. 1994. Productivity, Imperfect Competition and Trade Reform: Theory and Evidence. *Journal of International Economics.* 36 (1-2). pp. 53–73.

Hayakawa, K., T. Matsuura, and S. Takii. 2015. Does Trade Liberalization Boost Quality Upgrading? Evidence from Indonesian Plant-Product-Level Data. In C.H. Hahn, and D. Narjoko, eds. *Trade Policy Changes and Firm Adjustment: A Search for the Underlying Mechanisms.* ERIA Research Project Report 2014, Jakarta: Economic Research Institute for ASEAN and East Asia.

Helpman, E. 2006. Trade, FDI, and the Organization. *Journal of Economic Literature.* 44. pp. 589–630.

Helpman, E., M. Melitz, and S. Yeaple. 2004. Export versus FDI with Heterogeneous Firms. *American Economic Review.* 94 (1). pp. 300–16.

Hopenhayn, H. A. 1992. Entry, Exit, and Firm Dynamics in Long Run Equilibrium. *Econometrica.* 60 (5). pp. 1127–50.

Hopman, C., and H. Rojas-Romagosa. 2010. The Relation Between Competition and Innovation: Empirical Results and Implementation into Worldscan. CPB Memorandum. The Hague: CPB Netherlands Bureau for Economic Policy Analysis.

Iacovone, L., and B. S. Javorcik. 2010. Multi-product Exporters: Product Churning, Uncertainty and Export Discoveries. *The Economic Journal.* 120 (544). pp. 481–99.

Ito, K. 2011. Sources of Learning-by-Exporting Effects: Does Exporting Promote Innovation?" In C. H. Hahn, and D. Narjoko, eds. *Globalization and Innovation in East Asia.* ERIA Research Project Report 2010, No. 4. Jakarta: Economic Research Institute for ASEAN and East Asia. pp. 20–67.

Jovanovic, B. 1982. Selection and the Evolution of Industry. *Econometrica.* 50 (3). pp. 649–670.

Kohpaiboon, A., and J. Jongwanich. 2013. Global Production Sharing and Wage Premium: Evidence from Thai Manufacturing. In C.H. Hahn and D. Narjoko, eds. *Impact of Globalization on Labor Market.* ERIA Research Project Report 2012, No. 4. Jakarta: Economic Research Institute for ASEAN and East Asia. pp. 135–64.

Krishna, P., and D. Mitra. 1998. Trade Liberalization, Market Discipline and Productivity Growth: New Evidence from India. *Journal of Development Economics.* 56 (2). pp. 447–62.

Kuncoro, A. 2011. Globalization and Innovation in Indonesia: Evidence from Micro-Data on Medium and Large Manufacturing Establishments. In C. H. Hahn and D. Narjoko, eds. *Globalization and Innovation in East Asia.* ERIA Research Project Report 2010, No. 4. Jakarta: Economic Research Institute for ASEAN and East Asia. pp. 193–224.

Liu, L. 1993. Entry-Exit, Learning, and Productivity Change: Evidence from Chile. *Journal of Development Economics.* 42 (2). pp. 217–42.

Liu, L., and J. R. Tybout. 1996. Productivity Growth in Chile and Colombia: The Role of Entry, Exit, and Learning. In M. J. Roberts and J. R. Tybout, eds. *Industrial Evolution in Developing Countries: Micro Patterns of Turnover, Productivity, and Market Structure.* New York: Oxford University Press. pp. 73–103.

Mayer, T., M. Melitz, and G. Ottaviano. 2014. Market Size, Competition, and the Product Mix of Exporters. *American Economic Review.* 104 (2). pp. 495–536.

Melitz, M. J. 2003. The Impact of Trade on Intra-Industry Reallocations and Aggregate Productivity. *Econometrica.* 71 (6). pp. 1695–725.

Narjoko, D. 2012. Policy Reforms, Firm Entry, and Labor Productivity Change: Learning from Vietnamese Manufacturing. In S. Urata,

C. H. Hahn, and D. Narjoko, eds. *Economic Consequences of Globalization: Evidence from East Asia*. Routledge–ERIA Studies in Development Economics. London: Routledge. pp. 103–26.

Nguyen, N. A., P. M. Nguyen, D. N. Nguyen, and D. C. Nguyen. 2011. Trade Liberalization and Innovation Linkages Micro-evidence from Vietnam SME Surveys. In C. H. Hahn and D. Narjoko, eds. *Globalization and Innovation in East Asia*. ERIA Research Project Report 2010, No. 4. Jakarta: Economic Research Institute for ASEAN and East Asia. pp. 315–40.

Olley, G. S., and A. Pakes. 1996. The Dynamics of Productivity in the Telecommunications Equipment Industry. *Econometrica*. 64 (6). pp. 1163–97.

Palangkaraya, A. 2011. The Link between Innovation and Export: Evidence from Australia's Small and Medium Enterprises. In C. H. Hahn and D. Narjoko, eds. *Globalization and Innovation in East Asia*. ERIA Research Project Report 2010, No. 4. Jakarta: Economic Research Institute for ASEAN and East Asia. pp. 103–40.

Pavcnik, N. 2002. Trade Liberalization, Exit, and Productivity Improvement: Evidence from Chilean Plants. *Review of Economic Studies*. 69 (1). pp. 245–76.

Qiu, L. and M. Yu. 2014. Multiproduct Firms, Export Product Scope, and Trade Liberalization: The Role of Managerial Efficiency. ERIA Discussion Paper Series. DP-2014-06. Jakarta: Economic Research Institute for ASEAN and East Asia.

Qiu, L., and W. Zhou. 2013. Multiproduct Firms and Scope Adjustment in Globalization. *Journal of International Economics*. 91 (1). pp. 142–53.

Romer, P. 1990. Endogenous Technological Change. *Journal of Political Economy*, 98 (5). pp. S71–102.

Sjoholm, F., and S. Takii. 2003. Foreign Networks and Exports: Results from Indonesian Panel Data. ICSEAD Working Paper Series. Vol. 2003–33. Kitakyushu, Japan: International Center for the Study of East Asian Development.

Thangavelu, S. 2013. Trade, Technology, Foreign Firms and Wage Gap: Case of Vietnam Manufacturing Firms. In C. H. Hahn and D. Narjoko, eds. *Impact of Globalization on Labor Market*. ERIA Research Project Report 2012, No. 4. Jakarta: Economic Research Institute for ASEAN and East Asia. pp. 107–33.

Yeaple, S. 2005. A Simple Model of Firm Heterogenity, International Trade, and Wages. *Journal of International Economics*. 65 (1). pp. 1–20.

7

The Rise of the People's Republic of China and Its Competition Effects on Innovation in Japan[1]

Nobuaki Yamashita and Isamu Yamauchi

7.1 Introduction

As a reaction to import competition from low-wage economies, firms in developed economies would respond by upgrading their innovative activities, leading to so-called defensive skill-biased innovation. In this chapter, we examine this "defensive innovation" hypothesis, which was first discussed in Wood (1994) and subsequently formalized in Thoenig and Verdier (2003). In a broader context, the effect of competition on the rate of innovation has been one of the most studied areas in the literature (e.g., Aghion et al. 2005). In the study most relevant to our work, Bloom, Draca, and Van Reenen (2016) found that a large sample of European firms increased a wide range of their innovative activities (patenting, research and development [R&D] expenditures, computer use, and total factor productivity growth), driven by intensified competition from the People's Republic of China. This innovation was conducted within-firm.[2]

---

[1] This study is conducted as a part of the Mobility of Knowledge and Innovation Performance project undertaken at the Research Institute of Economy, Trade and Industry (RIETI). This study utilizes the microdata of the questionnaire information based on the Basic Survey of Japanese Business Structure and Activities, which is conducted by Japan's Ministry of Economy, Trade and Industry, and the Kikatsu Oyako converter, which is provided by RIETI.

[2] Amiti and Khandelwal (2013) find that increased import competition (measured by a decline in tariffs) spurs an economy's export quality (measured by market share) in the market in the United States (US).

Building on the foundation set by the previously mentioned studies, this chapter examines the causal effect of intensified import competition from the People's Republic of China on the innovative activities of a panel of Japanese firms for the period 1994–2005. We focus on patent usage data as an indicator of innovative outputs. Unlike other studies using patent statistics, this study adds to the literature by exploring strategic patent usage as a response to import competition from a low-wage economy (People's Republic of China). While it is generally acknowledged that patent statistics are meaningful proxies for firm-level innovation, firm-level patenting serves as more than just an indicator of knowledge capital output (Nagaoka, Motohashi, and Goto 2010). Well-known inventor surveys[3] have revealed that many of the patents are not used to introduce new products into the market; instead, they are used as effective strategic instruments to "block" other competitors from innovating or imitating. Boldrin and Levine (2013) present a case involving Microsoft, a market incumbent with a stockpile of patents blocking Google in the smartphone market.

Studying innovative firms' responses to import competition from the People's Republic of China provides an interesting and excellent testing ground for the following reasons: First, over the past decades, the People's Republic of China has emerged as a pivotal assembly-export economy of high-tech products (mainly, electronics), importing parts and components from other developed economies and exporting final products (including the famous iPhone). Accordingly, the country's export bundle has dramatically changed from labor-intensive goods to high-tech products, exerting considerable competitive pressures on firms in developed economies. Second, many of their exports compete at lower cost margins than most high-tech products. For instance, a study by Schott (2008) found that the People's Republic of China's export similarity index has become closer to that of Organisation for Economic Co-operation and Development (OECD) economies, but the unit prices of the People's Republic of China's exports have been consistently lower than those of OECD economies.

The finding suggests that the People's Republic of China's import competition leads Japanese firms to expand their innovative activities, as found by Bloom, Draca, and Van Reenen (2016). The expansion is partly driven by an increase in firms' numbers of unused patents, which reflect the strategic use of intellectual property protection.

---

[3]   For example, the survey jointly conducted by the Research Institute of Economy, Trade and Industry (RIETI) in Japan and Georgia Tech of investors in the US.

7.2 The Rise of the People's Republic of China in World Trade

Figure 7.1 depicts the rise of the People's Republic of China in world exports for 1990–2011. In 1990, the People's Republic of China's exports accounted for a tiny share (around 3%) of world exports. Since then, the country's share has gradually increased. In particular, its export growth has risen since the early 2000s. In the second half of the 2000s, the country achieved formidable export expansion by overtaking Germany's position as the world's largest exporter, accounting for more than 10% of world exports. The People's Republic of China's export share has been growing without any disruptions, while the world shares of Japan, the United States, and Germany have not grown during the same period. At the same time, the country has become an important economy in the world import market. While the United States still accounts for the bulk of world imports (around 15%–20% in world imports), its share has gradually been declining since 2000. By contrast, the People's Republic of China's share has steadily increased to close to 10% in 2011.

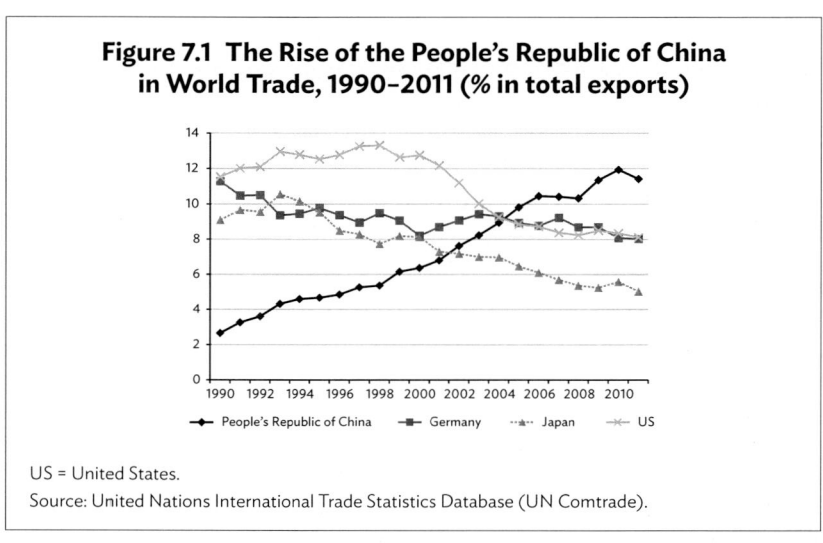

Figure 7.1 The Rise of the People's Republic of China in World Trade, 1990–2011 (% in total exports)

US = United States.
Source: United Nations International Trade Statistics Database (UN Comtrade).

With the rise of the People's Republic of China in world trade, its specialization has dramatically changed, as well. Figure 7.2 depicts the share of relatively more capital- and technology-intensive products (e.g., electrical machinery and household electric appliances) as compared to

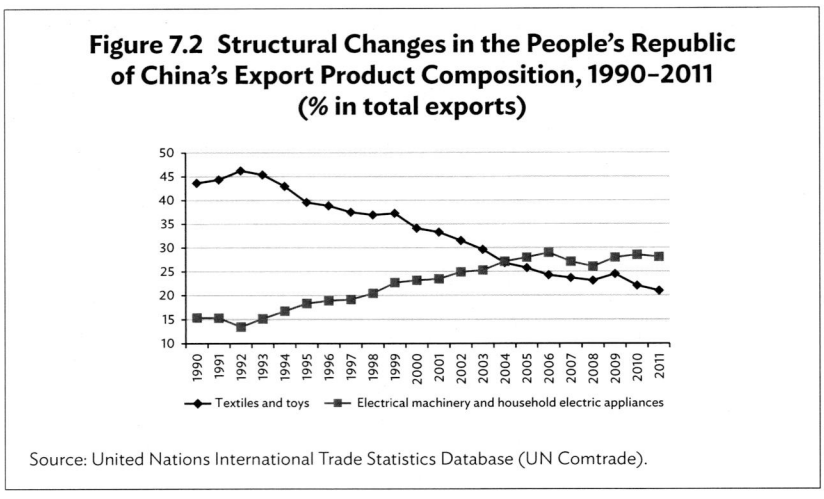

Figure 7.2 Structural Changes in the People's Republic of China's Export Product Composition, 1990–2011 (% in total exports)

Source: United Nations International Trade Statistics Database (UN Comtrade).

more labor-intensive products (e.g., textiles and toys). There has been a notable shift of comparative advantage from more labor-intensive products toward more capital- and technology-intensive products. In 1992, textiles and toys accounted for approximately 45% of the People's Republic of China's total exports. However, this share continuously declined and dropped to close to 20% in 2011. On the other hand, the export share of electrical machinery and household appliances doubled from less than 15% in 1992 to 30% in 2011. In this product category, the export composition is highly concentrated in information and communication technology products. Other important product categories include office machines and telecommunications sound equipment (including mobile phones).

Based on the income-weighted export bundle of goods from the People's Republic of China, some commentators argue that the technological capability of the country is showing signs of rapidly converging toward the technological frontier of developed OECD economies and is now directly competing with them in the export market. However, this should be interpreted cautiously. Allowing for intraproduct specialization, it is known that the People's Republic of China's export specialization still rests largely on the labor-intensive assembly stage rather than specialization in technological content (Athukorala and Yamashita 2006). In other words, the country's comparative advantage still rests on a labor-intensive segment in high-tech products, even though these products are exported from the country (a final assembly economy). This explains why Schott (2008) observes that the unit price of the People's Republic of China's export bundles are at the lower end of the price range, as compared to those of OECD economies (the price competitiveness coming from the People's Republic of China's lower labor costs). In sum, the bulk of the country's exports are mass-market commodities assembled with relatively low unit costs using imported high-tech parts and components from other industrial economies (notebook computers, mobile phones, etc.).

Table 7.1 displays first the top and bottom eight industries by degree of import competition from the People's Republic of China in 1994 (the beginning of the estimation period).[4] In the textile industry, where firms are considered to have comparative advantage, the degree of import competition was already strong in 1994: of Japan's import of textile products, 49% came from the People's Republic of China. That share continued to increase, reaching 77% in 2005. More strikingly, the largest increase in the People's Republic of China's share of Japanese imports is in office and service industry machines, rising from 19% in 1994 to 76% in 2005. Correspondingly, in the industries in which the People's Republic of China's share increased, there was a decline in the share of Asian newly industrializing economies and the United States. In the bottom eight industries, an increase in the People's Republic of China's share is palpable, with strong growth in electronic equipment and semiconductor devices. Production networks between Japan and the People's Republic of China may explain an expansion in import in those high-tech industries.

Table 7.1 Change of Import Competition by Source Economies in Japan's Manufacturing Industry, 1994 and 2005

	1994			
	People's Republic of China	Asian NIEs	SEA	US
Manufacturing, total	11.4	15.9	10.2	25.7
Top eight sectors in 1994				
Coal products	68.9	13.2	0.0	2.7
Textile products	**48.7**	**15.1**	**8.0**	**5.6**
Miscellaneous ceramic, stone, and clay products	34.4	19.1	3.0	13.6
Rubber products	33.4	18.3	10.1	15.7

continued on next page

---

4   Data from 1990 are used in an experimental stage, but the order-import completion-exposed industries are roughly the same in 1994.

Table 7.1 *continued*

	1994			
	People's Republic of China	Asian NIEs	SEA	US
Leather and leather products	26.5	19.9	5.8	5.2
Electrical generating, transmission, distribution, and industrial apparatus	24.4	24.1	19.5	19.6
Pig iron and crude steel	23.7	4.0	3.0	7.0
Office and service industry machines	**19.4**	**16.5**	**21.6**	**22.1**
Bottom eight sectors in 1994				
Chemical fibers	1.2	48.9	2.7	26.4
Petroleum products	1.0	22.4	12.0	6.2
Electronic equipment and electric measuring instruments	**0.6**	**3.1**	**0.6**	**63.9**
Pulp, paper, and coated and glazed paper	0.5	1.7	0.9	40.7
Semiconductor devices and integrated circuits	**0.4**	**41.7**	**8.2**	**49.1**
Printing, plate making for printing, and bookbinding	0.4	26.0	1.0	64.7
Tobacco	0.1	0.0	0.0	95.3
Motor vehicles	0.0	0.3	0.0	27.7

	2005			
	People's Republic of China	Asian NIEs	SEA	US
Manufacturing, total	28.6	12.8	10.9	15.2
Top eight sectors in 1994				
Coal products	92.2	1.5	0.0	0.5
Textile products	**76.5**	**3.5**	**4.0**	**2.0**
Miscellaneous ceramic, stone, and clay products	60.4	5.0	3.8	9.6
Rubber products	58.4	6.9	17.2	5.5
Leather and leather products	46.5	1.8	2.7	2.0
Electrical generating, transmission, distribution, and industrial apparatus	47.2	8.5	17.2	10.2
Pig iron and crude steel	29.7	6.7	1.5	1.7
Office and service industry machines	**76.2**	**8.2**	**7.7**	**2.7**

continued on next page

Table 7.1 *continued*

	2005			
	People's Republic of China	**Asian NIEs**	**SEA**	**US**
Bottom eight sectors in 1994				
Chemical fibers	13.9	34.2	15.5	13.3
Petroleum products	2.8	21.1	12.8	2.5
Electronic equipment and electric measuring instruments	**10.5**	**3.5**	**4.0**	**38.8**
Pulp, paper, and coated and glazed paper	7.3	6.5	13.4	33.5
Semiconductor devices and integrated circuits	**7.9**	**48.2**	**19.1**	**18.9**
Printing, plate making for printing, and bookbinding	13.5	11.2	4.5	23.3
Tobacco	0.6	0.1	0.1	89.6
Motor vehicles	1.4	1.9	0.9	8.8

	Change 1994–2005			
	People's Republic of China	**Asian NIEs**	**SEA**	**US**
Manufacturing, total	17.2	−3.1	0.7	−10.5
Top eight sectors in 1994				
Coal products	23.3	−11.7	0.0	−2.2
Textile products	**27.8**	**−11.6**	**−4.0**	**−3.6**
Miscellaneous ceramic, stone, and clay products	26.0	−14.1	0.9	−4.1
Rubber products	25.0	−11.5	7.2	−10.2
Leather and leather products	20.0	−18.0	−3.1	−3.3
Electrical generating, transmission, distribution, and industrial apparatus	22.8	−15.6	−2.3	−9.4
Pig iron and crude steel	6.0	2.7	−1.5	−5.3
Office and service industry machines	**56.7**	**−8.4**	**−13.9**	**−19.4**
Bottom eight sectors in 1994				
Chemical fibers	12.7	−14.7	12.8	−13.1
Petroleum products	1.8	−1.4	0.8	−3.7
Electronic equipment and electric measuring instruments	**9.9**	**0.4**	**3.4**	**−25.1**

continued on next page

Table 7.1 *continued*

	Change 1994–2005			
	People's Republic of China	Asian NIEs	SEA	US
Pulp, paper, and coated and glazed paper	6.8	4.8	12.6	−7.1
Semiconductor devices and integrated circuits	**7.5**	**6.5**	**10.9**	**−30.3**
Printing, plate making for printing, and bookbinding	13.1	−14.8	3.5	−41.4
Tobacco	0.6	0.1	0.0	−5.8
Motor vehicles	1.4	1.7	0.9	−18.9

NIE = newly industrializing economy, SEA = Southeast Asia, US = United States.
Source: Japan Industrial Productivity 2013 database.

7.3 Data and Variables

7.3.1 Firm-Level Patent Data

Patent statistics as an indicator for innovative outputs have recently become widely available to researchers because of the significant progress made in data accessibility (e.g., United States National Bureau of Economic Research patent data, Japan Patent Office, PATSTAT Worldwide Patent Statistical Database). Patent statistics carry important invention-related information such as bibliographic data, backward and forward citations, technology fields, name of inventor, and usefulness. However, it has been well-documented from survey-based studies that not all patents are in use (but are "sleeping"). In Japan, approximately 60% of pharmaceutical patents are reportedly not currently in use (Nagaoka, Motohashi, and Goto 2010).[5] Rather, firms obtain patents as a defensive blocking mechanism in response to technology competition.[6] "Blocking" patents might protect a firm's once-exclusive market as it becomes commercialized. This project, for the first time in the literature,

---

[5]   More generally, it is more common in the discrete technology industries. In the pharmaceutical industry, R&D can take as long as 10–15 years before new drugs can be introduced into the market. Hence, there is a substantial number of patents for drugs that are still in the process of R&D and not yet in the market.

[6]   It is important to note that those unused patents may simply reflect firms that lack the internal assets to commercialize or are searching for licensees.

empirically relates this unexploited nature of patent holdings to import competition from a low-wage economy.

For this purpose, we extracted the relevant data from a Japanese firm-level survey—the Basic Survey of Japanese Business Structure and Activities, conducted by the Ministry of Economy, Trade and Industry[7]— covering the period 1994–2005.

The firm-level patent usage data are then merged with industry-level exposures to the People's Republic of China's import competition, resulting in a unique dataset for the following aspects. First, it provides a panel dataset of patent usage as it relates to competitive pressures. The available surveys tend to report single-year responses, only depicting the static nature of patent usage.[8] Using a panel of firm-level data offers the perspective of within-firm variations of patent usage in response to import competition. Second, the data period is long enough to cover the People's Republic of China's changing comparative advantage from more labor-intensive to more skill- and technology-intensive goods. Third, using panel data allows firm-specific effects to be included, because (unobserved) managerial skills (assuming time-variant intrafirm elements) can be controlled, along with industry and year fixed effects. Clearly, in a cross-sectional setup, this cannot be controlled.

Based on firm-level information, we created the patent usage variables as shown in Table 7.2. In short, for each firm, we count the patents owned (PAT), the patents in use (USE) and patents that are not in use (NON-USE). Within PAT-USE, we have information for the number of patents based on internal inventions (DEV), and the number of patents that are licensed out (LICENSE). These variables form the dependent variables in the regression analysis that follows.

---

[7]   This survey is governed by the Japanese Statistics Act, and failure to reply results in a fine. The survey sample is restricted to firms that have more than 50 employees and capital of more than 30 million yen. It collects firms' accounting information (sales, employment, employment compensation, the number of establishments, R&D spending, exports, and imports). The industry classification is available at a three-digit level. For our purpose of analyzing the impact of import competition, however, we restricted the sample to only manufacturing firms. All individual firms are assigned unique identifiers, making it possible to track the operations of the same firms over time (the panel data).

[8]   Motohashi (2008) uses the data from the Survey of Intellectual Property Activities by the Japan Patent Office conducted in 2001 in order to classify patent usage. It was found that some of the patents are withheld by firms wishing to use them (or license them out) in the future. Others are kept because a firm needs them for future licensing negotiations. This practice is common in the electronics industry where cross-licensing occurs more frequently.

Table 7.2 Patent Usage and Variable Definitions

	Variable Symbol	Brief Explanation and Definitions
Patent owned	PAT	The count of patents owned (including those purchased and cross-licensed) reported by a firm in a given fiscal year. This includes the cumulative count of patents owned by firms, not just patents for which application has been made in a given year.
Use (including licensed out)	USE	Those patents currently in use.
In-house inventions	DEV	Patents based on internal inventions that are in use.
–use	NON-USE	Defined as PAT minus USE, including blocking and future commercial use/negotiation.
Licensed out	LICENSE	Total count of patents that are licensed out. Domestic and international segregation is available, as well as the amount of money received.

Source: Authors.

It is important to note several limitations. First, the patent statistics in our data are a patent pool: all patents in which the firms have ownership. Empirical work that uses patent statistics collected from a patent office normally covers those patents for which an application has been made, as well those patents that have been granted to the firm. In our data, all patents are presumably those granted (because the survey question asks how many patents a firm owns, rather than patents that have been applied for or are being granted). Since patent applications can indicate firms' innovative efforts, our measure may underestimate them.

Second, our patent data are simply the count. Other studies employing patent statistics usually weight the patent count to its (backward and forward) citations, thus controlling for patent quality. The higher-quality (or sometimes more basic) inventions attract more forward citations than lower-quality inventions (sometimes referred to as "patent thickness"). Without the ability to link our data on firm-owned patents with the citation information, we are unable to account for this quality dimension.

Third, our data do not adjust for the depreciation rate of outdated patents. It is appropriate to adjust for this, because some firm-held patents can become obsolete. However, with no identification of the grant (or application) date of each patent, the deprecation rate cannot be applied in our data. We therefore look at the growth rate of each patent usage (rather than a simple count), hoping to minimize the bias coming from the nondepreciation of the patents.

7.3.2 Japan Industrial Productivity Data

Industry-level variables used in the regression analysis are mainly sourced from Japan Industrial Productivity (JIP) Database (JIP 2013) stored in the online database in the Research Institute of Economy, Trade and Industry in Japan.[9] The JIP dataset is organized at the three-digit industry level (52 manufacturing industries).

Import Competition from the People's Republic of China
We use the value of imports originating from the People's Republic of China as a share of total world imports as a measure of the exposure to the country's import competition in a given JIP industry j:

$$\mathrm{CHM}_j = \frac{\text{Chinese imports}_j}{\text{Imports}_j}.$$ (1)

We also employ the conventional method of constructing import penetration by normalizing the People's Republic of China's import on domestic absorption (i.e., domestic absorption = value added + imports − exports).[10]

$$\mathrm{CHM}_j = \frac{\text{Chinese imports}_j}{(\text{Value Added}_j + \text{Imports}_j - \text{Exports}_j)}.$$ (2)

Instrumental Variable
While our motivation for the empirical analysis is to estimate the causal effects of the People's Republic of China's import competition on patent outputs, we encounter a possible endogeneity problem. Firm-level innovative activity for reasons other than import competition

---

[9]   See the appendix for further details on the JIP Database 2013 (http://www.rieti .go.jp/en/database/JIP2013/).

[10] "Value added" is defined as the difference between gross output and intermediate inputs. Gross output is measured as the sum of industry shipment, revenues from repairing and fixing services, and revenues from performing subcontracting works. Intermediate inputs are defined as the sum of raw materials, fuels, electricity, and subcontracting expenditure.

may also shape trade flows, altering the degree of import competition in the industry (e.g., more innovative firms might opt to do more offshoring to the People's Republic of China in order to facilitate their innovative home operations). For the same reason, the reverse causality is also a possibility. Imports from the People's Republic of China may be correlated with industry-wide technology shocks (to some degree, industry-specific fixed effects may take care of this concern, but it might not be sufficient). This makes ordinary least squares (OLS) estimators biased and inconsistent.

We use a measure of the People's Republic of China's (labor) productivity as an instrument for the endogenous import variables in the technology equation. This implied volatility strategy extracts any exogenous variations affecting the People's Republic of China's export supply capacity, while indirectly affecting the level of innovative activity only through the intensified import competition in Japan. This instrument is inspired by the use of an instrument in other studies. Autor et al. (2015) used the exposure to the People's Republic of China's import competition of eight developed economies[11] as instruments to measure the exposure of the United States to People's Republic of China's imports. The motivation for their implied volatility strategy was to extract supply-side productivity elements in the People's Republic of China's export performance. However, as the authors pointed out, their instrument faces a validity challenge, whereby industry technological changes among those developed economies must be separate incidents. In other words, the technological diffusions must be limited across those high-income economies. In our implementation of the implied volatility strategy, we directly use the productivity measure (labor productivity) of the People's Republic of China's industries, which undoubtedly has been behind the surge in the country's export growth yet is indirectly related to firm-level innovative activity. These data are extracted from the China Industrial Productivity (CIP) Database.[12] There is no strict industry correlation between CIP and JIP industries, so we arbitrarily assigned the corresponding CIP manufacturing industries to 52 JIP industries.

7.4 Empirical Specification and Results

We use the following linear specification to relate firm-level patent growth (for different patent usages separately) to the exposure of the People's Republic of China's import competition in industries:

---

[11]   Australia, Denmark, Finland, Germany, Japan, New Zealand, Spain, and Switzerland.

[12]   The CIP Database 2015 is available at http://www.rieti.go.jp/en/database/CIP2015/index.html.

$$\Delta\ln(\text{PAT})_{ijt} = \alpha_i + \alpha_{jt} + \beta_1 \text{CHM}_{JT-5} + \varepsilon_{ijt}. \quad (3)$$

where subscripts i, j, and t denote firm, industry, and time. For each firm i, we have the count of patents owned (PAT), the count of patents in use (USE), and patents that are not in use (NON-USE). Within the group USE, we also have information broken down by patents that are based on in-house inventions (DEV). We also have the count of patents that are licensed out (LICENSE). These variables form the dependent variables separately in the regression analysis that follows.

The dependent variable is the 5-year (log) change in the patent usage categories as an indicator of firms' innovative activity. An explanatory variable, CHM_{it-5}, is in level for the period $t-5$. This linear specification slightly differs from that in Bloom, Draca, and Van Reenen (2016), who use the 5-year log changes in both dependent (technology) and explanatory (exposure to the People's Republic of China's import competition) variables. The formulation of equation (3) is preferred in our data; it is intuitively more appealing because creating technology (and filing for patents) requires more time.[13] This specification tests the subsequent firms' innovative reaction to the People's Republic of China's import competition experienced in the period $t-5$.[14] Aghion et al. (2005) and Amiti and Khandelwal (2013) also use a specification similar to equation (3).

The baseline specification also includes both firm fixed effects (α_{it}) and industry-year fixed effects (α_j), to purge invariant shocks common in the respective dimensions (such as the unobserved managerial techniques within firms), as well as an industry-specific propensity to patent. It has been concretely reported that some industries are intrinsically prone to produce more patents than other industries because of effective patent enforcement (chemical and pharmaceutical).

We also form the patent production function to include other explanatory variables (in log form), which are drawn from the knowledge production function that treats patents as knowledge output and other firm characteristics as knowledge inputs: employment, age of firm, and R&D ratio to sales (R&D intensity).

---

[13] Growth rate is also preferred for a technical reason. Our data on the patent count include the cumulative number of patents in which firms claim ownership. Hence, by using growth rate, we only account for newer patents while discounting older patents.

[14] Even using the same specification as Bloom, Draca, and Van Reenen (2016), it turns out that the estimation results are quite similar. This goes to show the persistent impact of the People's Republic of China's import competition on the technology variables.

7.5 Results

Table 7.3 presents the benchmark results. We ran a set of regressions in OLS with firm and industry-year fixed effects. To aid the interpretation of the main results, descriptions of key variables are presented in the appendix (Tables A7.1 and A7.2). Column (1) of Table 7.3 indicates that import competition from the People's Republic of China provides an overall inducement for more innovative activities among Japanese firms, although its estimated effect seems to be relatively smaller than the one found in Bloom, Draca, and Van Reenen (2016): a 10-percentage-point increase in the People's Republic of China's import competition would result in a 0.37% increase in firm-level patents. Across the results, there is a visible position effect of import competition, with the exception of PAT-DEV and LICENSE.[15]

The most interesting finding is that the People's Republic of China's import competition also generates more unused patents (NON-USE). It appears that the estimated coefficient is consistently larger than the one

Table 7.3 Import Competition from the People's Republic of China and Patent Usage, 1994 and 2005

	OLS				
	(1) PAT	(2) USE	(3) DEV	(4) NON-USE	(5) LICENSE
CHM$_{jt-5}$	0.037***	0.013*	−0.019***	0.026***	−0.001
	(0.008)	(0.007)	(0.006)	(0.007)	(0.001)
Constant	−0.552***	−0.353*	0.359**	−0.447**	0.106***
	(0.191)	(0.198)	(0.169)	(0.171)	(0.033)
Firm fixed effects	Yes	Yes	Yes	Yes	Yes
Industry-year fixed effects	Yes	Yes	Yes	Yes	Yes
R-squared	0.394	0.346	0.342	0.298	0.289
N	35,200	35,200	35,200	35,200	35,200

OLS = ordinary least squares

Notes: *** denotes 1% significance; ** denotes 5% significance; * denotes 10% significance. Estimation is by ordinary least squares with standard errors clustered by industry. The dependent variable is in 5-year log differences of each patent usage type. Imports from the People's Republic of China as a fraction of total industry imports represent an explanatory variable. All columns include a full set of firm and industry-year fixed effects.

Source: Authors' calculation.

---

[15]   In fact, it is puzzling to see that the intensified import competition from the People's Republic of China would actually lower the rate of in-house invention patents, while it has no statistically significant impact on patents designed for licensing out.

estimated for a USE equation (column (2) in Table 7.3): a 10-percentage-point increase in the People's Republic of China's import competition would result in a 0.26% increase in unused patents (versus a 0.13% increase in patents that are in use). Notwithstanding a reservation about the limitation in this variable (i.e., not all unused patents are used for the purpose of "blocking"), the evidence suggests that Japanese firms would undertake more defensive reactions to the increased import competition.

The regression result indicates that lowering the People's Republic of China's import competition would trigger more patents based on in-house inventions (judging from the negative sign in a DEV regression, column (3) in Table 7.3) In addition, the People's Republic of China's import competition has no statistically significant effects on patents designed for licensing out (LICENSE), as shown in column (4).

These results and associated interpretations are reinforced upon taking an instrumental approach (Table 7.4). In the first-stage regression (not shown), labor productivity has a statistical significance that is on the level of the import competition.[16] The estimated coefficients in all regressions now show larger effects as compared to the OLS estimates.[17]

Table 7.4 Import Competition from the People's Republic of China and Patent Usage (Implied Volatility Regressions), 1994 and 2005

	Instrumental Variable				
	(1) PAT	(2) USE	(3) DEV	(4) NON-USE	(5) LICENSE
CHM$_{jt-5}$	0.113***	0.064***	−0.073***	0.077***	−0.009***
	(0.004)	(0.004)	(0.004)	(0.004)	(0.001)
Constant	−1.017***	−0.524***	0.366***	−0.828***	0.065**
	(0.090)	(0.091)	(0.094)	(0.098)	(0.030)
Firm fixed effects	Yes	Yes	Yes	Yes	Yes
Industry-year fixed effects	Yes	Yes	Yes	Yes	Yes
N	35,200	35,200	35,200	35,200	35,200

Notes: *** denotes 1% significance; ** denotes 5% significance; * denotes 10% significance. Estimation is by ordinary least squares with standard errors clustered by industry. The dependent variable is in 5-year log differences of each patent usage type. Imports from the People's Republic of China as a fraction of total industry imports represent an explanatory variable. All columns include a full set of firm and industry-year fixed effects.

Source: Authors' calculation.

---

[16]   A full set of tests needs to be carried out to establish the validity of instruments

[17]   In Bloom, Draca, and Van Reenen (2016), similar results were obtained.

In Table 7.5, the empirical specification follows a form of the conventional knowledge production function, treating patents as knowledge outputs. Even after we control for relevant firm characteristics, the People's Republic of China's import competition remains positive and statistically significant. With respect to firm size (measured by the number of employees), it indicates that smaller firms obtain more patents, and older firms (in terms of the age of the firm) engage in more innovative activity (interestingly, the estimated coefficients for firm characteristics remain much larger than a variable of capturing the level of import competition from the People's Republic of China): a 10-percentage-point decrease in employment leads to a 4.4% increase in innovative activity. Other than a PAT regression, we found the effect of the People's Republic of China's competition to be positive and statistically significant in a NON-USE regression (column (4)). Conditioned on relevant firm characteristics, the People's Republic of

Table 7.5 Import Competition from the People's Republic of China and Patent Usage (OLS with Firm-level Characteristic Controls), 1994 and 2005

	(1) PAT	(2) USE	(3) DEV	(4) NON-USE	(5) LICENSE
CHM_{it-5}	0.031***	0.010	−0.012*	0.021***	−0.000
	(0.008)	(0.007)	(0.006)	(0.007)	(0.001)
$Log(Emp)_{it-5}$	−0.445***	−0.113	0.023	−0.532***	0.029
	(0.096)	(0.098)	(0.106)	(0.098)	(0.028)
$Log(Age)_{it-5}$	0.517***	0.326***	−0.617***	0.372***	−0.089***
	(0.109)	(0.110)	(0.139)	(0.134)	(0.029)
$Log(R\&D)_{it-5}$	−0.253***	−0.372***	−0.696***	−0.032	−0.069**
	(0.056)	(0.101)	(0.118)	(0.075)	(0.026)
Constant	0.276	−0.714	2.564***	1.307**	0.266
	(0.597)	(0.589)	(0.556)	(0.634)	(0.165)
R squared	0.398	0.349	0.350	0.301	0.291
N	35,164	35,164	35,164	35,164	35,164

OLS = ordinary least squares.
Notes: *** denotes 1% significance; ** denotes 5% significance; * denotes 10% significance. Estimation is by OLS with standard errors clustered by industry. The dependent variable is in 5-year log differences of each patent usage type. Imports from the People's Republic of China as a fraction of total industry imports represent an explanatory variable. All columns include a full set of firm and industry-year fixed effects.
Source: Authors' calculation.

China's import competition would produce patents of a more defensive nature (unused patents) among Japanese firms.

Table 7.6 sequentially introduces the import competition indicators from other economies. We introduced import competition from Asian newly industrializing economies separately for those from high-income OECD economies (including the United States and high-wage European economies).[18] Overall, the main results remain the same. Increased import competition would make Japanese firms pursue more patenting, while import competition from other high-wage economies has no statistical significance. These findings conform to those found in Bloom, Draca, and Van Reenen (2016). The theoretical intuition drawn from the trapped-factor model is that import competition from high-wage economies is not a substitute for old products, which do not create incentives for innovation. There is positive and statistically significant effect on non-use of patents (NON-USE), while in other regressions the sign for CHM changes or loses statistical significance as compared to the benchmark estimation.

Table 7.6 Import Competition from the People's Republic of China and Patent Usage (OLS with Other Import Competition Variables), 1994 and 2005

	(1) PAT	(2) PAT	(3) USE	(4) USE	(5) NON-USE
CHM_{jt-5}	0.036***	0.033***	0.015***	0.007	0.025***
	(0.008)	(0.009)	(0.005)	(0.009)	(0.008)
NIE_{jt-5}	−0.003		0.005		−0.004
	(0.008)		(0.008)		(0.005)
$High_{jt-5}$		−0.007		−0.008**	
		(0.006)		(0.004)	
Constant	−0.494**	−0.144	−0.471*	0.126	−0.351*
	(0.238)	(0.366)	(0.233)	(0.336)	(0.200)
R-squared	0.394	0.395	0.346	0.347	0.298
N	35,200	35,200	35,200	35,200	35,200

continued on next page

---

[18]   In an experimental stage, import competition from other low-wage economies (such as those in mainland Southeast Asia) was included, but it turns out that it is not important, and does not change the estimated coefficient for CHM.

Table 7.6 *continued*

	(6) NON-USE	(7) DEV	(8) DEV	(9) LICENSE	(10) LICENSE
CHM_{jt-5}	0.023***	−0.021***	−0.019**	−0.002*	0.000
	(0.007)	(0.005)	(0.008)	(0.001)	(0.001)
NIE_{jt-5}		−0.007		−0.002	
		(0.007)		(0.001)	
$High_{jt-5}$	−0.005		−0.000		0.002*
	(0.008)		(0.005)		(0.001)
Constant	−0.170	0.512**	0.365	0.154***	−0.003
	(0.408)	(0.214)	(0.390)	(0.032)	(0.077)
R-squared	0.298	0.342	0.342	0.290	0.290
N	35,200	35,200	35,200	35,200	35,200

OLS = ordinary least squares.

Notes: *** denotes 1% significance; ** denotes 5% significance; * denotes 10% significance. Estimation is by OLS with standard errors clustered by industry. The dependent variable is in 5-year log differences of each patent usage type. Imports from the People's Republic of China as a fraction of total industry imports represent an explanatory variable. All columns include a full set of firm and industry-year fixed effects.

Source: Authors' calculation.

7.6 Conclusion

This chapter examined the impact of the People's Republic of China's import competition on the innovation responses of a panel of Japanese manufacturing firms for the period 1994–2005. Based on the unusually detailed firm-patent dataset, we have uncovered several heterogeneous dimensions of the impact of innovation in the case of import competition from the People's Republic of China. First, we found that, while increased imports from the People's Republic of China have induced Japanese firms to take out more patents, they are mostly of lower quality (i.e., patents with zero-forward citation). This was inferred as evidence suggesting that Japanese firms have increased the defensive nature of patents in order to protect their core inventions. This is similar to a strategy followed by firms in "continuous" technology-intensive industries in the field of information and communication technology; to build up the patent fence in order to deter new entrants in the technology field. This finding coincides with a sector that has been subject to intensified import competition from the People's Republic of China over the past 2 decades.

Second, when the sample of firms is split into globally engaged firms with positive importing (and exporting) activity and domestic-oriented firms, the former group has responded positively to import competition from the People's Republic of China by increasing its R&D intensity. Our interpretation of this result is that Japanese firms (and presumably more innovative firms) have built up their innovation capacity while moving away from low-cost manufactured goods, in which the People's Republic of China has more comparative advantages. In contrast, such effects are consistently muted for firms with a domestic market focus. These types of firms are completely insulated from the People's Republic of China's import competition.

References

Aghion, P., N. Bloom, R. Blundell, R. Griffith, and P. Howitt. 2005. Competition and Innovation: An Inverted U Relationship. *Quarterly Journal of Economics*. 120 (2). pp. 701–28.

Amiti, M., and A. Khandelwal. 2013. Import Competition and Quality Upgrading. *Review of Economics and Statistics*. 95 (2). pp. 476–90.

Athukorala, P., and N. Yamashita. 2006. Production Fragmentation and Trade Integration in a Global Context. *North American Journal of Economics and Finance*. 17 (4). pp. 233–56.

Autor, D., D. Dorn, G. Hanson, and J. Song. 2015. Trade Adjustment: Worker Level Evidence. *Quarterly Journal of Economics*. 129 (4). pp. 1799–860.

Bloom, N., M. Draca, and J. Van Reenen. 2016. Trade Induced Technical Change? The Impact of Chinese Imports on Innovation, IT and Productivity. *Review of Economic Studies*. 83 (1). pp. 87–117.

Boldrin, M., and D. K. Levine. 2013. The Case against Patents. *Journal of Economic Perspectives*. 27 (1). pp. 3–22.

Motohashi, K. 2008. Licensing or Not Licensing? An Empirical Analysis of the Strategic Use of Patents by Japanese Firms. *Research Policy*. 37 (9). pp. 1548–55.

Nagaoka, S., K. Motohashi, and A. Goto. 2010. Patent Statistics as an Innovation Indicator. In B. H. Hall and N. Rosenberg, eds. *Handbook of the Economics of Innovation*, Volume 2. Amsterdam: Elsevier. pp. 1083–127.

Schott, P. K. 2008. The Relative Sophistication of Chinese Exports. *Economic Policy*. 23 (53). pp. 5–49.

Thoenig, M., and T. Verdier. 2003. A Theory of Defensive Skill Biased Innovation and Globalization. *American Economic Review*. 93 (3). pp. 709–28.

Wood, A. 1994. *North-South Trade, Employment and Inequality: Changing Fortunes in a Skill-Driven World*. Oxford: Clarendon Press.

Appendix A7

Table A7.1 Descriptive Statistics

	PAT	NON-USE	USE	DEV	LICENSE	CHM
Year	Mean	Mean	Mean	Mean	Mean	Mean
1994	109.1	77.2	35.0	27.9	0.4	10.3
1995	107.2	75.2	32.2	27.8	0.3	12.5
1996	121.1	86.7	34.6	30.7	0.4	13.7
1997	98.6	64.3	34.4	91.7	0.6	15.1
1998	106.4	68.1	38.3	101.2	0.5	16.0
1999	115.2	73.3	41.9	108.8	0.6	16.8
2000	50.2	36.6	24.1	40.7	0.9	18.2
2001	123.3	75.4	47.9	38.9	0.8	20.5
2002	124.3	78.1	46.3	38.8	0.7	23.0
2003	142.5	91.9	50.5	41.4	0.7	24.1
2004	141.9	88.7	53.2	43.1	2.1	26.5
2005	130.9	81.0	49.9	43.2	2.3	28.9

	PAT	USE	NON-USE	LICENSE	# of Firms
Year	Sum	Sum	Sum	Sum	Sum
1994	46,908	16,118	30,790	200	6,374
1995	49,417	16,300	33,117	79	6,637
1996	53,485	17,650	35,835	300	6,614
1997	53,352	17,600	35,752	800	6,464
1998	52,119	17,200	34,919	228	6,513
1999	55,909	18,692	37,217	247	6,447
2000	43,166	9,800	33,366	344	6,340
2001	50,000	39,726	10,274	938	6,415
2002	47,000	24,670	22,330	301	6,269
2003	48,061	20,155	27,906	350	5,764
2004	47,166	43,000	4,166	8,930	6,088
2005	42,662	34,000	8,662	10,000	5,937

Source: Authors' calculation.

Table A7.2   Descriptive Statistics for Variables Used in Regressions

Variable	Unit	Obs	Mean	Std. Dev.	Min	Max
PAT	Count	75,862	113.8	1,102.1	0	55,909
USE	Count	75,862	40.4	433.2	0	43,000
NON_USE	Count	75,862	74.5	819.2	0	42,662
DEV	Count	75,862	53.1	653.8	0	55,909
LICENSE	Count	75,862	0.8	49.3	0	10,000
Emp. total	Unit	75,862	629.0	2,424.1	50	80,500
R&D expenditures	Value in yen	75,862	888.4	10,266.2	0	527,359
Est. year	Year	75,857	1,951.0	111.0	0	2,006
CHM	Percentage	75,862	18.6	16.2	0.02	98

Source: Authors' calculation.

8

Trade Reform, Managers, and Skill Intensity: Evidence from India[1]

Pavel Chakraborty

8.1　Introduction

International trade economists have long been interested in understanding the distributional implications of globalization or trade liberalization or product market competition. One of the crucial aspects of such distributional effects, which have received a lot of attention, especially from the 1990s onward, is how such forces divide the labor pie into skilled (or nonproduction) and unskilled (or production) workers. In other words, does an increase in trade participation or exposure to international markets result in an increase in returns for skilled or less skilled workers?

The theoretical underpinning of such an important empirical question originates from the predictions of a well-known theorem in international trade: Stolper–Samuelson. In a model with two factors, it states that "for a rise in the relative price of a good, it will lead to a rise in the return to that factor which is used most intensively in the production of the good, and conversely, to a fall in the return to the other factor" (Stolper and Samuelson 1941). For example, let us denote skilled and unskilled labor as two factors. Now, as countries reduce trade barriers, the Stolper–Samuelson theorem predicts a rise in unskilled-labor wages and a fall in skilled-labor wages in developing countries (as they have a big pool of relatively less skilled workers). The opposite is true in the case of skill-rich countries. In other words, the theorem points out that exposure to international trade or world markets can significantly

---

[1]   This chapter is based on Chakraborty and Raveh (2018).

affect the distribution of resources within the country and can generate substantial distributional conflict.

To investigate whether this is the case, a significant number of studies have tried to establish a causal link between the effects of competitive forces (in the form of trade liberalization) and skill premium or some other measure of wage inequality between skilled and unskilled workers: (i) Argentina (Galiani and Sanguinetti 2003; Bustos 2011); (ii) Brazil (Pavcnik et al. 2004; Gonzaga, Menezes-Filho, and Terra 2006; Menezes-Filhoz and Muendler 2011; Araújo and Paz 2014; Krishna, Poole, and Senses 2014); (iii) Chile (Beyer, Rojas, and Vergara 1999); (iv) the People's Republic of China (Chen, Yu, and Yu 2017); (v) Colombia (Attanasio, Goldberg, and Pavcnik 2004; Goldberg and Pavcnik 2005); (vi) India (Chamarbagwala 2006; Kumar and Mishra 2008; Chamarbagwala and Sharma 2011; Mehta and Hasan 2012); (vii) Indonesia (Smith et al. 2002; Amiti and Davis 2012; Amiti and Cameron 2012); (viii) Mexico (Feenstra and Hanson 1997; Revenga 1997; Harrison and Hanson 1999; Feliciano 2001; Verhoogen 2008; Frías, Kaplan, and Verhoogen 2009, 2012); (ix) Morocco (Currie and Harrison 1997); (x) Turkey (Krishna, Mitra, and Chinoy 2001); (xi) Viet Nam (McCaig 2011); and (xii) Latin American countries (Behrman, Birdsall, and Székely 2000; Haltiwanger et al. 2004).

The primary reason for such an overwhelming number of studies focusing on developing or emerging economies is that during the last 3 decades or so, many developing countries, most notably Latin American countries in the 1980s and early 1990s, India in the early 1990s, and the People's Republic of China joining the World Trade Organization in 2001, underwent a significant trade liberalization process that substantially increased their exposure to international markets. The main conclusion that emerges from these studies is that the skill premium rose in developing countries due to exposure to international trade. This is puzzling in a Heckscher–Ohlin context as developing countries have a comparative advantage in producing low-skill-intensive goods.

A handful of researchers have also investigated the demand for different kinds of workers in the case of developed countries, but between exports and non-exporters: (i) France (Biscourp and Kramarz 2007); (ii) Germany (Baumgarten 2013); (iii) Hungary (Koren, Csillag, and Kollo 2019); (iv) Portugal (Martins and Opromolla 2010); and (v) the United States (Feenstra and Hanson 1996; Bemard and Jensen 1997). Analysis across this set of countries finds strong evidence that an exporter wage gap, conditional on workers' skill levels, contributed to the growth in wage inequality. This finding is consistent with recent heterogeneous-firm trade models that feature an exporter wage premium as well as variability of the premium with respect to increasing trade liberalization.

Given this background, one issue that is currently at the center of economic debates regarding the dynamics of the labor market is how trade reform or exposure to international market(s) or product market competition affects a firm's demand for managers,[2] which in turn affects productivity and performance.[3] The literature on firms' managerial practices or demand for managers originates from a seminal paper by Garicano (2000).

He asks a simple question: What does a firm do? A firm solves problems. Problems arise during different stages of production, and managers solve not-so-common problems, whereas nonmanagers take care of routine problems. The demand for managers rises as the ratio of not-so-common problems increases. Garicano (2000) argues that this happens when a firm invests in technological deepening (of the production function). In other words, managerial inputs act as complements to technological inputs. Therefore, with greater adoption of technology (or technological inputs), the demand for skilled labor (or managers) increases. Caliendo and Rossi-Hansberg (2012) use this framework to show that participation in export markets also increases the demand for managers, as firms increasingly face new sets of not-so-common problems.

In a related context, Acemoglu (2003) develops a model to analyze the impact of international trade on wage premiums. He shows that wage inequality can also happen through skill-biased technical change because of increased international trade. And this may explain the rise in wage inequality without a rise in the relative prices of skill-intensive goods (both in the United States and less developed economies), which is the usual intervening mechanism in standard trade models.

Putting these two issues together, I argue that trade reform—or in my case a drop in input tariffs—can induce firms to adopt more technologically intensive inputs. Adoption of high-tech inputs can increase the demand for managers. On the other hand, managers make up a sizeable proportion of skilled workers. Therefore, I hypothesize that skill intensity may be a complementary channel through which trade may result in an increase in the demand for managers.

Adopting the case of India, I empirically study this nexus in a developing economy, through which we can unravel new dynamics that emphasize the distinctive features of such an economy in this context.

---

[2]   See Chakraborty and Raveh (2018), Chen (2017), Caliendo and Rossi-Hansberg (2012), and Marin and Verdier (2008, 2014).

[3]   Studies that link firm organization and managerial practices to firm performance and productivity include Garicano and Rossi-Hansberg (2004, 2006), Bloom and Van Reenen (2007, 2010), Bloom et al. (2013), and Bloom et al. (2014), among others.

All the previous studies investigating similar issues (skill intensity or premium) focus on either and/or both (i) differential returns for production and nonproduction workers; and/or (ii) skilled and unskilled workers, where the workers are sorted according to the number of years of education. I extend and complement the literature by focusing on one niche aspect of the group of skilled workers: the managers. To see whether managers can possibly represent skilled workers, I compute a simple correlation between managerial compensation (by aggregating firm-level data to industry) and the ratio of skilled workers or skilled intensity (nonproduction workers/total number of employees). The correlation coefficient is 0.56, suggesting that managers can fairly represent the skilled workers group.

Managers are the section of workers who manage or are associated with the production activities of a firm in the dataset that I exploit for this chapter.[4] The primary focus of this chapter is to investigate the effect of trade liberalization, as compared with changes in tariffs, on the demand for managers relative to nonmanagers, and in addition explore whether skill intensity can act as a complementary channel.[5] While previous studies examined components related exclusively to the managerial side, such as wages and bonuses (e.g., Cunat and Guadalupe 2009), very little attention, if any, has been given to the inclusion of the nonmanagers' side to consider relative terms and within-firm inequality.[6] I study the causal link and try to identify the underlying mechanisms through which it operates.

I start by presenting a simple link between trade (both exports and imports) and the relative demand for managers in a sample of Indian firms for 1990–2011 (Figure 8.1).[7] All three measures increase steadily throughout the period exhibiting a correlation of 0.85 between managerial compensation and exports, and 0.89 with imports. The surge in trade is a consequence of the 1990s trade liberalization exercise in

---

[4]   I exclude any manager who is associated with any kind of administrative duties in a firm, such as a human resources manager.

[5]   Managers are defined as any workers who manage at least one other worker (or who is the sole worker in the firm), with nonmanagers accounting for the remaining balance. I will further discuss this in detail in the empirical part.

[6]   An exception is Ma and Ruzic (2018). They study the impact of globalization on executives' income shares in firms in the United States using conditional correlations. In contrast, I try to establish a causal link and empirically identify the underlying channel, while examining a more general definition of managers.

[7]   The figure presents the yearly average of the share of total trade (exports plus imports) in gross value added and the share of managerial compensation in total labor compensation for a representative Indian manufacturing firm over 1990–2011. I proxy for the relative demand for managers using the latter. I discuss both the measures in more detail in the empirical part.

Figure 8.1 Trade and Managerial Compensation, 1990–2011

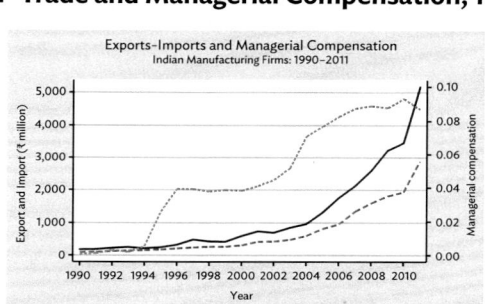

Exports–Imports and Managerial Compensation
Indian Manufacturing Firms: 1990–2011

Note: The figure presents the average trade (exports and imports) values and the average compensation share of managers, 1990–2011 ($\rho = 0.85$).

Source: Author's calculations.

India, which I discuss further later; the increase in the compensation share of managers is what I aim to investigate. I seek to understand whether there is indeed a causal relation between the two. To apprehend further whether such is the case, I divide the sample of firms into importing and nonimporting firms and plot the relative demand measure in Figure 8.2. The figure indicates that the surge (in the share of managerial compensation) is almost an exclusive feature of the former types. This motivates a focus on tariffs. To test whether, and how, the latter creates a causal effect, I exploit the exogenous nature of India's 1990s trade reform to study a rich dataset on Indian manufacturing firms that uniquely disaggregates labor compensation to managers and nonmanagers over a period of 2 decades.

I find a remarkably robust, persistent, and economically meaningful negative effect that, in line with the findings in the initial analysis, is entirely driven by input tariffs. The benchmark estimations indicate that a 10% decrease in input tariffs increases the share of managerial compensation (as well as their number) by approximately 0.5%–3.5%. This effect is robust to considering various controls, specifications, and estimation techniques. These results point to a quality-upgrading mechanism reminiscent of Caliendo and Rossi-Hansberg (2012),[8]

---

[8]   Studying a model of heterogeneous firms with knowledge-based hierarchies, they show that trade liberalization increases the number of management layers in exporting firms, as managers can solve more efficiently problems arising from increasing output than workers for whom costly knowledge needs to be acquired.

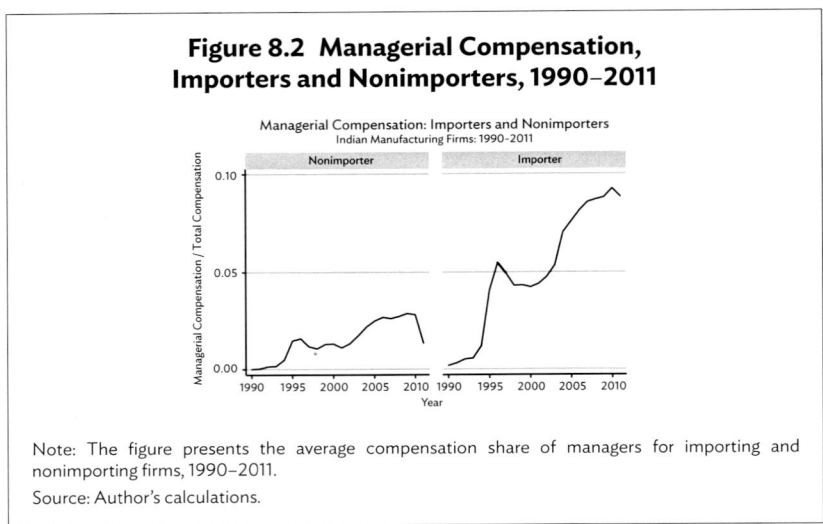

Figure 8.2 Managerial Compensation, Importers and Nonimporters, 1990–2011

Managerial Compensation: Importers and Nonimporters
Indian Manufacturing Firms: 1990-2011

Note: The figure presents the average compensation share of managers for importing and nonimporting firms, 1990–2011.

Source: Author's calculations.

adjusted to an importing-based economy: Firms import intermediate inputs of higher quality and greater variety. These, together with the products they produce, are embedded with new knowledge that in turn increases the relative demand for workers with skills to manage that.[9]

Next, in investigating whether skill intensity can act as a complementary channel resulting in demand for managers, my results suggest that the phenomenon is particularly significant for firms below halfv of the size distribution. In other words, as small and medium-sized firms start to import high-quality intermediate inputs (as a result of the trade reform) without any prior knowledge of how to use them in the production technology, this results in a higher demand for managers (relative to the top half of the size distribution) with suitable knowledge to use them. This increase in the demand for managers materializes in those sectors where there is a complementary effect of the drop in input tariffs and a higher ratio of skill intensity.

This chapter is primarily related to the literature on trade liberalization and the demand for skill or skill intensity in developing

---

[9] Interestingly, this is in contrast to previous studies that examined developed economies, pointing to a product market competition mechanism (e.g, Cunat and Guadalupe 2009; Bloom, Sadun, and Van Reenen, 2010), hence emphasizing the extent to which the case of a developing economy may present different dynamics and provide new insights.

economies. As discussed before, neoclassical trade theory, via the Stolper–Samuelson theorem, predicts that trade liberalization increases the demand for the abundant factor, which is expected to translate to an increased relative demand for low-skill labor in developing economies. Several studies, however, have documented the opposite (Goldberg and Pavcnik 2007). Various explanations have been offered, including trade-induced skill-biased technical change (Acemoglu 2003), credit constraints (Bonfatti and Ghatak 2013), improved exports (Zhu and Trefler 2005), import composition (Raveh and Reshef 2016), and quality upgrading (Verhoogen 2008). I check whether skill intensity can potentially be cited as one of the channels through which India experiences an increase in the demand for managers due to the trade liberalization episode.

Second, the chapter also contributes to literature regarding offshoring and wage inequality. Feenstra and Hanson (1996, 1997) show that purchasing an input from a foreign source can replace a task previously done by a worker and therefore can lower wages. On the other hand, the ability to use foreign inputs can raise wages (Grossman and Rossi-Hansberg 2008). Autor, Levy, and Murnane (2003); and Ebenstein et al. (2014) in the case of the United States; and Hummels et al. (2014) for Danish firms show that workers whose occupations involve routine tasks experience large wage drops with offshoring. I also find a similar result: increased use of foreign inputs results in a demand for managerial workers, but in the case of a developing country.

Last, the chapter is also closely related to the literature on how the adoption of technologically intensive inputs induces a skill wage gap between and within firms. However, as pointed out by Card and DiNardo (2002), a central issue regarding such an association is the problem of identifying a causal link between the adoption of new technology and a rise in skilled workers' wage. I use the drop in tariffs on intermediate inputs because of the trade liberalization exercise in India in the 1990s to identify a causal effect of technology adoption (in terms of adoption of high-quality technologically intensive intermediate inputs) on wage inequality.

8.2 Literature Review

As discussed earlier, a growing body of academic and policy debates on the merits and demerits of liberalization have centered on the internal distributional consequences and how they affect labor markets. This section presents all the other evidence from India on the impact of trade reform on wages. India offers an interesting case for studying the effects of trade reform for a couple of reasons. First, the magnitude of trade liberalization was very big (Kumar and Mishra 2008). The average tariff drop in manufacturing was more drastic than trade liberalization episodes in Latin American countries (e.g., Brazil, Colombia, and Mexico). In addition to tariffs, India has also reduced nontariff barriers since 1991. Second, trade reforms in India were exogenous and were in response to a severe balance-of-payments crisis in 1991. The objective of reducing trade barriers was based on the International Monetary Fund's conditionalities for assistance. Therefore, policy makers had less room to cater to special lobby interests.

The first paper to investigate the issue of wage inequality in India was by Chamarbagwala (2006). She uses data from the Employment and Unemployment Schedule of the National Sample Survey Organization for four rounds—1983–84, 1987–88, 1993–94, and 1999–2000—to investigate India's skill wage gap and gender wage differential during the 2 decades that coincide with the economic liberalization in India. Using a nonparametric methodology, she argues that economic liberalization contributed to the widening of the skill wage gap. In other words, demand for skilled labor increased, mostly due to skill upgrading within industries. On the other hand, the paper shows that international trade in manufacturing goods benefitted skilled men, but hurt skilled women, whereas outsourcing of services generated a demand for both male and female skilled workers. Dutta (2007) uses the same dataset for the same time period but estimates wage regression models using the augmented Mincer earnings equation controlling for human capital, industry affiliation, and various other characteristics. She also concludes that trade reforms have substantially increased wage inequality as the relative wages of the unskilled workers fell considerably.

Kumar and Mishra (2008) use household survey data from the Employment and Unemployment Schedule for the same four rounds to estimate the effect of a drop in tariffs on industry wage structure. However, since manufacturing is largely located in urban areas, they focus their attention on workers only in urban areas. In contrast to the abovementioned studies on India, they find that trade liberalization has led to a decrease in wage inequality between skilled and unskilled workers in India. This is because the magnitude of tariff reductions was relatively larger in sectors with a higher proportion of unskilled workers.

Azam (2010), using microdata for 1983–2005, investigates the role of the demand and supply of skilled workers in explaining the rise in skill premium in India. The paper presents the following findings. First, the tertiary (college)-secondary (high school) wage premium increased in India during the 1990s and 2000s, and this increase differs across age groups. Increases in wage premiums have been driven mostly by younger age groups, while older age groups did not experience any significant increase. Second, the increase in wage premium was due to demand shifts in favor of workers with a tertiary education, mainly between 1993 and 2004. He argues that the growth rate of the demand for tertiary-educated workers relative to secondary-educated workers was fairly stable in the 1980s and 1990s. This is due to the increase in the relative supply of tertiary workers during 1983–1993, which negated the demand shift. As a result, the wage premium did not increase much. However, between 1993 and 1999, the growth rate of the relative supply of tertiary workers decelerated and became virtually stagnant between 1999 and 2004. This resulted in an increase in the wage premium.

Chamarbagwala and Sharma (2011) investigate the relationship between industrial delicensing, trade liberalization, and skill upgrading during the 1980s and 1990s among manufacturing plants in India. They use Annual Survey of Industries data to test whether industrial delicensing during the 1980s and 1990s played a role in skill upgrading (as measured by the employment and wage bill shares of white-collar workers). Using both difference-in-differences as well as regression discontinuity techniques, they find two important results. First, industrial delicensing during the 1980s increased the relative demand for skilled workers via capital- and output-skill complementarities; second, trade liberalization did not play a major role in raising the relative demand for skilled labor during the 1990s.

Last, Mehta and Hasan (2012) examine the effects of trade and services liberalization on wage inequality in India. Their main finding is that labor reallocations and wage shifts due to services reforms are many times larger than those of manufacturing goods liberalization. Additionally, the paper also highlights that (i) a large proportion (30%–66%) of the increase in wage inequality is due to changes in industry wages and skill premiums that cannot be empirically linked to trade liberalization; and (ii) the bulk of the effects of trade liberalization do not remain in interindustry wage shifts and skill premiums but are subsumed by general equilibrium effects.

Overall, the evidence is mixed. The majority of the studies find trade liberalization to have increased skill premium, whereas others ascertain no effect. This chapter does not make any effort to investigate the direct effect of trade reform on skill premium but looks at whether trade reform affects the demand for managerial workers, where skill intensity acts as an intermediary channel. In doing so, I find that skill intensity can possibly be termed a complementary channel (in increasing the demand for managerial workers) for firms below half of the size distribution.

8.3 Firm-level Data

The firm-level data that I primarily use for this chapter are based on the PROWESS database, constructed by the Centre for Monitoring Indian Economy (CMIE). The PROWESS database contains information on approximately 27,400 publicly listed companies, all within the organized sector, of which almost 11,500 are in the manufacturing sector. I examine firms belonging to the Indian manufacturing sector. Firms are placed according to the five-digit 2008 National Industrial Classification (NIC) level and are reclassified to the 2004 NIC level to facilitate matching with the industry-level tariffs. The database reports direct measures on a vast array of firm-level characteristics, including sales, disaggregated trade components (imports and exports), research and development (R&D) expenditures, technology transfers, production factors employed, gross value added, assets, ownership, and others. In addition, it covers both large and small enterprises; data for the former types are collected from balance sheets, whereas the latter is based on the CMIE's periodic surveys of smaller companies.

PROWESS presents several features that make it particularly appealing for the purposes of this study. It is in effect a panel of firms, enabling their behavior to be studied over time. The (unbalanced) sample covers up to 8,000 firms, across 108 (four-digit NIC) manufacturing industries that belong to 22 (two-digit NIC) larger ones,[10] over 1990–2011, thereby covering the 1990s trade reform.

The unique feature of the dataset upon which the analysis is mainly based is that it disaggregates compensation data to those received by managers and nonmanagers, with a further disaggregation of compensation to wages and bonuses. Specifically, the division is done at three levels: nonmanagers, directors, and executives, with the last two comprising the managers group. While the definition of the former is that they do not manage other employees, directors are defined as managers without executive powers, as opposed to executives, who do possess such responsibilities. Executives include, for instance, the chief executive officer, chief financial officer, and chairperson, whereas directors cover positions such as divisional managers. In effect, directors are considered middle management, whereas executives are the top management. While there may be scope for subjective interpretation of this distinction by firms, it does not affect the main analysis where I

---

[10]   In terms of composition, approximately 20% of the firms in the dataset are registered as chemical and pharmaceutical industries, followed by food products and beverages (13.74%), textiles (10.99%), and basic metals (10.46%).

aggregate executives and directors. These features enable me to study the relative demand for managers and through that trace down the underlying channel that affects it.

Table 8.1 presents a conditional correlation matrix of the share of managerial compensation with exports and imports (with imports also divided into four different categories: import of raw materials, import of capital goods, import of stores and spares, and import of finished goods). Column (1) shows that the total imports of a firm and share of managerial compensation are significantly correlated at the 5% level. Columns (2)–(5) divide total imports into the four categories. The numbers indicate that the correlation is strongest in the case of import of capital goods (0.03) followed by import of raw materials (0.01), with no significance in the case of import of stores and spares and of finished goods. I also do not find any significant correlation between the exports of a firm (column (6)) and managerial compensation. Nonetheless, these numbers are merely suggestive and not conclusive, unless we control for any other policy effects and firm- and industry-level attributes.

Table 8.1 Correlation Matrix—Imports, Exports, and Managerial Compensation

	Total Imports	Import of Capital Goods	Import of Raw Materials	Import of Stores and Spares	Import of Finished Goods	Total Exports	MComp/ TComp
	(1)	(2)	(3)	(4)	(5)	(6)	(7)
Total Imports	1.00						
Import of Capital Goods	0.14*	1.00					
Import of Raw Materials	0.70*	0.02*	1.00				
Import of Stores and Spares	0.12*	0.02*	0.16*	1.00			
Import of Finished Goods	0.71*	0.00	0.008*	0.00	1.00		
Total Exports	0.97*	0.009*	0.75*	0.11*	0.63*	1.00	
Managerial Compensation/ Total Compensation	0.01*	0.03*	0.01*	0.002	−0.002	0.001	1.00

Notes: Numbers denote correlation coefficients. * denotes significance at 5% level.
Source: Author's calculations.

Figure 8.3 Managerial Compensation, across Industries, 1990–2011

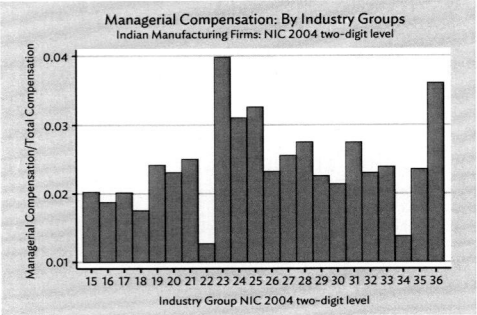

NIC = National Industrial Classification.

Note: The figure presents the average compensation share of managers across the 2004 NIC two-digit level industries, 1990–2011.

Source: Author's calculations.

The dataset provides much variation across firms and industries in the compensation characteristics of managers compared to nonmanagers. For instance, Figure 8.3 plots the average share of managerial compensation in total labor compensation across two-digit industries for 1990–2011.[11] It goes from a low of approximately 0.5% to a high of around 4%, and the difference across industries is clearly observed. This is also noted when measuring changes over time: Averaging annual changes over the same period, I observe that while in some industries the average annual rate of change is around 10%, in others it can get higher than 200%, thereby providing quite large differences. When this translates to the firm level, such variation will be even more prominent.

Last, the dataset has a relatively wide coverage, accounting for more than 70% of the economic activity in the organized industrial sector, and 75% (95%) of the corporate (excise duty) taxes collected by the Government of India (Goldberg et al. 2010). In terms of trade, it covers approximately 40%–45% of India's total export and import activity, presenting a reasonably good aggregate picture of India's trade position. In addition, it has been used in previous similar studies, providing some reassurance of its relevance and applicability to the particular

---

[11]   Note that all industry-level categorizations done throughout the chapter are based on the 2004 NIC classification.

issues studied.[12] All variables are measured in millions of Indian rupees, deflated to 2005 using the industry-specific Wholesale Price Index, and are outlined in the appendix. Table 8.2 presents descriptive statistics for all variables.[13]

Before proceeding to the regression analysis, it is imperative to clear up an important initial implication of the patterns outlined in Figure 8.2. The trend observed in terms of the increase in managerial compensation could be simply due to an administrative reclassification of workers. To show that this is not the case, I divide the sample of firms into four different quartiles by size (assets) and plot the share of managerial compensation for both importing and nonimporting firms across these four quartiles in Figure 8.4. A similar trend is observed across firms of all sizes: it is the importing firms for which the share is rising significantly. There is no plausible reason to argue that the firms across the size distribution in India are reclassifying their workers from nonmanagers to managers as the trade liberalization kicks in. This encourages me to look for an effect of trade reform where I use both firm-level import ratios and industry-level tariffs.

Table 8.2 Descriptive Statistics

	Mean	Median	Std Dev.	Min.	Max.
Panel A: Dependent Variables					
Managerial Compensation/ Total Compensation	0.02	0	0.07	0	1
Managerial Compensation	1.31	0	169.65	0	66,315.1
Nonmanagerial Compensation	95.53	14.4	631.83	0	47,619.5
Managers	1.56	1	0.72	1	7

continued on next page

[12]   See, for example, Goldberg et al. (2010), Topalova and Khandelwal (2011), Ahsan (2013), Ahsan and Mitra (2014), and De Loecker et al. (2016).

[13]   One pattern described in Table 8.1 deserves further comment. As reported, the maximum figures of various measures normalized using gross value added (GVA) can reach relatively high values. This is a feature of the definition of GVA (see the appendix), and occurs in cases of high purchases and low sales, such as in initial investments. All results are robust to omitting observations with GVA-normalized figures higher than 1; nonetheless, we maintain the full sample in the main analyses for the purposes of exploiting its full extent.

Table 8.2 *continued*

	Mean	Median	Std Dev.	Min.	Max.
Panel B: Firm-/Industry-level Determinants – Explanatory Variables					
Total Imports/GVA	0.89	0.04	39.63	0	7,323.5
Import of Raw Materials/GVA	0.68	0.15	10.25	0	1,142.67
Import of Capital Goods/GVA	0.40	0.02	12.66	0	1,192
Import of Stores and Spares/GVA	0.059	0.01	0.58	0	40.45
Import of Finished Goods/GVA	5.65	0.04	149.59	0	7,323.5
Technology Adoption/GVA	0.07	0	9.77	0	2,163
Capital Employed	8.82	1.76	128.57	0	16,789
Productivity	0.48	0.42	0.34	0	5.50
GVA	1,181.05	127.48	16,000.95	0.086	103,1605
Skill Intensity	0.26	0.25	0.07	0.04	0.71
Factories	3,870.49	3,304	3,021.15	15	13,893
Management Technology	2.49	2.48	0.42	0	3.17
Input Tariffs	73.02	48.83	49.40	17.34	202.02
Output Tariffs	75.93	50	57.14	14.5	298.07

GVA = gross value added.

Notes: Annual data at the firm level, covering 1990–2011. Monetary values are in real Indian rupees (million). "Managerial Compensation/Total Compensation" is the share of managerial compensation in total labor compensation. Compensation is the sum of wages and bonuses. With regard to managers, it is the sum for executives (top management) and directors (middle management), whereas for nonmanagers, it is all other employees. "Managers" is the total number of managers. "Total Imports" is Imports of Raw Materials + Imports of Capital Goods + Imports of Stores and Spares + Imports of Finished Goods. "Technology Adoption" is Research and development expenditure + Royalty payments for technical know-how. "Capital Employed" is the amount of capital employed. "Productivity" is a measure for firm productivity computed following the Levinsohn and Petrin (2003) methodology.[a] "GVA" is gross value added, defined as Total sales – Total raw material expenditure. "Skill intensity" is the ratio of nonproduction workers to total employees at the 2004 National Industrial Classification (NIC) three-digit level. "Factories" is the number of factories at the 2004 NIC three-digit level. "Management technology" is the management quality score obtained from Bloom and Van Reenen (2010) at the 2004 NIC two-digit level.[b] "Tariffs (input and output)" are at the industry level (NIC 2004 four-digit level).

[a] J. Levinsohn and A. Petrin. 2003. Estimating Production Functions Using Inputs to Control for Unobservables. *The Review of Economic Studies.* 70 (2). pp. 317–341.

[b] N. Bloom and J. Van Reenen. 2010. Why Do Management Practices Differ across Firms and Countries? *Journal of Economic Perspectives.* 24 (1). pp. 203–24.

Source: Author's calculations.

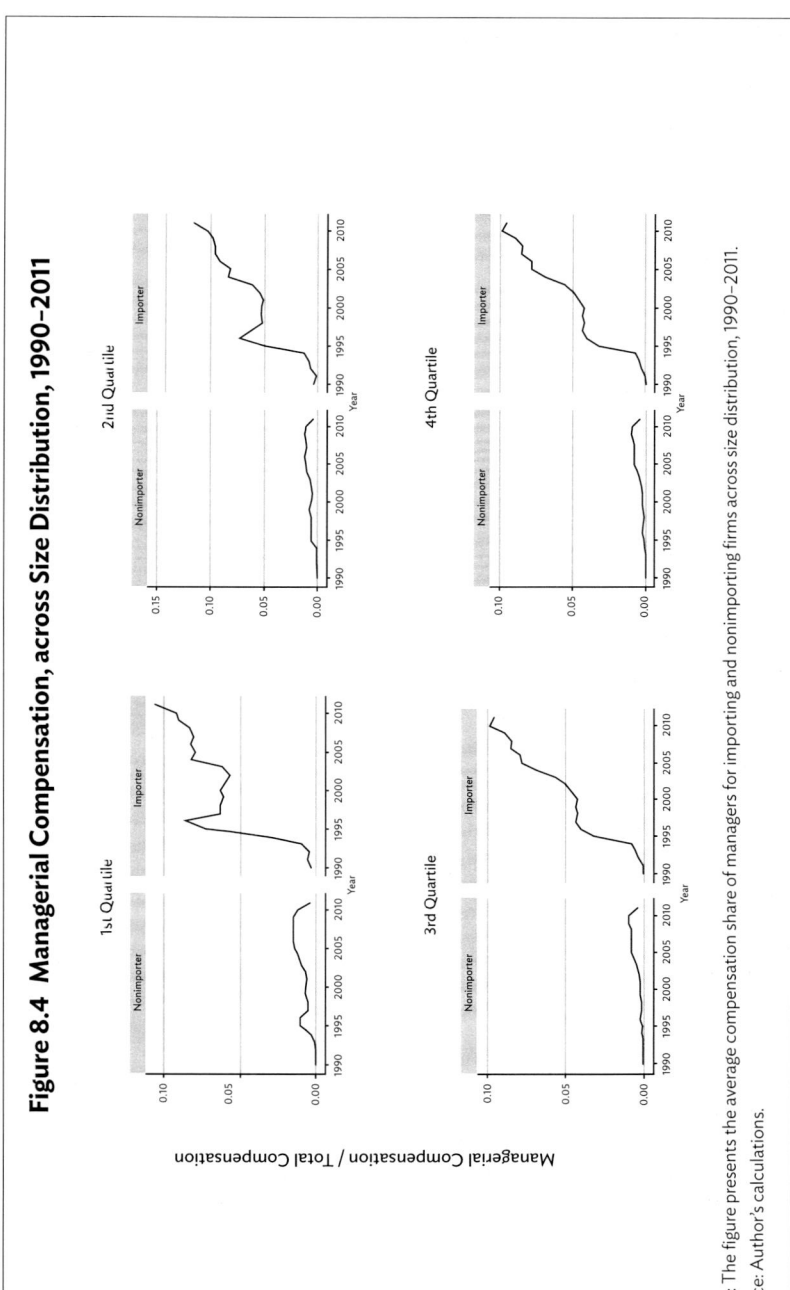

Figure 8.4 Managerial Compensation, across Size Distribution, 1990–2011

Note: The figure presents the average compensation share of managers for importing and nonimporting firms across size distribution, 1990–2011.

Source: Author's calculations.

8.4 Trade Reform and the Relative Demand for Managers

8.4.1 Preliminary Analysis

I start by testing the general association between trade and demand for managers through a firm-level analysis, using the data described earlier. Specifically, I use direct firm-level measures of trade, via import and export penetration, to see which form of trade flow is associated with demand for managerial workers. I consider the following equation for firm i, at time t:

$$\left(\frac{Mcomp}{Tcomp}\right)_{ijt} = \delta_i + \beta_T \ln(Trade/GVA)_{ijt-1}$$
$$+ firmcontrols_{it-1} + \eta_t + \theta_t^j + \varepsilon_{it} \qquad (1)$$

where *Mcomp* is the managers' total compensation, *Tcomp* is total labor compensation, *Trade* is either total imports or exports, and *GVA* is the gross value added of a firm i at industry j in year t. *firmcontrols* is a vector of firm-level characteristics. It includes firm age, age squared, and R&D intensity [(R&D expenditure + Royalty payment for technical know-how)/GVA]. δ_i and η_t are firm and time fixed effects. θ_t^j refers to interactions between industry fixed effects and time trends. It controls for other types of shocks (such as a change in labor policy or availability of more finance) at the industry level, which vary over time and may affect the compensation share of managers. I cluster standard errors at the firm level.

β_T is our coefficient of interest. It is the empirical association between normalized imports, or exports, and the relative demand for managers. In effect, the equation examines the determinants of the relative demand for managers, measured through the wage bill share of managers. Results appear in Table 8.3.

Starting with imports (*Imp/GVA*), column (1) presents the benchmark setting. As can be seen, the coefficient of interest is positive and significant. In addition, the magnitude is economically meaningful. A 1% increase in the GVA share of total imports increases the compensation share of managers by approximately 0.1%. In column (2), as I replace imports with exports (*Exp/GVA*), the effect vanishes. In other words, I do not find any effect of exports on the relative demand for managers. Column (3) uses both exports and imports. The significant effect of imports on the demand for managerial workers continues, with no effect from exports. Interestingly, this particular result depicts different

Table 8.3 Imports, Exports, and Relative Demand for Managers

	MComp/TComp				
	(1)	(2)	(3)	(4)	(5)
$(Imp/GVA)_{t-1}$	0.010*** (0.001)		0.010*** (0.001)		
$(Exp/GVA)_{t-1}$		0.002 (0.001)	0.0002 (0.001)	0.0003 (0.002)	0.001 (0.002)
$(ImpInput/GVA)_{t-1}$				0.008*** (0.001)	
$(ImpNInput/GVA)_{t-1}$				0.001 (0.003)	
$(ImpRaw/GVA)_{t-1}$					0.006*** (0.002)
$(ImpCap/GVA)_{t-1}$					0.010*** (0.003)
$(ImpStoSpa/GVA)_{t-1}$					0.002 (0.006)
$(ImpFin/GVA)_{t-1}$					0.001 (0.003)
Firm Controls$_{t-1}$	Yes	Yes	Yes	Yes	Yes
R-Squared	0.16	0.16	0.17	0.19	0.42
N	73,045	73,045	73,045	73,045	73,045
Firm FE	Yes	Yes	Yes	Yes	Yes
Year FE	Yes	Yes	Yes	Yes	Yes
Industry FE (four-digit) *Year Trend	Yes	Yes	Yes	Yes	Yes

FE = fixed effect, GVA = gross value added.

Notes: Columns (1)–(5) use the share of managerial compensation in the total compensation (*MComp/TComp*) of a firm as the dependent variable. Total compensation is the sum of compensation to managers and compensation to nonmanagers, where compensation to managers is the sum of compensation of all the management levels and compensation to nonmanagers is the compensation to all other employees. *Imp/GVA* is the GVA share of total imports (Import of raw materials + Import of capital goods + Import of stores and spares + Import of finished goods) of a firm. *Exp/GVA* is the GVA share of total exports of a firm. *ImpInput/GVA* is the GVA share of imports of capital goods and raw materials of a firm. *ImpNInput/GVA* is the GVA share of imports of stores and spares and finished goods of a firm. *ImpRaw, ImpCap, ImpStoSpa,* and *ImpFin* are import of raw materials, capital goods, stores and spares, and finished goods. GVA is the gross value added of a firm, defined as Total sales – Total raw material expenditure. *Firm Controls* include age of a firm, age squared, *TechAdop/GVA* and size of a firm. *TechAdop/GVA* measures the level of technology adoption, defined as Research and development expenditure + Royalty payments for technical know-how, normalized by GVA. I use "Assets" as the size indicator. All the dependent variables are in natural logarithm, measured in millions of Indian rupees, deflated to 2005 using the industry-specific Wholesale Price Index. Numbers in parenthesis are robust clustered standard errors at the firm level. Intercepts are not reported. *, **, and *** denote 10%, 5%, and 1% level of significance, respectively.

Source: Author's calculations.

dynamics than those presented in previous studies that emphasize the role of exports in developed economies (e.g., Caliendo and Rossi-Hansberg 2012), implying that the case of a developing economy may provide a new perspective on this.

Next, I exploit the classification of imports into several categories in columns (4) and (5). In column (4), I put together import of capital goods and raw materials and denote it as "import of inputs" (*ImpInput/GVA*), whereas I sum import of stores and spares and finished goods and classify it as "import of noninputs" (*ImpNInput/GVA*). The estimates show that the aggregate effect of imports on managerial compensation is completely driven by import of inputs. Column (5) regresses managerial compensation on exports and all the separate components of imports: import of capital goods (*ImpCap/GVA*), import of raw materials (*ImpRaw/GVA*), import of stores and spares (*ImpStoSpa/GVA*), and import of finished goods (*ImpFin/GVA*). Estimates demonstrate that the import of capital goods and import of raw materials are significantly and positively correlated with the share of managerial compensation, with the effect being higher in the case of capital goods.

To understand whether skill intensity can be termed one of the complementary channels for the increase in demand for managers, I interact the skill intensity ratio with the several import penetration ratios in Table 8.4. I define skill intensity as the ratio of nonproduction workers to total employees of an industry. This ratio is constructed at the three-digit level 2004 NIC. Columns (1)–(3) interact the skill intensity ratio with (*Imp/GVA*), (*ImpInput/GVA*), (*ImpNInput/GVA*), (*ImpRaw/GVA*), (*ImpCap/GVA*), (*ImpStoSpa/GVA*), and (*ImpFin/GVA*), respectively. The estimates do not show any evidence of the interaction effect of import ratios and skill intensity on the increase in the demand for managers.

Table 8.4 Imports, Exports, Relative Demand for Managers, and Skill Premium

	MComp/TComp		
	(1)	(2)	(3)
(*Imp/GVA*)$_{t-1}$ × *SkillInt*$_{t-1}$	0.003 (0.005)		
(*ImpInput/GVA*)$_{t-1}$ × *SkillInt*$_{t-1}$		−0.002 (0.007)	
(*ImpNInput/GVA*)$_{t-1}$ × *SkillInt*$_{t-1}$		−0.016 (0.021)	

continued on next page

Table 8.4 *continued*

	MComp/TComp		
	(1)	(2)	(3)
$(ImpRaw/GVA)_{t-1} \times SkillInt_{t-1}$			0.006
			(0.013)
$(ImpCap/GVA)_{t-1} \times SkillInt_{t-1}$			0.013
			(0.029)
$(ImpStoSpa/GVA)_{t-1} \times SkillInt_{t-1}$			0.003
			(0.006)
$(ImpFin/GVA)_{t-1} \times SkillInt_{t-1}$			0.002
			(0.006)
Firm Controls $_{t-1}$	Yes	Yes	Yes
R-Squared	0.61	0.61	0.61
N	73,045	73,045	73,045
Firm FE	Yes	Yes	Yes
Year FE	Yes	Yes	Yes
Industry FE (four-digit)*Year Trend	Yes	Yes	Yes

FE = fixed effect, GVA = gross value added.

Notes: Columns (1)–(3) use the share of managerial compensation in the total compensation (*MComp/TComp*) of a firm as the dependent variable. Total compensation is the sum of compensation to managers and compensation to nonmanagers, where compensation to managers is the sum of compensation of all the management levels and compensation to nonmanagers is the compensation to all other employees. *Imp/GVA* is the GVA share of total imports (Import of raw materials + Import of capital goods + Import of stores and spares + Import of finished goods) of a firm. *Exp/GVA* is the GVA share of total exports of a firm. *ImpInput/GVA* is the GVA share of imports of capital goods and raw materials of a firm. *ImpN'nput/GVA* is the GVA share of imports of stores and spares and finished goods of a firm. *ImpRaw, ImpCap, ImpStoSpa,* and *ImpFin* are import of raw materials, capital goods, stores and spares, and finished goods. GVA is the gross value added of a firm, defined as Total sales – Total raw material expenditure. *SkillInt* is the skill intensity of an industry, defined as the ratio of nonproduction workers to total employees of an industry at the 2004 National Industrial Classification three-digit level. *Firm Controls* include age of a firm, age squared, *TechAdop/GVA*, and size of a firm. *TechAdop/GVA* measures the level of technology adoption, defined as Research and development expenditure + Royalty payments for technical know-how, normalized by GVA. I use "Assets" as the size indicator. All the dependent variables are in natural logarithm, measured in millions of Indian rupees, deflated to 2005 using the industry-specific Wholesale Price Index. Numbers in parenthesis are robust clustered standard errors at the firm level. Intercepts are not reported. *, **, and *** denote 10%, 5%, and 1% level of significance, respectively.

Source: Author's calculations.

8.4.2 Causal Inference

India's Trade Reform

Prior to the 1990s, India was one of the most trade-restrictive economies in Asia, with high tariff and nontariff barriers. In 1991, following a balance-of-payments crisis, India turned to the

Figure 8.5 Tariff Reform in India, Manufacturing Industries, 1990–2011

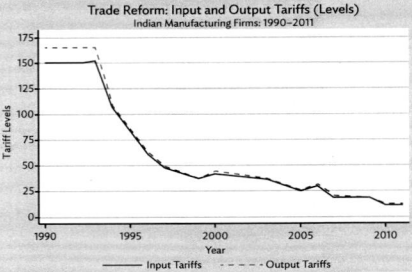

Note: The figure presents the average output and input tariffs across the 2004 National Industrial Classification four-digit level, 1990–2011.

Source: Author's calculations.

International Monetary Fund for assistance. The latter conditioned such assistance on the implementation of a major adjustment program. A major part of the adjustment program was to abandon the restrictive trade policies. As a result, average tariffs fell by more than half between 1990 and 1996 (Topalova and Khandelwal 2011). Nontariff barriers experienced a similar drop between the late 1980s and the mid-1990s (Goldberg et al. 2010). Figure 8.5 plots average tariff levels (both input and output) across manufacturing industries. Starting at around 150 in 1990, the average tariff level dropped to less than a tenth of that by 2011. These major tariff changes form the key policy measure I plan to exploit.

One major advantage with the tariff liberalization program is that it did not seem to have targeted industries within the manufacturing sector in a way that was related to prereform conditions (Goldberg et al. 2010). This establishes the plausibly exogenous nature of the reform. Next, there is much variation in the tariff changes across industries. The four-digit industry-level average annual decreases in tariffs range from as low as 2% to as high as 25%, with a mean of 6% and a standard deviation of approximately 2.5% (Chakraborty and Raveh 2018).

The tariff data are derived from the Trade Analysis Information System (TRAINS) and World Integrated Trade Solution (WITS) tariff database, at the Harmonized System six-digit level. These output tariffs are passed through India's input–output matrix for 1993–1994 to construct input tariffs. Next, both the input and output tariffs are then concorded to the four-digit 2004 NIC level using the Debroy and Santhanam (1993) concordance table. The tariffs are then matched with the firm-level data.

Empirical Strategy and Results

I estimate the following reduced-form equation to understand the effect of changes in tariffs on the relative demand for managers:

$$\left(\frac{Mcomp}{Tcomp}\right)_{ijt} = \delta_i + \beta_T \ln(Tariff)_{jt-1}$$

$$+ firmcontrols_{it-1} + \eta_t + \theta_t^j + \varepsilon_{jt} \qquad (2)$$

where $\ln(Tariff)_{jt-1}$ is the natural logarithm of tariff levels corresponding to industry j at period t-1. I use both output and input tariffs. The remaining notation follows that described previously. I follow Moulton (1990) to cluster standard errors at the industry level.

I start by using both input and output tariffs; results are reported in Table 8.5. Column (1) regresses the share of managerial compensation on lagged output tariffs, a number of firm controls (firm age, age squared, R&D intensity, and assets of a firm), firm fixed effects, year fixed effects, and interactions of industry fixed effects and year trends. The estimate shows that a drop in output tariffs or increase in product market competition significantly increases the share of managerial compensation. I additionally use lagged value of dependent variable in column (2); output tariffs continue to significantly affect managerial compensation. In column (3), I use both input and output tariffs. Including both input and output tariffs concurrently, the results show that the effect of output tariffs drops to 0 and a drop in tariffs on intermediate inputs now explains the rise in managerial compensation. Column (4) adds the lagged value of the share of managerial compensation. The previous finding continues: no effect of output tariffs and drop in tariffs on intermediate inputs explain the demand for managers.

This result (when using the input and output tariffs concurrently) also provides some insights into the potential underlying mechanism. While a decrease in output tariffs may stiffen product market (import) competition (Amiti and Konings 2007), a decrease in input tariffs increases the technological complexity of the production process. The latter is a feature of the higher quality and variety of imported inputs (Acemoglu and Zilibotti 2001; Eaton and Kortum 1996; Goldberg et al. 2010).

Table 8.5 Output Tariffs, Input Tariffs, and Relative Demand for Managers

	MComp/TComp			
	(1)	(2)	(3)	(4)
OutTariffs$_{t-1}$	−0.006**	−0.005**	−0.00002	−0.00006
	(0.003)	(0.002)	(0.003)	(0.003)
InpTariffs$_{t-1}$			−0.010**	−0.008**
			(0.005)	(0.004)
(MComp/TComp)$_{t-1}$		0.260***		0.263***
		(0.020)		(0.021)
Firm Controls$_{t-1}$	Yes	Yes	Yes	Yes
R-Squared	0.15	0.18	0.14	0.18
N	70,369	70,369	70,369	70,369
Firm FE	Yes	Yes	Yes	Yes
Year FE	Yes	Yes	Yes	Yes
Industry FE (four-digit)* Year Trend	Yes	Yes	Yes	Yes

FE = fixed effect, GVA = gross value added.

Notes: Columns (1)–(4) use the share of managerial compensation in the total compensation (MComp/TComp) of a firm as the dependent variable. InpTariffs/OutTariffs is input (output) tariffs at the four-digit National Industrial Classification 2004 level. Firm Controls include age of a firm, age squared, TechAdop/GVA, and size of a firm. TechAdop/GVA measures the level of technology adoption, defined as Research and development expenditure + Royalty payments for technical know-how, normalized by GVA. I use "Assets" as the size indicator. All the dependent variables are in natural logarithm, measured in millions of Indian rupees, deflated to 2005 using the industry-specific Wholesale Price Index. Numbers in parenthesis are robust clustered standard errors at the firm level. Intercepts are not reported. *, **, and *** denote 10%, 5%, and 1% level of significance, respectively.

Source: Author's calculations.

The dominating effect of input tariffs suggests that the observed increase in the relative demand of managers is triggered by changes in the production technologies rather than by a stronger competition in the final goods market. I continue my following analysis focusing on input tariffs.

Benchmark results. The benchmark results are presented in Table 8.6. In this table, I look at both intensive (price of managers or compensation of managers) and extensive (number of managers) margins of managerial demand in a firm. I start with the former. Columns (1)–(4) show that a 10% drop in input tariffs increases the relative managerial compensation of a firm by 0.8%–2.3%. In other words, the higher the usage of imported foreign inputs, the higher the demand for managers. Column (2) presents a dynamic version of Equation (2), providing a similar result.

Table 8.6 Input Tariffs, Relative Demand for Managers, and Skill Premium—Benchmark Results

	MComp/TComp					No. of Managers	MComp/GVA	Non-MComp/GVA
	(1)	(2)	(3)	(4)	(5)	(6)	(7)	(8)
$InpTariffs_{t-1}$	-0.015*** (0.003)	-0.023** (0.010)	-0.007 (0.005)	-0.0002 (0.003)	-0.014*** (0.005)	-0.312*** (0.104)	-0.010*** (0.002)	-0.004 (0.004)
$(MComp/TComp)_{t-1}$		0.657*** (0.031)						
$InpTariffs_{t-1}$ ×Importer			-0.008*** (0.003)					
$InpTariffs_{t-1}$ ×Importer Input				-0.013*** (0.001)				
Importer Input				0.067*** (0.006)				
$InpTariffs_{t-1}$ ×$SkillInt_{t-1}$					-0.005+ (0.003)			
$SkillInt_{t-1}$					0.013 (0.013)			
Firm Controls$_{t-1}$	Yes	Yes	Yes	Yes	Yes	Yes	Yes	Yes
R-Squared	0.12	N/A	0.12	0.62	0.61	0.58	0.31	0.43
N	70,369	70,369	70,369	70,369	70,369	27,975	70,369	70,369

continued on next page

Table 8.6 *continued*

	MComp/TComp					No. of Managers	MComp/ GVA	Non-MComp/ GVA
	(1)	(2)	(3)	(4)	(5)	(6)	(7)	(8)
Firm FE	Yes	Yes	Yes	Yes	Yes	Yes	Yes	Yes
Year FE	Yes	Yes	Yes	Yes	Yes	Yes	Yes	Yes
Industry FE (four-digit)*Year Trend	Yes	Yes	Yes	Yes	Yes	Yes	Yes	Yes

FE = fixed effect, GVA = gross value added.

Notes: Columns (1)–(5) use the share of managerial compensation in the total compensation (*MComp/TComp*) of a firm as the dependent variable. Columns (6)–(8) use number of managers, GVA share of managerial compensation, and GVA share of nonmanagerial compensation as the dependent variables, respectively. *Inp Tariffs* is input tariffs at the 2004 National Industrial Classification (NIC) four-digit level. *Importer* is a dummy variable that takes a value of 1 if a firm imports (either import of raw materials, capital goods, stores and spares, or finished goods). *ImporterInput* is a dummy variable if a firm imports either capital goods or raw materials. *SkillInt* is the skill intensity of an industry, defined as the ratio of nonproduction workers to total employees of an industry at the 2004 NIC three-digit level. *Firm Controls* include age of a firm, age squared, *TechAdop/GVA*, and size of a firm. *TechAdop/ GVA* measures the level of technology adoption, defined as Research and development expenditure + Royalty payments for technical know-how, normalized by GVA. I use "Assets" as the size indicator. All the dependent variables are in natural logarithm, measured in millions of Indian rupees, deflated to 2005 using the industry-specific Wholesale Price Index. Numbers in parenthesis are robust clustered standard errors at the firm level. Intercepts are not reported. +, *, **, and *** denote 12%, 10%, 5%, and 1% level of significance, respectively.

Source: Author's calculations.

Column (3) introduces an interaction term of input tariffs and an importer dummy (it takes a value of 1 for a firm that is an importer). The estimates show that the entire effect is concentrated for firms that are importing. In column (4), to understand the source of the previous effect according to the type of importing firm, I create an additional dummy where it takes a value of 1 if an individual firm is importing production units (capital goods and raw materials) and interacts with input tariffs. Likewise, in column (3), the results demonstrate that the magnitude of the effect increases by more than 1.5 times and the interaction term is significant at the 1% level. This gives additional support to the results shown in Table 8.3. Firms importing more intermediate inputs as a result of a drop in input tariffs (due to trade reform) require more managers to manage those inputs in order to utilize them in their production processes.

Column (5) introduces our key variable: skill intensity.[14] As before, I measure skill intensity through the three-digit industry-level ratio of nonproduction workers to all employees, with the standard skill intensity measure being used in the literature.[15] This measure is obtained from Ghosh (2014) (1990–2000) and the Indian Annual Survey of Industries (2001–2011). Previous studies indicate that globalization increases the demand for skill in developing economies (Goldberg and Pavcnik 2007). This, in turn, may affect the demand for managers. The main coefficient of interest, β_T, remains stable. Unlike the interaction terms between import ratios and skill intensity, the interacted effect of input tariffs and skill intensity explains the increase in demand for managers, but only at the 12% level of significance. In other words, *InpTariffs × SkillInt* indicates that there is an apparent differential effect across industries' benchmark skill intensity levels: The higher the drop in input tariffs, the higher the increase in the demand for skills, and thus

---

[14] At first glance, it may suggests that skill and managers might be correlated through the standard definition of skill in the literature, which considers nonproduction workers or otherwise those in white-collar occupations. Note, however, that this definition, while also covering managers, includes various additional occupations that are not necessarily managerial positions. For instance, in the cases of Berman, Bound, and Griliches (1994) and Zhu and Trefler (2005), skilled workers are defined as holding the following positions within the manufacturing sector: manager, professional, technician, and clerical worker. Indeed, managers represent a subset of that, though the other professions can fall under the nonmanagers classification.

[15] Proxying skill intensity by "nonproduction" is nontrivial, though this is common practice by necessity given data limitations. This measure is adopted by various studies on trade liberalization and skill in developing countries (e.g., Raveh and Reshef 2016; Zhu and Trefler 2005). In addition, Berman, Bound, and Griliches (1994) show that the production or nonproduction worker classification is a good proxy for skilled and unskilled workers.

the rise in managerial compensation. In other words, the demand for managers tends to rise in those sectors where there is a complementary effect of a drop in input tariffs and a higher ratio of skill intensity. This particular finding gives some possible indication of an increase in the skill premium through the import of high-quality intermediate goods by firms, which we investigate in column (8). On the other hand, the skill intensity variable is positively correlated with the demand for managers, but not significantly.

Column (6) uses the number of managers as the dependent variable. A drop in input tariffs also significantly affects the extensive margin of managers. I use the GVA share of managerial compensation in column (7). The benchmark result continues to be the same: a drop in tariffs increases the price of managers.

Lastly, column (8) exploits compensation of the other category of workers (i.e., nonmanagers) as the dependent variable. The reason to look at this category is to understand whether there is an opposite or differential effect of trade reform across different categories of workers. The point estimate shows that trade reform (or drop in input tariffs) has no effect on the demand for nonmanagers. In other words, the effect of tariff liberalization on nonmanagerial compensation is indistinguishable from 0. Based on these results, it is difficult to conclusively claim that higher demand for managers (as a result of trade reform) led to an increase in skill premium in India (although we find some evidence of skill intensity being one of the complementary channels).

Additional channels. Having identified the main effect, I now consider other possible complementary channels that may affect the demand for managers in Table 8.7. In each case, I focus on two points: first, the role of the additional control as an intermediate channel, by examining its direct effect, and second, via its effect through the main variable of interest (input tariffs).

I start with the potential connection between managers and capital employed. The key variable, intermediate inputs, is a flow measure of incoming equipment. The stock value of capital, which includes nonequipment stock as well, may also affect the demand for managers. For instance, capital-intensive production processes may involve automation and hence less problem solving and less demand for managers than labor-intensive production technologies. To test the role of capital intensity, I add firms' GVA share of capital employed in column (1). Its direct effect is indistinguishable from 0, providing no evidence that the stock of capital is correlated with the compensation share of managers. Importantly, the result does not change relative to the benchmark case, indicating that the effect of the incoming flow of equipment on the relative demand for managers holds regardless of whether the firm is relatively capital intensive. Notably, the interaction of this measure with input tariffs does

Table 8.7 Input Tariffs, Relative Demand for Managers, and Skill Premium—Additional Channels

	MComp/TComp				
	Capital Employed	Total Factor Productivity	Factories	Management Technology	
	(1)	(2)	(3)	(4)	(5)
$InpTariffs_{t-1}$	−0.003*	−0.00004	−0.009*	−0.013***	−0.035***
	(0.002)	(0.004)	(0.005)	(0.004)	(0.010)
$InpTariffs_{t-1}$ × $CapEmp_{t-1}$	0.001				0.005**
	(0.001)				(0.002)
$InpTariffs_{t-1}$ × TFP_{t-1}		−0.002			0.014***
		(0.003)			(0.004)
$InpTariffs_{t-1}$ × $Factories_{t-1}$			−0.001**		−0.002**
			(0.000)		(0.001)
$InpTariffs_{t-1}$ × MT_{t-1}				0.004	−0.029
				(0.004)	(0.019)
$CapEmp_{t-1}$	0.003				0.007
	(0.004)				(0.008)
TFP_{t-1}		0.016*			0.042***
		(0.009)			(0.016)
$Factories_{t-1}$			0.014***		0.019***
			(0.005)		(0.006)
Firm Controls_{t-1}	Yes	Yes	Yes	Yes	Yes
R-Squared	0.58	0.63	0.12	0.12	0.08
N	69,704	46,286	70,369	68,856	45,337
Firm FE	Yes	Yes	No	No	No
Industry FE	No	No	Yes	Yes	Yes
Year FE	Yes	Yes	Yes	Yes	Yes
Industry FE (four-digit) *Year Trend	Yes	Yes	Yes	Yes	Yes

FE = fixed effect, GVA = gross value added, TFP = total factor productivity.

Notes: Columns (1)–(7) use the share of managerial compensation (MComp/TComp) as the dependent variable. InpTariffs is input tariffs at the four-digit National Industrial Classification (NIC) 2004 level. CapEmp is the amount of capital employed by a firm. TFP is total factor productivity at the firm level estimated using Levinsohn and Petrin (2003).[a] Factories is the number of factories at the NIC 2004 three-digit level. MT is an index of Management Quality at the 2004 NIC two-digit level and has been sourced from Bloom and Van Reenen (2010).[b] Firm Controls include age of a firm, age squared, TechAdop/GVA, and size of a firm. TechAdop/GVA measures the level of technology adoption, defined as Research and development expenditure + Royalty payments for technical know-how, normalized by GVA. I use "Assets" as the size indicator. All the dependent variables are in natural logarithm, measured in millions of Indian rupees, deflated to 2005 using the industry-specific Wholesale Price Index. Numbers in parenthesis are robust clustered standard errors at the firm level. Intercepts are not reported. *, **, and *** denote 10%, 5%, and 1% level of significance, respectively.

a J. Levinsohn and A. Petrin. 2003. Estimating Production Functions Using Inputs to Control for Unobservables. *The Review of Economic Studies*. 70 (2). pp. 317–341.
b N. Bloom and J. Van Reenen. 2010. Why Do Management Practices Differ across Firms and Countries? *Journal of Economic Perspectives*. 24 (1). pp. 203–24.

Source: Author's calculations.

not point to any kind of systematic differential effects across capital intensity levels.

Next, I test for the effect of productivity. Previous research shows that trade liberalization increases firm productivity (e.g., Topalova and Khandelwal 2011). Higher productivity may increase the demand for managers due, for instance, to its potential effects on organizational design (Garicano 2000). To test whether it also acts as a complementary channel, I add a measure of productivity in column (2). I adopt the Levinsohn and Petrin (2003) methodology to construct firm-level total factor productivity.[16] The estimated coefficients indicate that the interaction effect of input tariffs and productivity is also not associated with the relative demand for managers.

Third, despite controlling for firm assets, I follow Acemoglu et al. (2007) and Bloom, Sadun, and Van Reenen (2010) to dig deeper into the potentially important effect of size on the demand for managers, by testing an additional related measure: the number of factories and plants at the three-digit industry level. I add this measure in column (3); the estimated coefficient   indicates that the main result is robust to this addition. The estimate also shows that a drop in input tariffs induced the establishment of more factories, which consequently led to an increase in managerial compensation, as local knowledge is important.

Last, an additional potential determinant relates to management technology. In a recent study, Chen (2017) makes a connection between trade liberalization and management technology. If better management technology requires a higher volume and quality of managers, it may represent a viable channel. To potentially test for this, I proxy management technology through the cross-country industry management survey carried out by Bloom and Van Reenen (2010). Surveying a large number of firms in various manufacturing industries in India (among other countries) throughout 2004, the authors construct a measure for management quality in different sectors. This index is a number between 1 and 5, with 5 representing the best quality. Estimates in column (4) indicate that input-trade liberalization does not have any systematically different effect on the relative demand for managers across industries' level of management technology.

In column (5), I include all the additional controls and their interactions with the input tariffs. This is a relatively demanding specification in terms of potential multicollinearity. However, the primary coefficient of interest remains negative and significant, similarly to the benchmark estimates.

---

[16]   The method controls for the potential simultaneity in the production function by using firms' raw material inputs as a proxy for the unobservable productivity shocks.

Firm characteristics. I now take a step further and look into several other firm- and industry-level characteristics to investigate which type(s) of firm or industry characteristic(s) is (are) driving the main result. An additional purpose is to check whether there is any kind of stronger evidence of skill intensity as a complementary channel for any subsample of firms that got masked in the aggregate results. The results are presented in Table 8.8.

I start by investigating the role of the size of a firm in column (1), more specifically whether the increase in the relative demand for managers is concentrated in one section of firms or differs across the size distribution. I divide the firms according to their size. I use the total assets of a firm as the size indicator. I use the following method: If the total asset of a firm is below the 25th percentile of the total assets of that industry, that firm belongs to the first quartile. Likewise, if a firm's total asset falls between the 25th and 50th, 50th and 75th, or is greater than the 75th percentile, it falls into the second, third, or fourth quartile, respectively. Since firms could move across quartiles over time, I use the average rank of the firms for the period of analysis. In order to find out the required effect, I interact the input tariffs with the respective quartiles.

The estimates reveal some interesting facts. All firms, except the big ones, show significant evidence of skill intensity as an additional channel due to a drop in input tariffs, with the effect being highest for the smallest firms. This is intuitive. As firms import more high-quality intermediate goods, due to trade reform, they require more managers. As a result, skill intensity acts as an additional channel through which demand for managers or managerial compensation rises. This is highest in the case of small firms, as they did not have any exposure before using these high-quality foreign intermediate inputs. On the other hand, the interaction terms of input tariffs and quartile dummies are significant across the size distribution, suggesting that skill intensity is not a channel (through which there is a rise in the demand for managers) for the big firms or the firms belonging to the fourth quartile.

Columns (2) and (3) divide the sample into exporters and nonexporters in order to understand whether there is any kind of premium attached to an exporting firm. As the results demonstrate, the effect of a drop in input tariffs on the demand for managers is observed for both exporters and nonexporters. However, the effect is stronger in the case of the exporting firms. Also, the evidence of skill intensity as a channel for the rise in demand for managers is stronger and greater for exporting firms than for nonexporters. The results point to an interesting outcome. The rise in the demand for managers or for a set of skilled workers is not only restricted to the group of exporters,

Table 8.8 Input Tariffs, Relative Demand for Managers, and Skill Premium—Firm Characteristics

| | Size | Export Orientation | | End Use | | Ownership | |
		Exporters	Non-exporters	Final Goods	Intermediate Goods	Domestic	Foreign
	(1)	(2)	(3)	(4)	(5)	(6)	(7)
$InpTariffs_{t-1}$		−0.021** (0.008)	−0.009+ (0.006)	−0.007 (0.006)	−0.017** (0.007)	−0.022*** (0.007)	−0.018 (0.019)
$InpTariffs_{t-1} \times SkillInt_{t-1}$		−0.012** (0.005)	−0.007* (0.004)	−0.004 (0.004)	−0.008+ (0.005)	−0.013*** (0.004)	−0.010 (0.013)
$InpTariffs_{t-1} \times Qr_1 \times SkillInt_{t-1}$	−0.020*** (0.007)						
$InpTariffs_{t-1} \times Qr_2 \times SkillInt_{t-1}$	−0.015** (0.007)						
$InpTariffs_{t-1} \times Qr_3 \times SkillInt_{t-1}$	−0.018*** (0.006)						
$InpTariffs_{t-1} \times Qr_4 \times SkillInt_{t-1}$	−0.007 (0.006)						
$InpTariffs_{t-1} \times Qr_1$	−0.054*** (0.010)						
$InpTariffs_{t-1} \times Qr_2$	−0.052*** (0.009)						

continued on next page

Table 8.8 *continued*

		MComp/TComp					
	Size	Export Orientation		End Use		Ownership	
		Exporters	Non-exporters	Final Goods	Intermediate Goods	Domestic	Foreign
	(1)	(2)	(3)	(4)	(5)	(6)	(7)
$InpTariffs_{s,t-1} \times Q_{r3}$	-0.054*** (0.010)						
$InpTariffs_{s,t-1} \times Q_{r4}$	-0.039*** (0.009)						
$Firm\ Controls_{t-1}$	Yes	Yes	Yes	Yes	Yes	Yes	Yes
R-Square	0.17	0.20	0.08	0.10	0.12	0.12	0.22
N	70,369	37,325	33,044	31,815	38,554	65,777	4,592
Firm FE	Yes	Yes	Yes	Yes	Yes	Yes	Yes
Year FE	Yes	Yes	Yes	Yes	Yes	Yes	Yes
Industry FE (four-digit)*Year Trend	Yes	Yes	Yes	Yes	Yes	Yes	Yes

FE = fixed effect.

Notes: Columns (1)–(7) use share of managerial compensation (*MComp/TComp*) as the dependent variable. *InpTariffs* is input tariffs at the 2004 National Industrial Classification (NIC) four-digit level. *SkillInt* is the skill intensity of an industry, defined as the ratio of nonproduction workers to total employees of an industry at the 2004 NIC three-digit level. Quartiles (Q_r) are defined according to the total assets of a firm. A firm belongs to the first quartile (Q_{r1}) if the assets of that firm are below the 25th percentile of the total assets of that industry to which the firm belongs and so on. *Firm Controls* include age of a firm, age squared, *TechAdop/GVA*, and size of a firm. *TechAdop/GVA* measures the level of technology adoption, defined as Research and development expenditure + Royalty payments for technical know-how, normalized by GVA. I use "Assets" as the size indicator. All the dependent variables are in natural logarithm, measured in millions of Indian rupees, deflated to 2005 using the industry-specific Wholesale Price Index. Numbers in parenthesis are robust clustered standard errors at the firm level. Intercepts are not reported. +, *, **, and *** denote 12%, 10%, 5%, and 1% level of significance, respectively.

Source: Author's calculations.

but rather it spans across the entire set of manufacturing firms. This is unlike the other cases, where the change in skill premium because of trade reform concentrates only on the exporters. In the case of India, the results suggest that the entire sector of manufacturing firms has undergone a change in their technological production processes.

Next, I categorize firms according to the end use of their goods: final and intermediate. The former comprises consumer nondurable and consumer durable goods, whereas the latter includes intermediate, basic, and capital goods. I follow Nouroz (2001) and match the firm-level dataset with the input–output classification. Columns (4) and (5) present the required result. The point estimates show us that the effect of the trade liberalization on the demand for managers is significant only in the case of the intermediate goods sector; similarly for the evidence of skill intensity.

Lastly, I investigate the ownership structure of an Indian manufacturing firm. I divide the sample of firms into two different groups: domestic (which includes both private and public firms) and foreign. The coefficients of interest in columns (6) and (7) tell us that the main result is entirely driven by the change in the managerial compensation ratio in the domestic firms, more so for the privately owned ones. While it is not entirely unexpected that privately owned firms have undergone a change in their production processes due to the adoption of high-quality foreign inputs, it is nevertheless surprising to see that only the domestic firms are the main drivers of change in the overall change in the demand for managers observed and not the multinationals.

8.4.3 Discussion of Results and Policy Relevance

Let us first summarize the main results of the empirical analysis and provide further interpretations. The key finding is that a drop in input tariffs, or increased use of imported intermediate inputs, increases the compensation (intensive) and number (extensive) of managers, with no effect on nonmanagerial workers. The effect is acute: (i) across firm-size distribution; (ii) whether a firm is an exporter or not; (iii) in firms producing intermediate goods; and (iv) in privately owned domestic firms. In addition, the results show some evidence of skill intensity as an additional channel, but only in the case of firms below the halfway point of the size distribution.

Two key questions arise. First, how may these findings be important for understanding the distributional effect, in terms of compensation of these two different kinds of workers (managers and nonmanagers), of trade policies? In particular, is the increase in wage gap between these two categories of workers solely due to an increase in the adoption of skill-biased technological inputs (due to a fall in input tariffs), or is there a simultaneous fall in the supply of skilled labor, which accentuated the wage premium? Second, what is the role of the government in responding to changes in the demand for more skilled workers through the supply of managerial skills and other types of skills? In order to address these questions, I draw on previous related research on India and consider a possible conceptual framework that can fit my findings into this broader picture.

I start by addressing the former. Input (output) tariffs relate to imported inputs (final goods). Goldberg, Khandelwal, and Pavcnik (2013) point out that because of the drop in input tariffs, due to the trade liberalization episode in India, imports of intermediate inputs saw the highest increase, of almost 300%; and the vast majority of the inputs are imported from the countries in the Organisation for Economic Co-operation and Development (OECD). Table 8.9 lists the top destinations in India's percentage of imported capital. It shows that India imports around 82% of capital goods from OECD destinations.

Table 8.9 Import of Capital Goods— Top 10 Destinations

Rank	Trading (1)	Imported Capital (2)
1	United States	20.14
2	Japan	16.80
3	Germany	16.73
4	United Kingdom	6.60
5	Singapore	4.98
6	France	4.96
7	Italy	4.63
8	Switzerland	3.10
9	Republic of Korea	2.18
	All Other	19.88
	Total	100

Note: Numbers in the table represent the share of capital goods imported by India from different destinations.
Source: I. Kandilov, A. Leblebicioglu, and R. Manghnani. 2016. Tariffs on Imported Capital and Firm-Level Investment in the Indian Manufacturing Sector, Mimeo, North Carolina State University.

Eaton and Kortum (2001) argue that the capital goods produced in the OECD countries are of high quality and R&D intensive. Thus, an increased use of imported inputs by a firm upgrades the technological intensiveness of the production technology it uses and therefore requires managers to cope with the new knowledge, thereby increasing their relative demand. Realizing the main effect is completely driven by the input side and hence implies that a quality upgrading channel is at work, operating via input-tariff liberalization.[17]

Previous studies on both developing and developed economies pointed to an export-based quality-upgrading channel (Caliendo and Rossi-Hansberg 2012) or product market competition (e.g., Cunat and Guadalupe 2009; Bloom, Sadun, and Van Reenen 2010). Verhoogen (2004) finds strong support for this hypothesis in the case of Mexico. Greater exports as a result of the peso crisis resulted in better-quality products being produced by the exporters. Since higher-quality products require a higher proportion of skilled workers, the relative demand for and returns to skilled labor increased. This chapter shows how a developing economy can present different dynamics regarding this.

Several hypotheses other than the "quality-upgrading" channel can be put forward to explain this rise in demand for managers and skill intensity. Some relate to economic reforms in general and not specifically to trade reform in driving the returns to skilled labor. According to this hypothesis, developing countries may experience higher returns to skilled-labor-intensive occupations such as professional, managerial jobs as a result of reforms that generate demand for individuals who can implement these reforms. The above results suggest that in India external sector reforms may have created more white-collar jobs. Empirical evidence is mixed: Cragg and Epelbaum (1996) find support for this hypothesis for pre-NAFTA Mexico, while Attanasio, Goldberg, and Pavcnik (2004) find no changes in the occupational returns between 1986 and 1998 in Colombia.

Further, outsourcing or global production sharing has also been identified as one of the reasons to explain the rise in skill intensity or premium and demand for skilled labor in developing economies. Feenstra and Hanson (1996, 2003) argue that trade liberalization by the developing countries allows their counterparts (developed countries) to transfer the production of intermediate goods and services. These

---

[17] To the extent that a higher demand for managers is associated with better management practices, these patterns are consistent with those documented by Bloom et al. (2016). They find that better-managed firms in the People's Republic of China and the United States use more imported inputs, and specifically more expensive and higher-quality inputs.

activities are skill intensive, which results in a greater demand for and returns to skilled labor. Therefore, the import of intermediate goods can benefit skilled workers in a developing economy, more so for firms that had the least exposure before the reform. Feenstra and Hanson (1997) find empirical support for this hypothesis for the case of Mexico.

The final one relates to skill-biased technical change. Wood (1995) argues that greater competition from foreign firms may induce domestic firms in a developing economy to either engage in R&D or to adopt new and advanced technologies in order to secure their market share in the domestic and international markets. Because of technology-skill complementarities, adoption of modern technologies raises the demand for and returns to skilled labor. He called this "defensive innovation." Harrison and Hanson (1999) and Attanasio, Goldberg, and Pavcnik (2004) found empirical support for this hypothesis for Mexico and Colombia, respectively. In the case of Ghana, Gorg and Strobl (2002) come to a similar conclusion (to mine): an increase in the relative wages of skilled labor (in my case, managers) brought about by skill-biased technological change induced through imports of technology-intensive capital goods. However, Pavcnik (2003) rejects the skill-biased technical change hypothesis for Chilean plants.

My analysis of managerial compensation of Indian manufacturing firms' documents large demand shifts toward managerial workers but does not find significant evidence of a shift away from nonmanagerial workers. I find that skill intensity played an important role in widening the wage gap between managerial and nonmanagerial workers in India between 1990 and 2011, but for small and medium-sized firms. These demand shifts were for both exporters and nonexporters as well as firms producing intermediate goods. The results also suggest that demand for managerial workers was primarily within industries during this period in India. This finding provides strong evidence for all the hypotheses discussed above: skill intensity as a result of external sector reforms played a major role in the creation of managerial jobs, thereby generating demand for skilled and managerial labor.

I now focus on the second question concerning the demand and supply factors influencing the role of skill intensity. Some of the existing literature (Dutta 2005; Kijima 2006; Chamarbagwala 2006) in India observes that the increase in wage inequality during 1983–1999 was mainly attributable to an increase in the returns to skills (as captured by educational attainment). However, Azam (2010) argues that the driving forces that led to the increase in wage premium for high-skilled workers (tertiary graduate workers) have not been fully explored. It is imperative to understand the determinants of the wage premium, as for policy

Table 8.10 Employment Share, by Educational Status

	1987	1993	1999	2004
	(1)	(2)	(3)	(4)
Below Primary	21.35	17.96	14.63	14.57
Primary	13.61	9.99	8.40	9.70
Middle	13.87	14.47	14.46	14.52
Secondary	29.47	31.14	32.72	31.50
Graduate and Above	21.71	26.45	23.79	29.71

Note: Numbers in the table indicate the share of regular employed male workers in urban India in the age group 23–57 years.

Source: M. Azam. 2010. India's Increasing Skill Premium: Role of Demand and Supply. The BE *Journal of Economic Analysis and Policy*. 10 (1). pp. 1–26.

makers it is important to know whether the increase in wage premium is driven by demand or supply, since the policy responses differ for these two scenarios. In addition, changes in wage premium have important implications for the evolution of wage inequality, and hence overall income inequality.

In order to understand whether the supply or demand factor played a role, I first look at the change in employment shares of different types of workers between 1987 and 2004. Table 8.10 divides workers according to educational status. The table uses data from four schedules (1987–1988, 1993–1994, 1999–2000, and 2004–2005) of the Employment and Unemployment Schedule administered by the National Sample Survey Organization. It shows that the employment share of workers with a graduate degree went up from 22% to 30% between 1987 and 2004. Though the supply of workers with a graduate degree and above increased between 1987 and 1999, it ceased to grow between 1999 and 2004. For the workers with primary and below primary education, the employment shares fell from 14% to 10% and from 21% to 15 %, respectively, between 1987 and 2004. However, the shares increased a little between 1999 and 2004. The employment share of secondary graduates also declined between 1999 and 2004.

Next, I look at the wage premiums. Figure 8.6 plots the wage premiums for graduate and secondary urban male workers. The figure shows two important things. First, the wage premium for graduate workers (calculated as the difference in mean log hourly wages between regular male workers with a tertiary or graduate degree and those with a secondary degree) increased from 0.37 to 0.52, whereas for secondary workers (wage premium calculated with respect to workers with

Figure 8.6 Wage Premium, Tertiary and Secondary Degree Workers, 1987–2004

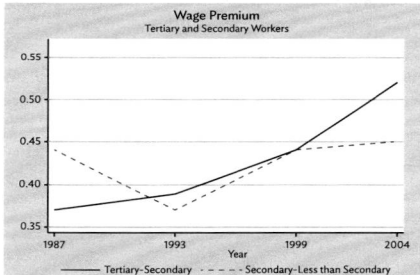

Note: The figure presents the wage premium for workers with a graduate degree and below a graduate degree, 1987–2004.

Source: M. Azam, M. 2010. India's Increasing Skill Premium: Role of Demand and Supply. *The EE Journal of Economic Analysis and Policy.* 10 (1). pp. 1–26.

below a secondary degree), it almost remained the same. Second, most of the increase in wage premium occurred in the 1990s, while it was relatively stable in the 1980s. Table 8.11 breaks down the wage premium estimates for all these years by different age categories. For the age group 23–27 years, the wage premium increased between 1987 and 1993,

Table 8.11 Tertiary-Secondary Wage Premium, by Age Group

Age Group	23–27	28–32	33–37	38–42	43–47	48–52	53–57
Year	(1)	(2)	(3)	(4)	(5)	(6)	(7)
1987	0.36	0.35	0.35	0.32	0.42	0.41	0.53
	(0.04)	(0.03)	(0.03)	(0.03)	(0.04)	(0.04)	(0.06)
1993	0.41	0.37	0.40	0.37	0.39	0.43	0.33
	(0.05)	(0.05)	(0.04)	(0.05)	(0.05)	(0.06)	(0.08)
1999	0.33	0.48	0.45	0.46	0.51	0.44	0.36
	(0.04)	(0.04)	(0.05)	(0.04)	(0.04)	(0.04)	(0.10)
2004	0.63	0.55	0.42	0.59	0.52	0.45	0.45
	(0.05)	(0.05)	(0.06)	(0.05)	(0.05)	(0.05)	(0.06)

Notes: The table entries are wage differential in mean log hourly wages between a tertiary graduate worker and secondary graduate worker. Numbers in parenthesis are robust standard errors.

Source: Azam, M. 2010. India's Increasing Skill Premium: Role of Demand and Supply. *The BE Journal of Economic Analysis and Policy.* 10 (1). pp. 1–26.

Figure 8.7 Wage Premium, Different Age Groups, Tertiary and Secondary Degree Workers, 1987–2004

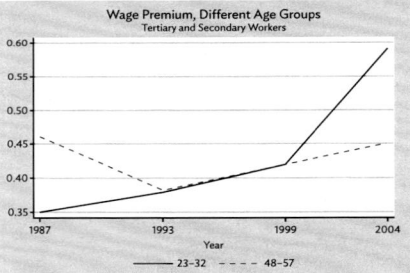

Note: The figure presents the wage premium for workers with a graduate degree and below a graduate degree for different age groups, 1987–2004.

Source: M. Azam, M. 2010. India's Increasing Skill Premium: Role of Demand and Supply. *The BE Journal of Economic Analysis and Policy*. 10 (1). pp. 1–26.

declined between 1993 and 1999, and then increased sharply between 1999 and 2004. The wage premium for the 28–32 age group increased continuously during 1987–2004. However, the wage premium for older age groups, 48–52 and 53–57 years, remained about the same between 1987 and 2004. This shows that the overall increase in wage premium of tertiary graduate workers between 1987 and 2004 was mostly driven by younger age groups. Figure 8.7 plots the wage gap between tertiary and secondary degree workers for the age groups 23–32 (younger group) and 48–57 (older group). It also shows similar trends.

Putting all these together, it can be argued that, as the relative supply of tertiary workers (or workers with a graduate degree or above) slowed down during the 1990s and 2000s, coupled with the increase in demand for them as the firms started to use more technologically intensive inputs due to a drop in tariffs, it led to a rise in wage premium. Further, this wage premium is particularly high for workers belonging to the 23–32 age group.

8.5 Conclusion

This chapter investigates the effect of India's trade liberalization episode in the form of a drop in tariffs on the demand for managerial workers during 1990–2011. Additionally, I check whether the demand for managers can be explained through a widely researched phenomenon, an increase in skill intensity. The study uses detailed data on compensation for Indian manufacturing firms and shows that a drop in input tariffs—and not output—significantly increases the demand for managers. A 10% drop in input tariffs increases the share of managerial compensation by 0.5%–3.5 %. The trade-induced demand shifts toward managerial workers find some support for quality upgrading, sharing of production activities, or the skill-biased technical change hypothesis, even though it is not possible to decompose the demand increase for managerial workers into its exact source.

The results also show that one possible channel for an increase in the compensation share of managers for firms below the halfway point of the size distribution may be through an increase in skill intensity. On the other hand, the estimates do not show any kind of demand shift away from nonmanagerial workers. Further analysis shows that the shortage in the supply of skilled workers during the late 1990s and 2000s, coupled with the increase in demand for these workers, led to an increase in wage premium for these workers. And this wage premium was highest for the workers belonging to the 23–32 years age cohort. This suggests that the demand for skill in the Indian economy was not solely due to an increase in the use of intermediate inputs but also to changes within the economy that were not related to trade. Dutta (2005) decomposes the wage regression functions to highlight that the industry affiliation of workers can also explain about a quarter of the wage inequality.

In India, low mobility between industries and a lack of transferable skills prevent workers from moving out of industries with declining relative wages in response to trade reform. All the results put together and this characteristic of the labor market in India suggest the current need to increase labor market flexibility through labor market and other institutional reforms. However, these reforms would also need to be supplemented by adequate provisions for social protection. Safety net programs for workers affected by trade reforms are necessary to minimize the short-run adjustment costs faced by workers from which there was a demand shift. There is also a need for a coherent strategy for social protection such as the rationalization of severance pay schemes, a movement toward insurance mechanisms covering both the organized and unorganized sectors, and skill development programs for workers.

References

Acemoglu, D. 2003. Patterns of Skill Premia. *The Review of Economic Studies*. 70 (2). pp. 199–230.

Acemoglu, D., P. Aghion, C. Lelarge, and J. Van Reenen. 2007. Technology, Information and the Decentralization of the Firm. *The Quarterly Journal of Economics*. 122 (4). pp. 1759–99.

Acemoglu, D., and F. Zilibotti. 2001. Productivity Differences. *The Quarterly Journal of Economics*. 116 (2). pp. 563–606.

Ahsan, R. 2013. Input Tariffs, Speed of Contract Enforcement, and the Productivity of Firms in India. *Journal of International Economics*. 90 (1). pp. 181–92.

Ahsan, R., and D. Mitra. 2014. Trade Liberalization and Labor's Slice of the Pie: Evidence from Indian Firms. *Journal of Development Economics*. 108 (1). pp. 1–16.

Amiti, M., and L. Cameron. 2012. Trade Liberalization and the Wage Skill Premium: Evidence from Indonesia. *Journal of International Economics*. 87 (2). pp. 277–87.

Amiti, M., and D. R. Davis. 2012. Trade, Firms, and Wages: Theory and Evidence. *The Review of Economic Studies*. 79 (1). pp. 1–36.

Amiti, M., and J. Konings. 2007. Trade Liberalization, Intermediate Inputs, and Productivity: Evidence from Indonesia. *The American Economic Review*. 97 (5). pp. 1611–38.

Araújo, B. C., and L. S. Paz. 2014. The Effects of Exporting on Wages: An Evaluation Using the 1999 Brazilian Exchange Rate Devaluation. *Journal of Development Economics*. 111. pp. 1–16.

Attanasio, O., P. Goldberg, and N. Pavcnik. 2004. Trade Reforms and Wage Inequality in Colombia. *Journal of Development Economics*. 74 (2). pp. 331–366.

Autor, D., F. Levy, and R. J. Murnane. 2003. The Skill Content of Recent Technological Change: An Empirical Exploration. *The Quarterly Journal of Economics*. 118 (4). pp. 1279–333.

Azam, M. 2010. India's Increasing Skill Premium: Role of Demand and Supply. *The BE Journal of Economic Analysis and Policy*. 10 (1). pp. 1–26.

Baumgarten, D. 2013. Exporters and the Rise in Wage Inequality: Evidence from German linked Employer–Employee Data. *Journal of International Economics*. 90 (1). pp. 201–17.

Behrman, J. R., N. Birdsall, and M. Székely. 2000. Economic Reform and Wage Differentials in Latin America. IADB Research Department Working Paper. No. 435. Washington, DC: Inter-American Development Bank.

Bernard, A. B., and J.B. Jensen. 1997. Exporters, Skill Upgrading, and the Wage Gap. *Journal of International Economics*. 42 (1–2). pp. 3–31.

Berman, E., J. Bound, and Z. Griliches. 1994. Changes in the Demand for Skilled Labor within US Manufacturing: Evidence from the Annual Survey of Manufactures. *The Quarterly Journal of Economics*. 109 (2). pp. 367–97.

Beyer, H., P. Rojas, and R. Vergara. 1999. Trade Liberalisation and Wage Inequality. *Journal of Development Economics*. 59 (1). pp. 103–23.

Biscourp, P., and F. Kramarz. 2007. Employment, Skill Structure and International Trade: Firm-level Evidence for France. *Journal of International Economics*. 72 (1). pp. 22–51.

Bloom N., B. Eifert, A. Mahajan, D. McKenzie, and J. Roberts. 2013. Does Management Matter? Evidence from India. *The Quarterly Journal of Economics*. 128 (1). pp. 1–51.

Bloom, N., L. Garicano, R. Sadun, and J. Van Reenen. 2014. The Distinct Effects of Information Technology and Communication Technology on Firm Organization. *Management Science*. 60 (12). pp. 2859–85.

Bloom, N., K. Manova, S. Sun, J. Van Reenen, and Z. Yu. 2016. Managing Trade: Evidence from China and the US, Mimeo.

Bloom, N., R. Sadun, and J. Van Reenen. 2010. Does Product Market Competition Lead Firms to Decentralize? *The American Economic Review Papers and Proceedings*. 100. pp. 434–8.

Bloom, N., and J. Van Reenen. 2007. Measuring and Explaining Management Practices Across Firms and Countries, *The Quarterly Journal of Economics*. 122 (4). pp. 1351–1408.

_____. 2010. Why Do Management Practices Differ across Firms and Countries? *Journal of Economic Perspectives*. 24 (1). pp. 203–24.

Bonfatti, R., and M. Ghatak. 2013. Trade and the Allocation of Talent with Capital Market Imperfections. *Journal of International Economics*. 89 (1). pp. 187–201.

Bustos, P. 2011. The Impact of Trade Liberalization on Skill Upgrading: Evidence from Argentina, Mimeo.

Caliendo, L., and E. Rossi-Hansberg. 2012. The Impact of Trade on Organization and Productivity. *The Quarterly Journal of Economics*. 127 (3). pp. 1393–467.

Card, D., and J. DiNardo. 2002. Skill-Biased Technological Change and Rising Wage Inequality: Some Problems and Puzzles. *Journal of Labor Economics*. 20 (S4). pp. S733–S783.

Chakraborty, P., and O. Raveh. 2018. Input-Trade Liberalization, and the Demand for Managers: Evidence from India. *Journal of International Economics*. 111. pp. 159–76.

Chamarbagwala, R. 2006. Economic Liberalization and Wage Inequality in India. *World Development*. 34 (12). pp. 1997–2015.

Chamarbagwala, R., and G. Sharma. 2011. Industrial De-licensing, Trade Liberalization, and Skill Upgrading in India. *Journal of Development Economics*. 96 (2). pp. 314–36.

Chen, C. 2017. Management Quality and Firm Hierarchy in Industry Equilibrium. *American Economic Journal: Microeconomics*. 9 (4). pp. 203–44.

Chen, B., M. Yu, and Z. Yu. 2017. Measured Skill Premia and Input Trade Liberalization: Evidence from Chinese Firms. *Journal of International Economics*. 109. pp. 31–42.

Cragg, M. I., and M. Epelbaum. 1996. Why Has Wage Dispersion Grown in Mexico? Is It the Incidence of Reforms or the Growing Demand for Skills? *Journal of Development Economics*. 51 (1). pp. 99–116.

Cunat, V., and M. Guadalupe. 2009. Globalization and the Provision of Incentives inside the Firm. *Journal of Labor Economics*. 27 (2). pp. 179–212.

Currie, J., and A. Harrison. 1997. Sharing the Costs: Trade Reform and Labor Market Adjustment in Morocco. *Journal of Labor Economics*. 15 (S3). pp. S44–S71.

De Loecker, J., P. Goldberg, A. Khandelwal, and N. Pavcnik. 2016. Prices, Markups and Trade Reform. *Econometrica*. 84 (2). pp. 445–510.

Debroy, B., and A. T. Santhanam. 1993. Matching Trade Codes with Industrial Codes. *Foreign Trade Bulletin*. XXIV (1). pp. 5–27.

Dutta, P. V. 2005. Accounting for Wage Inequality in India. *Indian Journal of Labour Economics*. 48 (2). pp. 273–95.

_____. 2007. Trade Protection and Industry Wages in India. *Industrial and Labor Relations Review*. 60 (2). pp. 268–86.

Eaton, J., and S. Kortum. 1996. Trade in Ideas Patenting and Productivity in the OECD. *Journal of International Economics*. 40 (4). pp. 251–78.

_____. 2001. Trade in Capital Goods. *European Economic Review*. 45 (7). pp. 1195–1235.

Ebenstein, A., A. Harrison, M. McMillan, and S. Phillips. 2014. Estimating the Impact of Trade and Offshoring on American Workers Using the Current Population Surveys. *The Review of Economics and Statistics*. 96 (4). pp. 581–595

Feenstra, A. D., and G. H. Hanson. 1996. Foreign Investment, Outsourcing and Relative Wages. In R. C. Feenstra, G. M. Grossman, and D. A. Irwin, eds. *Political Economy of Trade Policy: Papers in Honor of Jagdish Bhagwati*. Cambridge, MA: MIT Press. pp. 89–127.

_____. 1997. Foreign Direct Investment and Relative Wages: Evidence from Mexico's Maquiladoras. *Journal of International Economics*. 42 (3–4). pp. 371–93.

_____. 2003. Global Production Sharing and Rising Inequality: A Survey of Trade and Wages. In E. Choi and J. Harrigan, eds. *Handbook of International Trade*. Malden, MA: Blackwell. pp. 146–85.

Feliciano, Z. 2001. Workers and Trade Liberalization: The Impact of Trade Reforms in Mexico on Wages and Employment. *Industrial and Labor Relations Review*. 55 (1). pp. 95–115.

Frías, J. A., D. S. Kaplan, and E. Verhoogen. 2009. Exports and Wage Premia: Evidence from Mexican Employer-Employee Data, Mimeo.

_____. 2012. Exports and Within-Plant Wage Distributions: Evidence from Mexico. *The American Economic Review*. 102 (3). pp. 435–40.

Galiani, S., and P. Sanguinetti. 2003. The Impact of Trade Liberalization on Wage Inequality: Evidence from Argentina. *Journal of Development Economics*. 72: 497–513.

Garicano, L. 2000. Hierarchies and the Organization of Knowledge in Production. *Journal of Political Economy*. 108 (5). pp. 874–904.

Garicano, L., and E. Rossi-Hansberg. 2004. Inequality and the Organization of Knowledge. *The American Economic Review*. 94 (2). pp. 197–202.

_____. 2006. Organization and Inequality in a Knowledge Economy. *The Quarterly Journal of Economics*. 121 (4). pp. 1383–435.

Ghosh, S. 2014. Manufacturing Sector in India: Role of External Economies and Industrial Policy, Mimeo, Jawaharlal Nehru University.

Goldberg. P. K., A. Khandelwal, and N. Pavcnik. 2013. Variety In, Variety Out: Imported Input and Product Scope Expansion in India, In J. Bhagwati and A. Panagariya, eds. *Reforms and Economic Transformation in India*. New York: Oxford University Press. pp. 168–99.

Goldberg, P. K., A. Khandelwal, N. Pavcnik, and P. Topalova. 2010. Imported Intermediate Inputs and Domestic Product Growth: Evidence from India. *The Quarterly Journal Economics*. 125 (4). pp. 1727–1767.

Goldberg, P. K., and N. Pavcnik. 2005. Trade, Wages, and the Political Economy of Trade Protection: Evidence from the Colombian Trade Reforms. *Journal of International Economics*. 66 (1). pp. 75–105.

_____. 2007. Distributional Effects of Globalization in Developing Countries. *Journal of Economic Literature*. 45 (1). pp. 39–82.

Gonzaga, G., N. Menezes-Filho, and C. Terra. 2006. Trade Liberalization and the Evolution of Skill Earnings Differentials in Brazil. *Journal of International Economics*. 68 (2). pp. 345–67.

Gorg, H., and G. Strobl. 2002. Relative Wages, Openness, and Skill-biased Technological Change in Ghana, Mimeo.

Grossman, G., and E. Rossi-Hansberg. 2008. Trading Tasks: A Simple Theory of Offshoring. *The American Economic Review*. 98 (5). pp. 1978–97.

Haltiwanger, J., A. Kugler, M. Kugler, A. Micco, and C. Page. 2004. Effects of Tariffs and Real Exchange Rates on Job Reallocation: Evidence from Latin America. *Policy Reform*. 7 (4). pp. 191–208.

Harrison, A., and G. Hanson. 1999. Who Gains from Trade Reform? Some Remaining Puzzles. *Journal of Development Economics*. 59 (1). pp. 125–54.

Hummels, D., R. Jorgensen, J. Munch, and C. Xiang. 2014. The Wage Effects of Offshoring: Evidence from Danish Matched Worker-Firm Data. *The American Economic Review*. 104 (6). pp. 1597–629.

Kandilov, I., A. Leblebicioglu, and R. Manghnani. 2016. Tariffs on Imported Capital and Firm-Level Investment in the Indian Manufacturing Sector, Mimeo, North Carolina State University.

Kijima, Y. 2006. Why Did Wage Inequality Increase? Evidence from Urban India 1983–99. *Journal of Development Economics*. 81. pp. 97–117.

Koren, M., M. Csillag, and J. Kollo. 2019. Machines and Machinists: Importing Skill-Biased Technology, Mimeo, Central European University.

Krishna, P., D. Mitra, and S. Chinoy. 2001. Trade Liberalization and Labor Demand Elasticities: Evidence from Turkey. *Journal of International Economics*. 55 (2). pp. 391–409.

Krishna, P., J. P. Poole, and M. Z. Senses. 2014. Wage Effects of Trade Reform with Endogenous Worker Mobility. *Journal of International Economics*. 93 (2). pp. 239–52.

Kumar, U., and P. Mishra. 2008. Trade Liberalization and Wage Inequality: Evidence from India. *Review of Development Economics*. 12 (2). pp. 291–311.

Levinsohn, J., and A. Petrin. 2003. Estimating Production Functions Using Inputs to Control for Unobservables. *The Review of Economic Studies*. 70 (2). pp. 317–341.

Ma, L., and D. Ruzic. 2018. Globalization and Top Income Shares, Mimeo.

Marin, D., and T. Verdier. 2008. Power inside the Firm and the Market: A General Equilibrium Approach. *Journal of the European Economic Association*. 6 (4). pp. 752–88.

———. 2014. Corporate Hierarchies and International Trade: Theory and Evidence. *Journal of International Economics*. 94 (2). pp. 295–310.

Martins, P. S., and L. Opromolla. 2010. Exports, Imports and Wages: Evidence from Matched Firm-Worker-Product Panels, Mimeo.

McCaig, B. 2011. Exporting Out of Poverty: Provincial Poverty in Vietnam and US Market Access. *Journal of International Economics*. 85 (1). pp. 102–13.

Mehta, A., and R. Hasan. 2012. The Effects of Trade and Services Liberalization on Wage Inequality in India. *International Review of Economics and Finance.* 23. pp. 75–90.

Menezes-Filhoz, N., and M-A. Muendler. 2011. Labor Reallocation in Response to Trade Reform, Mimeo.

Moulton, B. R. 1990. An Illustration of a Pitfall in Estimating the Effects of Aggregate Variables on Micro Units. *The Review of Economics and Statistics.* 72 (2). pp. 334–8.

Nouroz, H. 2001. *Protection in Indian Manufacturing.* New Delhi: MacMillan Publishers India Ltd.

Pavcnik, N. 2003. What Explains Skill Upgrading in Less Developed Countries? *Journal of Development Economics.* 71 (2). pp. 311–28.

Pavcnik, N., A. Blom, P. Goldberg, and N. Schady. 2004. Trade Liberalization and Industry Wage Structure: Evidence from Brazil. *World Bank Economic Review.* 18 (3). pp. 319–44.

Raveh, O., and A. Reshef. 2016. Capital Imports Composition, Complementarities, and the Skill Premium in Developing Countries. *Journal of Development Economics.* 118: 183–206.

Revenga, A. 1997. Employment and Wage Effects of Trade Liberalization: The Case of Mexican Manufacturing. *Journal of Labor Economics.* 15 (S3). pp. S20–S43.

Smith, J. P., D. Thomas, E. Frankenberg, K. Beegle, and G. Teruel. 2002. Wages, Employment and Economic Shocks: Evidence from Indonesia. *Journal of Population Economics.* 15 (1). pp. 161–93.

Stolper, W. F., and P. A. Samuelson. 1941. Protection and Real Wages. *The Review of Economic Studies.* 9 (1). pp. 58–73.

Topalova, P., and A. Khandelwal. 2011. Trade Liberalization and Firm Productivity: The Case of India. *The Review of Economics and Statistics.* 93 (3). pp. 995–1009.

Verhoogen, E. 2004. Trade, Quality Upgrading and Wage Inequality in the Mexican Manufacturing Sector: Theory and Evidence from an Exchange-Rate Shock, Mimeo, University of California, Berkeley.

Verhoogen, E. A. 2008. Trade, Quality Upgrading, and Wage Inequality in the Mexican Manufacturing Sector. *The Quarterly Journal of Economics.* 123 (2). pp. 489–530.

Wood, A. 1995. How Trade Hurt Unskilled Workers. *Journal of Economic Perspectives.* 9 (3). pp. 57–80.

Zhu, S. C., and D. Trefler. 2005. Trade and Inequality in Developing Countries: A General Equilibrium Analysis. *Journal of International Economics.* 65 (1). pp. 21–48.

Appendix A8

Data

I use an annual-based panel of Indian firms that covers up to 8,000+ firms, across 108 industries within the manufacturing sector, over 1990–2011 (with the exception of specific cases, where specified). Unless otherwise specified, variables are based on data from the PROWESS database of the Centre for Monitoring Indian Economy (CMIE). All monetary-based variables are measured in millions of Indian rupees, deflated to 2005 using the industry-specific Wholesale Price Index. All industry-level cases are based on the 2004 National Industrial Classification (NIC).

Variable Definitions

o   **Managerial Compensation/Total Compensation:** Share of managerial compensation in total labor compensation; compensation defined as the sum of all salaries, and additional bonuses.

o   **Total Managers:** Total number of managers in a firm. This is the sum of the total number of managers at the top and middle management level.

o   **Managerial Compensation:** Total managerial compensation of a firm. This is the sum of all the management layers put together.

o   **Nonmanagerial Compensation:** Total nonmanagerial compensation of a firm. This is the sum of compensation of all nonmanagerial workers.

o   **Input/Output Tariffs:** Input/output tariffs at the four-digit industry level, obtained from Ahsan and Mitra (2014) for 1990–2003, with the balance collected from Chakraborty and Raveh (2018).

o   **Imp/GVA:** Share of total imports in gross value added.

o   **ImpRaw/GVA:** Share of raw material imports in gross value added.

o   **ImpCap/GVA:** Share of capital imports in gross value added.

o   **ImpSto/GVA:** Share of stores and spares imports in gross value added.

o   **ImpFin/GVA:** Share of final goods imports in gross value added.

o   **Exp/GVA:** Share of total exports in gross value added.

o   **GVA:** Gross value added, defined as the difference between total sales and expenditures on raw materials.

o **Skill Intensity:** The three-digit industry-level ratio of nonproduction workers to all employees, obtained from the Indian Annual Survey of Industries (2001–2011) and from Ghosh (2014) (1990–2000).

o **Capital Employed:** Total amount of capital employed by a firm.

o **Productivity:** Total factor productivity at the firm level is computed using the Levinsohn and Petrin (2003) methodology.

o **Factories:** The three-digit industry-level number of factories/plants.

o **Management Technology:** The four-digit industry-level management quality score in 2004, obtained from Bloom and Van Reenen (2010); the score is between 1 and 5, with 5 denoting the highest quality.

o **Technology Adoption:** Share of research and development expenditure and royalty payments for technical know-how in gross value added.

o **Assets:** Total assets of a firm. This is an indicator of size.

o **Age:** Age of a firm in years.

o **Ownership:** This indicates whether a firm is domestically owned or foreign owned.

9

Multiproduct Firms, Tariff Liberalization, and Product Churning in Vietnamese Manufacturing

Ha Thi Thanh Doan

9.1 Introduction

Multiproduct firms are the dominant players in international production and trade (Bernard, Jensen, and Schott 2010; Goldberg et al. 2010a). Moreover, these firms are active in alternating their combination of product varieties. In fact, Bernard, Jensen, and Schott (2010) have documented a frequent change in the product mix in the United States (US), where almost 50% of multiproduct firms change their product mix every 5 years. Indeed, firms' adjustment in product scope constitutes one important layer of firm heterogeneity (Nocke and Yeaple 2006).

Understanding firms' product adjustment is crucial for several reasons. First, changes in the commodity mix of manufacturing firms affect firms' output and productivity, through which they exert an impact on the economy's aggregate growth. For example, Bernard, Jensen, and Schott (2006) have demonstrated that the contribution to output growth of a product margin outweighs that of firm entry and exit. Goldberg et al. (2010a) have observed a similar phenomenon in Indian manufacturing, where changes in firms' product mix contributed to as much as 25% of output expansion. In this regard, the changing of product lines is a nontrivial channel of resource reallocation within firms. Second, switching production activities has important implications for the structural shift across sectors. For instance, a shift away from resource-based and primary products to more capital-intensive products, a source of industrial upgrading, will induce the economy to move to the next stage of the industrialization process.

Why some firms diversify their production is not a new question in the industrial organization literature. For instance, Penrose (1955) has suggested that product diversification provides firms with greater opportunities for market expansion, which can be limited if they only manufacture a single product. Recent studies on international trade and firm heterogeneity, however, have proposed a different approach. Most of the theoretical models on firms' responses to trade at the product level predict that product dropping is popular among all multiproduct firms (Eckel and Neary 2010; Mayer, Melitz, and Ottaviano 2014). Competition pressure instigates firms to narrow down their product range by dropping peripheral products and reallocating resources to their core competencies, defined as the product with the largest cost advantage compared to other products of the firm. Just as the least productive single-product firms are swept out of the market due to competition, the least productive product for each multiproduct firm should also be dropped.

However, several studies suggest a more heterogeneous picture, where an adjustment in product scope is contingent on the firm's position in the productivity distribution, firm size, or ownership type (Qiu and Zhou 2013; Lopresti 2016). Lopresti (2016), for example, examined changes in the product structure of US firms following the Canada–US Free Trade Agreement of 1989. Utilizing Bayesian econometric techniques, the author found that heterogeneity exists in firms' response conditioning regarding their engagement in global markets. In particular, more domestically oriented firms narrow down their product range, while more internationalized firms either add more products or do not respond to tariff reduction. Nevertheless, the adjustment is mixed when sales are used as an additional dimension of firm heterogeneity. Given these inconsistent theoretical findings, a conclusion remains an empirical matter.

This research adds to the growing literature on firm–product dynamics by investigating product turnover in Viet Nam's manufacturing, a developing country with impressive economic growth and a high level of trade openness. I utilize the Vietnam Enterprise Survey covering the 2010–2015 period. The research objectives are threefold. I first present several stylized facts about multiproduct firms, including their presence in manufacturing, their relative performance compared to single-product enterprises, and the frequency of product turnover. I then utilize the decomposition framework in Goldberg et al. (2010a) to examine the contribution of the extensive and intensive firm–product margin to aggregate output growth. Finally, I link product refocusing to trade liberalization as one of the most significant policy reforms during this period. In particular, this chapter addresses two questions. First, does a reduction in tariffs impact firms' product scope? Second, do responses vary depending on firms' trade status and ownership types?

To the best of my knowledge, this is the first study on Viet Nam. This chapter is closely related to Goldberg et al. (2010a), who examined product turnover in response to a reduction in tariffs in Indian manufacturing. However, my study deviates from Goldberg et al. (2010a) in two important respects. First, I consider the potential differences in scope decisions depending on firms' ownership. In Viet Nam, there exists a large gap in competitiveness and efficiency among multinational enterprises (MNEs), state-owned enterprises (SOEs), and small and medium-sized enterprises (SMEs). SMEs account for over 90% of firms and make an important contribution to job creation. However, this sector has low competitiveness and limited innovation and internationalization activities (Trinh and Doan 2018). Facing financial and managerial constraints, it is possible that these firms have limited flexibility to adjust their product mix. Foreign investors, on the other hand, are larger, more productive, and the main exporters.[1] Therefore, it is likely that MNEs are more proactive in product adjustment. Given the country's heavy dependence on MNE exports, MNEs' internal resource reallocation is expected to exert a nonnegligible impact on aggregate trade and industrial performance. The third group, SOEs, tend to behave differently from MNEs and SMEs, as profit maximization may not be their business target. This implies that the core-competency argument does not necessarily apply to SOEs.

In addition, I take into account differences in a firm's response to trade depending on its export status. More diverse output markets allow exporters to better cope with increased competition in one market, while their productive performance encourages them to take advantage of better market access to expand their scope. Lopresti (2016) has shown that domestic-oriented firms become leaner in response to trade shocks. In contrast, firms with a greater share of foreign sales expand. Baldwin and Gu (2009) have found that trade liberalization induces nonexporting firms to narrow down their scope, but there is no significant effect on exporters. Although I do not have data on exports by product, trade status could reveal potential heterogeneity according to firms' engagement in the international market.

From a policy perspective, this study can contribute in the following ways. First, to the extent that changes in product mix account for a

---

[1]   The foreign direct investment sector accounts for 50% of output and approximately 70% of export turnover in 2016.

nontrivial fraction of aggregate growth, a study on multiproduct firms can shed light on another important channel for enhancing allocative efficiency. While better resource reallocation is crucial for any economy, productivity improvement is currently one of the top priorities for policy makers in Viet Nam. As one of Asia's fastest-growing economies, Viet Nam has lifted itself out of poverty and achieved the status of a lower-middle-income country. However, impressive economic growth during the last 2 decades primarily originates from an extraordinary structural shift from agriculture and considerable labor expansion. The contribution of productivity, the third component of growth, remains limited (World Bank 2017). Second, examining the product scope decision can also facilitate understanding of the changes in the commodity composition of production observed at the aggregate level. According to Nguyen (2015), the contribution of resourced-based industries to overall manufacturing output has fallen markedly. For example, the ratio of output of the chemical products industry plunged from 7% to just 0.1%, while that of processed food fell from 32.4% to 24.2% over the 1995–2009 period. There has been a shift to more capital-intensive industries, such as electronics and computing. I expect, therefore, that this study can contribute to the discussion on industrial upgrading and sustainable growth.

9.2 Literature Review

This study is related to the literature on multiproduct firms and trade liberalization. On the theory side, most models predict that more competitive markets stimulate firms to drop their least profitable product and refocus on the product with the largest cost advantage, or the core product. Eckel and Neary (2010) have constructed a model in which globalization affects both the extensive and intensive margin of multiproduct firms through a competition effect and a cannibalization effect. Adjustment of internal demand linkages, or the cannibalization effect, allows firms to improve productivity by becoming leaner. In contrast, competition implies a decline in product variety. Bernard, Jensen, and Schott (2010) have extended Melitz's (2003) model by allowing firms to produce multiple products. The theoretical model suggests that severe competition in more liberalized industries drives the least productive firms and the least profitable products of firms out of the market. Mayer, Melitz, and Ottaviano (2014) assume that firms face a product ladder. Productivity or quality is negatively associated with the number of varieties produced. Tougher competition results in lower markups across products, rendering firm sales skewed toward core competences.

However, Qiu and Zhou (2013) have predicted product scope expansion for more productive firms. They argue that if we relax the assumption of a fixed fee for the introduction of each new variety and allow the fees to increase steeply, highly productive firms can still earn a profit by expanding their product scope. Dhingra (2013) has argued that the varieties produced by one firm are more substitutable than varieties across firms. Product expansion then reduces demand for existing products within the firm.

Inconclusive theoretical predictions suggest the essential role of empirical analysis. Baldwin and Gu (2009) have found that tariff reduction leads small firms to narrow down product scope, whereas large firms do not. Moreover, nonexporters drop products, whereas the impact on exporters is not significant. The authors argue that once firms enter the export market, they are more affected by factors other than tariffs, including learning-by-exporting, competition in the export market, and opportunities for better market access. Goldberg et al. (2010a) have identified a nonnegligible impact of changes in product mix on changes in output in Indian manufacturing. Trade liberalization (proxied as tariffs), however, does not have a significant impact on a firm's extensive margins. They postulate that strict industrial regulations in India may limit firms' flexibility in shedding existing product lines. Iacovone, Rauch, and Winters (2013) have found import competition from the People's Republic of China result in a fall in sales and number of products in the case of Mexican firms. The impact is highly heterogeneous across extensive and intensive margins. Smaller plants and more marginal products are negatively affected. In contrast, large firms and core products do not seem to be affected. Moreover, large firms benefit from access to cheaper imported intermediate inputs from the People's Republic of China. Arkolakis and Muendler (2010) have investigated the case of Brazilian exporters and demonstrated that the firm-product extensive margin is heterogeneous across firm sizes. Liu (2010) has noted that Canadian multiproduct firms are more likely to refocus on their core products in response to trade liberalization. The author constructed indices of product relatedness and demonstrated that the weaker the linkages between marginal products and the core product, the more likely it is that peripheral products are dropped. Goldberg et al. (2010b) have examined another aspect of within-firm reallocation, asking whether exposure to trade liberalization affects the input allocation of firms. The empirical results showed a positive impact of a lower input tariff on the introduction of new products thanks to better access to new intermediate inputs.

9.3 Data Source

My primary data source is the Vietnam Enterprise Survey (VES) provided by Viet Nam's General Statistics Office. Data have been collected annually since 2000, and the VES is by far the most comprehensive dataset available on Viet Nam's firms; it is the main source of firm-level statistics in the formal agriculture, industry, and service sectors.

The VES includes a general questionnaire covering basic statistics at the firm level, including ownership, assets and liability, employment, sales, capital stock, and industry code from January to December of a particular year. The survey covers all SOEs and foreign direct investment (FDI) without any firm size threshold. As for domestic private firms, however, a certain threshold is applied.[2] All formal firms with employment size above the threshold are included, while firms below the threshold are chosen by random sampling. Since 2010, the VES has also provided information on total exports and imports.[3] There is a consistent and unique tax code assigned to each firm, which allows us to track the firm across years.[4]

Apart from the general module, the General Statistics Office also designs industry-specific modules to survey the activities of each sector. For manufacturing, production data are provided at the plant level. The data comprise the list of products, the quantity produced for each product, the unit of measurement, the value of sales, and product codes, among others. The General Statistics Office applies an internal product classification developed based on the Viet Nam Standard Industrial Classification (VSIC) version 2007, European Classification of Products by Activity 2008, United Nations Central Product Classification 2.0, and Harmonized System 2007. Products are classified at eight digits, where the first five digits correspond to VSIC 2007. Under this classification, there are approximately 2,400 products in the manufacturing sector.

9.3.1 Variables

The key variables for our analysis are product codes and product sales. Product sales are deflated by the producer price index (PPI) at the

---

[2]   The threshold varies across years, provinces, and sectors. For example, in 2015, the threshold goes up to 100 in certain sectors for firms located in Ha Noi and Ho Chi Minh City. On the other hand, the maximum threshold for 2008 is only 10. For the census years (2006, 2011, and 2016), all formal firms were included.

[3]   Before 2010, trade status is only available for a few years.

[4]   A detailed description of the firm-level dataset is provided in Ha and Kiyota (2014).

two-digit sectoral level. Due to a change in product classification in 2010, my analysis is limited to the 2010–2015 period. In addition, we also utilize information on firms' unique identification to construct the panel, and firms' industry as indicated in the general module. Value-added deflated by PPI and employment data are used to compute labor productivity.

Given that the production module is at the plant level whereas the general module is at the firm level, I aggregate all data in the production module to firm level for consistency. As the production decision is made at the firm level, an analysis at the firm level is also more appropriate (Bernard, Jensen, and Schott 2010). Furthermore, I only focus on the manufacturing products of firms.

To complement the firm-product data, I use tariff data from the World Integrated Trade Solutions (WITS) database at four-digit International Standard Industrial Classification (ISIC) revision 3. I match ISIC with VSIC codes based on a concordance table provided by the General Statistics Office. I utilize effectively applied tariff, which is defined as the lowest available tariff. I favor trade-weighted tariff over simple average tariff, as the former can capture the relative importance of each industry's import share.

To account for the impact of trade liberalization on access to imported intermediate inputs, I also measure input tariff following Amiti and Konings (2007) as follows:

$$in_{st} = \sum_1^p a_{sp} * out_{pt}, \qquad (1)$$

where in_{st} and out_{pt} denote input tariff of downstream sector s and output tariff of two-digit upstream sector p, respectively. a_{sp} denotes imported input coefficients, defined as the value of intermediate imports from sector p over total output of sectors.[5] To compute input coefficients, we utilize the Organisation for Economic Co-operation and Development's Inter-country Input–Output Table (ICIO) edition 2016. ICIO provides annual information on inter-industry and across-country trade transactions for 63 countries including Viet Nam over the 1995–2011 period. Industrial classification is based on ISIC Rev. 3 at the two-digit level. Accordingly, 34 sectors are covered.

I favor the use of ICIO over Viet Nam's domestic input–output table for two reasons. First, ICIO adopts the ISIC classification, which can be

---

[5]   Note that we can only measure input tariff at the two-digit sectoral level due to data availability.

matched directly with output tariff data from WITS. Second, and more importantly, ICIO contains information on imported intermediates, which is not available in the domestic table. To better capture the impact of tariff changes on a firm's adjustment along the supply chain, it is more appropriate to measure the imported input coefficient than the domestic input coefficient. Although the database is available for 1995–2011, I only use ICIO for 2011, assuming that the structure of the economy is relatively stable across 2010–2015.

9.4 A Profile of Multiproduct Firms

This section documents the characteristics of multiproduct firms and the pervasiveness of product churning in Viet Nam's manufacturing during a 6-year period from 2010 to 2015. Following Goldberg et al. (2010a), I define sector and industry at the two- and four-digit levels of VSIC 2007, respectively. Product classification is defined at the eight-digit level.

Table 9.1 illustrates the presence of multiproduct firms in my sample. I include four groups of firms: firms that produce only one product, firms that produce at least two products, firms that operate in more than one four-digit industry, and firms with activities spread across two-digit sectors. Two features stand out. First, Viet Nam's firms are relatively specialized. On average, only 19% of firms produce more than one product. An average multiproduct firm manufactures 2.6 products. The proportions of multiple-industry and multiple-sector firms are

Table 9.1 Frequency and Output Share of Firms

	Single Product	Multiple Product	Multiple Industry	Multiple Sector
	Whole sample			
Share of firms	0.81	0.19	0.07	0.05
Share of output	0.59	0.41	0.24	0.20
Average number of products, industries or sectors per firm	1	2.62	1.45	1.28
	FDI			
Share of firms	0.81	0.19	0.07	0.04
Share of output	0.56	0.44	0.28	0.24
Average number of products, industries or sectors per firm	1	2.73	1.39	1.25

continued on next page

Table 9.1 *continued*

	Single Product	Multiple Product	Multiple Industry	Multiple Sector
SOE				
Share of firms	0.53	0.47	0.25	0.19
Share of output	0.26	0.74	0.50	0.46
Average number of products, industries or sectors per firm	1	2.93	1.80	1.50
Domestic private				
Share of firms	0.82	0.18	0.07	0.05
Share of output	0.72	0.28	0.13	0.08
Average number of products, industries or sectors per firm	1	2.58	1.45	1.28

FDI = foreign direct investment, SOE = state-owned enterprise.

Notes: FDI sector includes 100% foreign-invested firms and joint ventures of which the share of foreign capital exceeds 50% of total legal capital. Sector and industry are defined at the two- and four-digit levels of the Viet Nam Standard Industrial Classification 2007, respectively.

Source: Author's calculations from the Vietnam Enterprise Survey data.

even smaller, accounting for 7% and 5% of firm share, respectively. The figure is significantly lower than that reported in Bernard, Jensen, and Schott (2010) on the US and in Goldberg et al. (2010a) on India. Both studies documented a share of around 40% of multiproduct firms. The difference, however, is not surprising as in Viet Nam over 90% of firms are micro, small, and medium-sized firms with limited technological capability and low competitiveness.

Second, multiproduct firms tend to be larger. Despite the modest firm share, they contribute to 41% of total output, which is similar to the US and India, where the output share of multiproduct firms is also double that of firm share. Third, there exists heterogeneity across ownership types. Contrary to the overall trend, we observe the prevalence of multiproduct firms in the SOE sector. They constitute nearly 50% of total SOEs and account for 74% of output. The average number of products is also higher than the overall, reaching 2.93. In contrast, the FDI and domestic private sectors show a similar structure, closely in line with the overall trend.[6] One possible explanation for the specialization of MNEs is their exploitation of economies of scope. On

---

[6]   It should be noted that SOEs account for a minority of my sample. Therefore, it is likely that the overall trends are driven by domestic private firms and FDI.

Table 9.2 Superiority of Multiproduct Firms

	Multiple Product	Multiple Industry	Multiple Sector
Output	1.131	1.067	0.98
Export probability	0.161	0.143	0.153
Labor productivity	0.278	0.262	0.224
Employment	0.704	0.705	0.675
Capital intensity	0.25	0.22	0.185

Notes: Sector and industry are defined at the two- and four-digit level of the Viet Nam Standard Industrial Classification 2007, respectively. Each column reports the regression result of firms' characteristics according to status: multiproduct, multi-industry, and multisector. We use a dummy variable on the right-hand side to indicate each status. Industry-fixed effects are also included. All estimates are significant at the 5% level.

Source: Author's calculations from the Vietnam Enterprise Survey data.

the other hand, small capacity may limit domestic private firms in terms of diversifying their product portfolio.

Studies on multiproduct firms highlight the premium in terms of performance of more diversified enterprises. Firms face fixed costs when expanding their scope. Just as more productive firms self-select into export markets, only better-performing firms will choose to become multiproduct firms. I check if this is also the case for Viet Nam by looking at the relative characteristics of multiproduct firms compared to their single-product counterparts. Table 9.2 documents the characteristics of multiproduct firms. I find consistent evidence within the existing literature regarding their superiority. In particular, Viet Nam's multiproduct firms are more productive; they have higher labor productivity (0.27 log points), produce larger output, employ more workers, and are more capital-intensive. They are also more active in international markets, being 16% more likely to export. In short, multiproduct firms outperform single-product firms.

Having examined the frequency and overall performance of multiproduct firms, I now turn to the product structure of these firms. Table 9.3 presents the sales distribution of products within firms. It is clear that the distribution is highly skewed, meaning that a large proportion of firm sales is generated from few primary products, which is indicative of the core-competency hypothesis.

The average sales share of the largest product decreases from 74% to 42% as the firm's production increases from 2 to 10 or more. However, even for firms with a large number of products, sales of the "core" product account for at least 42% of total manufacturing sales.

Table 9.3 Sales Distribution across Products

Rank of sales in descending order	Number of Products Produced by the Firm									
	1	2	3	4	5	6	7	8	9	10+
	100	74	63	57	53	48	45	43	43	42
		26	26	25	24	24	23	22	21	21
			11	13	13	14	14	14	13	12
				6	7	8	8	9	9	8
					3	4	5	6	6	6
						2	3	4	4	4
							2	2	3	3
								1	1	2
									1	+1
										1

Note: The columns indicate number of products; the rows indicate the sales share of each product in firms' total manufacturing sales.
Source: Author's calculations from the Vietnam Enterprise Survey data.

9.5 Firm's Adjustment of Product Scope and Aggregate Output Growth

The existing literature suggests the importance of product churning for aggregate economic outcome. To investigate the issue, I begin this section by documenting the dynamics of product adjustment. I classify firms' activities into one of four mutually exclusive groups. The "No activity" category includes firms that do not change their product line in the period of study. "Add" refers to firms that produce new products in period t that are not in their product line in period $t-1$. "Drop" means that firms stop producing a product in period t, which was produced in period $t-1$. Finally, "Add and drop" includes firms that alternate their product mix by both adding and dropping. I focus on changes in product structure of the firm over time. Therefore, in this section I only use a subsample of continuing firms that appear in the sample throughout the whole period.

Table 9.4 shows the share of firms that alternate their product mix over 1-year, 3-year, and 6-year periods. A balanced panel is used for this analysis. The main findings from Table 9.4 are threefold. First, product churning is pervasive among Viet Nam's manufacturing firms. Sixty percent of all firms adjust their product range over a 6-year period. The corresponding numbers for 3-year and 1-year periods are 50% and

Table 9.4 Frequency of Product Turnover

| | Percentage of Firms (Unweighted) | | | | | | | | |
| | 6-Year Period | | | 3-Year Period | | | 1-Year Period | | |
	All	Single Product	Multiple Product	All	Single Product	Multiple Product	All	Single Product	Multiple Product
No activity	40.0	50.6	13.0	49.4	57.7	21.8	63.6	71.3	35.6
Add only	7.3	7.9	5.9	5.9	5.8	6.4	5.0	4.7	5.4
Drop only	8.8	NA	31.0	6.6	NA	28.5	5.7	NA	25.5
Add and drop	43.9	41.4	50.2	38.1	36.5	43.3	25.7	24.0	31.5

| | Percentage of Firms (Weighted by Sales) | | | | | | | | |
| | 6-Year Period | | | 3-Year Period | | | 1-Year Period | | |
	All	Single Product	Multiple Product	All	Single Product	Multiple Product	All	Single Product	Multiple Product
No activity	34.5	46.1	16.5	45.9	56.9	29.4	64.2	77.1	48.5
Add only	8.7	8.6	8.8	15.1	10.0	22.6	12.3	7.0	18.9
Drop only	10.3	NA	26.3	7.6	NA	18.9	6.5	NA	14.4
Add and drop	46.5	45.3	48.4	31.5	33.1	29.1	17.0	16.0	18.3

NA = not available.
Note: No activity means that the firm's product mix does not change between two consecutive periods. A product is added if it was produced in period t but not in the previous period. Similarly, a product is dropped if it was produced in period t−1 but not in period t. The statistics are computed on a balanced panel.
Source: Author's calculations from the Vietnam Enterprise Survey data.

40%, respectively. When I weigh our sample by firm sales, the number changes slightly, with 65% of firms changing their product mix over the whole period. The annual pattern, while less pervasive, also shows a high level of product turnover, with 40% of firms changing their product mix. Furthermore, I observe that multiproduct firms are more active in adjusting their product scope compared to single-product firms. Over 80% of the former group add and/or drop some products within 6 years. In addition, product dropping is much more popular than product adding. Firms that only add products account for less than 10% of the unweighted sample.

To further investigate the pattern of product churning, I categorize firms by ownership types. The FDI sector includes 100%-foreign-invested enterprises and joint ventures in which foreign capital accounts for at least 51% of total legal capital. The domestic private sector covers the rest of our sample. We conjecture that the behavior of these groups is heterogeneous along the product dimension given their performance gap. Table 9.5 reports the results.

Table 9.5 Product Turnover of Multiproduct Firms by Ownership Type

	MNEs	SOEs	Domestic Private	MNEs	SOEs	Domestic Private
	Percentage of Multiproduct Firms: Unweighted, 6-Year Period			Percentage of Multiproduct Firms: Weighted by Sales, 6-Year Period		
No activity	15.37	20.57	10.97	13.64	22.39	13.88
Add only	6.77	2.13	5.74	10.07	3.45	7.44
Drop only	35.12	24.82	29.66	23.39	31.6	29.94
Add and drop	42.74	52.48	53.64	52.9	42.56	48.74

MNE = multinational enterprise, SOE = state-owned enterprise.

Note: No activity means that the firm's product mix does not change between two consecutive periods. A product is added if it was produced in period t but not in the previous period. Similarly, a product is dropped if it was produced in period t–1 but not in period t. The statistics are computed on a balanced panel of multiproduct firms only.

Source: Author's calculations from the Vietnam Enterprise Survey data.

The left panel of Table 9.5 presents results without output weight, while the right panel includes output weight. The figures suggest that compared to SOEs, MNEs and domestic private firms are more active in adjusting their product mix: 85% of MNEs and 90% of domestic private firms change their product portfolio over a 6-year period. Moreover, albeit modest compared to the other three activities, the ratio of product adding is larger for MNEs and domestic private firms than for SOEs.

One may be concerned that the low percentage of product adding could originate from coding or reporting errors. However, if that is the case, one should also expect a lack of evidence on product dropping. My statistics demonstrate the opposite. Furthermore, if firms deliberately or mistakenly dropped some products in the survey, it is likely that the gap between total manufacturing sales reported in the general module and total product sales from the production module would be remarkable. I have compared the two datasets and found a good match. Third, if the list of products were not reported correctly, missing information on sales and quantity produced would probably constitute an issue. My database, on the contrary, provides detailed information on sales and physical output of each product with negligible numbers of missing values. Therefore, it is expected that the number adequately reflects the actual pattern of product churning.

Changes in the product mix make a nontrivial contribution to changes in the output of incumbents. To account for the sources of output growth, I decompose growth of gross sales into two components: changes in the product mix and changes due to existing products. I define these two sources as extensive margin and intensive margin. Growth of output can then be expressed as

$$\Delta Y_{it} = \sum_{j \in C} \Delta Y_{ijt} + \sum_{j \in E} \Delta Y_{ijt}, \qquad (2)$$

where Y denotes output (sales); and i, j, and t denote firm, product, and time, respectively. C represents the set of continuing products (intensive margin), and E represents the set of products that only appear in either period t or period $t-1$.

Following Goldberg et al. (2010a), I further decompose the net extensive margin into the contribution of added products (A) and dropped products (D). Similarly, the net intensive margin consists of two components: the fall (F) and rise (R) of individual product sales. Then aggregate output growth can be computed as

$$\Delta Y_t = \Sigma_i \left(\Sigma_{j \in A} \Delta Y_{ijt} + \Sigma_{j \in D} \Delta Y_{ijt} + \Sigma_{j \in R} \Delta Y_{ijt} + \Sigma_{j \in F} \Delta Y_{ijt} \right). \quad (3)$$

Table 9.6 presents the decomposition. Two major findings stand out. First, the contribution of the intensive margin, or the change in sales of individual products, exceeds that of the extensive margin. On average, out of a growth in output of 6.4 percentage points, 6 percentage points are from the intensive margin. Product churning only contributes to 0.4 percentage points. Second, on both the extensive and intensive

Table 9.6 Contribution of Product Turnover to Output Growth

	Gross Sales	Extensive Margin			Intensive Margin		
		Net	Addw	Drop	Net	Rising Products	Falling Products
2010							
2011	1.5	2.2	13.9	−11.7	−0.7	7.4	−8.1
2012	6.9	−0.8	12.7	−13.5	7.6	18.6	−11.0
2013	15.7	0.6	11.0	−10.4	15.1	24.8	−9.7
2014	1.6	0.5	9.4	−9.0	1.1	13.4	−12.3
2015	6.4	−0.5	11.7	−12.2	6.8	16.2	−9.3

Source: Author's calculation based on the Vietnam Enterprise Survey data.

margin, product adding or growing products makes a significant contribution to the net increase. In the case of the intensive margin, the growth is large enough to offset the negative impact of shrinking products, leading to high overall output growth. For the extensive margin, however, the negative impact of product dropping is too large to be compensated by product adding. The net extensive margin is thus relatively small. This observation is consistent with my previous analysis, where product dropping is prevalent.

9.6 Trade Liberalization and Product Turnover

The literature on international trade and firm heterogeneity emphasizes product churning as an important channel of resource reallocation as a result of free trade. While the theoretical predictions and empirical evidence do not provide a clear-cut picture of the direction of impact, most studies suggest a relationship between product dropping and trade liberalization. Given the high rate of product dropping found in the previous sections and the substantial trade reform that Viet Nam's economy has experienced, it is then natural to ask if the relationship holds in the case of Viet Nam. To shed light on this issue, this section examines the links between reduced trade costs and firms' extensive margin. In particular, I ask whether firms in industries with larger tariff changes experience product churning. I follow Baldwin and Gu (2009) to estimate the following equation on continuing firms:

$$Y_{jt} = \beta_1 out_{it-1} + \beta_2 in_{it-1} + \beta_3 X_{jt-1} + \beta_4 HHI_{it} + \alpha_s + a_t + u_{jt} \quad (4)$$

where Y_{jt} represents the number of product varieties of firm j in four-digit industry i at time t; out_{it-1} measures lagged output tariff of industry j at time t; in_{it-1} is lagged input tariff of sector s at time t; and X_{jt} is a vector of firm-specific characteristics, including employment, lagged export status, lagged export share over total output, and interaction terms between ownership type and trade variables. I include the Herfindahl–Hirschman concentration index HHI to capture competition at the industry level. Further, a_t is the year dummy and α_s the unobserved two-digit sector s fixed effect.

The main research question here is whether changes in the output tariff affect the number of products of the firm, controlling for the input tariff, export status and export intensity, and ownership structure of the firm. The choice of control variables is based on the literature. The input tariff, for example, has been widely used in studies on trade liberalization and firm productivity.[7] For the literature on product turnover, the input tariff is included in the analysis of Goldberg et al. (2010a, 2010b), among others. While the reduction in output tariffs could intensify competition pressure, a lower input tariff provides access to more intermediate inputs varieties. For a developing country with limited technological capacity such as Viet Nam, it is possible that advanced technology embodied in more advanced imported intermediates lowers the cost of innovation and encourages the development of new products, contributing to aggregate output growth.

In addition, as Lopresti (2016) suggests, the impact of trade liberalization on product scope depends on the extent of a firm's participation in the international market. A more globalized firm, defined as one with larger export sales over total output, tends to add more product or keep the product portfolio unchanged in response to lower trade costs. On the other hand, a more domestically oriented firm drops its product when facing international competition. To check whether this observation holds for Viet Nam, I include in my estimation export intensity, defined as the ratio of export turnover to a firm's total revenue, and its interaction term with the output tariff.

Table 9.7 reports the regression results. Columns (1)–(5) demonstrate the relationship between the number of products and tariffs in level. Columns (6)–(10) examine the determinants of firms' product extensive margins. Several findings are worth mentioning. First, in level, a higher output tariff is associated with a smaller number of products. The coefficient on the output tariff is negative and significant. Firms in industries with a lower output tariff are more likely to produce more products. One possible explanation is the competition effect, where firms diversify to reduce competition pressure. This finding is consistent with Dang (2017), who finds that import competition from the People's Republic of China stimulates Viet Nam's firms to introduce new products. The economic magnitude is small, however. Second, a higher input tariff is associated with a broader product range. I do not find evidence of expansion of product scope thanks to better access to more imported intermediates. One reason could be that, via access to more technologically advanced materials, firms are more likely to invest in quality upgrading of existing products.

---

[7]   See, for example, Amiti and Konings (2007), Topalova and Khandelwal (2011), and Bas (2012).

Table 9.7 Tariff Reduction and Product Churning

Variables	(1)	(2)	(3)	(4)	(5)
	Number of Products Produced by Firms				
Output tariff	−0.003***	−0.003***	−0.004***	−0.004***	−0.003***
	(0.001)	(0.001)	(0.001)	(0.002)	(0.001)
Input tariff		0.071**	0.078***	0.077***	0.073***
		(0.027)	(0.028)	(0.028)	(0.028)
Export dummy			0.038**	0.040**	
			(0.016)	(0.016)	
Export * output tariff			0.000	0.000	
			(0.001)	(0.001)	
SOE * output tariff				0.003	
				(0.002)	
FDI * output tariff				0.001	
				(0.002)	
Export intensity					0.041
					(0.036)
Export intensity * output tariff					0.000
					(0.003)
Δoutput tariff					
Δinput tariff					
Export * Δoutput tariff					
SOE * Δoutput tariff					
FDI * Δoutput tariff					
Export intensity * Δoutput tariff					
Employment			0.053***	0.054***	0.054***
			(0.011)	(0.011)	(0.011)
HHI			0.021	0.021	0.024
			(0.072)	(0.072)	(0.072)

continued on next page

Table 9.7 *continued*

Variables	(1)	(2)	(3)	(4)	(5)
	Number of Products Produced by Firms				
Constant	1.602***	1.490***	1.200***	1.204***	1.200***
	(0.148)	(0.156)	(0.165)	(0.165)	(0.164)
Observations	42,908	42,908	42,905	42,905	41,508
R-squared	0.004	0.004	0.006	0.006	0.005
Number of firms	7,294	7,294	7,294	7,294	7,257

Variables	(6)	(7)	(8)	(9)	(10)
	Change in Number of Products				
Output tariff					
Input tariff					
Export dummy			0.023***	0.023***	
			(0.008)	(0.008)	
Export * output tariff					
SOE * output tariff					
FDI * output tariff					
Export intensity					0.042***
					(0.015)
Export intensity * output tariff					
Δoutput tariff	−0.001	−0.001	−0.001	−0.001	−0.001
	(0.001)	(0.001)	(0.001)	(0.001)	(0.001)
Δinput tariff		−0.010	−0.011	−0.011	−0.016
		(0.017)	(0.017)	(0.017)	(0.013)
Export * Δoutput tariff			−0.001	−0.001	
			(0.001)	(0.001)	
SOE * Δoutput tariff				−0.000	
				(0.001)	

continued on next page

Table 9.7 *continued*

Variables	(6)	(7)	(8)	(9)	(10)
			Change in Number of Products		
FDI * Δoutput tariff				–0.000	
				(0.001)	
Export intensity*Δoutput tariff					–0.002
					(0.003)
Employment			0.010	0.010	0.009
			(0.007)	(0.007)	(0.007)
HHI			0.005	0.005	0.006
			(0.049)	(0.049)	(0.050)
Constant	0.276**	0.279**	0.219*	0.219*	0.227*
	(0.124)	(0.124)	(0.129)	(0.129)	(0.129)
Observations	35,591	35,591	35,588	35,588	34,430
R-squared	0.002	0.003	0.003	0.003	0.003
Number of firms	7,247	7,247	7,247	7,247	7,196

FDI = foreign direct investment, HHI = Herfindahl–Hirschman Index, SOE = state-owned enterprise.

Note: Robust standard errors in parentheses. *** $p<0.01$, ** $p<0.05$, * $p<0.1$.

Source: Author's calculation from the Vietnam Enterprise Survey data.

Third, the change in the output tariff does not have any significant impact on the extensive margin. One possibility is the increasing numbers of nontariff measures in Viet Nam (Ing, Cordoba, and Cadot 2016), some of which can be used with protectionist intent. If this is the case, the rise in nontariff measures can partly offset the impact of tariff reduction. Although it is desirable to incorporate nontariff measures in the analysis, distinguishing between protective and nonprotective measures is not a simple task. I shall leave this issue for further study.

Fourth, exporters produce more products and are more likely to add products. Coefficients on both export dummy and export intensity are positive and significant in both specifications. One observation is that exporters' extensive margin does not seem to be affected by tariffs. Coefficients of the interaction term between export status, including export intensity and export dummy, and output tariff, both in level and difference, do not show any significance. It is possible that once firms enter the export market, market diversification reduces the potential impact of the domestic market's competition on these firms.

Fifth, there is no significant impact of ownership on product churning. This result confirms findings from the previous analysis that the three groups of firms are not markedly different in terms of product turnover.

Several implications can be drawn from the regression analysis. First, my result further confirms the potential positive contribution of exporters to aggregate growth through product adding. Second, there is a need to consider other factors of trade policy reform, particularly the incidence of nontariff measures to capture another important aspect of trade liberalization. This study suggests that aside from common driving factors in the literature, the pattern of product turnover is heterogeneous across countries, depending on the regulatory environment and the competitiveness of firms, among other factors. This implication calls for careful country-specific analysis.

9.7 Conclusion

Here I have studied multiproduct firms in Viet Nam. The major findings are as follows. First, multiproduct firms are larger, more capital-intensive, more productive, and more likely to export. Second, while the share of multiproduct firms in Viet Nam is smaller than that found in the US and India, Viet Nam's multiproduct firms are active in the market. Approximately 60% of firms adjust their product scope within a 6-year period. Third, the contribution of firms' product extensive margin to aggregate output growth is limited due to the prevalence of product dropping, which offsets the positive impact of product adding to output growth. Most output growth during the period is thus generated by the intensive margin.

Turning to the link between tariff reduction and product shedding, I did not detect any significant impact. However, I found the important role of exporters in product adding, suggesting the potential contribution of exporters to aggregate growth through the channeling of product scope expansion. Contrary to expectations, this analysis offers limited support regarding the heterogeneity of product turnover across ownership types. While I find that SOEs are more likely to spread economic activities across products and industries, there are limited difference in terms of product churning among FDI, SOEs, and the domestic private sector.

The analysis provides several policy implications. First, as product adding contributes positively to aggregate output growth, firms should be encouraged to diversify their product range. This could be done through enhancing innovation, for example, through technology transfer and the enhancement of interfirm linkages and exports. Diversification also supports firms in reducing competitive pressure. Second, as multi-industry and multisector firms account for only 5% and 7% of firm share, respectively, whereas most product shedding occurs within narrowly defined categories, it is less likely that product churning or industry switching can represent a significant source of industrial upgrading toward more capital-intensive sectors. Therefore, rather than aiming at expansion across industries, a feasible policy option with respect to existing firms is to promote investment in process innovation to further increase the quality of existing products or expansion to closely related products, through which the intensive margin can be boosted.

References

Amiti, M., and J. Konings. 2007. Trade Liberalization, Imported Intermediate Inputs, and Productivity: Evidence from Indonesia. *American Economic Review.* 97 (5). pp. 1611–38.

Arkolakis, C., and M.A . Muendler. 2010. The Extensive Margin of Exporting Products: A Firm-level Analysis. NBER Working Paper. No. w16641. Cambridge, MA: National Bureau of Economic Research.

Baldwin, J., and W. Gu. 2009. The Impact of Trade on Plant Scale, Production-Run Length and Diversification. In T. Dunne, J. Bradford Jensen, and M.J. Roberts, eds. *Producer Dynamics: New Evidence from Micro Data.* Chicago, IL: University of Chicago Press. pp.557–92.

Bas, M. 2012. Input-Trade Liberalization and Firm Export Decisions: Evidence from Argentina. *Journal of Development Economics.* 97 (2). pp. 481–93.

Bernard, A. B., J.B. Jensen, and P. K. Schott. 2006. Survival of the Best Fit: Exposure to Low-Wage Countries and the (Uneven) Growth of US Manufacturing Plants. *Journal of International Economics.* 68 (1). pp. 219–37.

_____. 2010. Survival of the Best Fit: Exposure to Low-Wage Countries and the (Uneven) Growth of US Manufacturing Plants. *American Economic Review.* 100 (1). pp. 70–97.

Dang, D. A. 2017. The Effects of Chinese Import Penetration on Firm Innovation: Evidence from the Vietnamese Manufacturing Sector. WIDER Working Paper. No. 2017/77. Helsinki: World Institute for Development Economic Research.

Dhingra, S. 2013. Trading Away Wide Brands for Cheap Brands. *American Economic Review.* 103 (6). pp. 2554–84.

Eckel, C., and J. P. Neary. 2010. Multi-product Firms and Flexible Manufacturing in the Global Economy. *The Review of Economic Studies.* 77 (1). pp. 188–217.

Goldberg, P. K., A. K, Khandelwal, N. Pavcnik, and P. Topalova. 2010a. Multiproduct Firms and Product Turnover in the Developing World: Evidence from India. *The Review of Economics and Statistics.* 92 (4). pp. 1042–49.

_____. 2010b. Imported Intermediate Inputs and Domestic Product Growth: Evidence from India. *The Quarterly Journal of Economics.* 125 (4). pp. 1727–67.

Ha, D. T. T., and K. Kiyota. 2014. Firm-Level Evidence on Productivity Differentials and Turnover in Vietnamese Manufacturing. *The Japanese Economic Review.* 65 (2). pp. 193–217.

Iacovone, L., F. Rauch, and L. A. Winters. 2013. Trade as an Engine of Creative Destruction: Mexican Experience with Chinese Competition. *Journal of International Economics.* 89 (2). pp. 379–92.

Ing, L. Y., S. F. de Cordoba, and O. Cadot. 2016. *Non-Tariff Measures in ASEAN.* Jakarta: Economic Research Institute for ASEAN and East Asia (ERIA). http://www.eria.org/publications/non-tariff -measures-in-asean/.

Liu, R. 2010. Import Competition and Firm Refocusing. *Canadian Journal of Economics/Revue canadienne d'économique.* 43 (2). pp. 440–66.

Lopresti, J. 2016. Multiproduct Firms and Product Scope Adjustment in Trade. *Journal of International Economics.* 100 (C). pp. 160–73.

Mayer, T., M. J. Melitz, and G. I. Ottaviano. 2014. Market Size, Competition, and the Product Mix of Exporters. *American Economic Review.* 104 (2). pp. 495–536.

Melitz, M. J. 2003. The Impact of Trade on Intra-industry Reallocations and Aggregate Industry Productivity. *Econometrica.* 71 (6). pp. 1695–725.

Nguyen, T. K. 2015. Manufacturing Exports and Employment Generation in Viet Nam. *Southeast Asian Journal of Economics.* 3 (2). pp. 1–21.

Nocke, V., and S. Yeaple. 2006. Globalization and Endogenous Firm Scope. NBER Working Paper. No. w12322. Cambridge, MA: National Bureau of Economic Research.

Penrose, E. 1955. Limits to the Growth and Size of Firms. *The American Economic Review.* 45 (2). pp. 531–43.

Qiu, L. D., and W. Zhou. 2013. Multiproduct Firms and Scope Adjustment in Globalization. *Journal of International Economics.* 91 (1). pp. 142–53.

Topalova, P., and A. Khandelwal. 2011. Trade Liberalization and Firm Productivity: The Case of India. *Review of Economics and Statistics.* 93 (3). pp. 995–1009.

Trinh, L. Q., and H. T. T. Doan. 2018. Internationalization and the Growth of Vietnamese Micro, Small, and Medium Sized Enterprises: Evidence from Panel Quantile Regressions. *Journal of Asian Economics.* 55 (C). pp. 71–83.

World Bank. 2017. *Viet Nam 2035: Toward Prosperity, Creativity, Equity, and Democracy.* Washington, DC.

Index

Figures, notes, and tables are indicated by f, n, and t following the page number.